Police Selection and Training

NATO ASI Series

Advanced Science Institutes Series

A Series presenting the results of activities sponsored by the NATO Science Committee, which aims at the dissemination of advanced scientific and technological knowledge, with a view to strengthening links between scientific communities.

The Series is published by an international board of publishers in conjunction with the NATO Scientific Affairs Division

A	Life Sciences	Plenum Publishing Corporation
B	Physics	London and New York
C	Mathematical and Physical Sciences	D. Reidel Publishing Company Dordrecht and Boston
D	Behavioural and Social Sciences	Martinus Nijhoff Publishers Dordrecht/Boston/Lancaster
E	Applied Sciences	
F	Computer and Systems Sciences	Springer-Verlag Berlin/Heidelberg/New York
G	Ecological Sciences	

Series D: Behavioural and Social Sciences – No. 30

Police Selection and Training
The Role of Psychology

Editor:

John C. Yuille
University of British Columbia
Canada

Organizing Committee:

Ray Bull
North East London Polytechnic
United Kingdom

Karel J. Nijkerk
Erasmus University Rotterdam
The Netherlands

John C. Yuille
University of British Columbia
Canada

1986 **Martinus Nijhoff Publishers**
Dordrecht / Boston / Lancaster
Published in cooperation with NATO Scientific Affairs Division

Proceedings of the NATO Advanced Study Institute on "Police and Psychology",
Skiathos, Greece, May 7-15, 1985

Library of Congress Cataloging in Publication Data

ISBN 90-247-3369-3 (this volume)
ISBN 90-247-2688-3 (series)

Distributors for the United States and Canada: Kluwer Academic Publishers,
190 Old Derby Street, Hingham, MA 02043, USA

Distributors for the UK and Ireland: Kluwer Academic Publishers, MTP Press Ltd,
Falcon House, Queen Square, Lancaster LA1 1RN, UK

Distributors for all other countries: Kluwer Academic Publishers Group, Distribution
Center, P.O. Box 322, 3300 AH Dordrecht, The Netherlands

Printed in The Netherlands

PREFACE

The New Police Officer

During the past twenty years the tasks required of police officers have
expanded and changed with dramatic rapidity. The traditional roles of
the police had been those of law enforcement and the maintenance of
public order. As a consequence police officers were typically
large-bodied males, selected for their physical abilities and trained to
accept orders and enforce the law. Over the past two decades, however,
the industrialized nations have placed a variety of new demands on police
officers. To traditional law enforcement and public order tasks have
been added social work, mental health duties, and community relations
work. For example, domestic disputes, violence between husbands and
wives, lovers, relatives, etc., have increased in frequency and severity
(or at least there has been a dramatic increase in reporting the
occurence of domestic violence). Our societies have no formal system to
deal with domestic disputes and the responsibility to do so, in most
countries, has fallen to the police. In fact, in some areas as many as
60% of calls for service to the police are related to domestic disputes
(see the chapter in this text by Dutton). As a result the police officer
has had to become a skilled social worker, able to intervene with
sensitivity in domestic situations. Alternatively, in the case of West
Germany, the officer has had to learn to work co-operatively with social
workers (see the chapter by Steinhilper).

Another example of the changing demands made upon the police is in the
area of mental health. The past three decades have witnessed a profound
change in the treatment of the mentally ill. An impressive array of
drugs have been developed to control the symptoms of many forms of
psychosis. The result is that many psychotics can be released from an
institution and lead somewhat normal lives. Consequently, many large
mental institutions have closed during the past 25 years. A proportion
of the out patients who are on medication do pose an occasional problem
(the chapter by Monahan examines this issue). An individual may decide,
for example, to stop taking his medication, perhaps because he believes
he no longer needs the drugs or because of unpleasant side effects.
After he ceases the medication, he may have a psychotic episode, and it
is the police who are called to deal with the person. Thus the officer
has to deal, with skill and sensitivity, with a confused and sometimes
dangerous person who is in the midst of a psychotic episode. In short,
the changing pattern of the treatment of mental illness has led to the
police having to deal more directly with the mentally ill.

The addition of the new skills of social worker and mental health
worker are only part of the description of the modern police officer.
Reflecting the technological advances in dealing with forensic evidence,

the investigator of crime has had to add the skills of forensic scientist and technician to his/her repertoire. Due to the increase in hostage and terrorist situations, some police officers have had to become skilled negotiators. To deal with community relation problems stemming from racial, economic, and industrial tensions, the police require effective communication skills as well as an awareness of the roots of community tensions.

The end result of these societal changes is that law enforcement and traditional public order now comprise a relatively small proportion of police work (probably constituting less than 20% of an officer's time in urban settings). The contemporary demands placed upon the police raise the legitimate question of the capacity of one individual to meet all of these demands. It is likely that in the future we will see increased specialization in police work; however, for the present the police officer remains a generalist and has to perform a variety of tasks. Clearly, the modern police officer must be selected in a different fashion than he was in the past, and he or she requires a very different type of training than was provided in past decades.

The complexities of police selection and training have been amplified by the changing structure of police forces. Many forces have recognized the need to attract women into police work and a variety of training and organizational problems have to be faced (see the chapters by Reiser and by Tracy-Stratton). In centers of mixed ethnic and/or racial composition, there is a need to attract members of the minority groups into police work, and majority group members must be trained to work co-operatively with minority groups (see the chapter by Bull). As a result the demographics of police forces are changing, creating both positive results and adjustment problems.

A final problem area in policing which profoundly affects selection and training is the nature of police management. By and large, police management systems are antiquated and ill-prepared to meet the challenges of contemporary policing. Clinging to a military model, police organizations are too vertical in structure. Information flow is poor and decision making is often secretive and seemingly arbitrary. Police work, known to induce stress, must often be carried out in a management context which exacerbates rather than reduces tension. Changes in management style and method are the key to police organizations becoming flexible enough to deal with their new roles (see the chapter by Denkers).

Psychology and Police Selection and Training

Almost all of the changes that have occurred in police work relate to various areas of the discipline of psychology. As a result, psychologists have increasingly become involved in police work. At first, in the late 1960s and early 1970s, psychologists were employed by police in a clinical role.

Recognizing that police work is one of the more stress inducing occupations, police forces began to realize the necessity of providing therapeutic interventions to aid the members of their force. The United States took a leadership role in the development of police psychology, and Martin Reiser of the Los Angeles Police Department became the dean of police psychologists through his pioneering efforts in developing interventions and training programs for the police. Stress management and therapeutic interventions continue to be the major role of psychologists in the police context.

The early and continuing efforts of Dr. Reiser have born fruit; psychologists have expanded their involvement in policing, not only in the United States but throughout the industrialized world. Police psychology may be the most rapidly expanding aspect of psychology at the present time. Psychologists are now involved in the selection of police, both in the administration of tests and interviews, and in the development of selection procedures (see the chapter by Loo and Meredith). Psychologists are providing training to police in the areas of stress management (see Stratton in this volume), domestic intervention (see Dutton), communication skills (see Bull in this volume), de-escalation techniques, community relations (see Butler in this volume), interviewing and interrogation techniques (see the chapter by Yuille), and a variety of other areas. The chapters by Poole and by Nijkerk provide an overview of training issues in two national contexts. Psychologists are involved in developing and providing prevention and treatment programs for job related stress. Psychologists are aiding police operations in the areas of undercover operations, hostage negotiations, interviewing, and psychological profiling of criminals. As well as providing selection, training, and operational services, psychologists are deeply involved in doing research on all aspects of police work, providing scientific evaluation and assistance that has not been available to the police in the past (see in particular the chapters by Hare and by Mednick).

A First International Meeting

During the summer of 1982, at a meeting of the International Applied Psychology Congress in Wales, Ray Bull and I were discussing the tremendous growth and change in police psychology. We realized that this growth had led to several seminars, generally of a national nature, on topics of police psychology. However, to that point there had been no international forum for psychologists and police to share their common interests, and it was clear that there was a pressing need for such a forum. We decided at that time to try to organize an international meeting on the topic of police psychology.

Neither psychologists nor police have access to funds to facilitate an international meeting. It therefore became clear in our early planning that only a few sources of funds existed for the support of an international meeting, and that NATO provided the most appropriate program. The NATO Advanced Study Institute (ASI) program is designed to fund a meeting of a group of experts and students with a common scientific interest. The intent is to bring a group of people together for about two weeks to share, in depth, the current knowledge in their field. Ray Bull and I applied to NATO for funds to hold an ASI on the topic of police psychology. The NATO Scientific Affairs committee, headed at that time by Dr. Sinclair, expressed interest in the idea but asked us to add another member to our organizing committee and to narrow the focus of our program.

The request to add a third organizer was indeed a fortunate one. Dr. Karel Nijkerk agreed to join our efforts and his contributions were essential in the success of the meeting. Dr. Nijkerk played a leading role in contacting and aiding representatives from continental Europe who attended the conference. Dealing with a variety of languages, political structures, etc., was a difficult task but one that Karel managed with skill and diplomacy.

Karel Nijkerk, Ray Bull and I realized that the breadth of work of psychologists in police activities had become too great to cover in a single meeting. We decided to narrow our focus to the two related areas of the selection and training of police officers. In the end, a group of 63 police and psychologists from eleven nations met for several days. The locale was the Skiathos Palace Hotel on the Island of Skiathos, north of Athens, Greece. The location was beautiful and secluded. In spite of the natural attractions of the beaches and local villages, the common interests of the group kept almost everyone in the long daily meetings. Researchers and practitioners learned that despite local and national differences, there are a variety of common problems which police psychologists share.

Edited Proceedings

This book represents the edited results of many aspects of the May 1985 meeting in Skiathos. It is a special text in a variety of ways. First, there are very few texts on police psychology, a notable exception being the recent book Psychology for Police Officers by Bull, Bustin, Evans, and Gahagan. Secondly, there has been no text evaluating the role of psychology in the selection and training of police officers. Finally, this is the first text to provide a forum for sharing an international perspective on psychology and policing. Certainly the latter aspect was a major outcome of the meeting in Skiathos. A network of relationships was established which has significantly enhanced international co-operation in this field. The benefits will be felt for many years. In fact, a second international meeting was held at the FBI training facility in Virginia in December 1985. This conference, organized by James Reese, with the assistance of John Stratton and John Yuille, was a direct consequence of the Skiathos meeting.

The organization of this book is relatively straightforward. Section I contains chapters written by the major speakers at the meeting (as well as two chapters by individuals who did not attend the meeting but who represent important aspects of police psychology: Dutton's chapter on domestic intervention, and Hare's chapter on the criminal mind). The chapters in this section represent the major addresses which the lecturers provided at the meeting. Section II of the book contains a sample of the short presentations given by the participants in the conference. There is so much activity in this field that almost everyone who attended the conference had some research or report to present. Although these presentations were brief, space limitations precluded the inclusion of all of the short papers in this text, therefore, less than half of them are included here. They were selected to represent the variety of work and the variety of work contexts of current police psychology. A list of all of the participants is provided at the end of this preface and the reader may wish to write those whose work could not be included here to obtain fuller details about the current state of police psychology. (Additional address information may be obtained from the editor.)

Acknowledgements

An international conference requires a lot of planning and assistance. I would like to formally thank Ray Bull and Karel Nijkerk for their invaluable contributions in all aspects of the meeting. Also, the efforts and assistance of Doreen Kum were essential in making the meeting flow, and in making everyone feel comfortable and welcome. I would also like to thank the staff of the Skiathos Palace Hotel for their extra efforts in helping the meeting to be a social as well as a professional success.

The editing of this book involved the assistance of several people. Karel Nijkerk provided much needed assistance in organizing the papers found in Section II of the text. Judith Cutshall lent her considerable editing skills to overcome the grammatical and spelling limitations of the editor. Her contribution is gratefully acknowledged. Liz McCririck was very patient and dedicated in typing the manuscript.

John C. Yuille
University of British Columbia
Vancouver, B.C., Canada

LECTURERS

Ray Bull
North East London Polytechnic
United Kingdom

Anthony J.P. Butler
West Midlands Police
United Kingdom

Frans Denkers
Amsterdam Police Force
The Netherlands

Robert Loo
Royal Canadian Mounted Police
Canada

Sarnoff A. Mednick
University of Southern California
U.S.A.

John Monahan
University of Virginia
U.S.A.

Karel J. Nijkerk
Erasmus Universiteit Rotterdam
The Netherlands

Leslie Poole
Metropolitan Police Training School
United Kingdom

Martin Reiser
Los Angeles Police Dept.
U.S.A.

Gernot Steinhilper
Der Niedersachsische Minister Der Justiz
Federal Republic of Germany

John G. Stratton
County of Los Angeles
Hall of Justice
U.S.A.

John C. Yuille
University of British Columbia
Canada

DELEGATES

John Adams
Trent Polytechnic
United Kingdom

Robert Adlam
Bramshill Police Staff College
United Kingdom

Peter Ainsworth
University of Manchester
United Kingdom

Stanley Bailey
Northumbria Police
United Kingdom

William J. Barker
Calgary Police Service
Canada

Nouchka Barkhuis
University of Amsterdam
The Netherlands

H. Dale Baumbach
Mt. Diablo Hospital Medical Center
U.S.A.

Knud Eike Buchmann
FHS-Polizei
Federal Republic of Germany

Judith Cutshall
University of British Columbia
Canada

Graham Davies
University of Aberdeen
United Kingdom

Joseph M. Fabricatore
Los Angeles County Marshal's Office
U.S.A.

Guy Fielding
Sheffield City Polytechnic
United Kingdom

Nigel Fielding
University of Surrey
United Kingdom

Harvey A. Goldstein
Prince George's County Police Dept.
U.S.A.

Recep Gültekin
Ministry of Interior
Turkey

George E. Hargrave
Dept. of California Highway Patrol
U.S.A.

Deirdre P. Hiatt
Occupational Health Services Inc.
U.S.A.

Peter Horncastle
North East London Polytechnic
United Kingdom

Jens Cleeman Hors
Rigspolitichefen
Denmark

Pieter C. Immel
Holland Police Academy
The Netherlands

Robin E. Inwald
Hilson Research
U.S.A.

Sandra Jones
Brunel Univeristy
United Kingdom

Reinhold Korbmacher
Fachhochschullehrer
Federal Republic of Germany

Adelheid Kühne
Universität Hannover
Federal Republic of Germany

Robin Lewis
University of Southern California
U.S.A.

António Lourenço
High Police School
Portugal

Gerard Luyendyk
P/A L.S.C.
The Netherlands

Malcolm MacLeod
University of Aberdeen
United Kingdom

Henry Madamba
Atlantic City Police Department
U.S.A.

Mary Manolias
Home Office
United Kingdom

Colin Meredith
Abt. Associates of Canada
Canada

Eric Ostrov
Isaac Ray Center, Inc.
U.S.A.

Susan Phillips
University of Birmingham
United Kingdom

G. Ragna Ragnarsdótir
Ministry of Justice
Iceland

James T. Reese
FBI Academy
U.S.A.

Talib A. Rothengatter
Traffic Research Centre
The Netherlands

M. Gabriel Sciamma
Direction Personnel Formation Police
France

Ellen Scrivner
Prince George's County Police Dept.
U.S.A.

Nicolas Seisdedos
Seccion Estudios, TEA Ediciones
Spain

Eric Shepherd
City of London Polytechnic
United Kingdom

Manuel Alverez Sobredo
Policia Nacional
Spain

Frank Stein
Landespolizeischule
Federal Republic of Germany

Gerhard Steiner
Universitat Basel
Switzerland

Bud W. Stephenson
Weber State College
U.S.A.

P. A. Struijk
Nederlandse Politie Academie
The Netherlands

Barbara Tracy-Stratton
Psychological Services West
U.S.A.

Bryan Tully
Royal Hong Kong Police Force
Hong Kong

Frits Vlek
BIZA Directie Politie
The Netherlands

Roy Wilkie
Centre for Police Studies
Strathclyde Business School
United Kingdom

Roger G. Wittrup
Birmingham Psychological Services
U.S.A.

A. Daniel Yarmey
University of Guelph
Canada

TABLE OF CONTENTS

SECTION I
LECTURERS' CHAPTERS

RECRUIT SELECTION IN THE ROYAL CANADIAN MOUNTED POLICE

ROBERT LOO AND COLIN MEREDITH

The Royal Canadian Mounted Police (RCMP) has a history almost as long as that of Canada. Canada was established on July 1, 1867, and the North West Mounted Police (NWMP) was established by a Government Order-in-Council on August 30, 1873. Some six months later, the first Force recruiting poster was distributed with a statement of the following qualifications:
"Candidates must be active, able-bodied men of thorough sound constitution and exemplary character. They should be able to ride well, and to read and write either the English or French language".

Historically, we can look back upon that early period in the history of both the Force and the Canadian West and state that the caliber of recruits and serving members must have been quite high because these mounted policemen dressed in scarlet tunics earned the respect of white settlers and native peoples alike (R.C.M.P. publication, n.d.). Law and order characterized the settlement period of the Canadian West in the 19th and early 20th century.

Since those early days, the Force has evolved and currently has around 19,000 employees. Approximately 13,500 are regular members (peace officers), about 2,000 are civilian members who are recruited for their highly specialized skills (e.g., forensic chemists in Force laboratories), and about 4,000 are federal public servants who provide many support services. It should be noted that the Force has recruited females as regular members since 1974 and there are now about 500 female regular members serving in the Force across Canada.

As Canada's federal police force, the RCMP enforces federal statutes throughout the country and assists other federal government departments requiring their expertise in law enforcement. With the exceptions of the provinces of Ontario and Quebec which have their own provincial police offices, the RCMP enforces the Criminal Code and provincial statutes in the eight other provinces and in the Yukon and North West Territories. In addition, the Force has agreements with many municipalities to police their communities, enforcing local by-laws as well as provincial and federal statutes. Thus, it can be seen that the Force is involved at all levels of policing--federal, provincial, and municipal. To achieve its policing mission, the Force has over 600 detachments scattered across the country under a Divisional system of 16 Divisions plus the Force Headquarters in Ottawa, the nation's capital.

Like police forces around the world, the RCMP has continually introduced technological and managerial innovations into policing to enhance its law enforcement efficiency and effectiveness. Technological innovations such as computer/telecommunication applications and the forensic sciences combined with the increasing sophistication of society in general and the criminal subculture in particular stress the importance of attracting high quality recruits into the Force.

CURRENT RECRUIT SELECTION PROCEDURES

The basic requirements to become a regular member of the RCMP are that one must:
- Be a Canadian Citizen.
- Be at least 19 years of age (application may be made at age 18, but the applicant will not be eligible for engagement until his/her 19th birthday).
- Be physically and medically fit.
- As a minimum have successfully completed a secondary school education program.
- Hold a valid Canadian licence to operate a motor vehicle and have more than a minimal degree of driving proficiency.
- Be of a good character.
- Be proficient in either official language (French or English).

The Force's recruiting program is under the general direction of the Officer-in-Charge (Oi/c) Staffing and Personnel Branch which is part of the Organization and Personnel ("A") Directorate in the Force Headquarters in Ottawa. The Oi/c Staffing Branch provides functional direction in recruiting matters to Staffing Officers in the Divisions and the Staffing Officers usually report through an Administration and Personnel Office to the Division Commanding Officer. Recruit advertising, the formation of recruit troops for training at the Academy ("Depot" Division) in Regina, Saskatchewan, and the monitoring of recruitment activity are carried out centrally by the Staffing and Personnel Branch in the Force Headquarters. Actual recruit selection is done by the Staffing Officer and his staff, particularly the Staffing non-commissioned officers (NCO's), in each Division. The Staffing NCO's are highly experienced police officers who are thoroughly knowledgeable of both the recruit selection process and recruit training at the Academy and who are usually experienced interviewers. Except in a few large cities, the RCMP does not operate recruitment centres. Rather, each of the over 600 detachments and 39 sub-Division Headquarters across the country is considered a recruiting point for the Force. The detachment's role is to foster interest on the part of individuals in a career with the Force and to perform a preliminary screening of applicants according to the basic requirements.

The assessment of the applicant's satisfaction of the seven requirements noted above typically involves the following types of actions. Applicant documentation is examined to ensure that applicants meet the requirements of Canadian citizenship, age, formal education, and possession of a valid driver's permit. Canadian citizenship is stressed because our members should be knowledgeable of the society which they serve and be recruited from the society thereby making the Force representative of the society itself. Age and education requirements ensure that recruits have at least the basic education level required as a basis from which to tackle recruit training and that they adjust readily to the demands of police training and police life. A driver's permit ensures that candidates have at least basic driving skills and would be capable of achieving the necessary level of driving skills required for police work. A check of driving records also helps assess the candidate's driving behaviour in terms of driving infractions and accident involvement.

Physical and medical fitness are assessed through the combination of a comprehensive medical examination plus the taking of a personal and family health history. All recruits must be of sufficient physical stature, mental and physical health, and fitness to successfully complete recruit training and then fully perform their policing duties which can be physically and mentally demanding and which can involve the use of physical as well as deadly force.

Two paper-and-pencil tests, the Education Test and the Psychometric Test, are administered to help ensure that applicants have the learning potential to tackle not only recruit training but also police and managerial training later in their career. It is recognized that policing in a highly sophisticated, technological society requires the potential for high levels of investigative and administrative skills.

The Education Test is a three-hour test developed in 1964 (revised 1979) and it consists of two parts. Part I consists of 100 items divided among five subscales: mathematics, geography and science, social studies, general knowledge, and language. Part II is a requirement to write a composition of at least 300 words on one of four given topics. The Psychometric Test was constructed by Dr. George A. Ferguson in 1945 and is based upon the Canadian Army's "M" Test. Dr. Ferguson[1] was a Major serving with the Canadian Army at war's end in 1945 and because of his extensive training and experience in psychological test construction, he was directed by Colonel W. Line (Director Personnel Selection, Canadian Army) to follow through on Roderick Haig - Brown's report on recruit selection in the RCMP by constructing a test for the Force. The Psychometric Test consists of two timed parts (total 45 mins.) which stress both speed and accuracy. Part I consists of questions which deal with verbal analogies, vocabulary, and concept formation. Part II consists only of pictorial analogies questions.

The assessment of "good character" is conducted through a combination of documentation review, personal interview, and a security investigation. The main aims are to ensure that candidates have not been convicted of any significant crime and have a history of good social adjustment. The personal interview conducted by a recruiting NCO also focuses on the applicant's motivation for applying to the Force, his/her view of the police role, and desire to actively serve/participate in community life. The interview also covers the applicant's stability, industry, perseverance, loyalty, self-reliance, sociability, and leadership. The interview situation also permits the interviewer and applicant to focus on the applicant's values, life interests, attitudes, hobbies, sports, and achievements.

In the selection process, the Force draws from a potential pool which consists largely of 18-20 year-old high school graduates who meet the basic requirements identified earlier. Applicants who meet the basic requirements are invited to take the Education Test. Those who achieve at least the minimum acceptable score are invited to return to take the Psychometric Test and to be interviewed for up to three hours. Each component of the selection process is given a weight and points are tallied for each candidate. Candidates who are found to be acceptable are placed on a national waiting list where they remain for up to two years. It should be noted that the waiting list often contains about 1000 names and that in some years fewer than 100 candidates are actually sent to the Academy for recruit training. It is evident that with low

---

[1]Personal communication with Dr. Ferguson, 1985.

attrition in the Force and, subsequently low recruitment, the Force is able to select-in the "cream" of the eligible candidates.

Recruit training consists of a six-month program at the RCMP Academy in Regina, Saskatchewan, and then a six-month on-the-job training period in a detachment.

CONCERNS WITH PRESENT SELECTION PROCEDURES
Test Validation

Validation of the Education and Psychometric Tests has been of particular concern over the years. Several studies were conducted between 1945 and 1976. These studies found reliability coefficients ranging from about 0.40 to 0.80. However, none of the studies attempted a rigorous validation using different types of R.C.M.P. or applicant samples and various criterion measures.

Wevrick and Hung (1980) performed the most recent and most comprehensive reliability and validity studies of the Education and Psychometric Tests to date. Using anglophone (N=279) and francophone (N=342) samples of applicants[2] from the two-year period 1978-79, they found internal consistency reliabilities (Kuder-Richardson 20 formula) of 0.88 and 0.83 respectively for the Education Test and 0.89 and 0.90 respectively for the Psychometric Test using the 148 anglophones and 209 francophones who also completed the Psychometric Test.

In the validation study, scores on the Education and Psychometric Tests were validated against (a) the overall academic examination scores obtained in recruit training at the Academy; and (b) the on-the-job performance as indicated by performance evaluation scores obtained from the Force's computerized personnel information data base. A total of 3342 files for regular members engaged between 1975 and 1978 were included in the study. Of these, 558 were francophones. Validity coefficients in the form of Pearson correlations, uncorrected and corrected for restriction in range, are presented in Table 1.

While both the Education and Psychometric Tests were significant predictors of training performance at the Academy, they were not predictors of on-the-job performance. Secondly, the tests were better predictors for the anglophone than for the francophone group. This difference is not surprising given that the tests were developed in the English and later translated into French. Interestingly, when Weverick and Hung pursued the various interrelationships, they found that the correlation between training performance and job performance was only 0.21 for the anglophone group and 0.15 for the francophone group.

---

[2]Data are collapsed across gender.

Table 1
<u>Validity Coefficients</u>

	Anglophones		Francophones	
	Training	Performance	Training	Performance
Uncorrected				
Education Test	0.37***	0.11	0.21*	0.05
Psychometric Test	0.41***	0.03	0.31**	0.04
Corrected				
Education Test	0.53***	0.16	0.27**	0.06
Psychometric Test	0.44***	0.04	0.38***	0.04

*<u>p</u> < .05   **<u>p</u> < .01   ***<u>p</u> < .001

<u>Psychological Services</u>
  Psychologists have not played a role in recruit selection. However, with the Force commitment to develop in-house health services for its members came the decision to staff Regional Psychologists as program managers in the eight Force Health Centres across the country. Also, a Chief Psychologist would be staffed in "H" Directorate, a policy centre, in the Force Headquarters in Ottawa. Psychological services for regular members of the Force can be best described under the rubric of occupational clinical psychology; our mandate is to provide services to members as our end clients and, at this stage in our development, not to provide a forensic psychology function.
  The Regional Psychologists in the Health Centres can provide the following services in support of recruiting:
  - Advise NCO interviewers who have concerns over the psychological status of any applicant.
  - Provide formal psychological assessments on applicants referred by recruiters who are concerned over the psychological status (e.g., psychopathology) of applicants.
  - Participate and provide technical advice on the development of new selection tests, validation studies, and on test revisions.
  - Prepare position papers for Force use in defending the use of psychological selection tests for recruit selection.
  The participation of the Regional Psychologist in Regina where the Academy is located would focus on three main areas:
  - Acting as a resource person on behavioural issues to training staff.
  - Participating in recruit training by lecturing and by conducting seminars and workshops for recruits and, in the case of married recruits, their families.
  - Providing counselling services to recruits and, when necessary, performing psychological assessments and providing therapy.

THE NEW RECRUIT SELECTION TEST PROJECT
  A number of factors contributed to the decision on the part of the RCMP to develop a new job-related recruit selection test. This section discusses the most important of these factors.

Societal Changes

There have been a number of major changes in Canadian society since World War II. Many of these changes have had impacts on recruit selection and on the police role in Canada. For example, there has been large-scale immigration into Canada in the post-war period. Thus, the Canadian mosaic has become more richly represented by racial and ethnic groups from around the world. As well, there have been substantial changes in educational systems at all levels across the country. These changes should be considered in selection standards and selection tests. Also, there has been a trend for Canadian youth to stay in school longer and obtain post-secondary education through universities and community colleges. Finally, there has been a greater emphasis on the use of the French language in Canada and, therefore, a greater emphasis on bilingualism especially for those who deal with the public.

From its beginnings, the force has recruited men. However, in 1974 the Force began recruiting females and their number have increased steadily to the current level of about 500. The continued recruitment of female members will result in their increasing proportional representation in the Force and, therefore, the increasing representativeness of the Force of Canadian society.

Finally, the Canadian Human Rights Act forbids discrimination on the grounds of race, national or ethnic origin, colour, religion, age, sex, marital status, family status, pardoned conviction, and disability (mental or physical). Certain unavoidable exceptions are acknowledged. Relevant to the police selection area are bona fide occupational requirements (e.g., a job may be refused to a person who cannot perform it safely, efficiently, and reliably).

Questionable Validity of the Existing Tests

As discussed above the reliability and validity of the RCMP's current selection instruments were studied by the staff of the Ministry of the Solicitor General of Canada in 1980. Their findings indicated that the reliabilities of both the English and French versions of both tests were acceptable. However, the validity data showed that while the tests were related to academy training scores, they were not related to the RCMP's job performance measures. As well, English language applicants were found to score somewhat higher than French language applicants on the psychometric test. Clearly, it was time to develop new tests.

In 1983, the private firm of Abt Associates of Canada was chosen as the successful bidder to undertake the task of developing a new job related selection test for the RCMP. The activities performed in the conduct of this project are described in the sections which follow.

ORIENTATION

Several distinct tasks were performed to both familiarize the project team with current RCMP selection practices and performance measures, and to gain a more general understanding of police job analysis and selection practices.

Literature Review

The work began with a computerized literature search of the U.S. National Criminal Justice Reference Service bibliographic database in an effort to identify relevant references on police job analysis, selection practices and performance measurement. The project team also reviewed materials provided by the RCMP, and by the Ministry of the Solicitor

General. A number of useful references were located which assisted in the development of the job analysis survey form (discussed below). The search did not, however, succeed in finding any data collection instruments which were considered suitable for use in this project "off the shelf".

Interviews at Headquarters

RCMP members working in Training and Development and in Human Resources Planning provided our project team with briefings on current RCMP practices in selection and training. They also provided information and documentation on current performance measures taken during basic training, recruit field training and on the job as a constable.

Develop Job Inventory

A preliminary job inventory for RCMP junior constables was developed on the basis of both our literature review, and RCMP materials. Of particular relevance were Ericson's (1982) study of the Peel Regional Police, Rosenfeld and Thornton's (1976) Police Selection Test developed for the International Association of Chiefs of Police, and Spielberger's (1979) reference text on police selection. In terms of RCMP materials, the work categories in the Manhour Daily Report and in the Recruit Field Training Performance Record were particularly useful. The substance of the job inventory is reflected in the contents of the semi-structured protocol used in our interviews with constables (discussed below).

Site Visits and Interviews

In order to gain a broader understanding of the nature of the various duties performed by RCMP constables across the country, project team members visited both Depot (the national training academy), and a number of detachments across the country. At Depot, we were given an overview of the contents of basic training, and discussed the performance measures taken there. We also sought the views of the instructors at Depot as to what qualities they believed should be selected for in today's recruits.

We also interviewed five recruiting NCO's as well as 21 junior constables (including 7 females) from across Canada. The constables' interviews were conducted following a semi-structured interview format intended to provide the basis for the job analysis survey form.

The recruiting NCO's were asked their views on current selection and performance measurement practices, and on the qualities they look for in potential recruits. The NCO's identified such attributes as "common sense", maturity, emotional stability, interpersonal skills and self-confidence as characteristics they look for in potential recruits. The constables were asked what their jobs involved, and what qualities enabled someone to perform their job at a superior level. In terms of the desired attributes, the constables' responses were similar to those of the NCOs.

Finally, we interviewed representatives of the Toronto, Ottawa and Peel Regional Police, as well as the Ontario Provincial Police to gain an understanding of the selection practices of these relatively large police organizations. We also obtained a brief description of the selection procedures followed by the Montreal City and Quebec Provincial Police. We found that while these organizations make use of psychological tests to "weed out" unsuitable candidates, their selection criteria and procedures are not based on job analyses, and rely heavily on background checks, and on interviews with both individual officers and selection boards. In short, as far as we were able to ascertain at the time of our interviews, no police organization in Canada was employing selection procedures based on formal job analysis.

THE JOB ANALYSIS SURVEY

Our basis for developing a job-related selection test is quantitative job analysis. Quantitative job analysis is the only way to ensure that selection tests are clearly job-related. A complete job analysis provides several benefits:
- It helps ensure that selection tests both appear to be and are job-related.
- It meets the legal requirements that selection tests must be job-related.
- It provides a focus for the development of selection devices. Each element of the job analysis yields an element in the selection test.
- It facilitates future development of tests. That is, if the job is changed in the future, then changes in the selection test can be made more easily when the relationship between the selection test and the elements of the job is clearly specified.
- It is sound professional practice. In fact, job analysis of some type is required by the professional ethics of test development.

It was within this context of the central role played by quantitative job analysis data that we approached the mechanical task of collecting and analyzing job analytic data. One of the challenging aspects of this phase of the project was the complexity introduced by the fact that RCMP Constables perform various types of duties. There are two major groupings of duties performed by RCMP personnel in the field. These are referred to as contract policing and federal policing. Contract policing is work similar to that performed by municipal or provincial police forces. Federal policing, on the other hand, involves the enforcement of the federal laws and regulations relating to, for example, drugs, customs and excise, and immigration. All applicants selected for recruit training and placement in the RCMP must be suitable for both types of work.

Our first task was to develop a preliminary job inventory for RCMP junior constables. This inventory was developed on the basis of both our review of published literature, and on RCMP materials used to monitor recruit training, performance and work time allocations by operational staff. Categories in the job inventory were refined through a process of in-depth interviews with constables performing various duties across the country. The result of this process was a detailed job analysis form. The job analysis form was designed to take approximately 1/2 hour to complete. The constables completing the forms were asked to indicate both the percentage of their time spent and the average number of hours in a week spent in various work contexts. A somewhat novel aspect of this job analysis form was the basis used to allocate time to the different categories. Rather than first asking the respondents to indicate how much of their time they spent on a particular task, for example, doing paper work, we asked them to estimate how much of their time they spent working with various other individuals or groups. Specifically, they were asked to estimate how much time they spent working with other constables, with court personnel, with the general public on offense and non-offense related matters, and on their own. Next, they were asked to rate each of 10 general work categories according to whether each was a routine or less frequent part of their work, and important or unimportant to successful performance in their current position. Finally, the respondents were asked to indicate individual attributes which they believe make someone particularly good at each general activity. The respondents were instructed to focus on attributes which applicants bring to the organization rather than skills which are learned during training or on the job.

The job analysis forms were distributed to a random sample of 300 junior constables. This represents approximately a 25% sample of the total population of junior constables. Forms were distributed from and returned to RCMP headquarters in Ottawa. In all, 225 completed job analysis forms were returned to us, for a survey response rate of approximately 75%.

ANALYSIS OF THE SURVEY DATA

In developing the test blueprint, the survey data from all but the special constables were subjected to a series of standardizations. First, time spent in various environments was standardized such that exactly 100% of a constable's time was accounted for. The standardized times were then matched up with activities that constables undertake on a regular basis. This yielded a set of activity times for several types of duty: federal, highway, rural and municipal. Significant differences in activity times for different duties corresponded with significant differences that one would expect on a reasonable basis (e.g., driving time was significantly higher for highway patrol). The data were also internally consistent.

The steps in the analysis followed the order of the questions on the survey form:

Step 1

Section I of the survey asked constables to indicate how much time they spent in various roles including:
- Direct contact with other constables
- Working with court personnel.
- Working in contact with the public on offense-related matters.
- Working in contact with the public, but not in relation to a specific offense or investigation.
- Working completely alone.

Responses were given in terms of ranges of time spent per role, e.g., 11% to 20%. Ranges were recoded to their midpoint and treated as single points. The percentages for each role were summed and a total calculated. The resulting total times were less than 100% of time for one-third of the respondents and over 100% for the remainder.

In order to treat each constable's report equally, the percent time spent in each role was divided by the total percent time. This resulted in a standardized percent time per role with the property that the sum of all roles always equalled 100 percent.

Step 2

Section II of the survey was an activity breakdown. For each of the roles in Section I, constables were asked how many hours per month they spent doing a variety of associated activities. The hours for each role were also calculated. Using this information we calculated the percent time each constable spent per activity as:

% time per activity in role = $\dfrac{\text{hours per activity in role X \% time per role}}{\text{hours per role}}$

Using the percent time per activity in role as a basis, we calculated the percent time per activity. We did this by summing associated activity times from all roles that contained it. This led to percent time per activity for ten pre-identified activities: paperwork, looking for suspicious circumstances, preparing for court, testifying in court, interviewing, developing information sources, getting along with co-workers, sharing information with other members, community relations activities, and driving a patrol vehicle.

Step 3

As a check on the usefulness of our time calculations, we compared activities for a few key duties. We concluded the times were reasonable based, in part, on the following observations:
- Patrol for suspicious circumstances: in percent time we found highway duty higher than other duties.
- Interviewing suspects: a higher proportion of time is spent for municipal and rural duty than for highway.
- Time spent in contact with other members is higher for federal and municipal duty than for highway.
- Sharing information with other members is most significant for federal duty and of lowest importance for highway duty.
- Driving time is much larger for highway duty than for rural and municipal duty. In turn, these entail much more driving time than federal duty.

As a further check, we compared our derived activity times to ratings obtained in the survey. Here constables rated activities in terms of how often they did them. For nine out of ten activities there was a rank order match between activity times and ratings of activity frequency. Only for getting along with others did this not hold.

As well, we wanted to be certain that activity times were independent of how important an activity was, as indicated by constables' ratings of importance in the survey. For eight out of ten activities, time was independent of importance. Only for paperwork and for time spent patrolling for suspicious circumstances were importance and time spent significantly related.

Step 4

Activities were also rated for importance. In Section III of the survey, each respondent identified the three most important and three least important activities. The remaining activities were classed as medium importance. Optimal scaling (Nishisato, 1980) was applied to this data to establish the psychological distance between activities that best represented the perception of the constables surveyed.

Scale values and activity times were then combined to yield a single measure of the significance of each activity within the constable's work. This was done by multiplying the percent time per activity with its scaled importance rating. Since both variables have interval level measurement properties (or higher), the resultant scale value is also at an interval level of measurement. This single measure combined with psychological importance and time spent in an activity into a single Time-Importance Score (T-I Score). The T-I score for each activity for each type of duty constitute a basic job analysis.

Step 5

The T-I scores provide the basis for the needed translation into test

TABLE 2   The activity of attributes matrix

ATTRIBUTES	Paperwork	Alert for Suspicious Circumstances	Court Preparation	Testifying	Interviewing	Develop Into Sources	Get along with Peers	Share Info with Peers	Community Relations	Driving	ATTRIBUTE POINT TOTALS	RANK BY SIZE
Grammar/Spelling	1527		7								1534	2
Logical/Concise	2244		23								2267	1
Neat	897										897	6
Good Memory	157	241	11	33				8			450	12
Observant/Alert		1176							151		1327	3
Intuition/Curiosity		1052									1052	5
Common Sense		381				19					400	13
Persistent		452									452	11
Streetwise		150				178					328	14.
Suspicious		328									328	14.
Attention to detail			84								84	21
Confident			22	51							73	22
Verbal skills				128	833	38		45	100		1144	4
Mature/Reliable/ Responsible				8		4			12	613	637	7
Quick thinking/ Intelligent				8	134						142	20
Patient					543						543	10
Calm, Cool					237						237	17
Understand behaviour					636						636	8
Enthusiastic					31						31	23
Rapport						246					246	16
Considerate/Discrete						231					231	18
Crafty						9					9	24
Sociable/Easy going							251	374			625	9
Team Worker							15	159			174	19
ACTIVITY POINT TOTALS	4825	3780	147	228	2280	859	266	212	486	764		
RANK BY SIZE	1	2	10	8	3	4	7	9	6	5		

items and effort. For each activity we weighted the important qualities suggested for the activity by the T-I scores of the person suggesting the attribute. This yielded an activity by attributes matrix (Table 2). The elements in the matrix showed the T-I value of each characteristic within an activity. Non-testable characteristics were then eliminated, and related characteristics were combined. The result was a considerably condensed matrix of weights.

Step 6

We used the resultant matrix as a basis for subsequent factor analysis. Using Rao's method of factor analysis with varimax rotation enabled us to further combine circumstances. In fact, it yielded eight testworthy areas for further work (Table 3). Because we used Rao's method we can confirm that the characteristics we propose are a satisfactory fit to the data.

Finally, we assumed that a two-hour testing period could accommodate about 150 test items. Given this time allotment, each element of the matrix was assigned a portion of the test items corresponding to the proportion of T-I scores if represented.

The final result is a test blueprint that indicates which personal characteristics should be tested. These characteristics are matched with policing activities, so that a context for questions can be established. The number of questions per characteristic per activity is derived from the T-I score of that element in a way that clearly reflects job demands.

TEST CONSTRUCTION

At the present time we are in the process of preparing a draft instrument for pre-testing. Several mechanical constraints must be taken into account as we draft the instrument. First it must be administrable in no more than two hours. Secondly, it must be administrable by individuals with little if any training in test administration. Finally, it must be objectively and quickly scorable.

Items are now being developed to measure the eight attributes displayed in Table 3. The attributes are rank ordered according to their time importance weighting. As shown in Table 3, the first attribute we will be addressing is what we have called writing skills. We plan to employ straightforward multiple choice items to assess grammar and spelling. The extent to which applicants' writing is logical and concise will be assessed by a process in which the candidates will read brief descriptions of events and will select from a list of responses the three or four word headline which most correctly summarizes the contents of the paragraph.

To assess interviewing skills we plan to structure the candidate's interviews to some extent. Interviews as currently conducted will almost invariably involve some discussion of the content of the constable's job. We are considering providing a check list with probes for the interviewers to monitor the extent to which the candidate has achieved a detailed understanding of the job, and was able to identify and fill gaps in his/her knowledge. The interviewers will also rate the candidates' verbal facility.

Measurement of the extent to which candidates are observant will involve video presentations of scenes typical of police work. These scenes will include aspects which are "out of place" or incongruous. The candidates' task will be to identify these incongruities.

Table 3
Proposed Approaches to Attribute Measurement

ATTRIBUTE   MEASUREMENT APPROACH

WRITING SKILLS   – for grammar/spelling: Multiple choice items
                        – for logical/concise: Candidates select best
                          summary statement of contents of paragraphs
                          presented as text.

INTERVIEWING SKILLS   – for sociable/rapport: NCO inteviewer ratings
                        – for attention to detail: NCO asks candidate what
                          he/she thinks the job involves. Candidate then
                          reads brief and sketchy job description. NCO
                          asks what more if anything, candidate would like
                          to know about job. NCO rates perceived extent to
                          which candidate has achieved detailed
                          understanding of topic, and was able to identify
                          and fill gaps in his/her knowledge.

OBSERVANT   Candidate views video presentations of scenes
                        typical of police work. Scenes to include aspects
                        which are "out of place" or incongruous. Task is to
                        identify these incongruities.

GOOD JUDGMENT   Candidate views video presentations of scenes where
                        a police officer would face a decision on what to do
                        next, e.g., person fallen through ice, or auto
                        accident with injuries. Task is to select most
                        appropriate course of action from among alternatives
                        presented.

INTUITION/CURIOSITY   Similar format to 'OBSERVANT'. Candidate is to
                        identify 'what's wrong' with scenes presented in
                        video tape.

PATIENCE   Candidates will perform a timed, repetitive motor
                        task requiring attention to detail and neatness. An
                        example of such a task would involve transferring
                        numbers onto a machine readable scoring sheet. The
                        task would be scored for number of numbers correctly
                        transferred.

PERSEVERANCE   Candidates will perform a timed task in which they
                        are seeking something out of place in a long list of
                        similar items. Examples would be searching lists of
                        license plates or credit card numbers for previously
                        identified or incorrectly-formatted entries.

GOOD MEMORY   Candidates will perform three recall tasks in which
                        scenes will be presented to them visually, orally
                        and in writing. Following each presentation, the
                        candidates will answer multiple-choice questions
                        about the scenes.

The measurement of good judgment will involve video presentations of scenes where a police officer would face a decision on what to do next; for example, a person fallen through the ice, or an auto accident with injuries. The candidate's task will be to select the most appropriate course of action from among alternatives presented.

Measurement of intuition/curiosity will follow a format similar to "observant". The candidate's task will be to identify what's wrong with the scenes presented on a videotape, and will proceed to an additional step whereby the candidate will be asked to explain the nature of the incongruity.

Measurement of patience will involve having the candidates perform a timed repetitive motor task requiring attention to detail and neatness. An example of such a task would be transferring numbers onto a computer scoring sheet. The task would be scored for the number of numbers correctly transferred.

Measurement of perseverance will require that the candidates perform a timed task in which they are seeking something out of place in a long list of similar items. Examples would be searching lists of license plates or credit card numbers for previously identified or incorrectly formatted entries.

Finally, assessment of the extent to which the candidates have a good memory will involve having the candidates perform three recall tasks in which scenes will be presented to them visually, orally and in writing. Following each presentation, the candidates will answer multiple choice questions about the scenes.

The number of items to be developed for each attribute will reflect the individual attributes' Time Importance weighting.

One of the real challenges we face in developing a job-related selection test for police constables is achieving the appropriate balance between job content in the test, and assessing skills which can be expected to be developed during training or on the job. In many occupations, candidates for employment have usually acquired competence to perform the duties of the job prior to seeking employment. Truck drivers, for example, typically are licensed and know how to drive before applying for a particular position. Hence a job related selection test could involve actual performance of the work required of a truck driver. In police selection, this traditional approach cannot be followed since most applicants will have had no prior training in police work. In these circumstances, the selection process should focus on the ability of applicants to perform the duties of the job after successfully completing a training program. We must, therefore, be careful to avoid testing applicants for skills and abilities which they will be trained on later.

Finally, we should emphasize some of the advantages we see in using videotape equipment to administer some or perhaps all of the test items. One concern which is important in Canada is that of translation. To the extent that we can use videotape presentation of scenes of police work rather than having to describe the same scenes in words, we can avoid problems caused by inconsistent or inaccurate translation. As well, use of videotape to administer the test should yield some very real benefits in terms of the consistency of test administration. For example, we may be able to use the videotape equipment to provide all initial instructions to those taking the test, and to control the timing of individual components of the test. This should also simplify the task of test administration for individuals with no specific training in this area. Finally, by presenting the entire test via videotape, it will be possible to easily modify the test contents and maintain test security.

THE VALIDATION PLANS

Once a draft version of the test has been prepared, it will be pretested on a sample of individuals who are currently on the waiting list for admission to the RCMP. These will be individuals who have successfully passed the requirements of the existing selection procedure. The data gathered from these individuals will enable us to perform an item analysis on the draft test and correct any obvious problems. We are then planning to conduct a concurrent validation of the new test using performance data currently available for junior constables.

In anticipation of the planned concurrent validation of the new job-related selection test, we reviewed currently available performance measures used by the RCMP. We found that performance data for three distinct time periods are routinely available for junior constables (meaning 1-3 years of service).

Basic Training

Each recruit who completes basic training generates a record referred to as the "Basic Training Assessment". Form 2034 summarizes each recruit's training record in terms of their performance and attitude in 11 disciplines: law, operational training, human relations, technical services, communications training, firearms training, driver training, drill and tactical, swimming and lifesaving, physical conditioning and self-defence. These disciplines are rated on 12 point scales from A+ to D-. For each individual, a grade point average is calculated. Finally, each record includes an assessment of the recruit's estimated need for field supervison, which is rated as one of 'minimum', 'normal' or 'close'. These data, with the exception of the grade point average which is also entered into the RCMP's personnel database, are only available in each member's detailed personnel file at Headquarters and in the records at Depot. Consequently, these data will have to be manually recovered from paper files to be used in the validation. For the purposes of the concurrent validation, we will utilize all of these data with the exception of those variables which reflect physical performance (the last six disciplines listed above).

Recruit Field Training

Following basic training, recruits experience six months of 'Recruit Field Training' (RFT) during which time they are to be exposed to the full range of duties expected of a working constable. Training and supervision in these tasks is to be provided by the recruit's Detachment Commander or his designate. This individual is responsible for completing the recruit's training form which indicates for up to 275 separate tasks whether each was demonstrated to the recruit, performed by the recruit and performed satisfactorily by the recruit.

We were informed that there is considerable variation in the amount of supervision provided recruits during their field training period, depending largely on the size of the detachment, and the amount of time available to the NCO. Consequently, we do not propose to include any data from the RFT in our validation analysis.

On the Job

Constables typically experience their first formal performance appraisal three months after completing recruit field training. The second appraisal follows nine months later, and subsequent appraisals occur every twelve months thereafter.

The RCMP's Performance Evaluation Profile (PEP) system involves two distinct rating tasks. Part 1 employs a forced choice technique where the rater is required to rate sets of four statements, according to the extent to which each statement describes the ratee. Referred to as the "Tetrads", this component of PEP is not widely regarded as fairly and accurately reflecting individuals' performance, in part because the ratees do not understand the mechanics of the scores, and in part because some raters are believed to have "figured out" how the scoring works meaning that their subjective ratings can be introduced into the Tetrad scores. Although it appears to us to be a sophisticated and reasonably objective assessment instrument, the Tetrads reported lack of credibility among the rank and file discourages us from placing much emphasis on these data in our validation analysis. Even so, for exploratory purposes, we believe it would be useful to examine the Tetrad scores along with the other measures in attempting to validate the test.

Part 2B of the PEP requires the raters to score the ratees on 6 point scales from unsatisfactory to outstanding, reflecting 25 dimensions of their performance. Given their apparent acceptance among the members interviewed, we propose to use these data in validating our test. We should have at least two sets of these data for all constables who have completed more than 18 months of service.

THE STUDY GUIDE

A pre-test study will also be developed to be used in conjunction with the new test. It will explain the mechanics of the testing procedures to the candidates. Sample items of each type to be included in the test will be provided for the candidates to complete prior to beginning the test proper. Candidate's responses to the sample items will be reviewed by the test administrator to ensure that the candidate understands the format of each question type, and is entering his/her answers in the appropriate area of the test booklet.

FUTURE DIRECTIONS IN SELECTION

Future directions in the recruit selection area must attend to several major issues and consider the potential reinforcement of the new selection battery with other cost-effective selection procedures.

Comprehensive Validation

The new selection battery must be validated against recruit training performance. Such validation work should also take place within a larger context, specifically, a comprehensive validation of the total recruit selection procedure including the interview process. Clearly, a comprehensive validation would require a reliable longitudinal data base containing all relevant predictor and criterion variables.

Validation work would also address concerns over possible differences in predictive validity for anglophones and francophones, for males and females, and for minority groups (e.g., native people).

Screening for Psychopathology

Formal screening for personality factors or psychopathology is not currently done and it is recognized that such screening, especially, using paper-and-pencil inventories/tests is open to much criticism. However, it would be helpful to interviewers to be able to discuss specific applicants or to refer specific applicants to our Regional Psychologists when some specific concern is raised over the psychological stability of an apparently highly qualified applicant.

The Canadian Charter of Rights and Freedoms

In addition to our need to satisfy the conditions of the Canadian Human Rights Act mentioned earlier in the text is our need to satisfy Section 15 of the Charter of Rights and Freedoms which came into force in Canada on the 17th of April 1985. The text of this section is as follows:

"15(1) Every individual is equal before and under the law and has the right to the equal protection and equal benefit of the law without discrimination and, in particular, without discrimination based on race, national or ethnic origin, colour, religion, sex, age or mental or physical disability. (2) Subsection (1) does not preclude any law, program or activity that has as its object the amelioration of conditions of disadvantage because of race, national or ethnic origin, colour, religion, sex, age or mental or physical disability."

Clearly, employment testing will be seriously challenged in the courts over the years following enforcement of Section 15. It is essential that selection testing in the Force satisfy this section of the Charter but this will happen over a period of time because "landmark" rulings on this section have yet to be made by the courts. It should be appreciated that all organizations in Canada using personnel selection testing are operating in an environment which is in transition and somewhat ambiguous.

The Assessment Center Method

Current selection procedures rely mainly on documentation review, paper-and-pencil tests/exercises, and a personal interview. A (mini) assessment center approach, perhaps, as the final hurdle in the selection process might improve selection decisions. The assessment center approach can provide realistic (high-fidelity) police-type exercises to allow assessors additional opportunities for behaviour observation. Such exercises could help assess candidate's decision making under stress, interpersonal skills and style, and problem solving skills among other relevant dimensions.

It is recognized that the assessment center approach is expensive. However, if it is used as one of the final components in the selection process then a relatively small number of candidates are assessed. From the candidates' perspective, it would provide a realistic preview of policing and an opportunity to familiarize themselves with the Academy, perhaps the most practical location for the assessment center.

Closing Comments

The importance of recruit selection in any police force is underscored. Historically the RCMP has attracted many more qualified applicants than were required; thus, the Force has been able to select "the cream of the crop" to fill its ranks. Fortunately, this historical trend is expected to continue in the foreseeable future. The development of a new psychological selection battery as described in this paper will enhance the job relatedness of our procedures and the defendability of our procedures both professionally and legally.

It is also recognized that selection is only one component in a comprehensive recruitment to retirement career cycle. Psychological Services in the Force provides support to members throughout the career cycle under the rubric of occupational clinical psychology.

REFERENCES

Crosby, A., Rosenfeld, M., & Thornton, R. F. (1979). The development of a written test for police applicant selection. In W. Spielberger (Ed.), Police selection and evaluation. New York: Hemisphere.

Ericson, R. V. (1982). Reproducing order: A study of police patrol work. Toronto: University of Toronto Press.

Industrial Relations Center. Job functions inventory for police officers. Chicago: University of Chicago, Industrial Relations Centre, n.d.

McCormick, E. J. (1976). Job and task analysis. In M. D. Dunnette (Ed.), Handbook of industrial and organizational psychology. Chicago: Rand McNally.

Nishisato, S. (1980). Analysis of categorical data: Dual scaling and its applications. Toronto: University of Toronto Press.

Rosenfeld, M., & Thornton, R. E. (1976). The development and validation of a multijurisdictional police examination. Princeton: Educational Testing Service.

Royal Canadian Mounted Police. The origins of the R.C.M.P. A publication of the Public Relations Branch, n.d.

Spielberger, W. (Ed.). (1979). Police selection and evaluation. New York: Hemisphere.

Wevrick & Hung, C. K. (1980). R.C.M.P. selection study. Technical Report, Ministry of the Solicitor General, Ottawa.

CRITICAL ISSUES FOR THE POLICE PSYCHOLOGIST IN TRAINING POLICE

MARTIN REISER

This chapter focuses on important training issues in which the police psychologist will likely become involved. Starting with some of the common problems psychologists have experienced consulting in a police environment, the chapter then considers several critical issues such as an appropriate training model, the psychologically-based training needed for officers today, problems in training females for field police work, peer counseling training, supervisory and management training, and physical fitness-wellness training.

The author's comments are based largely on his 17 years of experience as a police psychologist within the Los Angeles Police Department (LAPD). Begun as a one-person operation in 1968, in-house psychological services at LAPD have gradually evolved into a comprehensive program of therapy, training, research, management consultation and crime-specific consultation. Over time, the Behavioral Science Services Section has come to be perceived as an important, integral part of the Department.

The police officer in modern society functions primarily as a social scientist (Singer, 1970). Most of the time, the officer deals with people problems rather than with crime situations (Bard, 1970). With minimal supervision and opportunity for consultation, the officer is required to make critical life and death decisions, often instantaneously (Bittner, 1970). In this executive decision-making role, the officer must use appropriate discretion, deal with considerable ambiguity, and perform as a leader rather than as a follower who is trained rigidly to go by the book (Reiser, 1974a; Waldhuber, 1979).

The complex demands of the police role, the structure of the police organization, the policing goals in regard to the community, and the basic philosophy of the department all influence the kind of training that will be provided ultimately and the ways in which that training will likely impact the officer's relationships with the citizens in the community, with peers and also with superiors in the police organization (Newman & Steinberg, 1970).

Problems Consulting with Police on Training

Police and mental health professionals have tended to view each other with suspicion, distrust, and apprehension over the years. Attempts at collaboration have typically involved a testing-out phase on both sides lasting from six months to a year before some of the strongly held prejudgments and stereotypes are partially dissolved (Reiser, 1982).

Mental health specialists may stereotype police as "dumb rednecks" who don't know how to communicate with people, while police tend to perceive psychologists and psychiatrists as "pie in the sky, ivory tower bleeding hearts" (Reiser, 1970). This state of affairs has resulted in serious problems in communication.

The attitude on the part of some consultants in approaching police administrators is that of omniscient savior condescending to educate ignorant and insensitive police types. As might be expected, this approach rarely makes friends or influences people (Hodges, 1970). If the neophyte consultant approaches the police administrator with an attitude of curiosity, of wanting to learn about the police environment and police problems and perhaps requests an opportunity to be a "student" for a period of time before giving advice or making recommendations, the response from the police manager is likely to be more positive (Reiser, 1970).

Another common problem occurs when the behavioral scientist sees himself as an agent of radical change in the police milieu (Caplan, 1970). Police organizations tend to be conservative, bureaucratic, and hierarchical, where change usually occurs in an evolutionary rather than a revolutionary way. The consultant who is impatient, unwilling to invest large amounts of time, who is unable to cope with the chronic frustrations linked to organizational and city politics, and the inherent resistances to change, is likely to become disillusioned, depressed and withdrawn (Gilbert, 1960).

The question of an in-house versus an outside consultant is still debatable (Mann, 1973). The inside consultant is subject to influences which can dilute or subvert his basic role if not countered. He may experience identity confusion with pressure toward acting and feeling like a police officer with the attendant attitudes and values. If so co-opted, the consultant may become an apologist in his over-identification with police and experience difficulty in maintaining his professional identity and necessary ethical standards (Reiser, 1972). The in-house consultant has more opportunity for acceptance, for access to privileged information inside the organization, and the ability to implement the kinds of research and programs that the outside consultant will not be able to do. However, the outside consultant may find it easier to maintain his professional distance from the police culture and to feel less stressed by organizational expectations and demands since his role and commitments are usually time-limited (Reiser, 1971).

The level at which the consultant gets plugged into the organization is an important consideration. In order to address significant issues and to have the necessary status and clout to get the job done, the consultant ideally should be connected at the top level of the organization and have the support of the upper management staff. If the consultant is forced to report to a first-line supervisor or middle manager, the filtering processes in the hierarchy will generate more opportunities for rejection of proposals than approvals. This could lead to a general tendency to down-play the importance of the psychologist's role and the psychological issues being addressed (Cohen, Sprafkin, Oglesby, & Claiborn, 1976).

The training consultant needs to view police officers as autonomous professionals who function in the field at the level of executive. The officer is de facto the primary mental health agent in the community on a 24-hour basis (Elkins & Papanek, 1966) whose main function is dealing with personal crises, violence, and a wide assortment of people problems (Caplan, 1970). In this connection, it is important that the consultant not underestimate or downgrade police needs for technical and professional sophistication (Reiser, 1974b, 1975).

Another significant problem area being examined currently is that of supervisory and management training in police organizations. The gradual shift in organizational structures and management styles from the authoritarian-bureaucratic toward more situational and participative models has been affecting police agencies as well as private industry (Archambeault & Weirman, 1983). This transition and the conflicts generated by countervailing forces have contributed to an increased need for human relations sophistication at the supervisory level and greater sensitivity to human resources and people problems by police managers (Bopp, 1984).

Training areas that require special knowledge for participation by behavioral science consultants include investigative hypnosis and hostage negotiation. Assisting police in setting up an appropriate hypnosis interview program to enhance the recall of victims of major crimes can be a meaningful contribution (Reiser, 1980). The consultant may also become involved with hostage negotiation training for police personnel and participate as a member of the negotiation team (Miron & Goldstein, 1978). He should be familiar with the material on suggestibility techniques used to influence hostage takers and other suspects (Reiser & Sloane, 1982).

A problem area in need of attention is that of designing and implementing the research needed to determine the cost benefits of the wide variety of training programs used in police agencies (Reiser, 1972). There have been relatively few longitudinal research projects done to evaluate the effectiveness of training and the influences of the police environment. The typical "quick and dirty" retrospective approach frequently avoids or leaves too many unanswered questions about the shaping influences of the police role and organization over time (Rossi, Freeman, & Wright, 1979).

At the Los Angeles Police Department there are currently several research studies in process. One is a longitudinal model utilizing measures of stress-proneness, hardiness, moral judgment, personality, and wellness (Hogan & Dickstein, 1972; Hogan, 1973; Kobasa, 1979; Holmes & Rahe, 1967; Shealy, 1977). Another study is looking at the interesting question of problems in relationships that develop between male and female officer partners in the field. This research will look at such issues as sexual manipulation interactions, gender-related power struggles, and perceptions of support and competence on both sides (Glaser & Saxe, 1982).

An interesting pilot study presently underway is looking at the effects of physical fitness training and its relationship to wellness and productivity. Three times weekly, on-duty officers in several divisions are given reinforcement training in self-defense and provided the opportunity to do some form of aerobics conditioning. Preliminary results indicate a significant drop in the amount of sick time used by participants in the program, a noticeable increase in morale and comaraderie, and a sense of improved organizational cohesion (Fitness for Life, 1983).

The Issue of an Appropriate Training Model

The need for discipline and accountability for the collections of relatively unorganized street enforcers led police organizations to adapt a military structure. Though this model served well for about a hundred years, the evolving of social mores and institutions led to calls for police reform and professionalization. As Neiderhoffer and Blumberg

(1976, p. 1) point out, "For all its seeming variety, law enforcement remains a slowly evolving creature of the past rather than a new institution born in recent decades and fashioned by the exigencies of the present."

One of the problems with the military model is that it tends to confuse authority with authoritarianism (Adorno, Frenkel-Brunswik, Levinson, & Sanford, 1964). Today, the utilization by the police service of authoritarian attitudes and modes of communication generates and aggravates problems with citizens in the community and among the various rank levels in the police organization. The modern officer cannot behave and function as an occupation trooper in a hostile village. He must operate as a crisis intervener and keeper of the peace with community support and approval (Reiser & Klyver, 1982).

Authoritarian communication tends to be framed in a parent to child mode rather than as adult to adult (Romano, 1981). This generates friction in police interactions and perpetuates the perception on both sides of inequality, with resultant hostility. The adherence to the quasi-military model of policing has contributed to role uncertainty in the minds of the police and public alike (Brown, 1981; Wilson, 1968).

The demands and expectations of the police have been changing over time, requiring an updating of the training model and philosophy of policing (Thibault, Lynch, & McBride, 1985). Police training has traditionally stressed the apprehension of criminals and the repression of crime. However, approximately eighty percent of the time police work deals with people problems rather than with apprehension of criminals (Bard, 1970; Brown, 1981). This reality has forced departments to devise more relevant training in communication skills and in psychological intervention techniques.

The professionalization of police has been a continuing process influenced by the complex needs of a changing society and the realization that knowledge and skills are more important than muscle in doing a credible job in the community. To meet the demands of diverse and challenging situations, police officers need to be flexible and resourceful in choosing strategies to manage difficult problems which defy arbitrary rules and procedures. This requires an ability to tolerate ambiguity in an open-minded rational way (Ingalls, 1979). In contrast to the military command structure, it is the lowest ranking person, the patrol officer, who has the greatest discretion in the police organization (Wilson, 1968).

Traditionally, police academies have utilized a high-stress military model for training recruits employing authoritarian role models and parent-child communications systems (Reiser & Klyver, 1982), this strategy has utilized personal hazing and demeaning of individuals who are slow to conform or catch on. This essentially negative discipline has been rationalized as a way to "separate the men from the boys". The artificially induced stressors were perceived as conditioning the recruits to face the challenges and rigors in the field.

However, the continued use of the authoritarian military model of training has had negative consequences. One such outcome is the exaggeration of the "John Wayne Syndrome" (Reiser, 1973). Recruits tend to internalize a model which includes the "badge heavy", intolerant, and overly aggressive behaviors of instructors. This model then provides the background for future complaints in the field from citizens and supervisors when acted out. This aggression modeling also appears linked to the development of later personal stress problems and authority conflicts within the police organization itself (LeDoux & McCaslin, 1981).

Earle (1973) hypothesized that authoritarian stress training was superior to non-stress training and conducted a longitudinal study at the Los Angeles County Sheriff's Department. He was subsequently forced to conclude that artificially stressed recruits tended to be more aggressive, less flexible, had more difficulty making decisions during crisis situations on the street and seemed less able to discriminate among the options available in use of force situations. It appears that the officer who is trained to be authoritarian-submissive tends to react by avoidance or aggressive acting-out in stressful confrontations rather than by using discretion, flexibility, and individual judgment (Levinson, 1976; Niederhoffer, & Blumberg, 1976).

Another problem emanating from the military model of training is for officers to develop a tunnel vision perspective of life, an "us against them" philosophy, and a tendency to see things in dichotomies, as good or bad, black or white, with no gradations of difference between. This contributes to feelings of insularity, isolation, and in-grouping wherein police only feel understood and comfortable in the company of other officers (Niederhoffer, 1967; Wilson, 1957). As Baker and Meyer (1980) state it, "Recruits in the academy are taught to see the world as composed of groups hostile to the purpose of the police. Police are portrayed as the upholders of the moral order, who must continuously fight others who are trying to subvert their cause. Such a world view creates difficulty for an officer who must deal with the gradations of intention and meaning that are found among members of the public" (p. 100).

Cantor (1956), in discussing the dynamics of learning, describes the effective teacher as a helper not a master. The teacher is not as likely to be effective if his primary objective is to control or to discipline students. Rather the teacher's main role is to guide and enhance learning which is basically a self-motivated activity. The instructor who respects the dignity and uniqueness of each student will earn respect and aid the student in developing self-respect.

Models of training are critical because they strongly impact trainee learning and subsequent behaviors (Bandura, 1973). If the instructor model is essentially hostile, authoritarian and overly aggressive, it is predictable that many students will employ the defense mechanism of identification-with-the aggressor as a way of coping with the situation. The internalized aggressor model will then more likely become operative when trainees encounter conflict and confrontation situations in the field. A rigid military training model for police will likely contribute to authoritarian management styles and a focus on punitive discipline strategies in attempting to regulate and control employee behaviors (Lipsky, 1980; Walsh, 1983; Waldhuber, 1979). When authoritarian-centered behaviors prevail in a police organization, growth is inhibited, dependency conflicts are emphasized, and much energy is dissipated in the attempt to solve self-generated internal problems.

Levinson (1973), in discussing the carrot and stick philosophy of human motivation, suggest that the power problems inherent in a bureaucratic structure are ultimately self-defeating. "An organization is a problem-solving mechanism. It is an educational institution that, for its own survival, must increase the psychological and economic competence of those who work in it. This conception calls for a different role for the leader; that of a teacher of problem-solving and a facilitator of human development" (p. 31).

Thus, the front-end training model has serious implications for the overall structure and management of the organization. Vroom (1972) points out that management by control is ineffective in motivating people whose basic needs are satisfied and whose ego-needs and self-fulfillment are dominant. The incentive for effective performance in the participative management approach are in the task or job itself, not in the consequences of task performance. In other words, it seeks to create conditions under which effective performance can be the goal, not the means to the attainment of the goal. It is based on self-control rather than organizational control (p. 106).

At the Los Angeles Police Department (LAPD) strains have been felt in regard to appropriate training models for the academy. Significant problems have been linked to this issue including communications difficulties, decision-making under stress, alternatives to the use of force, minority hiring, lawsuits, dishonesty behaviors among officers, stress disabilties, and organizational discontent. From the psychological point of view it appears that in some respects these difficulties are fostered by the old authoritarian values and methods that no longer appear workable. Obviously, these problems are complex and have many interacting variables, making it impossible to attribute causality to any one factor. However, it also seems clear that the training model at the front end of the system has tremendous residual power. It provides a continual reinforcement function on new and in-service officers. Over the years it is highly influential in affecting individual and organizational attitudes and values (Reams, Kuydendall, & Burns, 1975; Territo & Vetter, 1981; Norton, 1983).

In recent years the LAPD has formed a Human Resources Development Committee to assist with the process of self-scrutiny evaluation and criticism needed to make desirable changes in the organization (Fitz-Enz, 1984). It has also moved toward situational leadership philosophies (Hersey & Blanchard, 1982) and participative management (Ouchi, 1981; Peters & Waterman, 1982). Quality circles are being employed in different parts of the organization on a trial basis. Basic philosophies of policing and long-range goals are being re-examined (Carter & Gnagy, 1985).

Over time police training will likely move closer to the direction of the university model as opposed to the military version. Attitudes and communications will become more appropriate to the interaction of equal adults. This will have a profound influence on the self-image and professional approaches that police officers draw upon when interfacing with citizens in the community and with colleagues in the police organization.

The Issue of Psychological Training for Police Officers

In order to deal effectively with a wide-range of crises in the field, the officer needs to know himself and to develop skill in using himself as a positive instrument in crisis resolution (Parad, 1965; Specter & Claiborn, 1973). This requires a healthy self-concept, a positive sexual identification, an adult value system, and a sense of self-confidence and adequacy which permits interaction with others as equals (Reiser, 1974b).

In this context, the effective officer has developed his psychological sensitivity. He is aware that his police role, including his emblems of authority, automatically elicits a range of conscious and unconscious negative responses in people. Based on feelings linked to parents, dependency, punishment, criticism, and oppression, people act out toward the cop. Those individuals in the community who haven't worked through their dependency-authority conflicts adequately are more likely to perceive the police officer as symbolic punisher and critic. This automatic response to police officers is on an emotional basis with little awareness or interest in the officer as an individual human being. The trained, confident police officer learns to expect and to deal with these reactions without taking them personally (Reiser, 1973).

The field officer performs a triage service when confronted with individuals in crisis (Klyver & Reiser, 1983). He must decide when arrest is appropriate or when an individual should be hospitalized, referred for out-patient treatment, given brief counseling, or committed involuntarily for psychitric assistance. As the omnipresent mental health agent available in the community, the officer also must be knowledgeable about those who are severely depressed or suicidal, those with abuse problems, including child or spouse abuse, sexual assault, incest, drug abuse, as well as family disputes, and dealing with senile and developmentally disabled individuals (Green, 1976; Monahan, 1976).

In recent years, the plight of the victims of crimes has become a growing concern (McDonald, 1976). Consequently, more comprehensive training in victimology has become essential to the police officer's role (Salasin, 1981). In the past, because of insensitivity, lack of training or a tendency to "kiss off" situations requiring social services skills, officers may have unwittingly contributed a second injury to the victim (Symonds, 1980). This retraumatization of victims was sometimes a function of poor interview techniques involving interrogation methods or of an inappropriate attitudinal set which assumed that the victim was basically responsible for precipitating the crime in the first place (Bard & Sangrey, 1979).

It has become increasingly apparent that the professional officer must have a working knowledge of post-traumatic stress reactions in victims and what is required of him in providing constructive intervention, psychologically and legally (Schwartz, 1975; Banks & Romano, 1982). Victimology training emphasizes the importance of a supportive and non-judgmental role for the officer in all of his communications with and about victims and involved significant others (Zlotnick, 1979).

The Attorney General's Task Force Report (1984) and the American Psychological Association in its final report of the Task Force on Victims of Crime and Violence (1984) emphasized the need for training psychologists and other mental health personnel in these victimology issues as well as police officers and other criminal justice professionals in order to provide meaningful victim assistance and to avoid reinjury by those attempting to help (Parsonage, 1979).

Handling emotionally-loaded crisis situations is a highly stressful task for any professional (Symonds, 1970; Cox, 1978). Because a large proportion of the calls a field officer responds to involve significant human problems, the officer operates at a chronic high-level of arousal in coping with the unknown (Davidson & Veno, 1980; Carson, 1982; Alkus & Padesky, 1983; Terry, 1983). As in other professions, a constant, unrelieved high level of stress may eventually lead to burnout in a significant number of individuals (Maslach & Jackson, 1979; Daviss, 1982). This has been linked to an increasing number of stress disability pensions and related psychological problems among officers ranks in recent years (Haynes, 1978; Petrone & Reiser, 1985). It has become apparent that stress management training for police officers is an important and necessary component in the psychological training area

(Reiser, 1976; Singleton & Teahan, 1978; Stratton, 1978).

Another perennial issue of importance is that of community relations training which focuses on ethnic and cultural needs and differences among minority groups in the community (Steadman, 1972). Historically, there has been considerable experimentation with community relations programs (Watson, 1966). In New York, Bard (1970) initiated the family crisis intervention program. In Sausalito, California, Shev (1968) developed a small group consultation approach with police. In Los Angeles, Sokol and Reiser (1971) developed an Early Warning Mental Health Program for Sergeants. Other notable programs included the Houston police-community relations experiment (Sikes & Cleveland, 1969), a crisis intervention project in Dayton, Ohio (Barocas, 1971), and a program in Covina California designed to inrease empathy of police officers by having them experience being a jail prisoner (Johnson & Gregory, 1971).

Early training in community and human relations involved attempts to change the attitudes of officers in a more positive direction. Techniques included sensitivity training and other confrontational approaches (Petty, Ostrom, & Brock, 1981). However, the attitude change approach was basically unsuccessful (Tehman, 1975), a not surprising result given the outcome data on the difficulty of attitude change in general (Reardon, 1981; Rokeach, 1972). Currently, training in the area of community and human relations tends to focus more on outcome behaviors and desired goals rather than on personal biases or attitudes of the officer (Kusunoki & Rivera, 1985). It has been shown that it is quite possible for an officer to hold attitudes considered negative and yet perform his police role in a competent, professional fashion (Bem, 1970).

Another training question is that involving specialization. Over the years, there has been considerable debate about whether it is better to train officers as specialists or generalists (Bard, 1970; Reiser, 1973). Pragmatically, the generalist model allows all patrol officers to handle the wide variety of interpersonal conflicts encountered daily rather than farming out particular tasks to other specialized units. This approach avoids fragmenting of communications and dilution of service effectiveness to citizens. It also tends to raise the quality of police response across the department. It appears that many police departments including LAPD, have opted for the generalist model for field officers. For optimal training, this involves a small group format with active participation of trainees in acquiring specific skills necessary to the assigned task (Axelbard & Valle, 1979).

The role for the psychologist in the police training area has been fairly minimal until relatively recently. There have been resistances on the part of police administrators with a tendency toward insularity, feelings of skepticism about the usefulness of behavioral scientists, coupled with a desire to maintain control over all training parameters (Gammage, 1963). However, in recent years a growing number of police managers have found it advantageous to add behavioral science expertise. They have discovered that in the design of psychological training programs, in team teaching with police instructors, and in long-range planning for future training needs, psychologists can provide many benefits. These include higher quality training, an increased level of learning, a reduced level of stress among officers, and a greater acceptance of the reality that officers serve a legitimate social science function (Miller & Braswell, 1983).

At the LAPD, psychological training originally consisted of information about dealing with mentally ill and suicidal citizens. Outside behavioral science consultants volunteered their time to teach portions of the program. More recently, because of increased attention and community interest in the areas of uses of force, the plight of victims of crime, handling of alcoholics, and problems of mentally ill in jail, training has been deepened and broadened considerably in the psychological arena. Crisis intervention training has been established in the recruit and in-service schools, a new focus on victimology has been added, and the issue of updating the community and human relations training component is being addressed (Reasons & Wirth, 1975). Currently there are 24 hours of training in crisis intervention and victim management, approximately 10 hours in dealing with mentally ill and suicidal persons, eight hours of community relations, five hours of training in stress management, and six hours on positive communication skills.

Typically, psychological training involves a team-teaching format with a police psychologist and officer instructor sharing responsibility, presenting the material, and interacting with the trainees. They are able to share perceptions and perspectives from each vantage point and to enhance mutual credibility. Rather than straight lecture, a nuts and bolts, hands-on training approach is emphasized. Role-playing, simulations, and video-taped feedback are used to increase effective participant learning in the practicing of strategies and in working through a variety of problems when dealing with people (Breslin, 1978).

Issue of Females in Field Police Work and Training Implications

Traditionally, field police work has been primarily a male occupation with fraternal-type values and territorial imperatives. As in athletic locker rooms, women were perceived as unequal, as interlopers who didn't belong on patrol turf (Gross, 1984). As a consequence, the "policewoman" job classification was used as distinct and different from that of male police officers. Policewomen were relegated to safe areas such as juvenile, front desk, communication, selected detective assignments, jail, and administrative work. Underlying this system was the old philosophy that women really belong at home, in the kitchen, making babies, taking care of husbands, and staying out of "man's work" (Bell, 1982).

The evolution of women's rights and the related change in values and role definitions led to stresses and strains in police organizations attempting to maintain the old standards (Block, Anderson, & Gervais, 1973; Bass, 1982). In confronting resistances and artificial barriers to female equality in police organizations, courts have imposed legal requirements for achieving parity for females. In Los Angeles, a 1980 law suit led to a court-imposed mandate to increase the percentage of female officers in the department and gave it high visibility. It also led to a restructuring of assignment and promotional opportunities for women officers that had previously been more limited (Ayres, 1984).

However, it soon became obvious that there were continuing difficulties in achieving these goals. Assembling a qualified pool of female applicants was problematical and even more alarming was the high attrition rate among females during training. This was attributable mainly to difficulties with physical training and self-defense techniques and linked to female physiological and psychological shortcomings (Molden, 1985). The attrition rate for female recruits was approximately 50% between 1976 and 1980, compared to a 17% attrition rate for male recruits during the same period (Glaser & Saxe, 1982).

In addition to poor upper body strength, several psychological stressors were identified as negatively affecting female applicants and trainees. A significant problem for many females involved identity confusion. The need to be "one of the boys" and to function in the officer's authority role conflicted in many ways with femininity and traditional female role dimensions (Sherman, 1973). Another source of stress was a perceived lack of support for her new officer role both on and off the job (Scott, 1979). After a shift as an officer, the female is often expected to go home and put in another shift cooking, cleaning, and child rearing, while staying in a passive wife's role (Wexler & Logan, 1983). On the job, male partners may question the motives of the female for doing field police work, treat her as unequal, and as a sex object, thus reinforcing the self-doubt and confusion already present.

The directness and assertiveness required of field officers may be felt initially as not lady-like and therefore not ego syntonic. Some female applicants are motivated toward a police career by the romanticized version of it as depicted on television in programs such as Charlie's Angels. This fantasy notion of the police role is punctured during the rigors of academy training leading to disillusionment and withdrawal.

Another stressor experienced by many female trainees results from their emotional flexibility. Traditionally, females are permitted to react to affective situations more openly than are males. The need to keep emotions under tight control while functioning as an officer may require the utilization of suppressive defense mechanisms experienced as unnatural by females. This leads to overcompensation in some indiviudals with apparent emotional coldness and avoidance of prolonged interaction with people (Dilucchio, 1975).

The movement of more females into field police work has resulted in problems for male officers as well (Flanagan & Menton, 1984). Many have expressed a fear of not being backed-up in physical confrontations, observing that women cannot wrestle or fight well and therefore will not be able to perform in a situation of physical danger (Charles, 1982). Males may resort to sexual games in maintaining their superiority over females in the organization. This can range from demeaning jokes to outright sexual harassment (Martin, 1980). The wives of officers may add to the overall conflict by expressing anxiety over the intimacy perceived possible between male and female partners during long shifts in a patrol car. Because female probationary officers feel strong pressures to conform to please peers, training officers, and supervisors in order to be accepted and to achieve tenure in the organization, the possibility of relationship conflicts on the job is significant (Kroes, 1982).

In 1980, the Los Angeles Police Department implemented the Crime Prevention Assistant (CPA) Program in order to reduce female attrition by providing pre-training experiences for female applicants that would enhance performance. Major components of this program include physical and self-defense pretraining in order to condition the female applicants to meet the high standards at the academy rather than drop out; academic pretraining to establish the proper level of expectation and parameters required in order to successfully complete the training program; a module called Positive Orientation for a Winning Response (POWR) which was designed to enhance self-concept, to address assertiveness issues, to provide stress management training, and to help females deal with male colleagues by focused discussion and counseling around the variety of role conflicts to be expected. Now in its fifth year, this program is considered very successful. The POWR module has also been incorporated as a regular part of academy training for recruits. The attrition rate for females in the academy has dropped from 55% in 1980 to 11% in 1984 (Annual Report, 1984). Research is being done to evaluate the cost-effectiveness of the CPA Program over time. Data are also being collected to determine what happens to male-female partner relationships as more females are integrated into the patrol force and are considered less of a curiosity.

Issue of Peer Counseling Training

An informal system of counseling by fellow officers has existed in police departments from their beginning. However, the notion of a structured and organized peer counseling approach to assist officers with problems is a relatively recent development. Early peer programs tended to focus mainly on drinking-related disorders (DiGrazia, 1974). In August of 1981, officers of the Los Angeles Police Department initiated one of the first integrated peer counseling programs within a department. Rather than assigning officers as full-time counselors, the LAPD program adds the peer counseling duties as an adjunct to the employee's regular assignment. Peer counselors are available to deal with a wide range of problems including alcohol or substance abuse, financial difficulties, death and illness, relationship conflicts, marital problems, disciplinary issues, and other job-related problems (Wood, 1984). The program became operational in August 1981 and since that time approximately 200 peer counselors have been trained to respond to requests for service around the clock (Klyver, 1983).

The popularity of peer counseling among police personnel appears related to several factors. Many officers are resistant to seeking professional assistance because of anxieties and fears of being perceived as crazy or out of control. Professional services are usually more formal and office-bound as opposed to a more casual relationship with a peer. In this connection, officers often feel that only another police person can understand the relevant problems and pressures, that most mental health professionals do not communicate with that comprehension.

The initial peer counseling training at LAPD consists of a three-day format presented by a staff psychologist and a trained police instructor. Emphasized are role-playing, simulations, and a focus on critical issues in small groups. The course emphasizes skills development in assisting others with problems. Some of the content areas include crisis intervention techniques, reflective, listening, psychological assessment skills, methods of problem solving, alcohol and drug abuse, issues around death and dying, suicide risk assessment and management, and referral contingencies (Trimble, 1981). Officers not trained in positive peer counseling techniques may tend to interview and react to peers with traditional police interrogation methods originally designed to deal with suspects. The training enables the counselor to shift the approach to one of focused listening, open-ended questions, and joint problem-solving rather than taking charge and giving directions (Donahue, 1977).

That peer counselors can be extremely effective has been a consistent finding in empirical research; non-professionals with a modicum of training can function effectively in the counseling arena. Some studies comparing the effectiveness of professional psychologists with minimally trained paraprofessionals have shown that the non-professionals generally perform at least as well and frequently better (Durlack, 1979; Scully, 1981).

Getting counseled by a peer reduces the likeliness of stigmatization and allows for greater freedom in appointment setting. The majority of officers who require assistance with a problem do not need long-term, in-depth therapy. Typically, brief crisis-centered counseling is the intervention of choice in these situations (Truax & Carkhuff, 1977). Where referral is indicated, the peer counselors have available a wide range of referral resources for different problem areas.

Rather than utilizing a structured selection process, it was decided that the peer counselors would be self-selected volunteers. Those currently under investigation, in therapy, or not having the approval of their commanding officer were discouraged from participating in the program. In addition to the initial three-day training for the peer counselors, continuing education training is conducted periodically during the year. These workshops focus on critical incidents and issues which have been encountered, on improving counseling skills, on further practice using videotape feedback, and on discussion of relevant professional and ethical issues.

Although the peer counseling program started as a grassroots effort by officers themselves and is run by an autonomous board of directors, it was recognized that support from the very top of the organization was essential for the program's success. It was also very quickly decided that guidelines on confidentiality issues were necessary. In support of the program, the Chief of Police issued an administrative order establishing guidelines for the peer counseling program. This order legitimized the functions of the peer counselor and requested support from supervisory and command staff in making the program work (Administrative Order #3, 1984). The need for confidentiality was recognized, the only exceptions being violations of the law or serious misconduct. Uncertainties about what constitutes serious misconduct are addressed by the program directors on an individual basis as needed.

Peer counseling has caught on and is being initiated at other police agencies around the country. An example is the recent project developed at the Minneapolis Police Department using a similar format (Anderson & Baisden, 1984).

Issues of Supervisory and Management Training

Police organizations have commonly employed authoritarian management styles which are no longer optimal in today's society (Curran & Ward, 1975). These management behaviors approach people in a paternalistic way and establish unequal, parent-to-child communication processes (Romano, 1981). Employees in this system are viewed as unreliable children who will try to get away with things if not tightly audited and controlled. This approach emphasizes negative discipline and sanctions in controlling and motivating behavior (Schembri, 1983; Hersey & Blanchard, 1982).

A police department constitutes a symbolic family to its members (Reiser, 1974a). Psychodynamically, the Chief of Police is perceived as a powerful father figure who rules with an iron hand. He elicits a variety of ambivalent feelings including respect, resentment, awe, fear, and dependency. The hierarchical rank structure involves a pecking order utilizing seniority as a status measure in the "family" organization. High ranking "brass" are reacted to as powerful, older siblings who may tend to behave in a patronizing way towards subordinates. Rivalry and intense competition for recognition, acceptance, promotion, and increased adult status are important motivators in this structure (Medina & Galvin, 1982).

When authoritarian management approaches dominate, relatively less attention or concern is addressed to individual problems and human factors (Likert, 1967; McGregor, 1960). There is a tendency to view people in the organization as donkeys who can be moved only by dangling a carrot in front of the nose or by a whack over the head with a stick. Levinson (1973) has labeled this the great jackass fallacy. Increasingly, administrators are becoming aware that meaningful employee participation is necessary if some of the iatrogenic problems of the authoritarian organizational structure and philosophy are to be resolved (Eddy & Burke, 1980; Jacobs, 1971; Nash, 1983). At the supervisory and field training officer levels, problems may be compounded because of a preoccupation with logistical details or an absence of training in the teaching-learning area. Role conflicts around identifying as management or trying to be one of the guys often results from inattention to this area in training (Robinette, 1983).

In an attempt to address some of these issues at the supervisory level, a pilot project was launched at the Los Angeles Police Department in April of 1970. The purpose of this program was to train first-line supervisors in the early warning signs of emotional upset in officers, to provide them with brief intervention and assessment techniques, and to train them in referral contingencies. It was anticipated that by identifying a key component of the supervisory role as counselor-helper and providing the necessary training and supports the sergeants would likely become more sensitive to and aware of their officers as people. The one-year pilot project was considered successful and later was expanded to all eighteen geographic divisions. Five outside psychological consultants were hired on contracts to provide backup consultation to supervisors and reinforcement training at each police station as part of a continuing education process. The consultants provided the ongoing hands-on assistance necessary for program viability (Sokol & Reiser, 1971; Reiser, 1979).

In 1984 the program moved into phase two which was to provide assistance to Department middle-managers. The on-scene time of the psychological consultants in each geographic area was increased to enable more contacts with sergeants, lieutenants, and captains. A staff psychologist from Behavioral Science Services Section coordinates the program and acts as liaison between the contract psychologists and Department management. The specific training developed for middle managers consists of twenty modular units ranging from leadership styles to conflict management, team building, stress management, and communication and counseling skills. To date, the program has been considered successful and is continuing into its fifth year.

Managers are now being observed and evaluated more closely than ever by union and court observers in their employee decision-making (Levinson, 1972). Also stimulated in-house by an increase in stress-related disability pensions and serious discipline problems, managers have been forced to look more carefully at the issue of officer dysfunction and injury (Honig & Reiser, 1983). The realization has crystalized that the police officer is himself often a victim and is at risk for developing related symptoms of distress (Reiser & Geiger, 1984). Managers and supervisors are now becoming more familiar with the common post-traumatic reactions and experiences of the police officer (Greller, 1982). That the officer involved in a very stressful event will be in a crisis state with accompanying emotional instability, which can improve or worsen depending on the nature of the intervention, is being addressed by those in command (Reese, 1982). The traumatized officer, as do other victims, needs sensitive handling, support and personal consideration if additional injury is to be avoided. Specific approaches to assist these traumatized officers can be provided (LeDoux & McCaslin, 1981).

Programs currently in place at some police agencies include in-house psychological services, light-duty combined with a rehabilitation approach, stress management, and a mandatory referral system for officers involved in fatal or life-threatening situations (Lazarus, 1966; Monahan & Farmer, 1980).

Issue of Lifelong Physical Fitness and Wellness Training

Traditionally, police departments have been concerned about police officer strength and physical fitness in regard to job requirements (Booth & Hornick, 1984). Academy training has been geared toward getting recruits into peak physical condition, with an emphasis on endurance running and on self-defense capabilities (Kent, 1978). However, the physical training program during the recruit phase usually has not been validated adequately against actual physical requirements in the field (Price, Pollock, Getttman, & Kent, 1979). This training approach has raised credibility questions in the minds of observers and also has contributed to a reversion in some officers to their lesser physical status prior to recruit training. This is a particular problem where there are no provisions for a long-range, ongoing program to maintain fitness after academy training (Hogan, Cute, & Berg, 1979).

The relatively recent movement in private industry and in the general population toward getting and keeping physically fit is part of the overall concept of holistic health and wellness (Fitness for Life, 1983). It has helped motivate some police departments to design and implement lifelong physical fitness and wellness programs (Briley, 1984). It has been recognized that recruit officers in peak condition when leaving the police academy who then give up maintaining their physical state after assignment to the field are less productive in terms of overall performance and are a potential liability to themselves and to the agency in terms of stress disease and job effectiveness (Pollock & Gettman, 1977). As a result, the importance of a lifelong model of physical fitness and wellness is beginning to be appreciated in police circles (Gladis, 1978). Many traditional physical training programs tend to emphasize physical efficiency in handling suspects and criminals as a primary goal. Currently, more agencies are broadening the concept to encompass physical, psychological, and emotional wellness over the employee's career path and beyond (Prentice & Servatius, 1982).

An important rationale for this shift in emphasis has been the relationship of physical fitness and wellness to improved stress management, increased self and job satisfactions, and greater productivity (Stewart & Brook, 1983). Additionally, it is hypothesized that increased fitness and wellness will reduce the costs of stress illness, particularly for the burgeoning number of stress disability pensions (Honig & Reiser, 1983).

Although many models are currently in use for stress management purposes such as relaxation training, biofeedback, self-hypnosis and counseling, one of the most effective long-term strategies involves physical exercise (Pollock, Wilmore, & Fox, 1978). A comprehensive exercise program is the one proved method for reducing the number and severity of employee disabilities (Hogan, 1979; Witczak, 1984; Yamamoto, Yano, & Thoads, 1983). A National Institute of Law Enforcement and

Criminal Justice report (1979) recommended that all police agencies implement a preventive medicine program which includes an exercise module as well as educational information on developing good health habits.

Of the types of exercise possible, those which increase the capacity and the efficiency of the lungs and cardiovascular system appear to be most beneficial (Cooper, 1970; Pollock et al., 1968; Fixx, 1977). This type of aerobic exercise which includes running, walking, swimming, cycling, racquetball, and others, stimulates the heart and lungs and increases the amount of oxygen (aerobic capacity) that the body can process within a given time. Aerobic conditioning increases the body's ability to (1) rapidly breathe large amounts of air, (2) forcefully deliver large amounts of blood, and (3) effectively deliver oxygen to all parts of the body. It helps develop efficient lungs, a powerful heart, and a sound vascular system. Because aerobic capacity is linked to the condition of these vital organs, it is considered one of the best measures of overall physical fitness (Cooper, 1970; Serra, 1984).

Police officers in Dallas who participated in a controlled physical fitness program showed superior job performance, a significant decrease in days off because of sickness or injury, and fewer citizen complaints against them compared with a matched group of officers who did not exercise (Byrd, 1976). Hellerstein, Hornsten, Goldbard, Burlando, Friedman, Hirsch and Marik (1967) had 67 business executives who had been exhibiting physical symptoms, depressive reactions, and defensive behaviors, participate in an active exercise program. After six months, those in the exercise group exhibited fewer depressive symptoms, had improved self-image, and expressed feelings of greater satisfaction and well-being.

In February of 1983, at the Los Angeles Police Department, a department-wide, lifelong physical-fitness model was proposed. Because this model included significant costs for days off to be given as positive reinforcements for those achieving two desirable levels of fitness, it was decided to try an alternate model on a pilot basis that would not involve the dollar expenses for days off. As a result, five geographic areas comprising one bureau in the San Fernando Valley area of Los Angeles was selected for the research. Utilizing roll call periods three times weekly, officers voluntarily participate in self-defense and physical fitness training. Led by officer instructors and using a train-the-trainers concept, the program has generated almost total voluntary participation by officers as well as considerable enthusiasm for the program.

Over a one-year period, the use of sick time by participating officers has decreased approximately one-third, morale and espirit de corps has improved measurably, citizen complaints have decreased, and productivity has gone up significantly. One of the important ingredients needed to enhance the success of this type of pilot program is a human spark plug, an officer who is dedicated to the concept and willing to invest time and energy in making it work. Also critical to success is support from commanding officers in each of the involved areas since management attitudes affect subordinates' motivation. It is anticipated that, in one form or another, a viable model of lifelong physical training and wellness, incorporating information on stress management, proper nutrition, smoking control, and general lifestyle issues, will be implemented agency-wide at the Los Angeles Police Department in the near future.

Police training continues to evolve slowly in response to societal changes and demands. The traditional military model of training is largely outmoded, its continued viability questionable. Continued movement toward a university-type structure seems likely. As change continues, benefits will become more apparent. The reinforcement effect of traditional training on authoritarian attitudes and values will be displaced by an emphasis on adult communication skills needed to constructively handle people problems.

The officer's role in dealing with mental health issues, victims of crime, and family disturbances will continue to expand as the social scientist functions are legitimized. Primary prevention programs, with officers teaching in schools, will be more widely accepted as cost-effective and relevant.

In sum, the police psychologist of the future will be a key player in the police training arena addressing the broad spectrum of psychological problems faced by officers.

REFERENCES

Adorno, T. W., Frenkel-Brunswik, E., Levinson, D. J., & Sanford, N. R. (1964). The Authoritarian Personality, Volumes 1 & 2. Somerset, NY: Wiley.

Alkus, S., & Padesky, C. (1983). Special problems of police officers: Stress-related issues and interventions. Counseling Psychologist, II, 2, 55-64.

Anderson, B., & Baisden, H. (1984, April). Counseling for cops. Minnesota Police Journal, 43.

Annual Report. (1984). Behavioral Science Services, Los Angeles Police Dept.

Archambeault, & Weirman, C. L. (1983). Critically assessing the utility of police bureaucracies in the 1980's: Implications of management theory Z. Journal of Police Science and Administration, 11, 4, 420-433.

Attorney General's Task Force on Family Violence, Final Report. (1984, September). Washington, DC: U.S. Department of Justice.

Axelbard, M., & Valle, J. (1979). Effects of family by crisis intervention training on police behavior. Crisis Intervention, 10, 18-27.

Ayres, B. (1984). The women police manager. California Peace Officer, 13-15.

Baker, R., & Meyer, F. (1980). The Criminal Justice Game. Boston: PWS Publisher.

Bandura, A. (1973). Aggression: A social learning analysis. Englewood Cliffs, NJ: Prentice-Hall.

Banks, H. J., & Romano, A. T. (1982). Human relations for emergency response personnel. Springfield, IL: Thomas.

Bard, M. (1970). Training police as specialists in family crisis intervention. Washington, DC: Law Enforcment Assistant Administration.

Bard, M., & Sangrey, D. (1979). The crime victim's book. New York: Basic Books.

Barocas, H. A. (1971). A technique for training police in crisis intervention. Psychotherapy, 8, 342-343.

Bass, M. (1982). Stress: A woman officer's view. Police Stress, 5, 30-33.

Bell, D. J. (1982). Policewomen: Myths and reality. Journal of Police Science and Administration, 10, 112-122.

Bem, D. J. (1970). Beliefs, attitudes and human affairs. Belmont, CA: Brooks/Cole.

Bittner, F. (1970). The functions of the police in a modern society. Chevy Chase, Md: NIMH.

Block, P., Anderson, D., & Gervais, P. (1973). Policewoman on patrol. Washington, DC: The Police Foundation.

Booth, W. S., & Hornick, C. W. (1984, January). Physical ability testing for police officers in the 80's. The Police Chief, 39-41.

Bopp, W. J. (1984). Crises in police administration. Springfield, IL: Charles C. Thomas.

Breslin, W. J. (1978). Police intervention in domestic confrontations. Journal of Police Science and Administration, 6, 293-302.

Briley, M. (1984, January-February). Today's hottest perk: Fitness in the workplace. Dynamic Years, 12-16.

Brown, M. K. (1981). Working the street. New York: Russell Sage Foundation.

Byrd, D. A. (1976, December). Impact of physical fitness on police performance. The Police Chief, 30-32.

Cantor, N. (1956). Dynamics of learning. Buffalo, NY: Stewart.

Caplan, G. (1970). The theory and practice of mental health consultation. New York: Basic Books.

Carson, S. (1982, October). Post-shooting stress reaction. The Police Chief, 66-68.

Carter, D., & Gnagy, J. (1985, May). A Japanese management technique applied to local policing. FBI Law Enforcement Bulletin, 20-24.

Charles, M. T. (1982). Women in policing: The physical aspect. Journal of Police Science and Administration, 10, 194-205.

Cohen, R., Sprafkin, R. P., Oglesby, S., & Claiborn, W. L. (1976). Working with police agencies. New York: Human Sciences Press.

Cooper, K. H. (1970). The new aerobics. New York: Human Sciences Press.

Cox, T. (1978). Stress. Baltimore, MD: University Park Press.

Cummings, T. G. (1980). Systems theory for organization development. New York: Wiley.

Curran, J. T., & Ward, R. H. (Eds.). (1975). Police and law enforcement, Vol. II. New York: AMS Press.

Davidson, M. J., and Veno, A. (1980). Stress and the policeman. In C. L. Cooper & J. Marshall (Eds.), White collar and professional stress (pp. 131-166). New York: Wiley

Daviss, B. (1982, May). Burnout. Police Magazine, 13-18.

DiGrazia, R. J. (1974, July). Stress program. Boston Police Department, Special Order No. 74-85.

Dilucchio, J. A. (1975, April). Female officers in the department. The Police Chief, 56-57.

Donahue, J. J. (1977). Peer counseling for police officers: A program for skills development and personal growth. Unpublished doctoral dissertation, Boston University.

Durlack, J. A. (1979). Comparative effectiveness of paraprofessional and professional helpers. Psychological Bulletin, 86, 80-92.

Earle, H. (1973). Police recruit training: Stress, vs. non-stress. A revolution in law enforcement career programs. Springfield, IL: Charles Thomas.

Eddy, W. B., & Burke, W. W. (Eds.). (1980). Behavioral science and the Manager's role. San Diego, CA: University Associates, Inc.

Elkins, A. M., & Papanek, G. O. (1966). Consultation with police: An example of community psychiatry. _American Journal of Psychiatry_, _123_, 531-535.

Everstine, D., & Everstine, L. E. (1983). _People in crisis: Strategic Therapeutic interventions_. New York: Brunner/Mazel.

Fitness for life: A program for lifelong physical fitness. (1983, February). Los Angeles Police Department.

Fitz-Enz, J. (1984). _How to measure human resources management_. New York: McGraw-Hill.

Fixx, J. (1977). _The complete book of running_. New York: Random House.

Flanagan, J., & Menton, P. (1984). _Women in policing_. Ottawa, Ontario: Royal Canadian Mounted Police (Mimeo).

Gammage, A. Z. (1963). _Police training in the United States_. Springfield, IL: Thomas.

Gilbert, R. (1960). Functions of the consultant. _Teachers College Record_, _61_, 177-187.

Gladis, S. D. (1978, April). Run - to protect citizens and yourself. _FBI Law Enforcement Bulletin_, 21-27.

Glaser, D. F., & Saxe, S. (1982, January). Psychological preparation of female police recruits. _FBI Law Enforcement Bulletin_, 5-7.

Green, E. J. (1976). _Psychology for law enforcement officers_. New York: Wiley.

Greller, M. M. (1982, November). Police stress: Taking a department-wide approach to managing stressors. _The Police Chief_, 44-47.

Gross, S. (1984, January). Women becoming cops: Developmental issues and solutions. _The Police Chief_, 32-36.

Haynes, W. D. (1978). _Stress-related disorders in policemen_. San Francisco: R & E Research Associates.

Hellerstein, H. K., Hornsten, T. R., Goldbard, A., Burlando, A. G., Friedman, E. H., Hirsch, E. Z., & Marik, S. (1967). The influence of active conditioning upon subjects with coronary artery disease; cardiorespiratory changes during training in 67 patients. _Journal of the Canadian Medical Association_, _90_, 758-759.

Hersey, P., & Blanchard, K. (1982). _Management of organizational behavior: Utilizing human resources_. Englewood Cliffs, NJ: Prentice-Hall.

Hodges, A. (1970, January). How not to be a consultant. _Mental Hygiene_, 147-148.

Hogan, C., Cute, D., & Berg, G. (1979). _Preventing heart disease in public safety employees_. New Haven: The Connecticut Conference of Municipalities.

Hogan, R. (1973). Moral conduct and moral character: A psychological perspective. _Psychological Bulletin_, _79_, 217-232.

Hogan, R., & Dickstein, E. (1972). A measure of moral values. _Journal of Consulting and Clinical Psychology_, _39_, 210-214.

Holmes, T. H., & Rahe, R. H. (1967). The social adjustment rating scale. _Journal of Psychosomatic Research_, _11_, 2.

Honig, A., & Reiser, M. (1983). Stress disability pension experience in the Los Angeles Police Department: A historical study. _Journal of Police Science and Administration_, _II_, 385-388.

Ingalls, J. D. (1979). _Human energy_. Austin, TX: Learning Concepts.

Janis, I. L. (1982). _Stress, attitudes and decisions_. New York: Praeger.

Jacobs, T. O. (1971). _Leadership and exchange in formal organizations_. Alexandria, VA: Human Resources Research Organization.

Johnson, D., & Gregory, R. J. (1971). Police-community relations in the United States: A review of recent literature and projects. The Journal of Criminal Law, Criminology and Police Science, 94-103.

Kavanagh, T. (1980). The healthy heart program. Toronto: Van Nostrand-Reinhold.

Kent, D. (1978). Physical fitness programs for law enforcement officers: Manual for police administrators. Washington, DC: U.S. Government Printing Office.

Klyver, N. (1983, November). Peer counseling for police personnel: A dynamic program in the Los Angeles Police Department. The Police Chief, 66-68.

Klyver, N., & Reiser, M. (1983). Crisis intervention in law enforcement. The Counseling Psychologist, II, 2, 49-54.

Kobasa, S. C. (1979). Stressful life events personality and health: An inquiry into hardiness. Journal of Personality and Social Psychology, 37, 1-11.

Kroes, W. H. (1982). Job stress in policewomen. Police Stress, 5, 10-11.

Kusunoki, G. I., & Rivera, H. H. (1985, July). The need for human relations training in law enforcement. The Police Chief, 32-34.

Lazarus, R. S. (1966). Psychological stress and the coping process. New York: McGraw-Hill.

LeDoux, J. C., & McCaslin, H. H., Jr. (1981, October). Designing a training response to stress. FBI Law Enforcement Bulletin, 11-15.

Levinson, H. (1972). Organizational Diagnosis. Cambridge, MA: Harvard University Press.

Levinson, H. (1973). The great jackass fallacy. Boston: Harvard University.

Levinson, H. (1976). Psychological man. Cambridge, MA: The Levinson Institute.

Likert, R. (1967). The human organization. New York: McGraw-Hill.

Lipsky, M. (1980). Street level bureaucracy. New York: Russell Sage Foundation.

Mann, P. (1973). Psychological consultation with a police department. Springfield, IL: Charles Thomas.

Martin, S. E. (1980). Breaking and entering. Policewomen on patrol. Berkely, CA: University of California Press.

Maslach, C., & Jackson, S. E. (1979, May). Burned-out cops and their families. Psychology Today, 59-62.

McDonald, W. F. (Ed.). (1976). Criminal justice and the victim. Beverly Hills, CA: Sage.

McGregor, D. (1960). The human side of enterprise. New York: McGraw-Hill.

Medina, S., & Galvin, R. (1982, January-February). Corporations on the couch. Inn America, 118-119.

Miller, L., & Braswell, M. (1983). Human relations and police work. Prospect Heights, IL: Waveland Press, Inc.

Miron, M. S., & Goldstein, A. P. (1978). Hostage. Kalamazoo, MI: Behaviordelia.

Molden, J. (1985, June). Female police officers. Training implications. Law and Order, 12.

Monahan, J. (1976). Community mental health in the criminal justice system. New York: Pergamon Press.

Monahan, L. H., & Farmer, R. E. (1980). Stress and the police: A manual of prevention. Pacific Palisades, CA: Palisades Publishers.

Nash, M. (1983). Managing organizational performance. San Francisco: Jossey-Bass.

Newman, L. E., & Steinberg, J. L. (1970). Consultation with police on human relations training. American Journal of Psychiatry, 12, 1421-1429.

Niederhoffer, A. (1967). Behind the shield: The police in urban society. New York: Doubleday.

Niederhoffer, A., & Blumberg, A. S. (1976). The ambivalent force: Perspectives on the police. Hinsdale, IL: The Dryden Press.

Norton, W. M. (1983). Police officer characteristics and the performance of the order maintenance role. Presented at the Academy of Criminal Justice Sciences Meeting.

Ouchi, W. G. (1981). Theory Z. New York: Addison-Wesley Publishing Co.

Parad, H. J. (Ed.). (1965). Crisis intervention: Selected readings. New York: Family Service Association of America.

Parsonage, W. H. (Ed.). (1979). Perspectives on victimology. Beverly Hills, CA: Sage Publications.

Peters, J., & Waterman, R. H., Jr. (1982). In search of excellence. New York: Harper & Row.

Petrone, S., & Reiser, M. (1985). A home visit program for stressed police officers. The Police Chief, 36-37.

Petty, R. E., Ostrom, T. M., & Brock, T. C. (Eds.). (1981). Cognitive responses in persuasion. Hillsdale, NJ: Erlbaum.

Pollock, M., Wilmore, J., & Fox, S. (1978). Health and fitness through physical activity. New York: Wiley.

Pollock, M. L., & Gettman, L. R. (1977). Coronary risk factors and level of physical fitness in police officers. Police Yearbook. Gaithersburg, MD: International Association of Chiefs of Police.

Prentice, M. C., & Servatius, S. A. (1982, July-August). Physical exercise: A method of stress management. Police Stress, 10-12.

Price, C. S., Pollock, M. L., Gettman, L. R., & Kent, D. (1979). Physical fitness programs for law enforcement officers: A manual for police administrators. Washington, DC: National Institute of Law Enforcement and Criminal Justice, Grant #76-NI-99-0011.

Reams, R., Kuydendall, J., & Burns, D. (1975). Police management systems: What is an appropriate model? Journal of Police Science and Administration, 3, 4, 475-481.

Reardon, K. K. (1981). Persuasion: Theory and context. Beverly Hills, CA: Sage Publications.

Reasons, C. E., & Wirth, B. A. (1975). Police-community relations units: A national survey. The Journal of Social Issues, 31, 27-34.

Reese, J. T. (1982, June). Life in the high speed lane: Managing police burnout. The Police Chief, 49-53.

Reiser, M. (1970, September). A psychologist's view of the badge. The Police Chief, 224-226.

Reiser, M. (1971, January-February). The police psychologist as consultant. Police, 58-60.

Reiser, M. (1972). The police department psychologist. Springfield, IL: Charles Thomas.

Reiser, M. (1973). Practical psychology for police officers. Springfield, IL: Charles Thomas.

Reiser, M. (1974a, June). Some organizational stresses on police officers. Journal of Police Science and Administration, 156-159.

Reiser, M. (1974b, August). Mental health in police work and training. The Police Chief, 51-52.

Reiser, M. (1975). Policemen as mental health agents. In E. J. Lieberman (Ed.), Mental health: The public health challenge (pp. 184-188). Washington, DC: American Public Health Association.

Reiser, M. (1976, January). Stress, distress and adaptation in police work. The Police Chief, 24-27.

Reiser, M. (1979). Police consultations. In A. S. Rogawski (Ed.), Mental health consultations in community settings (73-83). San Francisco: Jossey-Bass.

Reiser, M. (1980). Handbook of investigative hypnosis. Los Angeles: LEHI Publishing Co.

Reiser, M. (1982). Police psychology - Collected papers. Los Angeles: LEHI Publishing Co.

Reiser, M., & Klyver, N. (1982). Needed: A modern police training model. Los Angeles Police Department (Mimeo).

Reiser, M., & Sloane, M. (1982). The use of suggestibility techniques in hostage negotiation. In M. Reiser (Ed.), Police psychology - collected papers (pp. 185-196). Los Angeles: LEHI Publishing Co.

Reiser, M., & Geiger, S. P. (1984). Police officer as victim. Professional psychology: Research and practice, 15, 3, 315-323.

Robinette, H. M. (1983, November). Police performance management. The Police Chief, 33-35.

Rokeach, M. (1972). Beliefs, attitudes and values. San Francisco: Jossey-Bass.

Romano, A. T. (1981). Transactional analysis for police personnel. Springfield, IL: Thomas.

Rossi, P. H., Freeman, H. E., Wright, S. R. (1979). Evaluation: A systematic approach. Beverly Hills, CA: Sage Publications.

Salasin, S. E. (Ed.). (1981). Evaluating victim services. Beverly Hills, CA: Sage.

Schembri, A. J. (1983, November). Educating police managers. The Police Chief, 36-38.

Schwartz, J. A. (1975). Domestic crisis intervention - evolution of a police training program. Crime Prevention Review, 2, 9-16.

Scott, S. (1979). Stress and the female cop. Police Stress, 1, 31-34.

Scully, R. (1981, March). Staff support groups: Helping nurses to help themselves. The Journal of Nursing Administration, 48-51.

Serra, R. C. (1984, January). Police officer physical efficiency battery. The Police Chief, 45-46.

Shealy, A. E. (1977). Police integrity: The role of psychological screening of applicants. Criminal Justice Center Monograph No. 4. New York: John Jay Press.

Sherman, L. J. (1973). A psychological view of women in policing. Journal of Police Science and Administration, 1, 383-394.

Shev, E. E. (1968, April). Psychiatric techniques in selection and training of a police officer. The Police Chief, 10-13.

Sikes, M. P., & Cleveland, S. E. (1969). Human relations training for police and community. American Psychologist, 23, 766-769.

Singer, H. A. (1970, April). The cop as social scientist. The Police Chief, 52-58.

Singleton, G. U., & Teahan, J. (1978). Effects of job-related stress and the physical and psychological adjustment of police officers. Journal of Police Science and Administration, 6, 355-361.

Sokol, R. J., & Reiser, M. (1971, July). Training sergeants in early warning signs of emotional upset. Mental Hygiene, 303-307.

Specter, G. A., & Claiborn, W. L. (1973). Crisis intervention. New York: Behavioral Publications.

Steadman, R. F. (Ed.). (1972). The police and the community. Baltimore, MD: The John Hopkins University Press.

Stewart, A. L., & Brook, R. H. (1983). Effects of being overweight. American Journal of Public Health, 73, 171-178.

Stratton, J. G. (1978). Police stress: An overview. The Police Chief, 45, 58-62.

Symonds, M. (1970). Emotional hazards of police work. American Journal of Psychoanalysis, 30, 155.

Symonds, M. (1980). The second injury. In L. Kivens (Ed.), Evaluation and change: Services for survivors. Minneapolis: Minneapolis Medical Research Foundation, 36-38.

Task Force Report on Victims of Crime and Violence. (1984, December). Washington, DC: American Psychological Associaton.

Tehman, J. E. (1975). A longitudinal study of attitude shifts among black and white officers. Journal of Social Issues, 31, 46-56.

Territo, L., & Vetter, H. J. (1981). Stress and police personnel. Boston: Allyn & Bacon.

Terry, W. C. (1983). The legitimation of police stress as an individual problem: Coalescence of administrative and psychological views. American Journal of Police, 1, 49-71.

Thibault, E. A., Lynch, L. M., & McBride, R. B. (1985). Proactive police management. Englewood Cliffs, NJ: Prentice-Hall, Inc.

Trimble, M. R. (1981). Post-traumatic neurosis. New York: Wiley.

Truax, C., & Carkhuff, R. (1977). Toward effective counseling and psychotherapy. Chicago: Aldine.

Vroom, V. H. (1972). The role of compensation in motivating employees. In D. R Hampton (Ed.), Behavioral concepts in management. Encino, CA: Dickenson Publishing Co.

Waldhuber, R. M. (1979, October). Police discretionary authority: A model for police training. The Police Chief, 91-92.

Walsh, W. F. (1983, November). Leadership: A police perspective. The Police Chief, 26-29.

Watson, N. A. (1966). Police-community relations. Washington, DC: International Association of Chiefs of Police.

Wexler, J. G., & Logan, D. D. (1983). Sources of stress among women police officers. Journal of Police Science and Administration, 11, 46-53.

Wilson, J. Q. (1968). Varieties of police behavior. Cambridge, MA: Harvard University Press.

Wilson, O. W. (1957). Parker on police. Springfield, IL: Thomas.

Witczak, T. J. (1984, January). Physical fitness with a pay incentive. The Police Chief, 50-51.

Wood, M. (1984, Summer). Help is only a phone call away. L.A. Police Relief Association Guardian, 1-7.

Yamamoto, L., Yano, K., & Thoads, G. G. (1983). Characteristics of joggers among Japanese men in Hawaii. American Journal of Public Health, 73, 147-152.

Zlotnick, J. (1979). Victimology and crisis intervention training with police. Crisis Intervention, 10, 2-17.

THE DEVELOPMENT OF TRAINING, AND THE NEED FOR IN-SERVICE TRAINING

KAREL J. NIJKERK

The Development of Vocational Training

Training given within the police force is one of the many branches of contemporary vocational training. Such training exists at many levels, ranging from basic vocational training, where so-called basic skills and the basic knowledge needed for a trade are taught, to specialized vocational training given at university level, such as for medical, legal and psychological professions, and the specialized technical training for engineers. Not only are there very different levels, but there are also an increasing number of fields in which vocational training is emerging. At the moment, for instance, a number of specialized types of vocational training are appearing in the field of automation and data processing. Technological innovations necessitate new branches of vocational training, also social developments lead to the creation of new professions, such as in the area of social work, social service and assistance.

If we view the development of vocational training in a more historical perspective, we can state broadly that during the second half of the last century, vocational training, which was originally intended to improve standards among artisans, raise the quality of handicrafts, and ensure the carrying over of skills, was introduced into industry for tasks related to certain specialized jobs. The spread of technology in industry and the growth in organizations necessitated setting up more training programs, and even entire factory schools were founded. In the twentieth century, central governments stimulated these developments by institutionalizing vocational education programs, while the factory schools and in-service training schemes expanded. Governmental and semi-governmental agencies, such as the railway companies, the postal services, local transport organizations, as well as the police, started their own training programs.

After the First World War, a great many vocational training schools were founded; they awarded official diplomas which were required in order to work as a skilled labourer. The Trade Unions also encouraged these developments. During the Great Depression, people became training conscious, and conscious of their learning potential as a means of maintaining and promoting their personal welfare. During World War II, training received a tremendous impetus from the Training Within Industry movement in the USA, and numerous on-the-job training schemes, most of them short, 10-hour training programs for supervisors and training officers. These programs were administrated to almost two million war production and essential service management staff. After World War II, management training emerged. In this sphere, the programs were conducted under the sponsorship and guidance of universities and colleges, and led by competent academics. In many countries, police training schools and academies were founded, following the development of training facilities within the army.

Police Training

Reflecting the general tendency toward professionalization, in the twentieth century the training of the police has become an increasing concern. As far as can be gathered from the literature, this development varies quite considerably from country to country. The role of police training is bound up with the place of the police in society, which means that there are wide divergences from country to country in the manner in which police training programs are set up. In some countries, police training is organized according to the military model. In other countries, precisely that military model has been abandoned, and police training has been linked to existing training schemes for administrative functions. In many areas of police training, notably in the basic training programs, traces of the military training tradition can still be found in the form of a comprehensive and punishment-oriented physical training program, encouraging strict protocol. Stratton calls this the 'stress approach' (Stratton, 1984).

The realization of police training sometimes had a curious history. In the 1920s, training in the Netherlands was given by senior police officers, who thereby earned a bit of extra pocket money. They transmitted their experiences to newcomers, and in this way police culture was shaped at the same time. Also, in the Netherlands it was primarily the trade unions that exerted themselves to obtain improvements in police selection and certification by means of national examination requirements and separate examination requirements for junior and senior police officers. The establishment of a police training school was partly brought about on the initiative of police officers.

A remarkable feature is that in those days the funds for police training were assembled via the annual proceeds from a lottery among the union members (Fijnaut, 1983; Van Reenen, 1983).

Since the Second World War, in particular, state-financed, official police training institutions have been established in many countries. On the European continent, the existing police organizations and police training were thoroughly reviewed in virtually all European states. In the Netherlands, a separate training program for senior officers was created in 1948. This was bound to the military model to such an extent, that members of the military were chosen by preference to follow this officers' training program, and the training itself was set up as a copy of the military officers' training. In Western Germany, the Polizei Führungs Akademie was started up in 1949. In the Anglo-Saxon countries, the development of a professional training system began somewhat earlier. Eastman and McCain (1982) give detailed information about the history of police training in the USA in the Journal of Police Science and Administration. In 1909, the New York City Police Department formally instituted its academy, which had evolved over more than ten years from its school of Pistol Practice. In 1916 came the point of conceptual divergence between police training and police education, as each became separately institutionalized. The New York Academy had, by then, become an influential model of department sponsored training (Eastman & McCain, 1982).

In 1924 J. Edgar Hoover, director of the FBI, started the National Police Academy, later called the National Academy. In 1928 the

University of Southern California started a full academic police training program within the department of Public Administration, and in 1936 Northwestern University started a nine month Training Police Administration training program. These data give a mere impression of the development in the USA. They indicate that professionalization of the police already has a fairly long history. The American case is unique in that the (existing) universities played an important role in the training of police officers, especially the senior ranks. This continues to be a feature of the development in the USA.

The end of World War II marked the beginning of the explosion in police education. In the allied countries, many men in military service had served in military police units, and veterans with the benefit of this education were encouraged to seek careers in civilian law enforcement. In the United States, the influx of a number of these men into universities helped to establish and expand police education programs as universities responded to a felt need. Others entered police agencies directly. They brought with them a consciousness of discipline and training, and contributed to the growing awareness of the need to improve police services. This awareness was partially translated, in turn, into a growing receptivity to the notion of education as one of the keys to professionalization (Eastman & McCain, 1982). In nearly all the Western countries, police became professionalized, and special schools and training institutes were set up to teach specific skills, such as detective work and traffic administration, necessary for developing the profile of the police.

The greater specialization in training reflects the specialization in the work of the police in general. A tendency which is initially indicated in practice is thus further strengthened by the specialized character of associated training. This also exemplifies the interconnectedness of professional activity and training, a relationship which can specifically be labelled "professional training" (or, as it is generally termed, vocational training).

We should also note that, as police training has become more important, facilities have been differentiated for the various hierarchical levels, which have been allocated their own specific training programs. In many countries, at least two, but sometimes three, separate police training programs have been developed: a basic or entry level (recruit level) training program; an intermediate level; and programs for senior ranking police officers. Some of these higher level programs may, in turn, include specialized courses, such as the different command courses at the Bramshill Police Staff College in Great Britain, and the Command Courses provided for officers in the Danish Police. Many countries today also provide a wide range of in-service and refresher courses for different specializations, as well as for different hierarchical levels.

This increasing differentiation is also characteristic of present-day vocational training. As a profession develops its profile, there is an increasing need for refresher courses. In the private sector, for instance, that is already a well established trend. These in-service and refresher courses are run by the existing training institutions, but also in the Netherlands, for instance, by institutions specially created for the purpose. Furthermore, local and regional police forces sometimes have at their disposal their own training departments which run refresher courses for the members of that specific police force. This is a form of in-service training which we shall return to in a later section of this exposition.

Horst Schult, from West Germany, reports that, at the moment of writing, 40,000 out of the 200,000 personnel in service in the police in that country were in some kind of training (Schult, 1981). It is certainly true that perfecting the training given and broadening the range of police possibilities occupies an ever increasing portion of the budget available for the police.

Some Critical Areas

The increased professionalization and the associated training needs have provoked, quite apart from the associated financial problems, a number of other problems. At the moment, the quality of training and the extent to which it corresponds to what is deemed necessary for carrying out professional duties correctly are the subject of a considerable amount of debate. The structure and content of the basic training program, in particular, are frequent points of criticism, both internally, from those who have experienced the training, and also from outside, where citizens have to deal with young, freshly-qualified police officers and find that their behaviour is not up to standard.

An American report from the National Advisory Commission on Higher Education for Police Officers, from 1981, is critical of the type of education given in police education programs. It argues that there has been far too much vocationalism in the college curriculum. A related observation by the Commission suggests that the quality of police educators has been quite low at colleges and universities (Eastman & McCain, 1982).

In the Netherlands recruits undergoing basic training have expressed fairly critical opinions of the wide gap between what is taught during the training and what occurs in practice (Algemeen Politie Blad no. 4, februari, 1985). A recent report about police training in the Netherlands, drawn up by an independent group of management consultants on commission from the general government, is extremely critical about the efficiency of virtually all police training programs in the Netherlands. It goes so far as to suggest a substantial reduction in staff at all training centres (Schoolrapport, 1985).

Similarly, in various papers, including those by Butler, Poole, and Reiser in this volume, critical comments are made about police training, particularly as it was given in the past. Frost and Seng (1983), who carried out a written survey about the developments of the police entry-level training in the USA over the last thirty years (1952-1982), are critical about the past, but write positively about the present situation. They concluded through their investigations that basic training has moved from the basement, as it were, into its own facilities, with its own separate status and identity.

There has been an increase in the size of the recruit training staffs in the past 30 years and also a marked improvement in the training facilities. Police entry training has risen from a unit to a division, from limited facilities to extensive often separate facilities and from a small to a full time staff. Such training is now well established and entry training is a stable function in that its administrative staff is full time and of command rank. Entry level training is recognized as providing a vital service to the operational units and is given sufficient facilities, personnel and support to provide these services (Frost & Seng, 1983).

In another study which focused on the instructors at recruit training programs, Frost and Seng (1983) concluded that prior to 1959 police recruit training programs were hastily arranged affairs, and instructor selection was accomplished by assigning a few veteran police officers to the task of informing groups of police recruits about the elementary functions of their job. Generally, the instruction consisted of dictating a series of questions and answers which were to be memorized by the recruits. From this study it appeared that, at present, recruit instructors are selected with greater care than was the case in the 1950s. In addition, it appears that the selection criteria are now more appropriate to the training task, so that instructors are selected through the use of relevant criteria. At present in the USA, instructors are trained and there is a formal evaluation by the trainees of their instructors, an evaluation which is mostly positive. Most instructors nowadays also meet state certification guidelines (Frost & Seng, 1983).

Leslie Poole's presentation in this volume describes a similar development in the case of the Metropolitan Police in London. He ,too, claims that twenty years ago "discipline and overall outlook were mainly punitive and the atmosphere militaristic. Learning was based almost entirely on rote and reinforced through practical exercises demanding set phrases and questions to establish details". As far as the instructors are concerned, Poole points out almost the same characteristics as Frost and Seng do in their American study: "The staff who taught were instructors in every sense of the word, a directive, didactic and controlling influence, as concerned with the transmission of social values as with delivering information....Initial provincial police training was similar in most respects, except of shorter duration". Poole reports, as do his American colleague researchers, that with respect to basic training, there have been many changes for the better partly through "the substantial contribution by the social sciences and of the discipline of psychology in particular".

I take it that in Great Britain, also, the quality of the instructors and teaching staff has improved substantially. The evaluative study carried out by Ray Bull (see chapter in this volume), reports the progress achieved in the recruit training program both through the input made by social studies and through the use of specially trained instructors (Bull & Horncastle, 1983). During my own visit to the Peel Centre, the imposing training centre of the London Metropolitan Police, I was impressed by the modern didactic methods which are employed there in the recruit and probationer training programs, and also by the openness with which both instructors and trainees spoke about their experiences of training to an outsider. Such openness and the critical attitude are probably additional consequences of the input of the social sciences in the training.

Training

In the above section, I noted a number of developments in the areas of professionalization and training. I would like to elucidate a few aspects of training, and make some comments with respect to training needs:

(1) In many countries, training opportunities and the possibilities of following refresher courses have been or are being extended considerably. This is happening because training is being considered more and more--and rightly so--as a norm of "education permanente". The opinion is gaining ground that policing should correspond to social developments and to the expectations held by society concerning policing in general, and the relations between the police and citizens,

individually or collectively.

Within the police system itself the conviction has also grown--partly as a result of developments in other sectors of society, particularly in trade and industry--that good training is of essential importance for the effectiveness of policing and for the quality of the police organization. Within this organization there is unmistakably a growing need for qualified leaders, leaders with managerial qualities. Experience in other sectors has made it clear that this entails giving extra instruction to those already holding positions of leadership and, also, training future leaders for their leadership functions. In this respect, stimulating ideas have emerged at the Police Staff College in Bramshill for the benefit of the British Police and the training programs given there. The research carried out by Mike Plumridge and Chief Inspector (and psychologist) Jim Gibson which assesses this and the publications by the same authors are impressive (Plumridge, 1983; Gibson, 1982).

(2) In various countries, serious attempts are being made to improve the quality of training, to link training more to what happens in practice, and to take account of training needs that emerge from practice. Robert G. Phillips carried out an interesting study recently in the USA on the training needs of personnel law enforcement agencies (Phillips, 1984). He sent questionnaires to more than 16,000 State and Local law enforcement agencies. He got a pretty good response to his enquiry. On the basis of the information compiled, he summed up the training priorities for both general and specialized police services. His impressions give an interesting picture of the training needs of law enforcement personnel. The ten highest priorities, taking all services together and in order of priority, are: (1) handle personnel stress; (2) conduct interviews/interrogations; (3) drive vehicles in emergency pursuit situations; (4) maintain an appropriate level of physical fitness; (5) promote a positive public image; (6) determine probable cause for arrest; (7) write crime incident reports; (8) handle domestic disturbances; (9) collect, maintain and preserve evidence; (10) respond to crimes in progress.

One of the author's conclusions is that: "one way to increase the efficient use of financial resources earmarked for law enforcement training would be to develop training modules on relevant activity groupings. These modules could then be assembled in a variety of combinations to meet the training needs of various law enforcement groups" (Phillips, 1984). Phillips' suggestion to set up modules is not a new one, and has already been utilized in various other sectors. In police training in general, however, there is still little talk of a modular approach.

As appears from Phillips' inquiry about needs, training with a view to stress-reduction is accorded high priority. He writes:

"Stress and the job burnout syndrome with which it is often associated are factors affecting performance in all types of human service organizations. The feelings of emotional exhaustion which result sometimes lead to cynicism towards the job and the citizens served, and seriously reduce organizational effectiveness. However, training in stress management is becoming widely available for law enforcement agencies, and it is therefore possible that the high priority rating given this area is due more to the training being 'en vogue' than to the actual need for increased expertise in coping with stress. On the other hand, since most training in this area is offered by health professionals, the high priority may reflect the inability of law enforcement agencies to pay for training of this type. Additional research would be required to resolve these conflicting possibilities" (Phillips, 1984).

That stress plays an increasingly important role in police services and that the stress factor in the work is increasingly recognized is corroborated by, amongst other things, the reports from various stress workshops organized in Great Britain and led by Mary Manolias (1983). These interesting workshops and reports give a good picture of the current problem areas in the work of the police at various levels and, also, of the need for training and refresher courses in the various areas of police work. Other authors have also pointed out the increasing stress which police officers individually, and the police organization as a whole, undergo. In practice, there are a range of training methods which are directly or indirectly concerned with stress-reduction. We may mention the Spouse Training Method described by Stratton, Tracy-Stratton and Allredge (1982) and the leadership training described by Steiner in this volume. Also of value are peer counselling techniques, emotional debriefing and other forms of response through which an attempt is made to reduce the stress with which the person involved has to deal.

It is notable that in Phillips' research, the need for training in communication skills is not explicitly mentioned. The priorities among training needs are accorded more to what I would refer to as classic law enforcement-related skills. There is an apparent conflict in the list of priorities drawn up by Phillips. On the one hand, there is a great need for stress reduction; on the other hand, there seems to be a great need for classic police skills, such as arriving quickly on the scene, good physical condition, techniques concerned with making arrests, techniques connected with crime reporting, etc. From the investigation into training needs, it seems that there is a desire to emphasize the criminal law aspect of policing even more. A probable explanation is that there is still considerable pressure, both from the side of the police themselves and from the public that the so-called "law and order" activities, in particular, should not be neglected; criminality should be fought even harder, etc. On the other hand, however, the public and individual citizens wish that individual policemen were able to communicate more adequately and were able to act appropriately in situations concerned with crises linked to or stemming from citizens' personal needs. The necessity of being able to communicate well and be of service in various kinds of situations is, in my opinion, insufficiently recognized both by the police themselves and by the public (see also Stratton, in this volume). Moreover, there is still only slight recognition given to the fact that communication skills can be learned through appropriate training. For social scientists, and particularly psychologists and professional helpers, the importance of social and communication skills is obvious. In many professions, the significance of communication skills is taken for granted; possession of such skills is considered by many as an inborn quality or a sort of personality trait. To return to stress in work situations, this is certainly not solely caused by a supposed lack of knowledge of professional skills, for instance in the field of law enforcement, but this stress is certainly partly caused by the fact that people have a faulty picture of the essential characteristics of the work situation and hold incorrect expectations about the nature of police work.

Part of a policeman's or -woman's work basically consists in rendering service and aid, in which respect, situations of crisis and emergency are often involved, as Reiser has also emphasized in his chapter in this volume. And it is precisely that part of the work which creates tension, because the police officers feel insufficiently equipped to deal with such situations. Through the conflict between role expectations, on the one hand, and the reality of day to day work, on the other, emerges a stress situation. The officer in question wonders, amongst other things, whether he or she has really chosen the right profession. That is an existential question which continues to worry one, and which comes up again each time one is forced into that service or help giving role. The question is then whether stress-reduction training methods actually only tackle the symptoms; they do not solve the underlying internal conflict. It is certainly important, even necessary, that during police training, a realistic picture is given of day to day work: that realistic role expectations are presented, that sufficient attention is paid to social and communication skills, and that experience of daily working practice is given at an early stage. In some training programs, for example, that of the Metropolitan Police of London, I think people have already gone some way towards achieving a training program which will prevent police officers from finding themselves in situations of stress later on. It is true here, too, that prevention is better than cure. I agree with Stratton when he claims that: "If policemen are effective communicators, they can take an emotional situation and lower anxiety and nervousness not only for themselves but also for others" (Stratton, 1984, p. 57).

The Analysis of Training Needs Through Job-Description

Research into training needs, such as that carried out by Phillips, is important and useful because it provides an interface between research and training needs. Nevertheless, such inventory-style research does not always give a complete picture of fundamental training requirements. The sort of training which should be given in order for people to be able to do their job adequately, i.e., at a qualitatively high level, must be determined above all on the basis of job-description and job-analysis. These two can give a clear picture of what is necessary in terms of knowledge, general insight, skills, etc., for the carrying out of a job or a trade. The basic training, as well as other training, in-service instruction, and refresher courses, should be built upon the basis of the most complete possible job-descriptions. To my knowledge, these are still mainly absent in the case of the police. At least, in the literature there is extremely little mention of them. In a recent article by the organizational sociologist Muller (in press), emphasis is yet again laid on the fact that it is of great importance to take job-descriptions as the starting point for setting up training and instruction courses. Such descriptions set out the aim of the job, the position of the job within the organization, the description of the duties to be performed, any special knowledge involved in performing the job, the external contacts to be maintained, the amount of independence and the degree of responsibility involved. In short, job-descriptions illuminate all the aspects necessary for good performance of a function. In addition, the various elements that make up the job are brought into view. Exposing the component parts of functions can also be significant in relation to other objectives, such as evaluation policy, promotion policy and career planning, and also often with respect to the

renumeration of the job. Of course, there is a certain effort involved
in composing job-descriptions, but for a large organization such as the
police, with a fair number of standard tasks, the composition of
job-descriptions would certainly be worthwhile. On the basis of
job-descriptions, instructors can check which skills and knowledge are
necessary for a particular function; further, they can make their
training methods and training programs correspond to what is set out in
the job-description with respect to what is required from those
fulfilling a certain function.

As long as the police fail to make use of job-descriptions, it will
remain difficult for instructors to put together balanced training
programs. Muller also points out that for good personnel policy, it is
important to have job-descriptions at one's disposal. In fact, on the
subject of personnel policy, there are a few things which should be said
with regard to the police. In most police forces, there is still not
much evidence of an advanced personnel policy; sometimes, one can .
scarcely speak of any personnel work at all, personnel problems being
simply dealt with at the hierarchical level. It is also important that a
close relationship should exist between, on the one hand, work concerned
with personnel matters and personnel policy and, on the other hand,
training policy. In various organizations, one sees that work to do with
training falls under the personnel department, and that a very close
cooperation exists between the two. Similarly, in private companies and
non-profit organizations (e.g., hospitals) which have their own training
facility, like the police, one often encounters close teamwork between
the personnel department and the instructing staff. I think that such
cooperation is most desirable for the police as well, and that
professionalization will benefit by it. The last point brings me to a
theme which, in my opinion, demands close attention: the relationship
between selection, training/instruction, and personnel performance.

The Need for In-Service Training

Many police training centres were, and still are, at least in a number
of European countries, rather closed, sometimes exclusive institutions.
Little publicity or even information is given to the outside world about
the nature of the training or the specific content of the training
program. The closed nature and exclusivity of police training holds a
number of advantages for the police organization. Police culture can be
carried over and, in fact, fostered. An esprit de corps can be achieved,
through which corps-solidarity can also be built up. People get to know
each other well, as members of an organization. There are, moreover, a
number of advantages for the trainees deriving from such a concentration
of exchanges of thought, amongst the trainees themselves and between the
trainees and the instructing staff. Furthermore, the curriculum can be
intensive, just as the mutual contacts among those present are. The
closed police training institutions are often based upon, or imitate, the
military, barracks-style-training situations. Where they differ from the
military basic and officer training, however, is that the latter are
often more closely linked to carrying out the job.

The military basic training is directly linked to military practice:
the recruits undergoing training are in active service straight away, and
on the whole, the officers are as well. At the police training
institutions, such a link with active service is present much less, and
sometimes even entirely absent. When one is discussing training or
instruction, an important question is whether a closed training system is

actually appropriate to the changed position of the police in society, and, in particular, whether it is still appropriate to the objectives of, as Denkers and others express it, managing to: "improve police-public relations, shorten emotional and physical distances between the public and the police" (Denkers, 1977).

In many publications emphasis is placed on the fact that the service-rendering function of the police is becoming more important within policing itself, and that the tasks of the police are shifting in the direction of the more service and help-rendering functions. In recent reports about police training, the trainees in training institutions complain that they are threatened with being socially isolated through the in-group culture and separation. One also'hears complaints from staff members about the isolating manner in which the training centres work. This isolation contradicts the changing tasks and function of the police whereby it is precisely the contact and communication functions which are emphasized, as most of the contributions to this volume indicate.

One may further wonder whether the nature of the work itself does not set certain requirements on the training situation. Policing can be characterized as "doing work". The average policeman is oriented towards action and variation. That is one of the attractive aspects of the profession and that aspect is also heavily stressed by the media, in the press, in police films and detective novels. Those who feel themselves attracted to the profession are, as a rule, people who are action-oriented. In an interview which I recently conducted with a deputy inspector, a head of department, in the framework of some research, the man complained bitterly about the great amount of administrative work that he was forced to do each day. "I hardly ever get out on the street", he complained. "If I had known that in advance, I might well have chosen a different career". The deputy inspector seemed to be strongly de-motivated by his administrative tasks, but he himself saw that in the organization as it is at present, it was virtually unavoidable for him in his position as an officer with responsibility.

Another example of the frustration resulting from lack of action that I came into contact with was in the detective force. When I was reporting a burglary to one of the detectives, I got an avalanche of complaints about the interminable office-work with which detectives are confronted. The detective who dealt with my report, and who had no idea that I had anything to do with the police, was backed up by other colleagues who were, likewise, at their typewriters, occupied with their daily portion of administrative work. "We aren't office clerks", the detective dealing with me said, looking at me reproachfully, as if I were the one guilty of keeping him from his work out on the street. "We want to get out on the street and do what we have been trained and appointed for", he added in my direction as he typed out my declaration.

Given the action-oriented professional image, the nature of the work itself, the variety of situations, and the contacts with people (very well illustrated in the American television series "Hill Street Blues"), it is important that training situations and programs are set up which correspond to the reality of the profession, and through which people learn from doing the work itself. In-service training is well suited to this. In-service training can be understood as a de-centralized training program where the focus is on task performance. With in-service training, the learning process is strongly related to what happens in daily work and to problems arising in connection with everyday activities. Few theoretical concepts are used, but trainees are particularly taught to reflect on the way they, and their colleagues approach and solve daily practical problems. The main goal of such training is to improve the quality of work done in general, as well as that of individual performance.

Industrial organizations already have a long tradition of in-service training programs for very different functions, and for the different levels within the organization. Apart from industrial organizations, in-service training is also taking a central place in service-orientated institutions, such as medical and nursing training. Other advantages of in-service training are the flexibility of the training program, and the possibility of altering both methods and content. The training curriculum is not fixed over a long period, such as happens in official training institutions where they are often bound by examinations and diplomas. Moreover, it is possible to know something about the effects of in-service programs, since direct feedback on the results is communicated via performance levels in practical work situations. A further advantage that has been revealed in the evaluation of certain Dutch in-service training programs is that such programs may influence work relations (Hulsman & Miedema, 1983). This method of "learning together" may have a cohesive effect. Recent research from the city of Amsterdam into the actions of the police in that city concluded, among other things, that: "improvement in the quality of policing and associated instruction should take place as far as possible 'in-service'" (de Klerk, 1983).

Of course, there are also some disadvantages which should be mentioned. In-service training programs may be labour-intensive and can only be effective if skilled teachers, trainers or coaches are available. Trainees need individual coaching in order to obtain the maximum benefit from this kind of training. In practice, it has also emerged that not everybody is suited to act as individual coach or supervisor of practical work, and that it may also be necessary to provide training courses for the coaches themselves (Nijkerk, 1983). A disadvantage can also be that only larger organizational units can employ in-service training programs: smaller units are seldom able to set up such training schemes unless they can make use of specific resources or can share the program with a larger unit. Also, because of its focus on practical aspects, in-service training offers little time or opportunity for theoretical deepening or various issues concerning the training.

It is self-evident that advantages and disadvantages should be carefully weighed against each other. Given that other organizations do have favourable experiences with this kind of training, the question arises whether the police should pay more attention to in-service training activities, in particular, in order to produce better qualified police officers at all ranks, but also to satisfy the growing need for ongoing education opportunities in the police force. Within the organization there is a great potential in terms of experience and expertise, and it is important that this should be utilized to the greatest possible extent. In the learning process which would do this, and in the setting up of in-service programs, psychologists can make an important contribution.

REFERENCES
Bo, J. (1984). The training of the Danish police. Police Studies, 7(3).

54

Buitenhuis, A. C. (1983, mei). Internaten of consentraten bij politie-
opleidings-instituten (Internship or concentration at police training
institutes.) Algemeen Politieblad, 11.

Bull, R., & Horncastle, P. (1983). An evaluation of the Metropolitan
Police Recruit Training in Human Awareness Training (HAT). London: The
Police Foundation.

Butler, A. J. P. (1983). Police management, the critical variable for
improving the police. In The future of policing. Cambridge: Cropwood
Conference Studies no. 18.

Denkers, F. A. C. M. (1977). Training en vorming geen Haarlemmerolie
(Training and social education, no panacea for everything.)
Tijdschrift voor de Politie.

Eastman, G. D., & McCain, J.A. (1982). Education, professionalism and
law enforcement in historical perspective. Journal of Police Science
and Administration, 9(2).

Frost, T. M., & Seng, M. J. (1983). Police recruit training in urban
departments: A look at instructors. Journal of Police Science and
Administration, 11(2).

Fijnaut, C. (1983). Politieopleiding en politie-apparaat in West Europa.
(Police training and organization in Western Europe.) Justitiele
Verkenningen, WODC The Hague.

Gibson, J. B. (1983, January). An investigation of the way that police
officers construe practical policing situations. University of
Manchester, Department of Management Sciences.

Hulsman D., & Miedema, J. (1983). Bezinning op de praktijk (Reflection
on practice). Algemeen Politieblad, no. 19.

de Klerk, P. (1983, November). Menselijke eenheid (Human unity).
Gemeentepolitie Amsterdam.

Kratz, G. (1984). Task and functions of the Polizei Fuhrungs Akademie of
the Federal Republic of Germany. Police Studies, 7(1).

Lawther, W. C. (1984). Successful training for police performance
evaluation systems. Journal of Police Science and Administration,
12(1).

Lester, D., Leitner, L. A., & Poster, I. The effects of a stress management training program on police officers. International Review of
Applied Psychology, 33.

Manolias, M. (1983). Stress in the police service. London: Home Office.

Muller, A. (in press). Job description in general, and especially for
the police, its use for training and selection in the Netherlands.

Nijkerk, K. J. (1983). Studying the police. Paper presented at the IXth
International Conference on Criminology, Vienna.

Phillips, R. G. (1984, August). State and local law enforcement training
needs. FBI Law Enforcement Bulletin.

Plumridge, M. (1983, July). A study of police management and command
roles. Bramshill Police Staff College.

Pots, L. W. (1981). Higher education ethics and the police. Journal of
Police Science and Administration, 9(2).

Schoolrapport. (1985). Schoolrapport Politie-Instituten. Ministerie van
Beinnenlandse Zaken. 's-Gravenhage.

Schult, H. (1981). Gibt es eine Konzeption für die Bildungsarbeit in der
Deutschen Polizei? Die Polizei, Heft 10.

Steinmetz, C. S. (1976). The history of training. In R. L. Graig (Ed.),
Training and development handbook (2nd ed.). McGraw Hill.

Stratton, J. G. (1984). Police passages. Manhattan Beach, CA: Glennong
Publications.

Stratton, J. G., Tracy-Stratton, B., & Allredge, G. (1982). The effects of a spouses training program: A longitudinal study. Journal of Police Science and Administration, 10(3).

Tannehill R., & Janeksela, G. M. (1984). Role and task analysis: An effective tool for manpower development and curriculum development in law enforcement education. Journal of Police Science and Administration, 12(1).

van der Schaaf , A., & Wouda, J. (1985). De HPO-stage, ervaringen van de pioniers. (Practical work, experiences of pioneers.) Alg. Politieblad, 4.

Wells, R. G. (1983). Training the police for the people. In The future of policing. Cambridge: Cropwood Conference Series, no. 18.

Yuille, J. C. (1984). Research and teaching with police: A Canadian example. International Review of Applied Psychology, 33.

THE PANACEA OF TRAINING AND SELECTION

FRANS DENKERS

About ten years ago my attention got attracted by an advertisement in the national newspapers. The Amsterdam city police were seeking a psychologist. Having been employed thusfar in the ivory towers of the University—six of those years I spent in a criminology department—I was attracted to the idea of working in a more practically-minded surrounding, one that is less protected. The job that was offered was not described in detail, but I thought that could be an advantage. I could be creative and "fill in" the job as I saw it.

That freedom proved to be relative. From the very beginning all sorts of informal expectations seemed to force me in my work. I remember having a conversation with one of the deputy-chief-commissioners; it was the second day of my new job, I think. He said to me: "What you should do, is improve the mentality and the motivation of the young cop!" Naively, I answered that seemed a proper thing to do, "but how about the mentality and motivation of the sergeant who was supposed to guide and supervise those young policemen. Don't you think that is equally important?" "Oh well", he said, "You just include those too". "But", I continued with unbroken naivety, "the inspectors, what about them?" I can still see the bewildered, even frightened expression on his face, and I can still hear him say: "But in that way you'll touch the chief-commissioner!" "Precisely, that is exactly what I mean", I said.

It is from that date, until this very day, that I foster a sense of allergy, even to the extent of a prejudice, for any proposal to improve by training or counseling upon the mentality and motivation of the young police personnel. Invariably, the solution to highly complex management problems involving aspects of an organizational, structural and cultural nature, are narrowed to proposals for improved selection, training and counseling of the lower echelons of the force, who are to do the actual job in the street. It seems like trying to improve international banking by building marble counters.

It is not just the inner circle of the police that shows reactions like these. Generally, when I am lecturing a group of laymen, and when I come to speak of the problems of police in society, the dilemmas of policing, the possibilities and the limits of policework, the inadequacies of police-public interactions, the reaction is the same: the understanding, sympathizing audience seeks to find the cure in training and selection and thus engages in the same stereotyped thinking that leads us into a pitfall, both as it concerns the police and others.

This pitfall exists elsewhere; that is, the quick and easy solutions are (in many organizations) located in training and selection. Consider, for example, the airline industry. When business executives return home after three months of alcohol abstinence in Saudi Arabia, it is the task of the stewardess and the purser to handle those passengers who are losing control after three whiskies. This level of personnel is selected and trained just for this job and the pilots (thanks to their rank) stay out of sight and out of trouble. Yet, if the cockpit crew would properly introduce themselves, by a simple appearance in the aisles before take-off, they would acquire a very effective authority to intervene in cases where this should be needed. But unfortunately, the cultural climate, the hierarchy, or company policy displays more interest in the management than the flying crew. Yet training and selection at the lowest level of the organization is not the panacea for management problems.

In my experience, my allergy for training of police officers and their selection still proves a useful prejudice. Let me be clear on one thing: I have nothing against selection and training as such! Within a broader framework of organizational activities and measures, improved selection and training may promote both the effectiveness and job satisfaction of the men and women working on the street. But I protest any suggestion that the problems linked with policework are to be reduced to deficiencies in selection and training.

Legal vs. Non-Legal Aspects of Training

In the first place, I think that when it comes to training (considerations of space force me to limit myself to training here) the call for improvement is a typical result of the past, when training was focused primarily on the knowledge of and application of the law. Nowadays police officers should be trained in social abilities like conflict management; they should develop a view on society and build their personality to a stable and mature form; and they should have the knowledge of the cultural aspects of the different minority groups with whom they deal. With this I fully agree, but not at the expense of a solid theoretical and technical knowledge of the law.

There are several reasons to call attention to old fashioned knowledge of law and general rules:

(1) Laws and regulations (like the constitution, criminal law, prosecutorial procedures, internal police regulations, and rules of behavior given by general orders) are all meant to make the police deal with everyday cases of crime, disturbances of the peace, and crises in a decent fashion. Decent means impartial, unprejudiced, restrained and without discrimination. Those law-like rules are, so to speak, the formalized decency norms; the utter essence of policing. For the execution and maintenance of this decency, a police force is called into life. These formalized decency norms are no means to catch thieves or maintaining order, on the contrary, thieves are caught and order is maintained for the sake of decency. Actually, any citizen can catch thieves or maintain order. Some can even prevent the suicidal jump from a roof and, given the suitable equipment, all of us can break up a peace-demonstration; a baseball team can do it. It takes little training and few social abilities to do just that. What is needed is restraint. Daily experience and history teaches us that without discipline and decency, without the guidance of rules, we make a mess of our society. Without explicit rules, emotions and personal or group considerations will prevail and then the law of the jungle prevails. For that reason we consented to leave the treatment of crime and peace-disturbances to a specialized branch of the authorities, the police. The proper task of the police is thus: react less emotionally, with more restraint to crime

and breaches of the law than we as private citizens are inclined to do.
This less emotional, more impartial, more decent behavior being the prime
task of the police, it is essential that the policeman and policewoman
keep informed in a theoretical and practical way of the legal instruments
by which the police must perform their task.

(2) There is another reason for an emphasis on the knowledge of legal
rules and that is on behalf of improved social abilities and societal
orientations. Knowledge of the law is indispensable for reaching the
instrumental goals of the police (maintaining law and order in the
broadest sense). Any officer may tell you that it is much easier to
check on the driver's license of an owner of a 1983 car, than to check on
the bulk of documents the driver of a lorry carrying ten tons of
dangerous chemicals is supposed to carry. The result is, more often than
not, that traffic control deteriorates to checking the drivers' licenses
while waving the big trucks to pass on. Gaps in the knowledge of
regulations may lead to gaps in the upholding of the law, and sometimes
to an unacceptable selectivity in law enforcement.

Two years ago, I, as a psychologist, prepared an overview of the prime
five articles in our criminal code regarding the discrimination of
minority group members. This overview was presented to top level
officials of the police who in return were "grateful to be introduced in
such an enlightening way to this legal stuff". This indicates the
intensity with which, until then, the problem of racial and other
discrimination had been met by top-ranking officials in a country where
10 per cent of the population consists of minority groups!

(3) There is still a third reason for keeping legal knowledge high on
the list of skills for the police. Most policemen and women do possess
sufficient social abilities for daily situations, but cannot rely on
these abilities in situations where specific, professional knowledge is
needed. Social skills are of help when the normal duty of the officer
brings him into a problematic encounter with the public, but these skills
are of no avail when those encounters are made problematic because the
officer in question does not know what the law requires him to do. In
those circumstances, the officer tends to lose self-confidence, becomes
insecure and, if the opposite party threatens to gain the upper hand, he
will readily fall into the behavior of most insecure people; in the
absence of moral authority backed by the law, he will rely on authority
backed by mere force. To stick to my earlier example of the truck driver
and his dangerous chemicals, the driver eithers bluffs himself out or is
taken with force from his truck to the office where the desk-sergeant is
called upon to provide his legal expertise. This is one of the classical
occasions for false arrests, police harassment, or excessive force which
could have been prevented if the officer knew the law and knew how to act
accordingly.

The Organization is the Key

I hope I have made my point clear that no training in social skills or
societal insight can substitute for legal knowledge. There is, however,
a more general objection to social and psychological training. A plea
for training in matters societal or psychological is nothing but the
charge that something is wrong with the ideas and mental constitution of
the police officers. The supposition is that there is too much of the
bad things or too little of the good things (or both) that we should want
them to have. I think it is very unfair and indeed dangerous to distort
a structural problem of any police force into a personal and individual

problem of the police officers. It is unfair because all failures of the police-organization in its normal, difficult task-performance are reduced to the individual characteristics, the personality-traits and the attitudes of the individual cop, who is subsequently blamed for those failures. It is dangerous because these individual characteristics and attitudes, the psychological make-up of the individual policeman or policewoman, is but one of the many aspects of the problem. And stress on these individual factors brings the danger of closing our eyes to the structural and cultural aspects of the organization in which the individuals are functioning. One of my favorite slogans is: cops are acting out as they are treated within their organization.

An example: the majority of the policemen and women are OK. This becomes evident if you speak with them face to face. It always strikes me how well-considered their opinions are when it comes to racial and cultural differences and how well they understand motives and drives of minority group members. But no sooner are they together with their mates and you get embarrassed by the racist utterances, and sometimes by their actual behavior towards foreign-born citizens.

What is the matter here? The individual cop is OK, most of the time. But, as we are all aware, it is the group culture, the dominating group norm and the informal opinion-leaders that determine the conversation and set its tone (see also Butler's chapter in this volume in regard to this issue). Also, policemen act, like we all do, in a manner so that they can function in their group without being laughed at. With this in mind, I doubt very much whether it would help to put those people together in a classroom and give them information on the cultural background of minority-groups as if the attitude of the individual policeman is at fault. Insofar as the individual policeman needs guidance and counseling, it would be better to help them resist the prevailing group-pressure in general. Of course, training could be very helpful, but training should not be aimed at attitude-change toward minorities, or special problems they meet in their jobs, but it should be aimed at a much broader and much more general human problem: how to be yourself, stay yourself as you were before you entered the force (or another version of the same person), and dare to stick your neck out. For this change of climate, the higher echelons cannot, of course, be kept out of the picture.

I mentioned the group culture expressed in meeting places like the canteen as one of the suppressing factors in the expression of sound individual feelings. In general, I tend to think that all 2500 executive police employees in Amsterdam (there are some 700 administrative workers) are OK, but, due to hierarchical structures, cultural pressures, styles of leadership and bureaucracy, they are permanently frustrated in being themselves. That is why I say that creating a cultural climate in the organization, creating new ways of dealing with one another, creating new styles of leadership such that the individual possibilities and talents are given free room instead of being frustrated, is the first thing to do. If we achieve that, and I think this is not just meant for the Amsterdam police force, then the remaining ten percent or so of the problem, would not pose such a challenge and perhaps could profit from further training.

Another example supporting my thesis that policemen act out as they are treated inside: In Amsterdam there have occurred a few large-scale disturbances in the last few years, especially in connection with evictions from houses in illegal use. It could be observed on television that the police used excessive force. Does this result from cooped-up or inadequately managed aggression on the part of the individual policemen whose inclination to do just that, should have been detected in the selection-procedures and, insofar as still present, should have been unlearned during training? I do not think so. Once we realize that the men who had to do the actual job, and keep the police away, have been on standby for a few days in advance, simply because a hesitating authority kept postponing the eviction, we should not be surprised to find that rioters from the police receive the blows that these policemen, having been caged for so long, would gladly have dealt to the ones who were responsible for this inactivity. The subsequent aggression is the responsibility of the Mayor. A psychologist cannot provide easy solutions in these circumstances and should not attempt to do so.

My last example of the acting-out-thesis is provided by the refusal of a detective to act against illegal card games in Turkish coffeeshops with the words: "But boss, how can you ask me to do that when you see us play for money every day during luncheon-break?"

Management by Punishment

My third objection to the "training and societal insight" panacea, as it is often advocated in the Netherlands, is that this training and insight are supposed to be directed at people who show a lack of something or other. As we have seen, this ignores the fact that most of the time it is not the individual shortcomings that are responsible for the discrepancy between the expectations and the actual results of city policing. It seems, however, that we forget that there are policemen, and these are not rare figures, who are functioning quite well, both in the eyes of the public and in the eyes of their superiors. How are these treated? I don't know how it is elsewhere, but in Holland the answer must be: nothing in particular is done. A cop gets reprimanded when he makes a mistake; when he acts substandard he is sent to a training program since he is supposed to be lacking something; but he is ignored when he excells. In this respect the organization acts towards its personnel in the same fashion as it acts towards its clients, the criminals: repressive and punitive. Rewarding well-functioning personnel, which most employers have found to be advantageous, is a practice almost absent in the police organization.

An illustration of this is a conduit-chart which is used in some forces. The chart, on a card with two sides, shows the punishments and rewards an officer has received during his career. Side 1 states: 'punishments'. Of course, when the card is turned around you would expect to see the entry: 'rewards'. Wrong! It also states: 'punishments', with only the bottom part of the conduit-chart reserved for the rewards. The designer anticipated the treatment of lower echelon personnel, or maybe he is just a bitter realist. Three quarters of the chart, and thus three quarters of the expected judgments about personnel, is expected to be negative in advance. Just one quarter is apparently supposed to be a positive comment. The good and clever things policemen do, are soon forgotten, if ever mentioned; the mistakes haunt them for the rest of their career. Preventive talks to house-occupants, football-vandalists, and minority-groups is shrugged off as something for the "softies", but I dare bet my life that in the last five years in cities like Amsterdam, Paris, and New York, normally, good willing policemen have prevented, just by being a softy, at least some thirty riots, which might have exceeded the Brixton riots at a factor of five or more.

I say it again: these excellent, preventive activities ought to be rewarded by their superiors. Unfortunately, you will see superiors react only after a riot has taken place. In order to assist these officials in their task of reinforcing behavior already exhibited, I intend, with a few journalist friends of mine, to spread the news on some particular day that no racial riots have broken out that day.

Social Responsibility

A fourth objection to the stress on training and insight is that by this route we hope to make the police deal with problems in an efficient, clever way, whether it concerns handing out speeding tickets or solving the domestic problems of a loudly quarreling couple. This presupposes that it is the policeman's job to solve or ameliorate societal problems. I am not so sure about that. In principle, the public should manage their own problems and conflicts. The police must point to these responsibilities and, if necessary, help the public to bear those responsibilities. If, for instance, the police in a small community had not noticed the behavior of a suicidal woman or had misinterpreted her behavior, the response to this dramatic event should not be training programs to "read" the signs of pre-suicidal behavior. What is indicated is that the police in that community should show their indignation that many members of that small community should have foreseen what was going to happen. By giving the community members their own responsibility, that community becomes the client of the police, not just the potentially suicidal members. The professionalism of the police is not to gather tasks and responsibilities which in turn must be met by further training. Professionalism consists here in delegating, or rather bringing back, responsibility where it belongs: to the community.

Attitude Training

I would like to make some remarks about a specific type of training: information on subgroups of the public that a policeman is likely to meet. The idea that a policeman needs more information on various groups in society rests on the fact that policemen are prone to form a negative view of human nature and as a result of their experience, form prejudices toward some groups. Three weeks of service in downtown Amsterdam, with its drug scene, drug-related crimes, prostitution and gambling joints is enough; from that moment on, the police officer may view Negroes as people who are to be put on a ship for sinking in the middle of the Atlantic, and this is just one example. To counteract these stereotypes, courses are given on practically every conceivable group from the general public: illegal house occupants, drug addicts, homosexuals, minority groups, ex-convicts, etc. Experts share their experiences, and sometimes direct confrontations with members of these groups are organized. All this is done to undermine, by direct experience and background information, the stereotype and negative image these groups usually have in the eyes of the police, thereby facilitating a more balanced, more adequate treatment by the individual policeman.

It is certainly true that knowledge of someone's background and motivation can be of help in approaching members of the public. A police officer is surely better prepared for what he is up against if he knows what an arrested Moroccan can expect in his country after he is expelled. An arrest will for that Moroccan have a quite different meaning than the arrest for a native-born Dutchman. However, I sometimes get the impression that the whole of the Dutch society is viewed as a conglomerate of minorities, each with its own right of differential treatment. This trendy approach has several very negative consequences.

In the first place there are very many minority-groups and they proliferate to such an extent that the police might never stop organizing background-information services. Yesterday the gay, today the illegal occupants, tomorrow the second generation Turkish immigrants, and who knows what's next. It becomes a full-time job to remember who already has had his turn.

In my opinion these training activities are redundant! What is at issue here? The inducement for additional information courses is the feeling on the part of some group that they are treated unfairly. Partisanship, discrimination and prejudice are working to their disadvantage and the problems that the group faces could, at least, be diminished by informing the police of their background and motives. This argument contains very dangerous reasoning. It makes the decency and integrity of the police dependent on their specific knowledge, which is better of some groups than of others. As I discussed earlier, the police officer is supposed to maintain decency and integrity in all situations, regardless of the other party, be it homosexuals, coloured people, house occupants, or "normal" citizens. For this purpose an elementary base of norms has been formalized in legislation, and the police have to stay within that specific charter, no matter to what religion, race, or sex the investigated persons belong. These principles and these principles only, and not some information-induced empathy with specific groups, should prevent the police from bullying or humiliating arrested persons. The same rules that tell citizens not to steal or engage in other unwanted activities tell the public what their norms are and ought to be: "only if somebody has done this or that you may arrest him and hand him over for proper trial".

A second negative consequence is the following. Suppose a course in the background of illegal house occupants is indeed effective. By the additional information and possibly peaceful confrontation, the house occupants are transformed in the eyes of the police from criminal elements into nice youngsters with a housing problem which they try to solve in a somewhat dubious fashion. Mutual insight and understanding have grown and, apart from the problem of how to tell your friends and colleagues, there is no real problem left. Is that true? Is it not more appropriate to say that one label has been exchanged for another? Of course, the label of rioter seems less friendly than the label of victim of an ill-conceived housing program, but they are both labels, that is, shorthand indications by which people are stereotyped. Such a person is regarded as a one-dimensional entity, not as a human being who deserves a normal amount of respect and who is responsible for his actions and who is to be taken into account. One-dimensional entities are not to be taken into account other than as numbers and elements of a technocratic policy. So the moment is not far away that new irritation arises; the victims will resent this role and will become the rioters again.

In a similar fashion, an excessive stress on the problems of acculturation may lead to an interpretation of a criminal act by a young Turkish girl as a sign of domestic problems resulting from the permanent discrepancy she faces between the rules and norms at home and the rules and norms of the Dutch society that she sees on the street and in school. Perhaps, however, she is just a bit love-sick, being abandoned by her boyfriend.

A more spectacular example can be found in the behavior of the chairman of F.C. Ajax, the one-time football club of Johan Cruyff. He appeared on television and in all other mass media when in one fortnight two big contracts were signed, involving millions. However, when he was asked to participate in a T.V. program on football-vandalism and to confront the fans of his team, he refused. I do not need a degree in psychology, nor a bunch of textbooks, to understand that those fans, who just like other human beings want some respect, felt deeply insulted by what they saw as contemptuous behavior by the chairman of their football club. And in some way, insofar as vandalism is a reaction to this sort of contempt, vandalism will stay with us, for that is a sign that these people are not yet bereft of their sense of dignity and have not fallen to apathetic acceptance of their subordinate position. In the face of contempt, vandalism may be the only healthy reaction.

A third negative consequence of viewing a society as a cluster of separate cultural groups is that the individual policeman in his contact with these groups is supposed to act in a well routinized manner that leaves little space for normal human needs and feelings that all human beings share. An anecdote may clarify that these normal needs and feelings often are more appropriate than techniques based on typical classroom knowledge. The daughter of a Turkish immigrant laborer had run away and was living with an older man, a Dutchman. The result was an enormous row and a call for police assistance. The police officer who was in charge clearly did not know what to do. He did not know the Turkish laws on this point nor did he know Turkish customs in these matters. Also, he could not understand the language, so the quarrel went way over his head. "You see how very important it is for policemen to learn about Turkish culture, their laws and their language?" a colleague remarked. I do not contest that, but the event showed another, equally important aspect. For after a while the officer got angry and irritated and did what no expert would have done with all his knowledge and all his compassion: he shouted "Now, for Pete's sake stop this gibberish and talk Dutch. If you don't, I'm off!" From that moment the Dutch speaking people were again party in the conflict. The Dutch police officer and the Turkish immigrant had met on common ground: no man, who is himself, wants to be made a fool of, and they both respected that.

In general, very often decisive interventions by policemen are not the result of careful deliberation and well rehearsed techniques. Breaking through the expectations connected with some situation is very wholesome, like one example of a policeman during a riot in Amsterdam. Against all regulations and educations, he stepped out of the line formed by his squadron and called to the stone-armed rioters: "Hey fellers, anything I can do for you?" This man, without helmet, disarmed more rioters than a few dozen squadrons. Such behaviour teaches us quite a lot: policemen should not always do what they have been taught.

A superior who is not afraid to become unpopular and has the courage to break through the norms of the group culture by saying after the second racist joke: "This is enough, stop it", can achieve by this one-second remark more than weeks of information in a training session. This should be encouraged, rather than organizing courses.

Conclusions

I repeat, I have nothing against selection and training as such. But if we agree that the behavior of the policeman is not only the result of selection procedures and training, but also and primarily of the structure, culture, policy, leadership, ways of interaction in his organization and the kind of responsibility he finds in his own organization, then we must not let ourselves be fooled into the role of behavioral experts who, by our actions in training and selection, keep the major part of the organization out of the picture. Behavioral experts, in their position as intellectuals, are not absorbed in the hectic everyday practice of executive policework, and must use this distance to consider the more fundamental problems of policy, structure and cultural norms. They are to pose the ever crucial question: what is the concrete product the police officer is expected to offer to his local community?

I think three "products" (or functions or goals) come to the foreground, and training and social education should be directed at these:

(1) to strive for and maintain a level of carefulness and decency that is higher than the normal, operant level that can be expected from the general public;

(2) to place the responsibility for human interaction where it belongs: with the citizens. This must be done whenever and wherever it is possible;

(3) to react to the emotions of the public in a way that can be recognized as real concern.

As to this latter point, this has to do with the historical grounds for creating a police force. I have elaborated that point already. In more primitive societies the private citizen had much more room to solve the problems generated by crime and disorder. The excesses that accompanied the unrestrained pursuit of emotional ideas of justice have evoked a counterforce that can be put into words in this way: "Fellow citizens, your feelings and ideas of just revenge are yours, they are legitimate, but they often result in illegal behaviour. So, let other people handle your problems and let them seek solutions that are effective and just. It may be the chief of the tribe, the king or his steward, or like today, the police and other criminal justice institutions, but from now on it is they who are going to deal with problems of crime and keeping order in a more detached, sober and honest way".

This history puts the burden upon the police to restrain their emotions, but also to show that they have taken over the job of the citizen: to find ways of a just and well-balanced answer to the distress that has been suffered, to give the public the information that some balance is restored or at least attempted to be restored. This is what the frontline policeman is confronted with: emotions that the public cannot and should not put to peace by its own actions. The public has the right to recognize their emotions in the actions of the authorities who have taken over for them.

These emotions, I stress, can be of a very diverse nature. Consider, for instance, somebody who comes to report a crime. This does not necessarily imply a deep rooted need that the perpetrator be arrested and punished severely. Women who come to report an attack or rape generally know that their attacker will not readily be found in the anonymous masses. Sometimes they want him found very badly, but very often that is not the only reason for their report. They want to be restored in their legitimate expectation that something is to be done about it and that they, and other women, can go out into the streets without fear. Fear and anxiety are problems for the policeman with a degree of reality and priority that equals the need to catch the villain. This problem of dealing with emotions cannot simply be dealt with by writing a report where the victim is used primarily as a source of information. Emotional witnesses are bothersome material, as any policeman knows, and the probing for reliable information interferes strongly with the help to be offered in overcoming the terrifying emotions. Some way must be found. A reaction that is definitely not right is expressing one's own sense of insecurity, such as a remark like "You feel unsafe, lady? Then what about us? We must go out there". This is a form of venting your professional worries at the expense of the public. A better way is to help somebody step over the barrier, like putting somebody behind the wheel after a car-crash. If you don't, he/she will never dare to drive again. In a similar way, an assaulted woman must be helped over the threshold to go out again. Otherwise, she will not go outside with a decent sense of security.

The help that the police give to the public is only partly the result of training. It is more important that the policeman himself can handle his emotions in a mature way; that he can handle and express his emotions within his own organization. In this respect, too, the policeman acts out as he is treated within his organization. And this is what worries me most: no other organization tends to suppress feelings and emotions of its personnel, making them systematically unfit to do their proper job of handling other people's emotions, more than the police.

TRAINING POLICE FOR SOCIAL WORK? - EXPERIENCES FROM A GERMAN PROGRAM

GERNOT STEINHILPER

THE SELF-CONCEPT OF POLICE AND SOCIAL WORK
Some assumptions and prejudices

Police and social work in general are opposed to each other. The police have the tasks of control and of crime prevention. Their main obligation is to detect crime, to clear up a case, to investigate and to convict a suspect. Their methods include the whole spectrum of forensic techniques and strategies. Police tasks are defined very clearly; their procedure is well regulated.

Social work is, according to its aims, methods, and self-concept, different from police work. Social workers try to analyze and understand the family in order to assist them in utilizing their own resources and those of the community to improve their situation. The methods of social work are counselling, crisis intervention, group services, and even long-term individual and family treatment. The differences between the two professions is clarified through the following positions: The police think that "Criminals make troubles"; the social workers think that "Criminals have troubles".

The interaction between police and social workers is by no means without problems; there is mutual reservation in both professional groups. The relationship is frequently ambiguous and sometimes hostile, or at least strained by prejudices and role conflicts. Communication and cooperation between the two professions is difficult, full of conflicts and emotions. The conflicts often result from the different tasks of the two professions within the same field of responsibility. Social workers and police officers are afraid of coming too close to each other.

The police say that social work doesn't work. According to this perspective, social workers only talk; they are not very efficient. In some cases social workers even identify with their clients against official agencies, especially against the police and the criminal justice system.

Social workers, on the other hand, say that the police control; they keep an eye on people they suspect. Police may also represent violence, and they are an authoritarian executive body of the government. A stereotype is the paramilitary operation of the police against demonstrators or the use of weapons when arresting someone. The police normally are very conservative in the sense that they are not flexible enough to react to changes in society; they are not sensitive to people's needs. Police primarily serve the state; social workers primarily serve the clients.

The above descriptions do not reflect reality, but rather the views of many citizens. Police officers are expected to guarantee public security and public order. Social workers are expected to be available at any time for almost everyone for many purposes (especially if someone is in a crisis situation, needs help, etc.).

The Situation in West Germany

This polarization of views might not exist in other countries, but describes the present situation in West Germany for two reasons:

(1) In the last century the police had jurisdiction for many services/tasks, for example for welfare, construction law, trade law, sanitary inspection and so on. Part of these tasks were taken away from the police gradually and given to other, more specialized agencies. But the impression of the omnipotence of the police is still alive within our population and creates a specific image of power associated with the police in West Germany. This image is supported by the bad experiences during the Third Reich, which broke down exactly forty years ago.

(2) German law does not acknowledge police discretion (for example, as practiced in Great Britain and in the United States). The police have no possibility, no right, and no opportunity to decide their response to a situation. They are not allowed to drop a case even if it is a minor crime. Each case, once reported to the police, must be brought to the prosecutor and, if necessary, to the court. Only the latter components of the criminal justice system have the power to decide whether someone must be punished or whether a case can be dropped. In other words, the police have no discretionary options, and they can play only one role in relationship to the public. This is especially problematic in the field of juvenile delinquency.

The Self-Concept of a Policeman

The self-concept of the police is quite different from the picture given above. According to a survey, 83% of police officers perceive their task in a negative light (Feltes, 1983), but nevertheless they believe their work is a service to the community. From a service point of view, this self-concept is correct because, on a general level, police have to guarantee the welfare of all citizens. In fulfilling that task, the police have a special source of information; they act in a zone where legal norms and social reality clash. The police perceive the human conflicts, personal helplessness, and stress situations of the citizen. They must deal constantly with the tension between law and reality. Because of their unique position, the police perceive themselves as having a task of social engineering; they must handle social conflicts, crisis intervention, counselling, and even compensatory administration of the law (for example, sometimes the police may remedy the inequalities among citizens that might originate in legislation).

Actual Reliance on Police Services

In their daily lives, citizens do not only expect public control and crime prevention from the police. They request many other services which often have nothing to do with crime such as: suicide, family disputes, neighborhood quarrels, runaway children, mentally disordered people, victims, drunken people, helpless elderly persons, marital disputes, and unsupervised children. These are more or less personal, individual, and social problems. A legal or police reaction is not necessary and often inappropriate; people only want to get information, help, suggestions, assistance, and support. The statistics all over the world tell us that these tasks account for a greater share of police jobs than search, investigation, arrest and other "typical" police activities. In Germany these non-crime-related tasks require on the average about 50% of police activities. According to all empirical findings, most victims of crime are initially interested in getting help in their situation and are less interested in the offender being punished.

There are many reasons why the situation is as it is. The main reason for charging the police with tasks beyond crime and public control is that the police are available around the clock (especially the emergency line). Social services, on the other hand, are not available outside office-hours and, as every policeman knows, those events which require social intervention normally occur during the night or from Friday afternoon till Monday morning (i.e., during the weekend) when social agencies are not on call.

Social work by the police?

Although the role of the police may vary slightly from country to country, generally their role is akin to social work in the wider sense, i.e., to help, to care, to assist, to intervene in crisis situations. This situation, however, is problematic for the police:

(1) Lack of training. Normally, a police officer is not prepared for social crisis intervention (either by training programs or by practice). Most of the training he receives deals with the law, with the procedures of the criminal justice system, with forensic techniques, with the use of weapons, and so on. Indeed, this aspect of his training sometimes seems to be over-stressed. Of course, there are many general or specific training programs in crisis intervention, stress management, family counselling, etc., as part of police training. However, if one examines them in detail, one cannot avoid the impression that even these additional training programs are more a strong desire than a realization. Even if a policeman is trained in a variety of fields such as psychology, sociology, social work, and so on, it is doubtful that he really can achieve competence as a psychologist, sociologist, and social worker, in addition to being a good investigator, law enforcer and so on.

(2) Lack of time and low priority. There are practical considerations which also limit the effectiveness of the police officer as social worker. Even if the police officer is a good social worker, does he have the time to extend his social work as far as it is needed? For example, if a woman is raped, what is the first task of the police officer? He has to collect evidence, search for the offender, clear the case, convict the suspect. The victim, who needs advice, help, and support immediately, may have a low priority for the officer. The police officer has to be concerned with crime first, and only secondarily, if there is enough time, with social work.

The police function comes first for another practical reason. A police officer's career is primarily affected by the number and nature of cases he clears up. For career advancement, it does not count very much to be a good social worker (for example, to talk to an old lady who will thank the policeman very much). One may regret this state of affairs, but in many countries it is a fact.

Inaccessible and Tangled Network of Social Services

In Germany (like in many other countries), there ia a nationwide network of social services with highly qualified experts. This system works splendidly on paper! In reality the network is so specialized that it is more like a jungle: It is very difficult to find one's way through it, to find the right person at the right time for the right problem. Even those working in that system have difficulty finding the right bureau responsible for a problem. For a police officer responding to a night call, it is much more difficult to find the appropriate social agency. The appropriate social agency in Germany depends upon, among other things, the age of the client, the type of help needed, sex, ethnic group, religion, area of residence, marital status, etc.

As noted earlier, the police have many reservations about doing social work, but nevertheless they believe that social work is needed in many cases. German policemen believe, in about 25% of their cases, that traditional social work is needed or at least helpful. Table 1 indicates the types of events for which social work is seen as useful, and Table 2 provides comparable data for persons (from Feltes, 1983).

Table 1
Proportion of Events Amenable to Social Work as Perceived by Police

Categories	%
drug problems	88.2%
alcohol problems	86.1%
psychiatric disturbance	74.2%
suicide (attempts)	70.2%
family disputes	58.7%
helplessness	57.3%
violent crime	18.6%
theft	10.4%

Table 2
Types of Persons Benefiting from Social Work as Perceived by Police

Categories	%
elderlies	78.4%
youngsters	79.2%
kids	72.6%
victims	64.7%
helpless persons	60.6%
adults	20.4%
suspects/offenders	19.0%

Social workers believe their services are needed especially in dealing with juvenile delinquency. In this instance the self-concept of the social worker differs from the expectations of the policeman.

"PREVENTION PROGRAM POLICE/SOCIAL WORKER" (PPS) IN HANNOVER

This section describes a pilot project that was tested in Hannover called the "Prevention program police/social worker" (abbreviated: PPS). After an experimental phase of five years, it became a permanent program in Hannover. Many other cities in West Germany are interested in establishing similar projects because there is a need to fill the gap between police and social services. So far, their program establishment has been prevented by financial restrictions.

Basic Idea and Origin of PPS

The basic idea of PPS is to respond to the social work needs of the police that have been outlined earlier. The main assumption of the program is that the police normally are not able to handle the social aspects of these problems in a manner which is adequate and has lasting effects. Social service in terms of crisis intervention, family counselling and therapy is not the commission and function of the police. The police have time restrictions and educational deficits.

On the other hand, the cooperation between police and responsible social services is not such that psychosocial assistance to offenders, victims and other persons in crisis situations is guaranteed. One problem is the availability of social services—particularly on weekends and during the night, when social conflicts are most likely to occur. On Friday afternoon at three o'clock, social agencies are closed and remain so until Monday morning at nine o'clock. Although some social services are on call, social workers can't be contacted outside regular office hours.

The basic idea of PPS (see Figure 1) is to install social workers in the police station available immediately and nearly around the clock (during the weekend and during the night).

Figure 1
Basic Concept of PPS

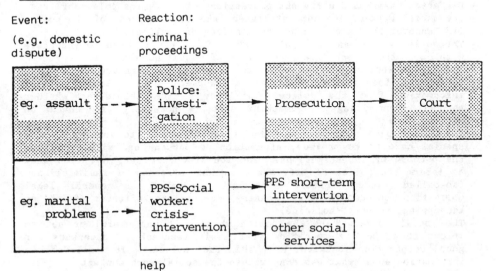

Event: Reaction:

(e.g. domestic   criminal
dispute)   proceedings

help

The impulse for new cooperation between police and their "own" social workers came from the U.S.A., where Harvey Treger (1975, 1979, 1981) directed a model called "Social Service Project" (SSP) in the Chicago area communities of Wheaton, Niles, and Maywood. This project was replicated in about fifty other Illinois cities as well as in the United Kingdom; in Devon and Cornwall in the so-called "joint-bureau". These projects assumed that criminal prosecution (investigation and detection) and social work (counselling and so on) are clearly distinct tasks, which should be fulfilled by two separate professions who do not interfere with each other. Thereby, role-conflicts can be avoided.

The Organization of PPS

Hannover is a city with approximately 500,000 inhabitants (situated in the north of Germany). The 9th police district is an area with some 80,000 residents (11% foreigners, mostly Turks, Greeks and Spaniards). Statistically, it has a relatively high crime rate with local centers of criminality but also with areas of low criminality due to social and housing conditions. Eight social workers have been provided with their own office within the building of the 9th police precinct. They are competent, well-trained, and available for the whole area of Hannover. The social workers have their own telephones independent of the police lines. The social workers are available to citizens even without referral by the police. Most of the time, however, the social workers are informed by telephone or radio or are seen personally by the policemen concerned. Another possibility is that the police may suggest to a potential client that he or she contact the social worker. The first talk between social worker and client takes place either in the office of the social worker or immediately at the place the event happened.

The Principles of PPS

The key-elements of PPS are:
- Different tasks need different professions; this avoids role-conflicts.
- The social workers are not integrated into the hierarchy of the police (in Hannover they are paid by the ministry of justice).
- The social worker and the police officer are not allowed to interfere with each others work (i.e., principle of mutual non-interference).
- The social workers have no power to investigate; they are not allowed to hinder the police. The social workers obtain their initial information from the police, but they decide themselves whether support, counselling or something else is necessary and should be offered.
- The police have no right to order a social worker to intervene in a special case or to provide information on persons and situations for the purpose of investigations. The social worker does not even need to inform the police of previously unknown offences of their clients (so-called hidden crime). There is, however, a general legal obligation to report the planning of serious offences (such as kidnapping, robbery, homicide).
- The social workers tell the police whether it was useful or not to inform them about a specific event. This feedback is necessary for good cooperation between PPS and the police. It includes no information about what was done within the social work contact.

The social workers play the role of a social fire brigade. Social work can be directed to the actual problem situation. Social work in

crisis situations promises greater success than tackling the problem
after a delay of days, weeks or even months. The social workers offer
social work at the "critical time of need". Very often the case would
come through the ordinary channels with a lot of useless paperwork after
several weeks to a social service which feels responsible.

Some Experiences of PPS
Figure 2 indicates the distribution of different demands placed upon
the social workers.

Figure 2
Events with which the PPS-social Workers were Concerned

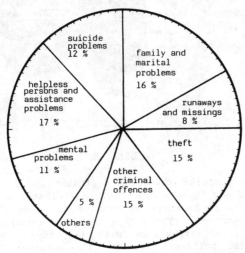

Figure 3
Hourly Distribution of Demand for Social Services

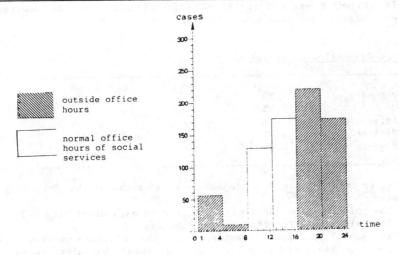

74

Figure 4
Weekly Distribution of Demand for Social Services

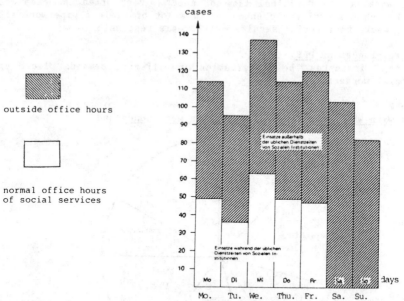

Figures 3 and 4 describe the time distribution of the demand for social services, and how these demands were distributed over the week.

The police officers in Hannover were asked to assess the cooperation of the PPS—social workers. Table 3 summarizes the responses of 237 policemen. After brief experience with the social workers in the program, most of the policemen came to the opinion: "Our PPS—social worker Meyer, whom I know very well, is OK; he is a good social worker". But this opinion does not mean that the policemen have lost their prejudice against social work in general. On the contrary, in general discussions they usually reject social work.

Table 3
Police Evaluation of Social Work

very good	14.8%
good	37.6%
satisfactory	32.1%
sufficient	8.9%
inadequate	6.8%

The success of the PPS—project can be seen in the following three points:
(1) The policemen and the social worker know each other very well;
(2) Both sides work together on the same case;
(3) The social workers are available for the policemen whenever they are needed; their availability in the same building seems to be important.

The main goals of PPS are:
- Prevention or interruption of criminal developments which are still below the threshold of criminality (for example, family quarrels) or have already passed it (shop-lifting). Because social problems very often lead to crime, the intention of the project is to intervene as soon as possible to prevent an event exceeding the threshold of crime.
- Improvement of psychosocial assistance to victims. (Insofar as Germany does not offer many programs; even private programs are rather rare.)

Besides these positive effects of PPS, there are, of course, some objections to the project. In particular, the union of the social workers opposed the whole approach. They suspected something like hidden police officers in the disguise of social workers. They did not trust the police and feared that confidentiality between the social worker and client would be breached. However, during the time of the PPS-project, there was no case in which a client refused services offered by the social worker of PPS.

Another objection is that people can be overprotected by official agencies. Nearly all professions (for example policemen, advocates, doctors, social workers) claim to serve human beings. However, one must be careful that this new kind of care does not lead to a netwidening effect of social control.

One of the most important results which came out of our project was that the police were astonished how effective social work can be. Thereby the police became more sensitive to the need for social work without being obliged to perform social work by themselves. They became more secure in their diagnosis concerning when help is needed.

PPS is only a model. It does not seem to be necessary if other social services are available for all the police around the clock. As long as social services are not available and guaranteed, organizations like PPS can be useful.

CONCLUSIONS
- It is not necessary to provide in-depth training in social work for the police.
- Police need not perform social work extensively. It seems to be enough if they are able to discover a social problem, and decide if social work is needed or not.

REFERENCES
Feltes. (1983). Soziale Probleme des Alltags - Aufgabe von Polizei oder Sozialarbeit? Kriminalistik, 234-237.
Michaels, R., & Treger, H. (1973). Social work in police departments. Social Work, 18(5), 67-75.
Schwind, H-D. (1977). Das Chicagoer "Social Service Team" (SSP-Modell) - Harvey Tregers Experiment mit einer neuen Form der Zusammenar-beit zwischen Sozialarbeitern und Polizei. Kriminalistik, 530-530.
Schwind, H-D. (1978). Sozialarbeiter im Polizeirevier: Das SSP-Programm von Chicago; in: Empirische Kriminalgeographie (eds.: Schwind, Ahlborn/1 Weiß), Wiesbaden (BKA-Forschungsreihe, vol. 8), 368-369.
Schwind, H-D., Steinhilper, G., & Wilhelm-Reiss, M. (1980). Prevention program police/social workers (PPS): A model-project in the lower saxony department of justice. Hannover, Federal Republic of Germany. Police Studies 3(2), 15-20.

Schwind, H-D., Steinhilper, G., & Wilhelm-Reiss, M. (1980). Präventions-
programm Polizei/Sozialarbeiter (PPS). Ein Modellversuch des
Niedersächsischen Justizministeriums. Kriminalistik, 58-64.
Steinhilper, G. (1981). Schließt oder schafft das "Präventionsprogramm
Polizei/Sozialarbeiter" (PPS) eine Lücke im System der psychsozialen
Versorgung? In A. Kreuzer & M. Plate (Eds.), Polizei und Sozialarbeit
(pp. 63-77). Wiesbaden.
Steinhilper, M. (1982). Das "Präventionsprogramm Polizei/
Sozialarbeiter" (PPS) - Modellbeschreibung, Berichte aus der Praxis,
Bewertung und Diskussion. In H-D. Schwind & G. Steinhilper (Eds.),
Modelle zur Kriminalitätsvorbeugung und Resozialisierung (pp.
45-111). Beispiele praktischer Kriminalpolitik in Niedersachsen
(Kriminologische Forschung, vol. 2). Heidelberg.
Steinhilper, M. (1983). "Präventionsprogramm Polizei/Sozialarbeiter"
(PPS) - Modellversuch wird Dauereinrichtung. Kriminalist, 15-20.
Steinhilper, M. (1984). PPS: 455 "Fälle" bis 6/84. Noch immer
aktuell: Zusammenarbeit von Polizei und Sozialarbeitern.
Kriminalistik, 524-525.
Treger, H. (1975). The police-social work team (a new model for
interprofessional cooperation). Springfield, Illinois, USA.
Treger, H. (1979). Wheaton-Niles and Maywood police-social service
projects. The Proceedings of the 1978 Cranfield Conference on the
Prevention of Crime in Europe, London, 107-117.
Treger, H., Thomson, D., & Jaeck, G.S. (1979). A police-social work
team model. Crime and Delinquency, 3, 281-290.
Treger, H. (1981). Police-social work cooperation: Problems and
issues. Social Casework: The Journal of Contemporary Social Work,
426-433.
Wilhelm-Reiss, M. (1981). Sozialarbeit als präventive Maßnahme im
Handlungsfeld der Polizei: Modellversuch Hannover. In H-D. Schwind,
F. Berckhauer, & G. Steinhilper (Eds.), Präventive Kriminalpolitik
(Kriminolohische Forschung, Vol. 1) (pp. 405-417). Heidelberg.
Wilhelm-Reiss, M. (1981). Modellversuch Hannover: Eine neue Form der
Zusammenarbeit zwischen Polizei und Sozialarbeitern wird erprobt. In
H. Kury, & H. Lerchenmüller, (Eds.), Diversion. Alternativen zu
klassischen Sanktionsformen, Vol. 2 (pp. 575-597). Bochum.
Wilhelm-Reiss, M. (1981). Erfahrungen mit dem Präventionsprogramm
Polizei/Sozialarbeiter (PPS) in Hannover. In Arbeit e. V. (ISA)
(Eds.), Institut für soziale. Sozialarbeit und Polizei. Münster.

THE CONTRIBUTION OF PSYCHOLOGY TO THE DEVELOPMENT OF POLICE TRAINING IN
BRITAIN (WITH PARTICULAR EMPHASIS ON METROPOLITAN LONDON)

LESLIE POOLE

INTRODUCTION
   It is my intention to paint a comparative picture of British police
training in 1965 and 1985 and examine the various components involved. I
want to examine the issues initially from a historical then from a
developmental perspective. In doing so I hope to correct some commonly
held misconceptions regarding the impetus for change in police training
in Britain. I will examine the origins of and support for those changes,
and the degree of acceptance and development achieved to date. Analysis
has been confined in the main to Constable training but not in isolation
from the more important developments in other areas of police training.
   Perhaps it would be appropriate here to make a definitive statement
about those aspects of psychology which I intend to examine. Firstly,
I'll emphasize the incorporation of applied psychology into the content
of police training, a gradual process over the past 20 years. Secondly,
I'll trace those elements of psychology which have contributed
significantly to educational theory, teaching skills and pedagogy, most
noticeable in the 80s. Finally, I'll examine some of the behavioural
responses to introducing social sciences to police training in an aura of
organizational scepticism and then later, in one of organizational
support.

London 1965-1971: The Origins
   Twenty years ago initial police training in London was fairly narrow in
terms of curriculum, and the environment was fairly harrowing.
Discipline and overall outlook were mainly punitive and the atmosphere
militaristic. An external observer might have described it as an
environment of depersonalization and desensitization. To this day,
officers newly attested are 'recruits' and their tutors 'instructors',
not the terminology of learner and teacher in most forms of educational
establishments outside the military. Learning was based almost entirely
on rote and reinforced through practical exercises demanding set phrases
and questions to establish details. No account was taken of individuals'
learning nor their inability to absorb knowledge at the set rate.
Students' performance was assessed mainly subjectively by means of
written examinations and a number of practical tests. Hunches and 'gut
feeling' were essential ingredients of assessment rather than observable
and measurable methods. In terms of comparison with established
educational practices elsewhere, police training compared favourably with
the general education system.
   The instructors were a directive and controlling influence as concerned
with the transmission of social values as with delivering information by
formal lesson method. In terms of the social context of the time the

staff training was efficient, effective and brought accolades from outside teaching organizations regarding its high standards and professionalism. Initial provincial police training was similar in most respects except of shorter duration.

Management training was concerned with police procedure and supervisory duties rather than the theory and practice of management. However, 1965 saw the introduction of the concept of 'man management' to police training, a term little understood by supervisors in a hierarchical organization staffed predominantly by men with experience of the British armed services. It was nonetheless an attempt to develop some consideration amongst police managers for personnel and managerial skills. This was a significant move from training wholly concerned with the technical and mechanical, rather than the human issues involved in achieving organizational efficiency. By the time a Working Party on Probationer Training sat in 1969, it had become abundantly clear to a few senior police officers that changes in society and the increasing demands of informed public opinion, required a "greater all round ability and versatility from police". They required a more flexible approach from officers. The question was how should this be done?

Certainly, adopting new methods of policing and the changing role of police in society were making new demands on officers. The Report on British Race Relations (Rose, 1969) emphasized the need for officers to be trained in the controversial and problematical aspects of policing as they related to the social role of the service and the relationships between police and community. Demands were made to ensure officers 'understood their role in social and humanitarian terms'. The Working Party emphasized the need for knowledge of issues, mainly sociological with a smattering of psychology and social psychology topics such as 'Perception' and 'Attitudes'. These social, behavioural, and constitutional studies were to be entitled Social Studies and would form most of the first 3 weeks of the course. At the same time the basic course was to be extended by 3 weeks to 16 weeks of which one would be spent in the practical situation at a police station under supervision. These major changes were to be incorporated into training in January 1971.

Once implemented, the lesson presentation naturally followed the established and formal style: delivering information, despite the more sensitive nature of the issues. Lessons were presented by police officers, not academics, to classes of about 20 officers. Some forces, including Metropolitan London, used police officers with related degrees to teach these subjects. Even then, the animosity towards the topics, the emphasis placed on doctrine, correct terminology, and its often unrelated nature, ensured this content would be treated with disdain. Arguments for retaining specialist instructors were based on the overall lack of knowledge by most staff and therefore the inexpert teaching which would result from a generic presentation. It was only by using the most proficient instructors with high credibility among their colleagues and sound attitudes that gave even the specialist instructors a chance of success. Absence of any form of testing of content in an otherwise rigidly examined syllabus was the final blow.

Developments Elsewhere

The subjects were presented in provincial training centres in Britain in mass lecture form, using academics from appropriate disciplines often addressing over 100 officers at a time. That method was found to be ineffective and unpopular, impractical and inconsequential. Both content and format were inappropriate. The former was left to the lecturers who invariably did not relate their topics to police work or use police examples, and who used copious amounts of jargon appropriate to their own disciplines. Where their delivery was relevant and linked to policing, the lecture proved a bad medium for presentation. Officers saw little relevance to the job they had to do and even less interest in matters being presented by non-police officers.

London 1972-1979: Review and Development

Whilst the rest of England and Wales pursued the external lectures, the Metropolitan Force tinkered with its system. Some tests were devised, concerned wholly with the regurgitation of information and knowledge of social studies subjects (Management Services, July 1976, Aug. 1977; Oct. 1978; March 1980). Teaching passed from specialist to generic instructor but lacked supervision, or general agreement and appropriate attitude of the staff. In 1977 the Metropolitan Police Commissioner expressed his concern about the quality of his training and set up a Steering Committee to examine the system. A clinical psychologist, Evelyn Schaffer was invited to examine Social Studies training and tendered her report (Schaffer & Poole, 1978; Schaffer, 1980). This report indicated that the aims and objectives of this aspect of initial training were already established but there were various counter-productive elements within the organization which prevented their achievement. The aim was given as follows:

"To produce a less abrasive, more mature professional Police Officer, whose foresight and understanding of social problems and human behaviour have been developed to assist him to assess situations and deal firmly but courteously with all members of the public."

The objectives were:
(1) To develop an awareness of social problems and cultural backgrounds of minority groups by the objective presentation of information aimed at destroying myths on which prejudices are based.
(2) To develop an understanding of human behaviour so that the policeman may understand and handle his own feelings, limitations, and reactions and anticipate those of others.
(3) Produce a more professional well-rounded Police Officer with more 'client sensitivity' and better able to deal adequately with the public.

These aims and objectives were supported by an internal report of Force psychologists in 1978 (Management Services, Oct. 1978), when the concept of the community manager was born:

"People are the police force's most important resource; therefore, mastery of social psychological arts such as leadership, communication and motivation is a pre-requisite to successful management, especially at the lower levels. Furthermore, the same skills which facilitate effective management of subordinates also facilitate successful communication with the public, whether it be the Constable controlling a situation in the street or the Chief Superintendent engaged in meetings with representatives of the local community".

These aims and objectives were laudable enough but the Schaffer report suggested that topics were still being inadequately handled by staff unfamiliar with the content, and teaching to their limit. Jargon and complex concepts detracted from relevance, and poor instruction was damaging the subject matter and image still further. The report stated "A great deal of teaching at Hendon is aimed at pouring in knowledge;

social studies should stimulate and draw it out of the students". It was further suggested that some form of examination be given and projects introduced as a means of assessment. There was a need to mix active learning with the familiar monotony of the course. Dedicated specialist staff were proposed as a means to effective teaching.

As a result of circulating this report and the statistics concerning the earlier social studies tests, it was suggested as recently as 1978 that teaching social sciences to police officers was time wasted. The statistics showed there had been no gain in knowledge in these subjects. Essential subjects and the requirements of the professional field were said to be of greater importance. Note the dichotomy between operational police practice and materials of an apparently unrelated nature, a fundamental issue.

Fortunately, the idea of abandoning this area of teaching, whilst not an untypical view was eventually rejected. It was accepted that an implicit objective of this part of the curriculum was one of affecting attitude if not one of attitudinal change. Instructors' courses were extended to include social skills teaching and a right of veto was introduced to exclude instructors whose own attitudes were most extreme and authoritarian. This was a real step forward in the long term, towards a genuine and acceptable generic instructor covering the entire training syllabus.

Meanwhile the specialist staff were retained to give time for better trained staff to develop and the generic system to have a greater chance of success. Small steps forward began to be taken in changing the format of the social studies teaching. Specialist staff were encouraged to alter the classroom geography from straight rows of desks to a horseshoe formation. At once a different concept of authority was introduced. A few began to facilitate discussions and use videotapes to assist them in exploring some controversial social and behavioural issues. Chunks of knowledge became less important in those lessons than the social and communicative skills of staff and students. It was quite evident however, that 10% of the syllabus, content and teaching style could not counterbalance the remainder.

The Social Studies report highlighted another area hitherto unexplored in Britain. It raised crucial issues concerning the pressure of petty discipline and victimization on young officers under training. This was seen to be associated with an approach by some training staff to toughen students up to withstand pressure on the street. It was suggested that confidence was accordingly undermined, particularly in practical exercises where staff over-reacted and the public were seen to be problems who abused or misused police. Undoubtedly the staff were role models for students and it is clear that socialization of students is an important ingredient of a basic training course. The real question posed was how to produce an authoritative not an authoritarian officer. Can a predominantly autocractic, hierarchical and authoritarian system imposing external discipline produce an authoritative, sensitive, responsive, self-disciplined policeman?

Some of the reservations expressed in the Schaffer report were reflected in the observations of another psychologist, albeit with a different emphasis. Dr. Alex Main, an educational psychologist, was appointed consultant to the force on educational method. Certainly the issues he raised of confidence building, punitive staff attitudes, and petty discipline were common themes with the Schaffer report. Similarly, a lack of variety in teaching methods and artificial practical situations excluding personal feedback, discouraging self-criticism, and in an atmosphere of ridicule for the student and hostility from the 'public', were all clear threads linking those two independent reports. It was suggested that "attempts to teach strict conformity with 'perfect' police behaviour reduced students' natural ability to communicate or to use common-sense in handling situations" (Main, 1979).

The major conclusions of Main's report elaborated on those themes and examined the training system in greater detail. The most important findings were that the development of students was the most crucial element of the course. In a very wide mixed ability group stretching from a first class honours degree to those with no formal educational qualifications at all in any given class, the teaching methods were inflexible. Rote learning was extensive with understanding less important than repetition of sections of law. Attrition rates were high due to pressure of work out of class, and the system providing no support or remedial training for the slow learners, let alone provision for counselling individuals. A major question posed to all similar police training establishments is whether their task is to train or to act as a further mechanism to select out students?

The clear direction for the future was one of variety of presentation using different methods in combination, to increase the students ease of learning and taking account of the fact that students learn in different ways. It was proposed that training instructors might concentrate more on method than content. It was suggested that any new course could include to good effect, sessions on counselling, facilitation, interpersonal skills, building in time for educational innovation.

Meantime in the late 70s, sergeants under training were being introduced to videotaped role play sessions on interpersonal skills. This proved problematic primarily because it formed less than a half day on a 4-week course and many of the supervisors involved did not, after only 6 months in their new rank, see themselves as managers at all. Some who did, responded positively whilst others thought interpersonal and communicative skills were obvious, unteachable and merely common sense. On occasion, the stress of the unfamiliarity of this training brought problems of adjustment. Evaluation of their performance was sketchy and inconclusive. Nevertheless, the management training was slowly but inexorably moving toward facilitation and less didactic methods of teaching as it began to include some areas of social skills training.

Whilst a narrow and somewhat unprogressive view of police training has been presented, I believe it reflects a fairly true representation of how things developed in the 1960s and 1970s[1]. It is important, however, to keep this in a realistic perspective. As to teaching methods, who else

---

[1]It differs little from similar comments made both before 1968 and after 1978, for example, Reith (1952) who said 35 years ago "It can be said of police training schools that the recruit is taught everything except the essential requirement of his calling, which is how to secure and maintain the approval and respect of the public whom he encounters daily in the course of his duties," and Alderson who said in 1979 "The basic education of the police is far too legalistic. As young people enter the service and go out to face the complexity of their problems on their beats they are bemused and disoriented by the seeming inadequacy of their training....Police training will have to take much more into account than it does at present, and start at the bottom level; the shift from its heavy legal orientation is long overdue."

had anything to offer to develop our style except perhaps a few pioneers in the management field? Even then, many of them were using methods considered highly unorthodox, even dangerous, and certainly they were methods educationally untried if not unsound. The wider world of education in universities, schools and teachers' training colleges was often surprised by what they saw as the good quality of our teaching. Few could match it, let alone surpass it, so where was the need to change?

The police in the main had been an organization never before required to be introspective and never renowned for either creativity or liberal ideas. Certainly since 1945 policing had been done in a familiar, relatively homogeneous, stable and unquestioning society. Naturally enough there remained an air of complacency about police training achievements and a predominant desire to preserve the status quo. So, from where would the impetus for change come?

Initially, the changes in society, the advance of technology (e.g., the use of unit beat police cars), the xenophobia of parts of the indigenous population, and the impact of the media all called for a greater versatility and flexibility from police. A few isolated examples of academic study related to policing indicated that the greater proportion of police activity was spent in social service rather than on law enforcement (Mallian, 1974; Punch & Naylor, 1973; Shane, 1980). This all reinforced the need to improve the police communication process with the public. A few senior police officers with vision and those officers connected with the flourishing new community relations departments were the vanguard of those advances in training which were to herald the demands made on urban police forces in Britain in the 1980s.

Quite evidently a start had been made towards the introduction of social science and social skills. Police were now aware of their shortcomings as seen by external professionals, all, as it happens, from the discipline of psychology. My hypothesis, however, is that if Metropolitan Police training had not suffered through these growing pains for a number of years it would not have made the significant advances it has made in the last 6 years. Achieving an acceptance by policemen of the relevance of developing skills to handle people and understand society was a lengthy process itself affected by further changes within society.

Gathering Momentum 1980-82

The 1980s have seen a substantial number of changes in training. The social disorders in Brixton and Toxteth, and the subsequent report on those events by Lord Scarman (1981), have been seen by many as a watershed in implementing entirely new initiatives. My foregoing comments indicate the glibness of such an explanation. The seeds had already been scattered and a few survived. These outbreaks of social disorder certainly brought the impetus for major changes to take place in police training and the finance to support them. They did indicate, once again, the very special and sensitive situation of the police officer who is the first line of attack in any major, violent confrontations between the people and the government. Unfortunately, neither the emphasis in Scarman's report nor the ensuing financial expenditure went far enough to rectify the overall breadth of the problem. The report seems to emphasize the police contribution to the disorders to the extent that over 3/4 of the 154 page report relates to 'the police and the law' as do 48 of the 64 recommendations. Less than 1/4 of the report refers to the underlying and insidious causes which contribute so much to the fermentation of discontent, i.e., housing, unemployment, education, and community representation.

Yet it was this very emphasis on the function and role of the police which in tangible terms, gave a boost in resources to police training in London. Priority was given both to enforcement in respect of public disorder training, deployment of riot shields, etc., and to handling people in the newly named human awareness training. Initial training was extended from 15 to 20 weeks. It was supported by in-service training at local level using Street Duty Tutors at police stations to supervise officers for their first 10 weeks before being allowed to patrol on their own.

The human awareness programme itself is the subject of the chapter in this text by Dr. Ray Bull. Suffice it to say that the programme has been evaluated externally (Bull & Horncastle, 1983) and is still developing now under the name of 'policing skills'. In the context of previous developments in the social science aspects of training, it is important to keep the impact of human awareness training in perspective. The threads taken forward from the earlier social studies lessons and now essential ingredients of this new programme are those concerning communication, attitude, and role. Elements of constitutional law and history were abandoned in order to re-direct more of the effort into areas of self-awareness, interpersonal skills and community relations. In essence then, the materials were an expansion of previous work with a greater bias towards the practical and away from the theoretical.

But other factors had changed; namely, the time allowed, the expenditure on such items as video cameras and a general climate of support for new initiatives in this field. Above all, the animosity of training staff towards these subject areas had decreased appreciably. Officers became more aware of the concepts, more concerned with developing as many tools as possible to insulate themselves from physical attack and confrontation, and an explicit respect for the practical skills to be learned.

External consultants assisted with the initial training of staff in the appropriate areas (Shepard, 1984). The right of veto on those deemed unsuitable to present these lessons was retained but only to exclude them from human awareness teaching. It did not preclude their acceptance as members of staff. Eventually, when staff training in its entirety was returned to Hendon in 1983, that veto ensured the exclusion of anyone from the staff considered to have insufficient potential to teach these subjects. Even then, this process did not redress the problems of indifferent attitude, change of teaching style and internal discipline, which were still untackled.

Organizational Support 1983

The final thrusts for change came in 1982/83 when a new Commissioner was appointed to the London Metropolitan Force, culminating in the publication of the 'Policing Principles' (1985). Committed to providing a better public service, multiagency cooperation in tackling crime, better communication with the public directing police activity towards community concerns, and a more cost effective police service, his philosophy has helped pave the way for more effective training in those skills necessary to handle people and to exercise discretion (Reports of the Commissioner, 1982; 1983). Above all, those set objectives were a statement of intent by the Commissioner that he would give his full support to the training necessary to achieve his objectives. Once again the concept of the Constable as a community manager resurrected itself.

In London's increasingly multi-racial and cosmopolitan community, many of the traditional policing and social values are now lost, and it is in the idea of the community manager and with the Commissioner's philosophy that our new traditions will be rooted. Such major changes of strategy involve massive organizational implications not least of which is the pursuance of a more harmonious and well-tuned relationship between the local populace and its police. For training, the ultimate question is how can this best be achieved?

In a service where officers spend 90% or more of their time operating alone, it would seem more important for training to emphasize personal decision-making, to develop initiative and even to encourage creative and proactive solutions to problems. Concentration on reactive solutions and procedural content rather than method, with reliance on rote learning and instructional staff with a prescriptive answer to all problems, are likely to prove counter-productive. Suddenly a black and white world with easy snap answers to all questions which was feasible in policing terms in a less complex and not so well informed world of 30 or 40 years ago, becomes nonsense which is not only unattainable but is also undesirable.

In a country where there is no third force between the military and the police, it is essential to train officers to respond almost mechanically to commands to deal with public disorder and sporadic, widespread violence. How does one counter-balance that very minimal part of their duty with the demands of daily policing? How stressful is it to transport the Home Beat Officer from a quiet pleasant suburb of London after talking to 5-year-olds in a school where the youngsters play with his helmet and whistle and then place him behind a riot shield in a situation which is frequently frightening in an area of urban decay and discontent? How stressful is it to cope with conflict and deal with the crises of others and how much does this produce crisis in the police officer himself? How those stresses are coped with will depend in part on his own personality--hence the psychological testing research--part on his level of preparation and training for these traumas, and part on the responsiveness and support of the organization to his needs. This too, is now being looked at and concern is being expressed about the relationship between training and preparation for the more rigorous aspects of police work (Metropolitan Police, 1984).

A Systems Approach

In 1969 the Central Planning Unit was set up as a central resource for police training for the whole of England and Wales except London. It trained instructors, revised lesson notes, planned curricula and set examinations. Its strength lay in the area of adopting a systems approach to training, in setting aims and objectives that were observable and measurable. Whilst this remains an effective means of testing knowledge and procedure, it has considerable shortcomings when creating new training programmes and accommodating changes in philosophy which are aimed at achieving a change in a police officer's outlook and behaviour.

As a result of recommendations in Professor Main's report, a Planning Unit was created in 1980 to deal with Metropolitan Police training. It took the best of the Central Planning Unit experience and then went on to meet Metropolitan needs. In creating its own evaluation unit, it remained strongly in favour of the systems approach. Adhering to such an approach becomes more questionable when one is looking at practical, interpersonal and communication skills, or where one is helping young officers explore their own aggression or hostility, or exploring sensitive issues such as race relations.

The assessment of technical proficiency lends itself to systems analysis. In contrast, morale or integrity, feelings and attitudes can't easily be quantified. Only by qualitative means can one establish whether the staff or public are fairly content with things and how responsive they are. Such measures are indicators of success. Cronbach (1976) and Weiss (1972) have pointed out the extensive difficulties of evaluating behavioural programmes in regard to both sampling and measurement. For the police service, the changes proposed in 1969 were not aims and objectives, they were almost unanalyzed pious hopes. It will take years, even decades, to test the effectiveness of the programme. Evaluation on such a macro level is rare. To evaluate changes in our training programme aimed at achieving different police behaviour, the component parts have to be so designed that certain short-term changes are assumed to be necessary conditions for achieving the long-range goals. The programme fails if the proximate goals are not achieved. The philosophy fails when the achievement of those proximate goals do not lead to the desired outcome. To meet policing needs in the 1990s, a reduced reliance on a systems approach is almost inevitable. The overall direction is no longer in doubt. What we have to establish is a series of short-term goals which we consider are preconditions to achieving the long term strategy. There are a number of major advances which have been made as steps towards that end. They are perhaps most readily identified under the headings of Method and Style, Content and Assessment.

Method and Style 1983-85

A major contribution to method was the new Training Manual proposed by Professor Main, 3 years prior to the present Commissioner's appointment. Coincidentally, the publication of the Manual occurred almost at the same time (in January 1983), having taken almost 3 years to prepare. It included all the Policing Skills lessons and was a far more effective aid to learning. It is a well laid out, illustrated manual where complex law and police practice are simplified to accommodate and stimulate individual learning. In contrast, the previous turgid, close-typed textbook is a dinosaur in learning terms, sufficient to demotivate the most highly motivated individual and the best cure for insomnia ever written. All in all, an adequate textbook but a poor educational tool.

The production of the Manual, however, was only the beginning. To simplify presentation, it provides notes for the trainer, introductory reading sheets and then full notes for the student, with further test questions to recap on learning. This posed a number of problems for the organization in terms of our teaching style. Moreover, where that style has been steeped in rote learning with a philosophy less concerned with understanding than prompt repetition, and sometimes unaware of principles and objectives, it is essential that the teaching style change. Resistance to that change from the police culture has been complicated by the relative success of our methods compared with other teaching agencies. I suggest that rigid, inflexible teaching encourages rigid, inflexible and unthinking police officers with automatic responses to complex situations.

Once again, and in support of Dr. Main's findings, the Joint Working Party of the Commission for Racial Equality and the Police who examined community relations training in 1981 emphasized the need for more learner centred training (Joint Commission, 1981).

By means of seminars for existing staff, in correlation with the 'Principles of Policing' (1985), it has been possible to actively encourage a shift in the style of teaching of established trainers (Styles of Teaching, 1984). New methods and techniques are being encouraged by management, and trainers are being introduced to their use and the relative merits of each one. Projects are now given to all students. Buzz groups, discussion groups, unsupervised private study and class presentations are becoming familiar methods of teaching. Trainers have been introduced to facilitation methods and given specific training in the use of role play, feedback, and use of video as a method of feedback and counselling.

New staff now embark on a 97-week development programme. Initially they are given a 10-week training course followed by 10 weeks of teaching practice supervised by an experienced tutor. That is followed by a further 2-week development course comprised of role play, video feedback, assessment methods and police discretion. Next they progress through teaching the 6th to 20th week of the course at least twice in 5-week blocks, i.e., weeks 6-10, 11-15, 16 to 20. They are then prepared for a tutor role in a further 2-week advanced training course (Instructor Development Programme, Nov. 1984). Throughout the first 76 weeks their progress is assessed, though decreasingly so, to ensure our objectives are being met. Flair and creativity are encouraged. It is as essential to ensure that the style of lesson presentation changes when giving law and procedure lessons as when presenting those on policing skills. Variety is important and pedestrian or rigid lessons or lecture presentations are discouraged and can lead to officers being posted out of training.

As a means of establishing the credibility of the staff, all have the option of obtaining a Teaching Certificate in Further Education as an externally valid teaching qualification accepted in the academic world. Next year it is hoped that the Force will be its own validating agency for that course. We consider that the elements of proper staff selection and training are essential keys to any major shift in emphasis in the training programme. The breadth of developments will be discussed later, in dealing with Content.

In order to further enhance trainer credibility, officers will be returned to operational duties after 21 months for a period of 6 weeks. This time will serve as an operational update, and a natural refresher of practical skill in the field. It will also reduce animosity from operational staff by limiting comments concerning "those who can, 'do' and those who can't, 'teach'".

Young police officers introduced to Policing Skills from 1982 onwards are now being supported in the field. In January 1986, a new Constables' Development Course of 2 weeks' duration will commence. It is primarily concerned with self-awareness and self-development particularly in terms of individual officers' problems and the demands made on them in their working environment. This course will form the basis of Constables' training which will recur every 3 years throughout his service, in the training unit closest to his workplace (Constable Training, 1984). A catching up process for the rest of the force has also started in terms of the Policing Skills Development Course. This is a 2-week course aimed at updating ranks from PC to Inspector in these topics. Once again, facilitation is the method of presentation.

The teaching style is, and I suggest could only be, facilitative in nature. Small groups, student and learner centred, discussing local policing problems and their effects on individual officers requires a trained catalyst with specialized skills. There is no room in this programme for prescriptive, teacher directed answers to problems.

A similar approach is being made at the Police Staff College at Bramshill where the most promising young Constables are trained on the Special Course to prepare them for accelerated promotion and managerial responsibility. There, the emphasis is placed on the entire development of the officer, his values, attitudes, direction and his ability to be critical of his own performance. Learning through self-development and awareness of self are viewed as the most effective means of learning and that most appropriate to accepting new responsibilities. For a pro-active police service intent on creative responses to old problems and new initiatives for emerging ones in the 21st century, didactic teaching becomes an atavistic prototype due for prompt abandonment.

Whilst some emphasis is placed on self-development, part of senior management training at Bramshill is aimed at the contrary position: the examination of an organizational culture. It looks at those mechanisms within the service which could negate such initiatives as those of the Special Course, and where the lack of support systems for those officers could jeopardize and stifle progress. Such are some of the contributions of professional psychologists on the Bramshill staff to a thorough examination of the dynamics within the police organization.

Metropolitan Police management and Detective training are also being tackled by a facilitative approach to teaching. The tutor acts as catalyst by active listening and contributing as and when necessary. The student body gain confidence in themselves, develop their self-expression and are encouraged to contribute their viewpoints and debate them. Obviously some formal input and a variety of styles of presentation are important and necessary particularly where technical and mechanical skills and information are to be learned. The overall shift, however, is towards information and knowledge sharing, using the tutor as a resource.

An unexpected effect of this change of emphasis in teaching style has arisen. For the less able trainer, the absence of the structure and constraints of formal teaching can be frightening. The image of the 'instructor' as a font of all knowledge has become so fixed in the mind, that the loss of that notion can have pronounced psychological effects. 'Structure' spells 'safety', spells 'familiarity' spells 'comfort'. Facilitation indicates the alternative destiny of flexibility, lack of direction and distinct discomfort. This has to be faced and dealt with.

Content

The pie chart in Figure 1 clarifies the relevant parts of the initial 20 week training course. The changes since the 1971 proposals were implemented are significant in terms of time allotted and methods employed. The increase in time is from 59 periods of formal theory lessons on social studies to 98 periods now on Policing Skills. This extension of time is not a cosmetic exercise. In real terms the overall percentage has increased and now forms 14% of the total course, and it has a much more practical emphasis. The majority of the theory lessons in Policing Skills occur in the first five weeks of the course as the fundamental basis of policing. Communication, asking questions, recording information, recollection and perception are all interlinked. Aims and objectives of lessons have been rewritten in a realistic

88

manner and are directed towards enabling objectives which contribute to achieving the ultimate target: a better service to the public.

Figure 1
Training Course Content

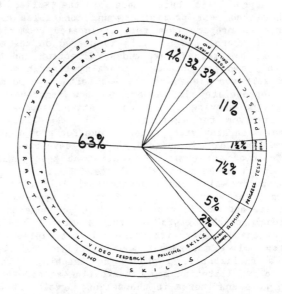

The three main components of Policing Skills remain as self-awareness, interpersonal skills and community relations (McKenzie, 1984). Our approach has been a personal one related to individuals on a generalist basis. The aim is to improve relations and individual interactions with the public yet not to train policemen as social workers. The shift has therefore been away from pure law enforcement training. The self awareness aspect is best reflected in the use of video feedback. It develops a knowledge of self and recognizes one's own problems and those of others. This tends towards a sense of empathy to situations and to the problems of others, an essential tool in tackling communication and understanding it in its social setting. A major part of that self-development process is the ability to be reflective on one's own performance, a start to the introspective process which helps the individual respond receptively to constructive criticism.

Practical exercises in communication and conversation techniques are videotaped and performance in relation to interpersonal ability is fed back to individuals subsequently. There are thirty 50-minute periods of classroom feedback throughout the syllabus. As soon as officers begin to report offenders for traffic matters and to practice making arrests, their practical performance is videotaped and analyzed later in the classroom. Such analysis is not confined to knowledge, control and application but addresses itself to handling skills. Many practical exercises are now prepared, and structured role plays use the students themselves as participant actors in policing situations. This is often more effective than using experienced staff who tend to respond in a predetermined rather than natural way.

Building confidence and improving performance are the primary targets
of these role play exercises. Scripting, using students as actors,
videotaping incidents and assessment of performance all contribute to the
closer reality of the 'real world' and minimize opportunities to ridicule
students. Maybe 10% of the clientele dealt with on the training roads
are unreasonable, a better representation of 'real policing'. The
improvement in confidence is very marked where trainees have the
opportunity of exercising their interpersonal skills in a supportive and
positive atmosphere rather than a derogatory and negative one.

Interpersonal skills involve an understanding of the communication
process and conversation skills which are applicable in any social
interaction (see Shepherd's chapter in this text). Role play and buzz
group work is important in this sphere too. Also relevant for the police
officer is the ability to elicit facts, obtain information, and acquire
interviewing techniques. These involve some knowledge of territory,
proximity and nonverbal behaviour to assist in interpretation and
response. Video recording is again the principal tool we use to develop
those skills in simulated police situations, either on the street or in
the police station. Hopefully, the often quoted but probably imaginary
case of the police officer delivering a death message with the well-worn
phrase to the deceased's wife of "Hello, are you Widow Jones" can at last
be put to rest. We have barely commenced work in the area of crisis
intervention or family dispute training per se (see chapter by Dutton in
this text).

The community relations component is aimed at 'better public service'
and modifying police behaviour to enhance that aim. Information, in
lesson format, discussion of feelings and various exercises specifically
tackle racism at a number of levels, including the individual, the
institutions, and culture. Skin colour is only one dimension of this
subject. Our community is now so heterogeneous and police have a need to
respond to all aspects of it. Our underlying aim is therefore to tackle
human relations in its widest context, and examine race as a particularly
significant and presently intractable area of that study. The local
community in any given area is going to be different and the racial mix
and level of knowledge similarly diverse. At the same time, the need to
build up a rapport, to understand their needs, and respond in a positive
fashion are clear. In achieving this we believe the other two threads of
self-awareness and interpersonal skill are indispensable in achieving any
level of success with local communities, regardless of origin.

The 'Policing Skills' and police duty in its broadest sense are
therefore interlinked as far as possible. They form the basis of a
'Fabric approach' in which the lessons on law and practice are interwoven
with the principles and application of skills training. In many
instances it is not possible to differentiate lesson content between
Policing Skills and practical police work particularly in the practical
context. They become one and the same yet the training emphasis has
changed towards a more behavioural approach. First, the training is as
experiential as possible in a sheltered training environment. Secondly,
the base has shifted from one of pure knowledge to one of real skill
encompassing those social attributes essential to successful policing.
Training hitherto almost totally concerned with 'the job' is now
concerned with 'self' and the development and understanding of that
concept.

A recent and valuable addition to our training is a Listening
Laboratory. It is there to improve communicative ability, particularly

listening skills, to reinforce the need to ask questions, to accurately recall and record information, and to develop empathy. The latter is achieved by presenting tapes of various groups in society whom many people have difficulty in understanding, and may frequently be stereotyped as retarded or inept because of some language or speech problem. For instance, spastics, the deaf, those with heavy foreign accents, or those who speak in either a heavy British or Commonwealth patois. Only careful, concentrated listening and a sympathetic hearing will facilitate understanding.

With 22 outlets and individual headphones, the trainer can control the input to each student. He can therefore compare results of different types of behaviour, responses to directions, preconceptions and listening errors of students. He can listen in and monitor performance by any of his class and they are unaware of it. Learning is consolidated through practice and officers are taught the rudiments of interviewing and statement taking which is developed to proficiency.

Staffing

Inevitably these alterations in lesson content and use of equipment require a more sophisticated approach to the content as well as the style of instructor training. Basic counselling, giving nonjudgmental feedback, confidence building and supportive analysis become necessary ingredients for staff training. Each part not terribly difficult one might say, but for a police service established and endowed with active practitioners, it places a strain on police resources. The best respond magnificently, but a number are excluded from training by virtue of its increasing complexity and the demands made on staff. Nevertheless, we subscribe to the belief that the best model for a uniformed, disciplined service should be a uniformed, disciplined and experienced police officer. To enhance credibility we have retained a minimal jargon approach rather than extolling the virtues of the underlying disciplines. 'Real' policemen who both believe and practice the art of handling people with sensitivity, in a cooperative rather than a coercive manner, are great assets to our training programme and excellent role models for their students.

Discretion

The persistent recurrence of the term 'discretion' in the Commissioner's Policing Principles, has led us to place even greater emphasis on this chartless and unbounded sea—those nuances, innuendos, and shades of grey which determine the variety of policing and the excitement of doing 'the job'. There are five formal lessons on discretion; analyzing its ingredients and personal nature, the demands of the organization and its expectations of its members. It is related to traffic and criminal matters, family disputes and public disorder situations. It attempts to address some vexing questions for police officers: when a conscious decision NOT to act is as effective and positive as one to make an arrest; of how to balance two of the basic police duties when they are in conflict, i.e., maintaining public order and enforcing the law. It aims to produce an appreciation that though an officer has certain powers it is not always either prudent or appropriate for him to exercise them to the full, and that this is not an automatic sign of weakness but one of strength. This is a very different concept of police authority, more far-reaching and quite in accord with the Commissioner's Principles. It requires some adaptability in reactions and flexibility of solutions.

In support of those 5 theory lessons, there are at least 15 fifty minute periods of practical lessons which encourage the real use of discretion according to set criteria discussed in the classroom. As a result, no officer should finish his initial training feeling that his only course of action is to utilize his power to the full regardless of role or circumstances. A workbook of brief case studies form part of the testing for this subject. With no simple and precise answer to the questions, the method of dissecting the problems and supporting the decisions is emphasized. It also examines students' ability to reason and rationalize. The mere fact that there is no single conclusive solution to a given problem will itself be likely to have a fundamental effect on the values of the officers and how they see their duty.

In these various ways, discretion is analyzed in a rational and clinical way. What was once referred to as common sense, the indefinable, is carefully dissected. What took years of experience and was done therefore without any formal training or analysis, is now examined and talked out and the stresses caused by its lack of clarification reduced.

Assessment

Evaluation of our work has begun. Our planning Unit has reported on the effects of the Training Manual and the relevant advantages and otherwise of our role plays and practical exercises. It assisted with the setting up of a Training Support Unit to assist those with learning difficulties. It also assessed the effectiveness of internal staff training. Such objective evaluation is taken as an effective means of feedback on our performance. Criticism is not taken personally but capitalized on to improve existing and future programmes and planning.

The creation of the Training Support Unit has been beneficial in helping slow learners and in eradicating problems of unclear phraseology in the Manual and teacher inefficiency in specific areas. Students use the facility on a voluntary or compulsory basis. The former often only want to reinforce their confidence about a particular subject, but having staff available to assist outside normal teaching hours helps to allay their doubts. The Unit is also responsible for the major part of staff assessment, maintaining records of staff performance and making visits to lessons on a structured basis until it is considered that no further assistance or supervision are required.

Other advances relate to student assessment and testing. With a view to making a more objective evaluation of student performance we are presently experimenting with various methods of assessment. We are examining the possibilities of a profiling system, collating assessments from a number of testing situations, primarily practical, including personal subjective observations of staff (Report on Policing Skills Assessment, June, 1984). Much of this relates to the assessment of handling skills. In constructing the Profile Checklist we are using BARS (Behaviourally Anchored Rating Scales). Our ultimate aim is to provide the student with an objective view of his performance and to provide his new supervising officers at his police station some clear indications of the standards attained. We believe this will be more helpful than the present 'A+, A, A- etc.' gradings with minimal feedback in verbal form of what those grades represent.

Despite the unsatisfactory attempt at testing social studies in the 70s, we are committed to some form of testing. Following the

recommendations in the Social Studies report in 1978 and the Phase I evaluation of Human Awareness in 1982, we are exploring a number of options. The projects are an obvious candidate for assessing effort and commitment. Question writers have been appointed to write both objective and subjective questions regarding the Policing Skills content. The writers are serving Constables with degrees in psychology and knowledge of methodology and testing techniques. Provided we do not fall into the trap of testing pure knowledge, trivia, and jargonese, we have some chance of enhancing the credibility of the material and relating it to practice. For example, a definitive test question on aggression referring to whether or not it is repressed or sublimated is valueless if the knowledge being tapped has no effect on how the officer deals with aggression in himself or how he responds to it in others. Using such definitive terminology without any reference to practice and example cost us dearly in the 70s and now is not the time to propound doctrinaire principles. In the same fashion, the practitioner's knowledge and application must be tested to demonstrate its (undoubted) reference to policing and the training curriculum. The case-books on discretion, video feedback comment, and practical profiling are all elements of that testing process. We believe they pave the way for the achievement of the 'new' police ethic and philosophy. The development of reliable forms of assessment is a substantial element in the success of our programme, and we still have to evaluate their utility.

The Ethos of Training

The respective parts of method, style, content, assessment, and staff training all have a part to play in the change in training atmosphere; the initially imperceptible shift in attitude which gradually becomes the ethos of the training establishment. It cannot be quantified, but no external observers in 1985 could suggest there has not been a significant change of mood and style in Metropolitan Police training in the past 10 years. All the changes mentioned are under way. Emphasis is laid on what will fit the officer for the practical world outside the training environment. Fulfilling special criteria to suit the dogmatism and personal preferences of individual trainers is eradicated. Selection of appropriate staff with reasonable attitudes, good communicative skills, and without the need to be pedantic and narrow in viewpoint or approach, ensures that young officers will have very professional and credible role models during their training. The tutors concern must be attuned to those of the organization and its demands, and the need to not only act but to believe in a 'people-oriented' approach where social skills, law enforcement, and servicing community needs are of equal importance. Our staff training enhances the talents the trainers bring with them and hopefully develops some of them into being more effective and successful individuals. It is still a 'tall order' to successfully train 20-year-olds to handle people (including themselves), find out facts, and apply the law and procedure correctly.

Self-discipline has been substituted for petty schoolroom discipline. That type of discipline is more associated with training non-compliant, mediocre teenagers or 'crack' response troops than mature adults required to act on their own initiative. Self-discipline is more appropriate for individuals who must think for themselves and work on their own in 90% of their working lives. Penalities for petty misbehaviour involve advising the miscreants that their misdeeds will be brought to the notice of the senior officer at the station at which they will be serving and placed on their training record. Far more effective it seems than administering meaningless internal punishments, instantly mocked and just as promptly forgotten.

Inevitably, the critics, not least the autocrats, will suggest that these developments will produce more questioning officers who are less responsive to blind discipline. If this means fewer automatic responses to unreasoned commands, then there is nothing to fear. Thinking individuals should still be smart, self-disciplined, polite and professional. That does not preclude querying a directive from management if it is done courteously and properly thought out. Neither does it mean that officers should not be trained to respond to immediate commands in violent or public order situations, which involve such a small proportion of an officers' time. Such disciplined response without question is essential for the police service. That does not mean that for the rest of the time, 85% plus, officers should respond in an identical way. Flexibility and adaptability to such changes of conditions are part of the everyday lot of the officer--why should he respond in only one way?

The traditional lack of introspectiveness and 'play it close to the chest' policies of the past have always given an impression that the police have something to hide. The force policy of community liaison, the creation of consultative committees, the free press, and more vociferous if not always accurate critics, have led us to an 'open door' policy for press and public. There were 249 visits to Hendon Training Centre in 1984 involving 1,721 visitors, many of them magistrates, police committees, and local organizations. This is a time consuming but essential commitment to community policing which on occasion has to be checked to prevent complete disruption of the training schedule. Criticisms are made and responded to and no special programmes are put on for visitors. They see the Metropolitan Police as it is.

Every six weeks a group of 60 or so youths and their community leaders come to Hendon on a Sunday to engage in sporting activities and social interaction with police officers under training. This has been going on for almost 2 years now and is proving very successful in breaking down mutual stereotypes and providing interface in non-confronting situations. Hitherto our extensive facilities had not been utilized by external groups at all. The presence of such visitors, as well as appointed consultants and researchers, will make it difficult to remain a purely reactive and introverted organization for long.

Organizational Support

The organizational support from the Force has not only come in the form of statements of intent but in physical terms. For two years we have set ourselves planning tasks which have been approved centrally at Scotland Yard. In the ensuing months we have had to meet our targets and appraise the senior management of our success or otherwise. This process of Management by Objectives, whilst not without its traumas, ensured that plans were expressed in writing and pursued until conclusion. Documentation of principles ensured clarity of thought and identification of objectives. A number of the advances and changes made were as a result of targets being set and given operational and managerial support throughout the Metropolitan Police. The importance of that central organizational support cannot be over-emphasized. It has enabled my Senior colleagues and myself to prepare a statement of philosophy on training which gives an unequivocal declaration of intent. The specifics of the training program are presented below.

Initial Training (D8(1))

The aim of initial training is to produce police officers who are self-disciplined; have a good standard of appearance and physical fitness; acknowledge the need to treat people with a positive attitude, with some compassion and sensitivity; and who recognize the need for police to provide a better service to the public. In pursuit of a professional standard, it is sought to avoid turning out unthinking, insensitive officers with a verbatim knowledge of their powers but lacking any concept of discretion or proper understanding of how such powers should be exercised. Throughout the 20-week initial course at Hendon, teaching is conducted in an atmosphere which encourages self-discipline but which at the same time encourages individual learning in a student participative environment. The curriculum focuses upon the acquisition of a good level of knowledge and understanding not only of the powers of a police officer but the processes in which he is involved. The student is introduced to the Commissioner's Principles of Policing and almost a quarter of the course is concerned with the development of interpersonal skills, self-awareness, and community policing. Students are introduced to this skills part of the course during the first five weeks and for the remainder of their course are expected to demonstrate those skills in the many practical exercises undertaken. All aspects of the course are based on a high level of communicative ability, a wide range of social skills, a growing need for practical expertise, an understanding of police discretion, and the ability to apply it to a number of situations in an increasingly complex society.

The basis of theoretical learning is an educationally sound Training Manual written in straightforward English. Many well accepted methods continue to be used in teaching the syllabus. However, a much greater emphasis is placed on practical training with video taped incidents being discussed in the classroom to establish the knowledge, control, and interpersonal skill used in achieving set objectives. Discretion is also looked for and analyzed in practical situations. In essence, therefore, the course has moved from a knowledge to a skills based approach.

Training staff are expected to create an atmosphere which is conducive to student involvement and which encourages the display of initiative and creativity by using as broad a variety of teaching methods as possible. The trainers' role is to bring their practical experience into the classroom and relate it to practical exercises. They are encouraged to produce a group of smart, caring professionals, who can think for themselves and who have a real understanding of the breadth of the role of a police officer.

Arrangements are made for officers undergoing initial training to be taught to work as a team in appropriate situations, as for example, in handling Public Order incidents where immediate response to command is essential. The staff are, therefore, encouraged to balance fair discipline in a structured uniformed organization with the development of confidence and initiative in individuals.

The overall atmosphere is one where student learning is paramount, and where positive, wide ranging responses and solutions are encouraged. In this way, Initial Training can make a substantial contribution to the Commissioner's overall strategy for the future, in that it will help develop the sort of individual able to cope with the substantial changes which are now occurring and those likely to take place in the service in the future.

It is only with the support of management that the entire strategy will be effective. Problems will remain where those in the organization choose not to adapt and reinforce the 'old' and 'proper' ways. Reinforcement of these organizational changes has taken place in the form of legislation, namely the Police and Criminal Evidence Act, 1984. That enactment provides legislative impact on a change in policing style, emphasizing the elements of 'reasonableness', accountability, and the balance of power in society.

CONCLUSION

In relatively few years, most elements of initial police training in London have moved towards being learner-centred rather than teacher-based. This in itself requires a more skillful teacher, crucial to the success of the entire approach. Training is becoming more behavioural and less cognitive, emphasizing skills rather than pure knowledge. The learning environment and atmosphere has changed. Young officers are leaving training school better equipped than ever before, for a job more complex and demanding than hitherto. Social skill and discretion are important elements of that equipment. With experiments in Neighbourhood Policing and other initiatives it is the Constables who have to talk to their local communities, attend residents association meetings, and indicate local police policy on a given topic. They are the ambassadors and the managers and must have the skills to do those jobs. The advances discussed in this chapter, ranging from a Training Manual, through lessons on discretion, to organizational support and welcoming visitors, all indicate the breadth of the impact that is essential in order to make fundamental organizational change.

Impetus for change has come from within the service as well as from interested parties outside. Now supported by the organization in style and emphasis, the machine can move forward, building on the work of the past 20 years and hopefully learning from its mistakes. Without that historical introduction we would not have advanced as far as we have. We are probably only at the beginning of a number of massive changes both in society and the police service, and our young officers must have the capacity to respond to them. The key seems to be to move away from a training system geared to train a standing army to respond collectively to public needs on a formal, routine and law enforcement basis. The answer is to produce a programme aimed at training individuals to respond as such to local demands and on occasion as a collective group. The emphasis has to continue to move towards personal development, independent response and improving communication, thus reducing the reinforcement of peer group solidarity and group responses to situations.

Modern advances owe much to the application of psychology to its methods, thinking and content. The pursuance of professionalism through careful analysis and a willingness to be self-critical, are likely to both enhance the service and make even greater use of psychology in the future. These various strands are closely interwoven. They are the means by which we will produce the sort of police officers, male and female, consistent with the modern demands being made on them to be community managers: effective, confident communicators, knowledgeable and approachable, who will exercise their authority in accordance with the law but tempered with discretion. Without those qualities, community support and cooperation are figments of the imagination.

This is not the end. It is not even the beginning of the end. But it is perhaps, the end of the beginning (Churchill, 1942).

REFERENCES

Alderson, J. C. (1969). A report of the working party on working party on police training. Part 1: Probationer training. New Scotland Yard.

Bull, R., & Horncastle, P. (1983, July). An evaluation of the metropolitan police recruits training programme in human awareness: Interim report.

Churchill, W. (1942, November). Speech at Mansion House concerning the Battle of Egypt.

Constable Training. (1984, May). Proposals for a 30 year career span – Hendon.

Cronbach, L. J. (1976). Essentials of psychological testing. Harper & Row.

D8(1) Instructor Development Programme (1984, November). Hendon Training School.

Joint Commission for racial equality and police community relations working party report. (1981, December).

Main, A. (1979). Teaching and learning in recruit and probationer training in the metropolitan police.

Mallion, D. (1974, April). The police and the community: A Scottish survey, Focus.

Management Services Department reports, evaluation of social studies training. (1976, July; 1977, August; 1978, October; 1980, March).

McKenzie, I. (1984). Some details expanded on in "The essential requirements of his calling – police training in the 1980's". Police Journal, LVII(3).

Metropolitan Police. (1984, December). Force working party on stress, Phase I report.

Metropolitan Police. (1984). The principles of policing and guidance for professional behaviour.

Punch, M., & Naylor, T. (1973, May). The police: A social service. New Society.

Report of the Commissioner of Police of the Metropolis to the Home Secretary. (1982). Cmnd. 8928, H.M.S.O.

Report of the Commissioner of the Police of the Metropolis to the Home Secretary. (1982). Cmnd. 9268, H.M.S.O.

Report on policing skills assessment. (1984, June). Hendon Training School.

Rose, E. J. B. (1969). Colour and citizenship. O.U.P.

Scarman, Lord. (1981)., The Brixton disorders: Report of Lord Scarman, O.B.E., Cmnd. 8427, H.M.S.O.

Schaffer, E. B. (1980). Community policing. Croom Helm.

Schaffer, E. B., & Poole, L. (1978). Social studies aspects of police training.

Shane, P. G. (1980). A comparison of five countries. Mosby.

Shepherd, E. (1984). Values into practice: The implementation and implications of human awareness training. Police Journal, LVII(3).

Styles of teaching and the training manual. (1984, September). Hendon Training School.

AN EVALUATION OF POLICE RECRUIT TRAINING IN HUMAN AWARENESS

RAY BULL

In his 1952 book on policing, Reith made the claim that, "It can be said of police training schools that the recruit is taught everything except the essential requirements of his calling, which is how to secure and maintain the approval and respect of the public whom he encounters daily in the course of his duties". This paper focusses on the extent to which this may no longer be true in London, over thirty years on.

The Metropolitan Police began its 'Human Awareness Training' (HAT) for recruits in April 1982. We began our evaluation of this training in June 1982 as a result of an initiative by the London Metropolitan Police, who asked the newly established Police Foundation to set up a training evaluation team in order that HAT could be examined. The Police Foundation (U.K.) is an independent British charity set up with the aim of improving the efficiency and effectiveness of policing through research. Funding for the evaluation was provided by the Metropolitan Police, but it is to the Foundation that we were required to report.

It should be noted that, contrary to the established principles of effective evaluation, we were asked to undertake the evaluation not only after HAT had been designed, but also after it had commenced. We were therefore unable to ensure that the customary contributions of evaluators toward design, implementation and running of a programme to be evaluated were made. Though regrettable, such a state of affairs is not unusual in the police context. Clark (1979) in Police and the Community noted:

Somewhere along the line there may be a claim that certain objectives are the reason for a programme of action, but there may be no way of exactly determining when that objective is reached because of the vague terminology used in describing the objective. In such a case the evaluator is forced to design his own measures and apply them. This can result in very unhappy consequences to the project's promoters, and a bitter colloquy ensues with charges and counter-charges of the inadequacy of measures and performances. The remedy is really so simple: set up criteria for evaluation before the project ever gets off the ground, in the planning stage if possible, but certainly before actual implementation.

Even though the stated objectives of HAT were vague (see, for example, Burns-Howell, McKenzie and Kember, 1981), we attempted to conduct a worthwhile evaluation of this training which is undertaken by over one thousand new recruits each year.

A BRIEF HISTORY
In 1971, a social studies input was authorized in the recruit training

school in London, although at this time it was not incorporated into the syllabus at the police training centres outside London. Recruits received this training during the first two weeks at their initial training course, where it was presented as an uninterrupted block of study. The training was soon judged by the London Metropolitan Police not be very effective. The level of input was rather 'academic' and this appeared to cause many recruits to lose interest in this part of their training. The content of the input (and the way in which it was presented) was thought to clash with the law enforcement image which many of the recruits were believed to hold of police officers. Rather than being abandoned, the social studies input was developed and improved during the period 1973-1981. The content of the first two weeks of the course was spread throughout the whole of the syllabus, and, in particular, the social studies inputs were related to appropriate police duty subjects. The input comprised Social and Public Administration, Sociology, and Social Psychology. Some coverage was also given, although in little depth, to the areas of communication.

Due to the fact that social studies were now running throughout the entire training course, the title of the course was changed to 'Integrated Police Studies' (IPS). It was felt that the training should be further developed in recognition of the fact that the constable on the street is in reality a manager of people. The provision of person-management skills for constables was one of the main objectives of IPS. It was also felt that recruits should be provided with information regarding the society which they were to serve. March 1981 (before the riots in London and other parts of Britain) saw the beginning of further developments in recruit training. A working party of police officers was formed to examine and report on current methods of formal and informal behavioural training for recruits and to make the recommendations for improvements in these areas. From the findings of the working party came recommendations (Burns-Howell, et al., 1981) for what became the Human Awareness Training (HAT) programme which was implemented in London in April 1982. HAT (which has since been renamed 'Police Skills Training') comprised three identifiable but related areas of training: interpersonal skills (said to comprise self-knowledge and participation in structured experience); self-awareness (said to comprise self-knowledge and participation in structured experience); and community relations (said to comprise race awareness and cultural awareness). When this new form of training began, its goals were not adequately specified, in fact they were hardly any more explicit than in the previous sentence. Only after the receipt of our evaluation was a comprehensive list of goals drawn up by the police. The HAT sessions were distributed throughout the 20 week, full-time training programme and comprised 25% of it. The training takes place both in the classroom and in simulated street situations. In the classroom, however, the training is rarely simply of a didactic nature, instead the trainer (and the session handouts) imparts information which is discussed by the group as a whole. Not only in mock-up streets but also in simulated situations in the classroom, the trainees role-play being a police officer. The trainer usually gives feedback to the role-play participants (whilst other trainees look on) and the role-playing is often video-taped and then played back during feedback sessions. Between the advent of HAT and the completion of this evaluation, some changes and improvements to the programme have been made: these are described later.

AN OUTLINE OF THE PRESENT EVALUATION

A main component of the evaluation was the administration of three well researched and standardized questionnaires to a large number of recruits. These questionnaires were chosen after an extensive search as being the extant questionnaires most relevant to the (vaguely stated) aims and objectives of HAT. They were drawn from the behavioural sciences and are recognized as being reliable and valid. They were completed at the beginning (Week 1) and end (Week 20) of initial recruit training, and then again six and twelve months later. They were: (1) a social-evaluative anxiety questionnaire which measures social avoidance and distress, and fear of negative evaluation; (2) a self-esteem questionnaire which measures need to establish satisfactory relationships, need to control such relationships, and need for affection. To these three questionnaires we added a fourth which, though not yet comprehensively tested in Britain, seemed promising and was said by its developers to provide a personal profile which measured influence on others, dominance, steadiness and compliance. In all, across the four testing occasions six groups of officers completed these questionnaires. (Four groups each completed one of the four questionnaires, one group two of the questionnaires, and one group all four questionnaires).

Since none of these four questionnaires seemed to focus precisely on what HAT was trying to achieve, we decided to design a questionnaire (called the recruit training questionnaire (RTQ)) which focussed directly on HAT-related aspects of policing. Two groups of officers filled in the RTQ on the four testing occasions. (Further details of this questionnaire are presented later in this paper).

In conducting this investigation we were, of course, guided by previous evaluations of police training carried out in various countries. One of the main criticisms of much evaluation in policing (and elsewhere) is the lack of control groups (i.e., groups who, by design, do not receive the training being evaluated). Although this dismays the scientist, it is a common state of affairs in the evaluation of real-life (as opposed to laboratory-based) endeavours. Once the present evaluation began in June 1982, it was not possible, HAT having commenced in the previous April, to have a group of Metropolitan Police recruits purposely undergo the training which HAT replaced. Consequently, for the purposes of the evaluation, it was not possible to have adequate control groups. We did consider administering questionnaires to recruits being trained in other police forces but the clear limitations of concluding anything directly relevant to HAT from any such comparisons, plus the understandable reticence of other forces outside the Metropolitan Police whom we informally approached with this notion, persuaded us not to pursue this idea. The absence of control groups does not, however, preclude an adequate evaluation being conducted. Many evaluations of real-life training endeavours employ time-series analyses in which data from the trainees are gathered both during and after the training to see whether its aims and objectives are being met. Such analyses cannot prove that any improvements are definitely due to the training (as opposed to other factors which may take place during or after training) but if the methods of gathering data are chosen with care, then worthwhile conclusions can be drawn.

Even though the use of questionnaire control groups within the Metropolitan Police was precluded, it was decided that information from constables who were trained in the last months before the introduction of HAT would be of value. Consequently, over one hundred such constables filled in a fairly extensive, specially designed questionnaire concerning their views, in the light of their policing experience, of the IPS training they had received. In addition, over one hundred constables who had received HAT several months earlier completed a similar questionnaire concerning their views on its strengths and weaknesses.

We have attempted to evaluate HAT using instruments we believe are sensitive to the objectives of 'awareness' training. Although participant observation has been used to a limited extent as an evaluation technique in some previous policing studies, we did not employ behavioural observation in this initial evaluation of HAT. This decision was made for a variety of reasons, but mainly because the necessary resources and time needed for the development of reliable and appropriate behavioural observation checklists were not available. We also felt that before it is applied to behavioural outcomes, any evaluation should focus on answering the most basic questions surrounding training, i.e., examining whether or not awareness skills can be successfully taught and whether instructors are adequately prepared to cope with the training needs of recruits. If and when it is decided that HAT is achieving its objectives within the training school, then a more behaviourally based evaluation of the performance of those patrolling officers who have received HAT would be warranted. We have recently been asked by the London police to undertake such a study.

EXTANT QUESTIONNAIRES GIVEN TO RECRUITS

In this section will be presented information concerning the four extant questionnaires which recruits completed. The following section will then present the information concerning the questionnaire we designed especially for this evaluation.

It was decided that the recruits should fill in the questionnaires at the beginning (Week 1) and end (Week 20) of their initial training and that they should do so again during continuation training, six and then twelve months after the end of initial training. This was done in order not only to determine whether any changes might occur across the full-time initial training period of 20 weeks, but also to see whether any changes were maintained, reversed or enhanced during the twelve months after initial training was completed.

During Week 1 and again in Week 20, one training period (approximately 45 minutes) was devoted by the training staff to the completion of the questionnaires. On each of these two occasions an intake class of recruits (n=30) completed (in the presence of one of the evaluation team) one or more questionnaires. (The group which completed all four questionnaires was allocated two training periods for this).

The Social-Evaluative Anxiety Questionnaire

This questionnaire (which was designed by Watson and Friend, 1969) contains two sub-scales, the fear of negative evaluation scale (FNE) and the social avoidance and distress scale (SAD). Subjects are briefed that "the questionnaire is concerned with the way in which you behave with people in various situations". Social evaluative anxiety was defined by Watson and Friend as "the experience of distress, discomfort, fear, anxiety, etc. in social situations"; as "the deliberate avoidance of social situations"; and "a fear of receiving negative evaluations from others". The SAD scale taps the first two aspects, the FNE scale taps the latter aspect. Police work, by its very nature, produces many stressful social encounters for officers on the beat. Individual officers will inevitably vary in the amount of distress over their negative evaluations. However, through the social encounters component of their Human Awareness Training, individuals might well demonstrate a positive shift along the SAD and FNE dimensions as a result of their training, particularly as several of the (vague) HAT objectives relate to the SAD and FNE scales.

Rosenberg's Self-Esteem Questionnaire

When one speaks of an individual with high self-esteem, one is referring to a person who respects himself and considers himself worthy. Such an individual recognizes his limitations and expects to grow and improve. Conversely, low self-esteem implies self-rejection, self-dissatisfaction and self-contempt. The individual lacks respect for the self he observes and wishes it were otherwise. In his study of the self-image in adolescents, Rosenberg (1965) claimed that not only was low self-esteem a psychologically distressing state in itself, but that it also leads to several other states which are equally distressing, e.g., anxiety (which is sometimes characterized by Rosenberg as a "blockage in communication"). Furthermore, Erlich (1973) claims that "negative self-attitudes are strongly linked with prejudice". The questionnaire was presented to the recruits with written instructions explaining that the questionnaire"...asks about your feelings towards yourself and towards other people...". Rosenberg identifies certain interpersonal qualities of the individual with low self-esteem which are not present in the individual with high self-esteem. Some of these qualities are relevant to the objectives of human awareness training.

The FIRO-B

The FIRO scales are a series of measuring instruments derived from Schutz's (1958) theory. The FIRO-B (fundamental interpersonal relations orientation - behaviour) is said to be a measure of a person's characteristic behaviour towards other people in the areas of inclusion, control and affection. The primary purpose of the FIRO-B is to measure how an individual acts in interpersonal situations. Two aspects of behaviour in each dimension are assessed: the behaviour an individual expresses towards others and the behaviour he wants others to express toward him. The fundamental interpersonal dimensions of the FIRO theory may be defined behaviourally as follows:
(1) inclusion (I) - The interpersonal need for inclusion is the need to establish and maintain a satisfactory relationship with people with respect to interaction and association.
(2) control (C) - The interpersonal need for control is the need to establish and maintain a satisfactory relationship with others with respect to control and power. Control behaviour refers to decision-making processes between people.
(3) affection (A) - The interpersonal need for affection is the need to establish and maintain a satisfactory relationship with others with respect to love and affection.

The FIRO-B thus comprises six scales: Expressed and wanted behaviour in the areas of Inclusion, Control and Affection. The interpersonal orientation measured by FIRO-B seems applicable to awareness training. The FIRO-B has proved to be useful in the measurement of interpersonal relationships during and following sensitivity training. The differences among occupational groups are very striking and, for the most part, consistent with occupational stereotypes. High overall scores are attained by professions requiring a great deal of contact with other people.

Personal Profile Analysis

The personal profile analysis (PPA) has recently been designed by Thomas International Systems as an attempt to assess certain personal characteristics. No published literature is yet publicly available concerning this questionnaire but its developers claim that people display four basic characteristics, namely dominance, influence on others, steadiness, compliance. Thomas International Systems claim that the personal profile has been recently validated in client companies in a wide range of jobs and cultures throughout the USA and Europe. Although not yet a 'proven questionnaire' like the three others reported here, the PPA was used in this evaluation because of its claimed focus on factors relating to HAT. The PPA scores are said to reveal three profiles:

(1) profile A - 'How others see me': This is said to indicate how the individual feels he is expected to behave in order to be successful.

(2) profile B - 'Behaviour under stress': This is said to indicate how the individual behaves under pressure, and is believed to reveal the individual's limitations.

(3) profile C - 'How I see myself': This is said to indicate the person's self-image. It is believed to show whether the individual can communicate and whether he can make decisions.

RESULTS FROM EXTANT QUESTIONNAIRES

The Social-Evaluative Anxiety Questionnaire

There were considerable differences in scores obtained by the various individuals. These large individual differences were in line with our expectations and they emphasize the need to compare an officer with him or herself over the passage of time, rather than comparing one group of officers with another group of individuals. The proposed time-series method of evaluation can cope with these differences in scores among the trainees.

For both groups of individuals who completed this questionnaire there was a statistically significant decrease (Page's L test) in SAD, FNE and total scores across the four testing occasions. The scores became lower, indicating that the officers' social avoidance/distress and their fear of negative evaluation in social situations decreased over time. Comparisons were made between pairs of the four testing occasions in order to determine more precisely when these decreases in scores occurred (Wilcoxon Signed Ranks Test). Few significant changes in scores took place (i) between the end of initial training (i.e., Week 20) and six months later, and (ii) between six months and twelve months after the end of initial training. A number of significant decreases in scores occurred during the training and this suggests that the training was meeting its objectives by there occurring during the training period a decrease in SAD for one group, a decrease in FNE for the other group, and a decrease in total score for both groups. These improvements in scores are all the more worthy of note when one considers that the norms (or average scores) for members of the public on this questionnaire are noticeably higher than those evidenced by the recruits even on Week 1. Thus, even though the police recruits' scores were already rather low at the beginning of their training, these scores become even lower across time. (Very few females were present in the groups who filled in the Watson and Friend, Rosenberg, FIRO-B or Personal Profile Analysis questionnaires and consequently no worthwhile conclusions regarding sex differences can be drawn.)

The Self-Esteem Questionnaire

The raw scores revealed, as did the social-evaluative anxiety data mentioned above, that there were considerable differences between individual officers in their scores which tended to be maintained across the four occasions. When the raw scores on each sub-scale and the total raw scores were compared statistically across the four occasions (using Friedman's Analysis of Variance rather than Page's L test because there are few linear trends revealed in the data), no overall statistical difference effect was found for any of the three groups. There was an almost significant effect for the score of one group on the self-esteem sub-scale, and further statistical analysis revealed that this was entirely due to there being a significant difference (Wilcoxon Signed Ranks Test, p < .05) between scores on Week 1 and Week 20. For this group their self-esteem increased significantly during the training period, but then it progressively decreased after training. However, too much should not be made of this isolated finding. Examination of the data also revealed that whereas the changes across the four testing occasions were not similar for all three groups of officers for 'self-esteem', 'sensitivity to criticism' and for the 'total scores', the changes follow a somewhat similar pattern for 'faith in people' and for 'interpersonal threat'. Consequently, the data from all three groups of officers were pooled to see if larger combined sets of scores might reveal any differences. When this was done, some significant differences were found. For 'faith in people' and for 'interpersonal threat' significant differences were found, these differences being due to the scores at Week 1 being significantly different from the scores at Week 20, at six months and at twelve months. The lack of difference on these scales among the latter three occasions means that 'faith in people' and 'interpersonal threat' scores changed only during training. It can be concluded that during initial training, officers' 'faith in people' and 'interpersonal threat' decreased. The latter finding that over the training period the officers' feelings of 'interpersonal threat' decreased would seem to be meeting the objectives of the training, but the former involving a 'faith in people' decrease does not. Although these changes are real, it should be remembered that they were not revealed separately in each of the three groups of officers studied, but only when the data from the three groups were combined. Nevertheless, these findings are worthy of note.

The FIRO-B

When the raw scores on each sub-scale and the total raw score were compared statistically across the four occasions (using Friedman's Analysis of Variance), no overall statistical difference was found for any of the three groups. There was an almost significant effect for the scores of one group on 'inclusion-expressed' and further statistical analysis (Wilcoxon Signed Ranks Test, p < .05) revealed that whereas there was no difference in scores between Week 1 and Week 20 there was a significant difference between Week 20 and six months later (the differences between Week 1 and six and twelve months were significant as was the difference between Week 20 and twelve months). An examination of the relevant mean scores for the other group's 'inclusion-expressed' similarly found that although during the initial 20 week training there was no change in this score, once out of training school for six months the officers' expressed need to establish and maintain satisfactory relationships with people decreased.

Whereas the changes across the four testing occasions were not similar for all three groups of officers for 'expressed inclusion', 'wanted control', 'expressed affection', 'total expressed' and 'total expressed minus wanted', the changes followed a somewhat similar pattern for 'inclusion-wanted', 'control-expressed', 'affection wanted', and 'total-wanted'. Consequently the data from all three groups of officers were pooled to see if larger combined sets of scores might reveal any differences. When this was done some significant differences were found, though none for 'control-expressed'. For 'inclusion-wanted' there was no overall decrease between Week 1 and Week 20, but there was a gradual decrease between Week 1 and twelve months. For 'affection wanted' there was a significant decrease during the initial 20 week, with Week 1 also having a higher score than at six months or twelve months. There was no significant decrease for 'affection-wanted' in the period after Week 20, although the scores tended to continue decreasing. For 'total-wanted' the decrease between Week 1 and Week 20 was not significant but that between Week 1 and twelve months was (with that between Week 1 and six months being almost significant), as was that between Week 20 and twelve months.

What these changes suggest is that scores on most of the wanted aspects of this questionnaire (i.e., 'inclusion', 'affection', and 'total', but not 'control') decreased gradually and progressively across the four testing occasions.

The Personal Profile Analysis

The data for one group produced only one significant change ($p < .05$) within the four testing occasions (Friedman's Analysis of Variance) and for the other group, one difference approached significance ($p < .10$). That is, one group's score for 'steadiness' on profile C did not change significantly between Week 1 and Week 20, but it did significantly decrease between six months and twelve months ($p < .01$; with the difference between Week 1 and twelve months being even more significant, $p < .005$). The other groups's score for 'compliance' on profile C was significantly more negative on Week 20 than on Week 1, and on Week 20 than at six months. When the data from the two groups of officers were combined, no further significant changes were found.

The significant changes observed mean (i) that whereas the profile C 'steadiness' decreased across the entire testing period, this occurred more once the initial 20 week training period was over, and (ii) that although profile C 'compliance' became lower during the initial training it reached its week 1 level again within six months of the end of initial training.

CONCLUSIONS FROM EXTANT QUESTIONNAIRES

The data analyzed in this section reveal that at least the social-evaluative anxiety questionnaire was an appropriate measuring instrument to be employed in this evaluation. It revealed that during the 20 Week initial training period, worthwhile improvements (i.e., the lowering of scores) often occurred. Watson and Friend (1969) point out that their questionnaire has test-retest reliability. Therefore, the change in officers' score on this questionnaire found in this evaluation cannot be due merely to the passage of time, but must be due to what actually happened during the time periods. Given the composition of the human awareness training, it seems appropriate to conclude that the improvements found to occur during the 20 week initial training period are due in considerable part to the training. If once they left the training school the probationers had received no further training, then this would militate against such a conclusion since some further improvements in scores occurred after initial training had been completed. However, in its wisdom the Metropolitan Police decided to try to improve its post initial training for probationers before and during the period of this evaluation of the effectiveness of initial training. Consequently, the continuing improvement in scores beyond initial training could well be due to this 'improved' post initial training.

The other three extant questionnaires found few within-group differences in scores across the four testing occasions. However, Rosenberg's self-esteem questionnaire did find that during the 20 week initial training period 'self-esteem' for one group of officers did improve, and for the three groups of officers combined 'interpersonal threat' significantly decreased. This questionnaire also found that for the three groups combined their 'faith in people' decreased rather more during initial training than during later periods. The finding for 'interpersonal threat' suggests that during initial training the trainees came to feel less threatened in interpersonal situations. This is in line with the aims and objectives of HAT. However, their 'faith in people' decreased. Whether this reflects badly upon HAT or signifies the beginning of what Niederhoffer (1967) called 'reality shock' in policing is hard to say.

The FIRO-B questionnaire also found few within-group differences across the four testing occasions. For one group whereas 'expressed inclusion' (the expressed need to establish and maintain satisfactory relationships with people in social interaction) significantly decreased during the post initial training period, it did not do so during initial training. This could possibly be taken to reflect well on the training, but since this was the only one of the 27 within-group statistical comparisons found to be significant it could be no more than a chance finding. More important are the findings from the combination of data from the three groups of officers. For 'wanted affection' there is a significant decrease during initial training, and this decrease continues after initial training. For 'wanted inclusion' and 'total wanted' the scores do not decrease during initial training, but in the period after that there are strong suggestions of a decrease. Such post-initial training decreases in the extent to which officers want others to establish and maintain satisfactory relationships with them could well reflect how policing experience, once they have left the training school, affects probationers in a non-HAT way.

The personal profile analysis also found few changes. For one group of officers, profile C 'steadiness' significantly decreased after, but not during, initial training. Thus this group of officers' self-perceived/ self-image of 'steadiness' (which could be deemed to be largely a pro-HAT concept) decreased considerably once they left the training school. For the other group, profile C 'compliance' decreased during training and then afterwards it increased again to its beginning of training level. Since a decrease in profile C 'compliance' can be taken to suggest an increase in self-image of a more confident interpersonal style, then one could conclude that the initial training has a worthwhile effect which was dissipated by post-training school experiences.

Overall, the data and analyses in this section suggest that at least for 'social avoidance and distress' and 'fear of negative evaluation' in social situation, there is significant improvement during initial training. The other three extant questionnaires employed found rather few changes, but this may well be only as expected given that they were used because no other valid and reliable yet more appropriate questionnaires were believed to exist. Where these three questionnaires did find changes, these were broadly of three types. One type (e.g., Rosenberg's 'self-esteem, 'interpersonal threat' and personal profile analysis profile C – 'compliance') consisted of significant changes during the 20 week initial training which could be taken to reflect well on the training. A second type (e.g., FIRO-B 'wanted affection') involved significant changes during initial training which could possibly be taken to reflect badly on the training. The third type (e.g., FIRO-B 'wanted inclusion', 'expressed inclusion', 'total wanted') consisted of significant changes found in the period after, but not during, initial training which could be taken to reflect badly on post-training school experiences.

A SPECIALLY DESIGNED RECRUIT QUESTIONNAIRE

It was pointed out above that no extant questionnaires really adequately focussed on what HAT appeared to be trying to achieve. We therefore decided to construct our own recruit training questionnaires (RTQ). Even though there were neither resources nor time within the present evaluation to assess fully the predictive validity and reliability of the questionnaire, we attempted to design one which had content and face validity.

Selection of Items for Inclusion in the RTQ

To enhance the ecological validity of the Recruit Training Questionnaire, items were selected from literature relevant to police psychology. The resultant population of items was reduced from a total of 160 to a smaller sample of items which would be suitable for inclusion in this questionnaire. (Details of some of these items are provided below). Items thus selected were non-ambiguous, parsimonious and relevant to HAT objectives. The items were then categorized according to the area of police work to which they were applicable. Fifteen areas were identified: police-community relations; use of social skills; police training programmes; ethnic minority groups; training-general aspects; prejudice; human relations; effective policing; domestic disputes; perceived role of police officers; foot patrol; society/general public; complaints against the police; recruitment and selection; discretion; miscellaneous. The questionnaire contained roughly the same number of statements in each of these categories. This balance ensured that officers did not perceive the instrument as threatening. It appeared to focus on many aspects of police work rather than on one or two sensitive areas such as 'prejudice' or 'complaints'. On the basis of a pilot test the questionnaire was reduced from 32 pages to 19-page booklet consisting of twelve questions, in seven of which respondents were asked to rank order several statements, in two of which they were required to indicate how much they disagreed with various statements, and in three of which they were asked to indicate to what extent they 'would' and 'should' do something.

One criticism which could be made against the use of extant psychometric devices in this evaluation is that they may not measure the effect of HAT alone, but could also measure a general training/training environment effect as well. Although this is valid criticism (which is impossible to overcome), it was our intention to design an instrument which is particularly sensitive to the objectives of awareness training.

The Data Gathered From the RTQ

Two groups of around 30 trainees completed the RTQ on the four testing occasions. In both groups of trainees very few (n=2) of the respondents who completed the questionnaire on all four testing occasions were female and so no worthwhile comments regarding sex differences can be made. When one group completed the questionnaire at the training school, the initial training was only of 16 weeks duration; but by the time the other group commenced their training, the initial course had been redesigned to consume 20 weeks. (This major change in what we were evaluating took place after the evaluation had commenced.)

In this section are presented brief details of the extent to which each group of officers' responses changed significantly within the four testing occasions. First, statistical comparisons were made across the four testing occasions combined and where this comparison indicated that some reliable change in score had occurred, then further statistical tests were performed to determine exactly where within the four testing occasions this effect took place. Since space limitations prevent discussion of all the changes found for the twelve questions, only a sample will be presented here. (For a full presentation of our analysis of the RTQ data the reader should consult Bull and Horncastle, 1985).

Question 3 required respondents to indicate the extent of their agreement or disagreement with each of 13 statements. For one group there was a significant change in the extent of agreement/disagreement with the statement, 'The teaching of social studies and community relations is useful in preparing police officers for their forthcoming role in society'. Further statistical analyses revealed that the scores at Week 1 differed from those at Week 16, at six months (both $p < .05$, two tail) and at twelve months ($p < .001$). For the other group, there were very similar changes: again, scores at Week 1 significantly differed from those at Week 20 ($p < .001$), at six months ($p < .01$) and at twelve months ($p < .001$). For both groups no other changes on this item were significant, save that for one group, scores at Week 16 significantly differed from those at six months ($p < .05.$, two tail).

The most important conclusion from Q3 is that for both groups there was a significant decrease in agreement with the view that 'The teaching of social studies and community relations is useful in preparing police officers for their forthcoming role in society'. This change is by no means solely brought about by the probationers' post-initial training course experiences since for both groups the differences in scores between the beginning and the end of their initial training course are significant. In the first week of their initial training course, overall the trainees showed across the 13 statements least disagreement with this clearly pro-HAT statement. However, by the end of their initial training course the amount of agreement with this statement had significantly decreased. These within training school changes in the trainees' views concerning the usefulness to them of teaching in social studies and community relations could be due to their initial views being pro-HAT (i.e., for both groups the mean Week 1 agreement score was half way between 'strongly agree' and 'agree') and the human awareness training not living up to their expectations, or to the non-HAT part of their initial training playing down the importance of HAT. Both explanations are, of course, possible. For both groups their views changed very little between six and twelve months after training, and in only one group did the judged usefulness of this training decrease after leaving training school.

Whereas the above data concerning Q3 do not reflect well on the initial training, the answers to several other aspects of Q3, though not apparently affected by training, can be considered to be pro-HAT.

Question 4 contained behavioural intention rating scales. For each of five statements respondents were required to indicate the extent to which they 'would do this' and 'should do this'. For one group there were significant differences of both 'would' and 'should' regarding the item, 'As an efficient police officer I try to understand the customs, viewpoints and traditions of as many minority groups as possible.' For this group both the 'would' and 'should' scores significantly decreased (p < .02) between the beginning and end of the initial training course. (For the 'would' data the difference is also significant between Week 16 and twelve months (p < .001) and for the 'should' data between Week 1 and twelve months (p < .01)). For the other group there were also significant differences regarding the 'would' aspect of this item. Again, the 'would do this' score significantly decreased (p < .01) across the initial training course (with the scores at six and twelve months also differing significantly (p < .02) from those at Week 1). This group's 'should' scores also were less (numerically but not statistically) at Week 20 than at Week 1. Furthermore, the difference between 'would' and 'should' scores for this item increased over time. This means that although at the beginning of their initial training course trainees felt strongly that they 'would' and 'should' as efficient police officers 'try to understand the customs, viewpoints and traditions of as many minority groups as possible', by the end of the training course they felt less strongly that they 'would' and 'should' do this. There is here a strong suggestion that whereas at the beginning of their initial training course the trainees' views are very much in line with HAT aims and objectives, by the end of the initial course their views, whilst still somewhat pro-HAT, have become less so.

Question 6 required the trainees to rank in order of importance ten 'aspects of stopping somebody in the street'. For one group, analysis across the four testing occasions for each of the ten aspects found no significant differences. For the other group, the item 'not to let the suspect's age, sex, colour or background influence the way I talk to him or her' produced some changes in that at six and twelve months after initial training this item was ranked as being of lesser importance (p < .02 and p < .01 respectively) than at the beginning of training and, because the scores for the beginning and end of initial training did not differ, the difference between Week 20 and twelve months was also significant (p < .05, two tail). The data from the other group for this item reveal a similar, though nonsignificant, pattern of decreasing importance.

One could take the decreased importance of this item, found outside the initial training course, to reflect badly on the probationers' post-training school experiences. However, one needs to consider for which items the rank scores were correspondingly increased for the same time intervals. Although none of these changes were sufficiently reliable to be statistically significant; making an arrest (if necessary) unobtrusively, being relaxed but firm with the suspect, and being wary of all suspects, were all ranked as being more important outside the initial training course than within it.

Question 8 required the respondents to indicate their agreement or disagreement with each of 13 statements. For one group there was a significant change for the item, 'Spending a lot of money training police officers in social skills is largely a waste of time.' At the beginning of training there was strong disagreement with this statement, but by the end of training there was significantly less disagreement ($p < .001$). This difference also applied for Week 1 vs six months ($p < .01$) and vs twelve months ($p < .001$). Similar differences were revealed in the data for the other group. Here again the amount of disagreement with this statement, though initially high, became less at six and at twelve months (both $p < .02$), with the beginning vs the end of training difference not quite reaching significance. Such changes could be taken to reflect badly on HAT but it must be noted that the probationers' views have changed from Week 1, when they were somewhere between 'strongly disagree' and 'disagree', to somewhere between 'disagree' and 'undecided'. Nevertheless, the fact that both groups of trainees came to disagree less with the statement cannot be ignored.

Other changes revealed by Q8 involved for one group the statements 'Problems can be caused by the inability of police officers to understand ethnic minority groups', and 'Most racial prejudice comes from coloured people themselves.' For the former statement, mean disagreement scores were higher outside the training school than at the beginning of training. Thus, although probationers tended to agree with this statement whilst at the training school, they became rather more 'undecided' about it once out on district. Similarly, for the statement, 'Most racial prejudice comes from coloured people themselves', there were significant differences ($p < .01$) between scores at Week 1 and six and twelve months after the end of initial training. Here, although at the beginning of their training officers were 'undecided' on this issue, once they had been out serving in a police station for six months they came to agree with it. Similar (though non-significant) trends are revealed in the data for the other group. These scores suggest that once initial training has been completed, the probationers' views concerning racial prejudice and understanding ethnic minorities undergo changes which are counter to the aims and objectives of HAT.

Question 9 contained behavioral intention rating scales. For one group the scores for, 'As a police officer I try to devote most of my time to catching criminals and leave welfare work to social workers and the like', increased both for the 'would' and for 'should' between Week 20 and six months ($p < .01$) with no differences during training or between six and twelve months. For the other group there was a similar increase on this item for 'should' between Week 1 and six and twelve months ($p < .02$). The responses to this item indicate that after several months out at police stations probationers feel that they now 'would do this', whereas during initial training they would not. Thus post-initial training experiences increase the likelihood that probationers feel they 'would' and 'should' devote their time to catching criminals and leave welfare work to social workers and the like. These data produced in response to question 9 (only some of which are reported here) suggest changes in views concerning law-enforcing aspects of policing which are not necessarily contrary to the principles of HAT. Those items in Q9 which more closely focussed on HAT issues (e.g., those concerning 'person to person' contact, and on the use of 'discretion') reveal that at the beginning of training, trainees had pro-HAT beliefs which were not significantly affected by training.

Question 10 asked respondents to rank the importance of 11 items 'for high morale among police officers'. For one group the rankings for 'good community-police relations' changed in that at Week 1 it was ranked significantly higher ($p < .05$, two tail) than at Week 16 or at six and twelve months. From initially being ranked overall second at the beginning of training, it dropped to fifth place by the end of training (and then non-significantly to sixth and seventh). A corresponding significant increase from Week 1 to six months ($p < .05$, two tail) occurred in the rank given to 'superior officer you can get on with', with 'good pay' showing a non-significant increase outside the initial training period. The data for the other group show a similar, though statistically non-significant, decrease in ranked importance for 'good community-police relations', and a lowered ranking for 'fewer accusations of police corruption' at twelve months compared with the beginning of training ($p < .01$). The answers to Q10 show that, particularly during the initial training period, the ranked importance of 'good community-relations' for high morale decreases. This can only be taken as being contrary to the aims and objectives of HAT.

Question 11 required the probationers to rank the importance of six items for 'studying why people behave the way they do'. For one group the item, 'Because it makes a police officer more effective in his job', was ranked as being of lower importance at the end of initial training than at the beginning ($p < .02$) and at six and twelve months (both $p < .01$). At first glance this within-initial-training decrease in the ranking of a pro-HAT item might appear to be a cause for concern. However, there was a corresponding (though non-significant) increase in the ranking of another of the pro-HAT items in this question, namely, 'Because it aids communication between the police and the public'.

The data for the other group revealed that for the item, 'Because police officers play an important role as social workers', the ranking after six and twelve months was significantly less than at the beginning of training (both $p < .01$), with the ranking at twelve months also being lower ($p < .01$) than at the end of initial training. The decrease in the ranking of this item once the officers were out at police stations could be taken to reveal an anti-HAT development since the only items which numerically increased their overall ranking after the end of initial training are not HAT objectives and reveal some naivety regarding the validity of being able to predict human behaviour (i.e., the items 'So that a police officer can tell which people look like criminals' and 'So that a police officer can tell when a person is lying').

Conclusions Concerning the RTQ

A number of conclusions can be drawn from the responses to the questions contained in the RTQ. The first is that the questionnaire did seem sensitive enough to identify some changes across the four testing occasions in the two groups of respondents. In all, some 36 of the statistical analyses across the four testing occasions were significant enough to justify further statistical comparisons within pairs of testing occasions.

The second conclusion to be drawn is that few of the changes in scores between the beginning and end of training reflect well on the HAT aspect of the initial training course. A few changes do so (e.g., in the ranking on Q1 of 'Being just an ordinary person with a job') but these are in the minority. Where changes do occur between the end and the beginning of training these are mostly of an anti-HAT nature (e.g., in Q3 there became more disagreement with, 'The teaching of social studies and community relations is useful in preparing police officers for their forthcoming role in society'; in Q4, trainees 'would' as efficient police officers try less 'to understand the customs, viewpoints and traditions of as many minority groups as possible'; in Q7, 'the community as a whole' ranked higher in terms of having decreased in its respect for the police; in Q8, there became less disagreement with the statement, 'Spending a lot of money training police officers in social skills is largely a waste of time'; and in Q10, the ranked importance for morale of 'good community-police relations' decreased). Consideration of these developments contrary to the aims and objectives of HAT should be tempered by noting that on a number of aspects of several questions the answers given at the beginning of training clearly revealed pro- HAT attitudes, views and beliefs held by the trainees. Consequently, in many instances it would perhaps be expecting too much of HAT to strengthen these views still further by the end of initial training. This last point notwithstanding, the proponents of HAT may be disappointed by the outcomes of the comparisons of scores between the end and the beginning of initial training.

A third conclusion which can be drawn is that there occurred a number of changes once the officers were out serving in police stations which are not in line with the (admittedly vague) aims and objectives of HAT (e.g., in Q4, probationers 'would' as efficient police officers try less 'to understand the customs, viewpoints and traditions of as many minority groups as possible'; in Q6, 'not to let the suspect's age, sex, colour or background influence the way I talk to him or her' was ranked as being of lower importance once out of initial training: admittedly this item could be deemed ambiguous, but its anti-HAT meaning is the most likely one; in Q9, when serving in police stations the officers indicated that they would 'as a police officer devote most of my time to catching criminals and leave welfare work to social workers' whereas during training they said they would not; in Q11, the ranked importance of 'Because police officers play an important role as social workers' decreases). Such changes as these, which occurred once the initial training was completed, suggest that the community relations aspects of the training may require strengthening and that the post-initial training experiences which the probationers undergo could in certain ways have an effect counter to that wished for HAT.

PROBATIONER FEEDBACK QUESTIONNAIRE

We devised another questionnaire which was given to 109 probationary constables approximately a year after they had undergone Human Awareness Training as recruits. This questionnaire examined these officers' views of the training they had received and it contained 69 questions, some of which had several parts. Space permits only a summary of its findings to be presented here.

General Attitudes Towards HAT

Throughout the questionnaire there was little or no evidence to suggest that respondents had merely given what could be deemed desirable responses to the questions they had answered. Overall, the probationers seemed to recognize the need and importance of HAT, but there were indications that a sizable minority, 36% of the sample, felt that the training they had received was either inadequate or unsatisfactory in preparing them for their role as police officers. Approximately the same percentage of officers chose to criticize HAT in the final section of the questionnaire.

HAT: A Before and After Look

An exploration of probationers' present attitudes to HAT compared with what they remembered as being their first impressions of it revealed a high percentage of respondents who retained favourable attitudes to HAT once they had undergone training and were out serving in police stations. For those whose answers suggested a change in attitude, some strong, positive shifts occurred in favour of HAT.

Perceptions of HAT Relative to Other Experiences

HAT was perceived as being of limited importance in aiding the probationers interactive skills when compared with their experiences prior to joining the force and with subsequent experience encountered as a probationer. Of those experiences gained outside the training environment, probationary experiences tended to be valued more than pre-recruitment experiences in terms of their perceived facilitatory effect on interpersonal skill.

When asked for their opinions about contributory factors to morale, 'an understanding of human behaviour' and 'good police-community relations' were ranked as being of little importance for morale. Skills-based aspects of HAT ('helping the public' and 'communicating well with others', for instance) were seen as being important aspects of a police constable's job, while knowledge-based aspects (e.g., 'an understanding of human behaviour') tended to be ranked lower. The probationers seemed unable to see how the two aspects of 'understanding' and 'skill' could be related. Results for the more procedural aspects of training revealed the opposite, e.g., 'knowing the law' (i.e., knowledge-based) tended to be ranked high, while skills-based aspects (e.g., 'making arrests') tended to be ranked low.

A Framework for Training

Most probationers felt that HAT and the more procedural aspects of police work should (and could) be fully integrated. However, three quarters of the sample felt that this integration was not fully achieved during their recruit training. Nevertheless, few probationers reported difficulties in integrating some HAT skills into their procedural repertoire, whether in the training or the policing environment. Nearly half of the probationers felt that 'politeness had been mistaken for weakness' in their work, but very few regarded HAT as an obstacle to good policing. A majority of respondents indicated that both supervisory pressure to get 'figures' and a shortage of manpower did have an adverse effect on their HAT-type dealings with the public.

Quality of Training, Uses, Flaws and Possible Improvements

Only 62% of probationers felt that the HAT which they had received had been sufficient for the job. The handouts they had been given during training were considered by most probationers to be satisfactory, although some negative comments on these were made and 33% judged the handouts to be too simple. Forty-one per cent of the sample commented negatively upon their practical, role-play training. The most frequent criticism was that the role-play practicals lacked realism. Roughly half the sample felt that HAT in general had not assisted in their handling of practicals.

Fifty-four per cent of the probationers felt that the input on ethnic minorities was unsatisfactory in preparing them for this aspect of policing. Sixty-four per cent of those who had anticipated more visiting speakers during their recruit training requested more participation from speakers of ethnic minority groups. Sixty-two per cent of respondents who wanted more outside speakers as part of their recruit training also wanted psychologists for this input. A majority of those who wanted more visiting speakers did so for reasons sympathetic to HAT. HAT was generally perceived as being of use in dealing with different groups of victims and there were very few individuals who felt that their HAT was inadequate in dealing with various target groups.

When asked about more practicals, more community attachments and stress training, a majority of probationers saw these as areas in which their training might have been improved. However, when asked whether training could be improved by expanding and continuing HAT, the majority of respondents disagreed (and many respondents were ambivalent on this issue). Few respondents agreed that only HAT-sympathetic individuals should be recruited into the force.

Assessment and Feedback

A majority of probationers agreed with the assertion that HAT tends to be taken lightheartedly by recruits partly because they know that they will not be examined on it. Further, 97% of the sample felt that asessment would improve the efficiency of the training.

Discretion

Fifty-six percent of the sample were encouraged to use discretion at training school, while 33% were criticized for using it (either at training school or later out on district). Some evidence was obtained to suggest that the probationers held positive attitudes towards the use of discretion in their work, although in the hypothetical situations given, roughly one third of the sample indicated a mismatch between what they felt they would do and what they felt they should do in discretionary situations.

The 'Canteen Culture'

HAT no longer seemed to be a source of discussion for many probationers. Most of the sample agreed with the assertion that HAT itself was not a waste of time, but that problems arose in putting it into practice out on district. Many probationers had experienced sarcastic or humorous remarks made to them about HAT when they were probationer constables, but few had experienced direct hostility or derision aimed directly at them rather than at HAT. Nearly 70% of the sample had been asked about HAT by other officers (apart from fellow probationers), although half of these were made to feel defensive when explaining it. Only 34% of the sample had experienced these officers showing a genuine interest in the subject. Some 40% of the sample felt that their senior officers had a false impression of what HAT was about.

CONCLUSION

As feedback exercise, the questionnaire has provided some useful insight into probationers' perceptions of HAT. Although many of these are somewhat critical, it should be remembered that the content, approach and quality of HAT has been constantly refined in the several months since the probationers in this survey underwent their recruit training. Nevertheless, it is important to note that whereas 38% of the sample felt that the HAT which they had received had been sufficient for the job, no fewer than 36% of the sample felt that the HAT which they had received was either inadequate or unsatisfactory in preparing them for their role as a police officer. Although no wholly conclusive evidence can be extracted from this questionnaire as to why this is the case, many findings do give the impression that during recruit training HAT is seen by probationers as an acceptable (and accepted) part of the training programme, but that its impact is lessened by virtue of the fact that it does not in their opinion operate efficiently. One of the reasons for this perceived lack of operating efficiency is lack of formal assessment of HAT. Coupled with this is the probationers' view that for HAT to be successfully employed, they are not necessarily required to understand anything about human behaviour, merely to have a repertoire of HAT-based skills which can be used when they are deemed appropriate.

Any lessening of the impact of HAT upon individual probationers will undoubtedly be reinforced by one or more aspects of the so-called canteen culture. Several possible drawbacks of this canteen culture on the impact and efficacy of HAT were identified in the questionnaire and further study of such effects seems desirable. Given that HAT appears, using this questionnaire, to be having some desired effects upon probationers, evaluation of the extent to which their policing behaviour reflects these desired effects appears warranted.

EXPERIENCED OFFICERS' QUESTIONNAIRE

We distributed another questionnaire to constables who each had approximately three years experience of being a police officer. These constables' initial recruit training had involved that which Human Awareness Training replaced (i.e., Integrated Police Studies - IPS). The questionnaire was somewhat similar to the one we gave to probationary constables a year after they had received HAT (see the previous section). One hundred and six officers completed this questionnaire, indicating their views of the training they had received in the light of their policing experience. Space permits only a summary of the findings to be presented here.

The Experienced Officers' Questionnaire (particularly when contrasted with the Probationer Feedback Questionnaire) served to illustrate both deficiencies in the old style IPS training and the new style HAT. Overall, HAT-trained probationary officers seemed to hold more favourable views about their human awareness training than did experienced officers towards their IPS training. It is debatable whether difference in length of service alone could have caused this shift towards a more positive attitude. That less criticism of practicals was made by HAT-trained officers (who also seemed to attach greater importance to communicating well with others) is testimony to the success of HAT over the old style training. It would seem that the greater emphasis on communication skills in HAT has paid off insofar as officers' views are concerned (this still leaves unanswered the question of whether they are more effective communicators out on the street). Although the experienced officers as a whole were equally divided in their opinion as to whether IPS training should be expanded or continued, this does not necessarily imply that they would be receptive to HAT-style training. Such attitudes are probably based more on the fact that some of them saw their IPS training as ineffective. Few instances were quoted where IPS training had been of specific use to officers in interacting with members of the public. The requests from non-HAT trained officers for training improvements were frequently about topics on which HAT now focusses (e.g., training for controlling situations, greater practical training, a greater emphasis on the role of discretion) but other requests (particularly concerning stress) are not met by HAT.

Knowing about law and police procedure was seen as important for the police role largely, it seems, because it promotes greater confidence in the police officer when he deals with a situation. The success of any training programme such as HAT is therefore dependent upon the extent to which the two areas of training (procedure and HAT) are integrated. Similarly, the theoretical side of training needs to be fully integrated with the practical aspects of training (this did not seem evident in the experienced officers' IPS training). In recent months, HAT has begun to improve in this respect, although there is still some evidence to suggest that there is a void in the training between the knowledge and the skill aspects of human behaviour.

HAT is very much an improvement over IPS training in that far greater emphasis is placed on the skills of police work. The increase in the amount and complexity of practicals with video feedback undoubtedly increase the face validity of this type of training for the recruits. HAT-trained probationers were far less critical of this area of training than were the experienced, IPS trained officers, although there is still room for improvement in terms of the amount of realism and flexibility achieved by these sessions.

Both the HAT-trained probationers and the experienced officers were critical of the method used to assess HAT-type skills. To impart an awareness to recruits of human behaviour and the more discretionary aspects of their role as police officer is commendable, but the impact such knowledge will have is likely to be seriously undermined if recruits are not assessed (at least partly) along these dimensions, or if considerable pressure is exerted on them to satisfy the demand for arrest and process figures during their probationary period whilst serving in police stations.

One further area of improvement lies in the area of community relations training. Neither the experienced officers nor the HAT-trained probationers demonstrated much enthusiasm for the race awareness part of their training. It seems likely that as this area of training moves away from the traditional (IPS) 'chalk and talk' approach to a more dynamic approach, so attitudes of officers towards this area of training may improve.

Evidence from both surveys did indicate that probationers do not always work in an environment which is conducive to exercising their HAT knowledge and skills. With the emphasis on obtaining process and arrest figures for the first few years of a police officers' service, serious thought must be given to the attitudes which may prevail in London's police stations towards HAT and its objectives. The longitudinal data produced by cohorts of recruits in this evaluation do show some changes for the worse in attitudes towards community relations issues as officers progress through their probationary period. Given the great importance which both experienced officers and HAT-trained probationers attached to street experiences in determining their ability to be effective police officers, it seems important that attitudes in police stations are brought more into line with HAT objectives.

OUR JUDGMENT ON THE TRAINING HAVING OBSERVED IT

We sat in on a considerable amount of the training and we also talked at length to the trainers and the trainees. The Police Foundation and the Metropolitan Police asked us to produce an interim report after the first 12 months of our 30 month long evaluation. In this interim report we made a number of suggestions concerning HAT, even though the data reported on in the present paper were not available at that time. The force appears to be acting upon these points, although some of these actions are receiving more impetus than others. In short our suggestions were that:

(1) There should be a substantial increase in the amount of the training that is concerned with the principles and processes governing and underlying behaviour.

(2) Due to the fact that the training in community relations is woefully inadequate, this main component of the training needs to be considerably improved upon.

(3) Since the assessment of recruits' HAT performance is far too infrequent and informal, far more rigorous and regular testing procedures should be adopted.

(4) Because the majority of trainers are not properly equipped to be effective HAT trainers, better provision for their needs is required and far more realistic role-playing is necessary.

The staff of the Recruit Training School were not unaware of several of the shortcomings of HAT referred to here, but it may well be that comments from external evaluation may provide the necessary impetus for essential improvements to be made. In its first years of operation, one cannot expect such an outstanding achievement to be fully operational and the following comments should be read in this light.

The Absence of Sufficient Training Concerning the Principles Governing and Underlying Human Behaviour

It is very likely that the training which HAT replaced was insufficiently based on the behavioural aspects of practical policing skills. The previous training concerning the understanding of human behaviour was far too academic and classroom-based. One of HAT's greatest achievements is the training of human awareness as an integral part of policing skills rather than as a separate entity which could be seen as different from real policing. However, the reactions to the gross inadequacies of the previous form of training (which is still practiced by many British police forces) may well have had too strong an effect in at least one crucial respect. The worthwhile emphasis on the behavioural skills required of a police officer was so strong in HAT as to leave little time for explaining to the trainees how and why they were being taught to behave in certain ways. We stated that the training should include information explicitly designed to inform the trainee of the principles and processes underlying and governing human behaviour so that (1) the trainee can more effectively (a) assimilate the training material, and (b) generalize from the situations encountered in training to those encountered when on duty, and so that (2) the trainer can more effectively offer explanations concerning what is being taught. Furthermore, a far greater imparting of the principles governing and underlying human behaviour would also equip the trainee to learn more effectively from his probationer experiences once he has graduated from the training school, and most importantly would act to insulate the officer from the possible effects of being told, once working in a police station, to "forget all that rubbish you learned at the training school, we experienced officers will tell you what it is really like."

The absence of sufficient information of this type is one of the major reasons why the training in self awareness and especially community relations (two of the three main components of HAT) was inadequate. Neither the trainers nor the trainees were sufficiently knowledgeable concerning the general principles governing behaviour, even though Burns-Howell et al. (1981) claimed that HAT "will give recruits an organized theoretical framework for analyzing interpersonal situations, evaluating their own performance and for devising ways of responding to a variety of citizens". Although it is not appropriate to go into details here, a few examples may be illustrative. There was, in the training, insufficient or no mention of such factors as (1) how expectancy and anxiety predispose the use of abuse and affect decision-making; (2) the psychological processes which a police officer may experience when finding himself under stress and/or in a crisis situation; (3) how and why authoritarian behaviour is likely to occur when a police officer finds himself in socially ambiguous or uncertain circumstances; (4) how prejudice and/or fear often leads to derogation and deindividuation. A greater emphasis on these and many other processes is desirable and is certainly possible.

Some people have recently claimed that HAT succeeds in this regard (e.g., Shepherd, 1983), "The 'theory' requirement of police training based on human awareness is substantial. A recruit is now required to grasp the conceptual, particularly psychological, behavioural and ethical bases of human thought, feelings and actions", but it seemed most unlikely in 1983 that HAT was achieving this. The 1967 U.S. President's Commission on Law Enforcement Task Force Report on the Police stated that, "The police officer should be provided with a basis for understanding the various forms of behaviour with which he must deal", and that trainees "must acquire information and understanding concerning human relations". It was our belief that HAT was successful in imparting information of behavioural nature but that it could do much more to provide an understanding of human relations. Trainees will by no means necessarily acquire the latter merely from receiving a considerable amount of the former. It seems of limited use for trainees to have acquired a substantial amount of behavioural interpersonal skill if they do not understand the psychological principles which govern such skills. The greater dissemination within the training of psychological principles should not, of course, be in the form of academic theory and jargon. Instead it should be in a form that is comprehensible by the trainees and which is seen by them as relevant to policing skills.

The Inadequate Training in Community Relations

Community relations training is one of the three main components of HAT and it was clearly the weakest. The stated aim of this part of the training is to provide recruits with race awareness and cultural awareness. With regard to both of these topics the training was woefully inadequate. Neither the nature of prejudice and racism nor knowledge of the various cultures and groups which exist in British society were sufficiently covered. The insufficiency of the training concerning the nature and dynamics of prejudice stemmed in a large part from the lack of concern (referred to above) with the principles and processes underlying and governing behaviour. It is unreasonable to expect human beings to be able to control behaviourally the prejudices which they all undoubtedly have without providing them with (1) an adequate understanding of the processes involved and (2) the means whereby they may become conscious of their own biases so as to be able to prevent these from affecting their policing.

The rather factual information which made up the training on community awareness was in need of considerable improvement. The community awareness training lacked breadth, depth and dynamism. It failed to explain the points of view of citizens who had different cultural backgrounds from the trainees and it did not adequately deal with the cultural differences which exist in the interpretation of behaviours and acts. In short, the race relations training aspect of HAT was too simplistic.

The Lack of Adequate Trainee Assessment During HAT

Assessment of each trainee's progress is vital. However, the assessment was conducted in a rather subjective, haphazard and infrequent manner. Furthermore, by no means all the trainees were followed through training by the same trainers. At some points during the training programme, the trainers did make a special effort to check whether each trainee was performing satisfactorily. However, we suggested that a much more formalized and rigorous assessment programme should be introduced, even though some exploratory but unsuccessful attempts were made some time ago. Not only should the assessment of behavioural skills become more rigorous (and the trainers adequately taught how to do this), but also the expected increase in recruits' self-awareness and knowledge of community relations should be formally monitored on a constant basis.

One of the reasons for the need for constant formal assessment of recruits' self-, race-, and cultural-awareness is that this part of the course needs to be seen both by the trainees and the trainers as equally important for successful graduation from the training school as other parts of the recruit training programme which are already regularly assessed in a formal way. An even more important reason for the need for a greater amount of regular assessment of trainee progress throughout HAT is that of feedback. If trainee progress is not constantly, formally monitored then there is little chance that the recruits could benefit from information which informs them (and the trainers) of their strengths and weaknesses. Such feedback would also point to weaknesses in the training programme.

There was some assessment of recruit performance, but this focussed almost entirely on the interpersonal skills' component of HAT and even this assessment could be improved, especially if the role-playing exercises were made more realistic. Assessment of recruit progress regarding the other two components of HAT (self-awareness and community relations) was either minimal or non-existent. An understandable reason for this is the inadequate training provided on these topics. If training school staff know that despite their own best endeavours the coverage of these topics is insufficient, then one can comprehend why there was little regular assessment relating to these two important components.

The 1967 U.S. President's Commission of Law Enforcement Task Force Report on the Police pointed out that "since current selection methods cannot screen out all persons who are unsuitable for police work, a comprehensive evaluation of recruits during probation is extremely important". The fact that selection procedures in British police forces still do not adequately discriminate among applicants on the basis of their human awareness potential underlies the need for regular evaluation of recruits during HAT.

Other Limitations of the Training and of the Trainers

The majority of trainers had little knowledge, other than that provided by their own life experiences, of the principles and processes governing and underlying behaviour. This resulted in there being too exclusive an emphasis on the behavioural components of HAT. We suggested that if it were possible to provide trainers with appropriate manuals/booklets which appropriately outline and explain the principles governing and underlying the behaviour which they are training, then they could incorporate these into their teaching. The provision of such materials would require a substantial input from outside police since there exist as yet few, if any appropriate texts. [Even our Psychology For Police Officers (Bull, Bustin, Evans & Gahagan, 1983) by no means covers all of HAT; see also Bull, 1984).]

Most of HAT quite rightly focussed on role-playing exercises. However, the role-playing sessions conducted towards the end of the course lacked realism, even though Burns-Howell et al (1981) noted the importance of having realistic exercises. "The learning is to be of a real-life type which will enable the recipients to develop such skills throughout their police service...Recruit training...must realistically prepare an officer for operational duty". The person in the exercise who played the role of the citizen with whom the recruit interacted was rarely from an ethnic/cultural group different from that of the recruit. Usually the role of the citizen was played by one of the trainers and while this had some value in that the trainer thus controlled the behaviour of the 'citizen', this advantage was likely to be more than outweighed by the fact that the trainees knew that the 'citizen' was a trainer and usually one with whom they were acquainted. The resultant interaction is unrepresentative and unrealistic. Early on in the training programme, the use of role-playing trainers with whom the trainees are acquainted may be justifiable but later on in the training and in assessment, the role of the citizen should not be played by the kind of person typically present at the training school. What is required is a programme of even more difficult role-playing exercises which take place at intervals throughout the training course.

In our interim report we stated that "HAT was conceived, organized and implemented by experienced police officers, some of whom possess bachelor's or master's degrees in psychological/social sciences. Given the limited amount of formal knowledge of human behaviour and of education that even such persons would possess, it should not be at all surprising that certain aspects of HAT could be considerably improved upon. The resources and levels of competence available within the Metropolitan Police Force have fortunately been sufficient to enable such a worthwhile package as HAT to commence and be sustained. (Many other forces throughout the world have tried to mount human awareness training and have failed, partly due to the lack of competence). However, it should not be at all surprising that this level of competence is not sufficient to ensure that all aspects of HAT are as effective as they could be".

The above summarizes our 1983 comments on the Metropolitan Police's HAT and it is to the force's credit that it requested outside evaluation and has decided to act, as it sees fit, on these criticisms.

METROPOLITAN POLICE RESPONSE TO IMPROVE HAT

Since the presentation of our interim report, there have been a number of developments at the training school, some of which are responses to our criticisms concerning HAT. The title has changed from Human Awareness Training to Policing Skills Training. This has been accompanied by a greater focus on skills-based training. The revised HAT syllabus now involves 29 separate sessions of videotaped practical exercises fed back in the classroom to the students. HAT lessons now form the majority of the first five weeks of the initial course and they are considered the fabric on which all the subsequent training is said to be based.

In all practical exercises after the first ten weeks, discretion is introduced as an element of each exercise. The assessment of practical ability will form the basis of a profile of the students' performance throughout the course. A question writing team of police officers (who are psychology graduates) has recently been set up to prepare a variety of assessment questions related to HAT. This material will be tested throughout the course by written examination. That part of the syllabus concerned with community relations has been extended and developed. The time spent on and the range of these topics has increased substantially. The training of trainers has been extended to ten weeks followed by a further ten weeks in which trainers interact with classes and assist more experienced tutors with the first five weeks of initial training. This training emphasizes that the HAT subjects are essential ingredients for the rest of the course. The assessment of the trainers' teaching ability continues for another twelve months and includes two further courses of a developmental nature dealing with role play, counselling and video exercises. These crucial improvements in the training are very welcome and they point to the value of having external evaluators involved.

CONCLUDING COMMENTS

Several important conclusions can be drawn from this evaluation. One is concerned with the feasibility of an outside team of evaluators closely monitoring some of the activities of Britain's largest police force. At the inception of this project, a number of people appeared to be of the opinion that a close examination of recruit training would simply not prove to be possible. Previous experience of working with other police forces argued against this possibility, but we were nevertheless concerned that our attempted evaluation might not be well received generally within the Metropolitan Police. Such concern was not, in fact, warranted. We have received the fullest co-operation, not only from the training staff and officers in charge of training, but also from the trainees and others.

A second important conclusion is concerned with the fact that many of the measuring instruments (i.e., the questionnaires) used in the evaluation did actually manage to quantify relevant views, beliefs, attitudes and opinions. In the behavioural sciences it is by no means always the case that something can be quantified merely because it is believed to exist. Some of the questionnaires given to trainees across four testing occasions found few changes over time. When such null outcomes occur one has to make a professional judgment concerning whether no relevant changes therefore occurred, or whether changes may have taken place but gone undetected. The data from the social- evaluative anxiety questionnaire suggest that the finding of null differences is an important outcome. Many previous attempted evaluations of police awareness training around the world have found no or little effect of the training. Many such outcomes could be due to the use of inappropriate measuring instruments rather than to ineffective training. Often it is difficult to tell which of these two is the correct conclusion, though much of the training evaluated appears to be ill thought out and naive.

By and large, the data we have collected subsequent to making our 1983 constructive criticisms support these. The community relations/race awareness aspects of the training still seem in need of considerable improvement and one hopes that the extension and development described will be substantial enough. If the planned formal assessment of HAT turns out to be competently conducted, then this should readily help determine if trainees' race and community awareness has been sufficiently affected by the training.

With regard to the practical exercises, there is strong evidence that this aspect of training is a vast improvement over that which preceded it. There is much more realism in these sessions under HAT than under IPS. However, there is still some room for improvement, particularly regarding the question of who plays the role of citizen in these videotaped encounters. The aspect of the training to which these sessions most strongly relate, i.e., interpersonal skills, is clearly the best, and although even now we consider this to be among the best in the world, the more extensive training of the trainers can only serve to make it even better.

The much more extensive training to be received by the trainers should also help them to include more in the training on the principles and processes underlying human behaviour. When this is done the apparent gap between understanding/concepts/notions on the one hand, and skills/practice on the other will hopefully be bridged so that trainees will no longer be under the illusion that the very wide range of interpersonal skills required of a police officer can be effectively and appropriately exhibited without an enhanced understanding of human behaviour.

In conclusion, of the three components of HAT, 'interpersonal skills' is clearly the best; the component described as 'self-awareness' is of a reasonable standard; and that described as 'community relations' is, as yet, rather poor. However, should one in an evaluation merely compare that which is being evaluated with some ideal, or should one focus on a comparison with what it replaced? If the latter (and we feel this is the more appropriate perspective), then there can be little doubt that HAT is a very substantial improvement over that which it preceded. HAT also compares very favourably indeed with training in other forces around the world. When the planned improvements are fully operational, it could well be considered the best that we humans have yet come up with for training police in human awareness. We have seen very little evidence that police recruit training in the rest of Britain even approximates the Metropolitan Police's HAT.

The Metropolitan Police's initial recruit training programme in human awareness is a very worthwhile achievement of considerable substance and promise. However, the desirable achievements of the initial training seem to some extent dissipated by post- initial training experiences. Now that the force's initial recruit training in human awareness appears likely to be operating with considerable efficiency, it seems appropriate to determine the extent to which the effects of this training are manifested in constables' policing behaviour.

REFERENCES

Bull, R. (1984). Psychology's contribution to policing. In D.J.
  Muller, D.E. Blackman and A.J. Chapman (Eds.), Psychology and law.
  Chichester: Wiley.

Bull, R., Bustin, B., Evans, P. & Gahagan, D. (1983). Psychology for
  police officers. Chichester: Wiley.

Bull, R., & Horncastle, P. (1983). An evaluation of the metropolitan
  police recruit training programme in human awareness: Interim report.
  London: The Police Foundation.

Burns-Howell, A., McKenzie, I., & Kember, R. (1981). Human awareness
  training for recruits and probationers. Metropolitan Police Training
  School Report No. OG9/31/37.

Clark, R. (1979). Police and the community. New York: Franklin Watts.

Ehrlich, H. (1973). The social psychology of prejudice. New York:
  Wiley.

Neiderhoffer, A. (1967). Behind the shield - the police in urban
  society. New York: Anchor.

President's Commission on Law Enforcement and Administration of Justice.
  (1967). Task Force Report: The Police. Washington: U.S. Government
  Printing Office.

Reith, C. (1952). The blind eye of history: A study of the origins of
  the present police era. London: Faber.

Rosenberg, M. (1965). Society and the adolescent self-image.
  Princeton University Press.

Schutz, W. (1958). FIRO-A three dimensional theory of interpersonal
  behaviour. New York: Holt, Rinehart and Winston.

Shepherd, E. (1983). Values into practice: The implementation and
  implications of human awareness training. The Police Journal.

Watson, D., & Friend, R. (1969). Measurement of social-evaluative
  anxiety. Journal of Consulting and Clinical Psychology, 33, 448-457.

THE LIMITS OF POLICE COMMUNITY RELATIONS TRAINING

ANTHONY J.P. BUTLER

The Objective

Police work is a complex occupation undertaken in a complex world by members of a complex organization. A statement of the obvious, but nonetheless worth making because there is a tendency to see activities undertaken by the police, such as police community relations training, as having a value in themselves without any reference to the reasons why. Therefore, the role the psychologist can fulfill in the evaluation of police community relations training cannot be achieved without some definition of what the training is seeking to accomplish. For the purpose of this paper, the objective of police community relations training will be stated as follows: To promote the achievement by police officers of socially acceptable standards of behaviours in their face-to-face encounters with citizens.

The Problem

The purpose of training is to establish, maintain or improve the quality of encounters between citizens and police officers. Therefore it is implicit in this notion that socially acceptable standards do not occur "naturally", therefore they have to be established or improved, and furthermore, when established, these standards of behaviour have to be reinforced to prevent degeneration. Thus training has to intervene at the point of initial recruit training and at various stages in a constable's career to set and maintain standards. The organization also shapes officers' perceptions and behaviour, and therefore training will be appropriate as part of a manager's development. The development of training concepts, material, and strategies in England are described elsewhere (see chapters by Bull and by Poole in this volume). This chapter is concerned with some strategies which have been developed to attempt to describe the nature of the problem and evaluate existing training methods. In essence, the paper is seeking to identify the nature of the problem to be solved and in so doing, point to the most likely avenues to achieve the objectives of promoting socially acceptable standards of behaviour in police-citizen encounters.

The Nature of the Problem

A major examination of police-citizen encounters in the United States was commissioned by the President's Commission on Law Enforcement and Administration of Justice in the late 1960s. The report of this research by Black and Reiss (1967) provides a useful starting point for the definition of the problem of understanding police-citizen encounters. In the opening pages of the report, the complexity of police-citizen encounters is explored. A primary task of the police in responding to a call from a citizen for assistance, or investigating an apparently suspicious situation or merely meeting a person informally during the normal course of their work, is the judgments about the role and status of the actors in this situation. The actor will have social status such as his sex, age, race, ethnic or social class and a situational status which is more complex and is liable to change as it depends upon the particular circumstances or relationships which exist in the encounter. A situational status can be as a neighbour, customer, employer, husband, wife or stranger, and overlaid on this categorization a person may be the one who called the police as a complainant or a person who is a suspected or an alleged offender. In some encounters the police may have a third category of person, namely those who are witnesses, victims or merely bystanders who form an audience.

Black and Reiss (1967) observed that police officers "like most other actors, prefer ordered and routine social encounters to disorganized or unorganized and unpredictable encounters". This observation would fit conventional wisdom and touches upon a central issue in relation to police-citizen encounters. The police officer has a monopoly of power insofar as he is endowed by the state with the authority to use force if necessary to achieve the legitimate goals of policing. The police officer exercises this power through the use of actual or symbolic authority which causes police-citizen encounters to have an underlying ambiguity and ambivalence which is crystalized in the following passage by Black and Reiss:

"Not infrequently a police-citizen encounter takes the form of a precarious balance of officer control and citizen submission. Police control not uncommonly is more apparent than real. Many officers realize that as they exercise authority, like other incumbents of such positions, they are in an important sense dependent for co-operation upon those over whom they control. Unlike many persons in situations where authority is exercised, the police sometimes are faced with a dual set of clients in an adversary situation. Those who call the police are prepared to accept the police officers authority at least at the outset. Those who are to be policed often do not. The major form of control open to the officer in such situations is to assert authority." (p. 11)

In situations where a person requesting police assistance concurs with the officer's interpretation of the situation and agrees with his proposed course of action, and the suspect submits to the officer's authority and becomes a willing participant in the scenario, the officer and all the participants to the encounter are likely to be satisfied. It is in circumstances where this ideal is not achieved that the officer has some difficulty. Where the suspect does not accept the interpretation made by the officer, he can become difficult by denying the authority of the officer, by challenging that the officer has power to undertake the course of action or by the simple threat or use of physical force.

When an officer has a compliant customer and adversary, he has a broad range of options consistent with his legal discretion; however, as difficulties arise that range of discretion is reduced to the point that he may feel obliged to make an arbitrary decision merely to extricate himself from what is becoming a difficult, if not impossible, situation. It is in these scenarios that the quality of police-citizen encounters is inevitably bound to be damaged, thus the ability of an officer to control any situation is likely to have a direct correlation with the perceived quality of the encounter.

Evidence of the Quality of Police-Citizen Encounters

Data from the British Crime Survey were analyzed to provide a profile of contacts between police and public (Southgate & Ekblom, 1984). The conceptual framework for the analysis of these data made a distinction between three types of police-citizen encounters. The public were conceived as being either:

(1) Consumers of police services seeking to receive assistance in connection with crimes, physical plights, disturbances or disputes.

(2) As actual or suspected adversaries, stopped, questioned, searched, moved on, or arrested.

(3) As citizens not personally involved in crime or other problems but nevertheless co-operating with the police.

Obviously the purpose of the encounter from the citizens perspective will be a significant element in his judgment of the quality of the interaction. Of the data examined, "97% of the contacts initiated by the public were classed as consumer related with the remainder involving the reporting of traffic accidents. Of those initiated by the police, 86% were classed as adversarial" (p. 5). The report asserts that the marked contrast shown in these data, reflecting who initiated the encounter, is a central issue in understanding the relationship between the police and the public. Just over half the sample of 6,329 had not had any encounters with the police in the preceding 14 months. Of the 47% who had encountered the police, 31% had encountered them only as consumers and 6% had encountered them only in an adversarial context. The remaining 10% had encountered the police both as consumers and as adversaries.

The British Crime Survey, consistent with previous research, found that just under half of all police contacts initiated by the public related to issues not involving the reporting of a crime. There were variations in the frequency of contact with the police and although more than half of the sample had not initiated a contact with the police, those that had were likely to have contacted them for a number of reasons on different occasions. The most likely profile of a person contacting the police for help was that of a young middle class male.

Contacts initiated by the police were only half as frequent as those initiated by the public. Taking all respondents, 14% had gone to the police to report a crime, while 16% had been approached by police as a suspect of a crime or offence. Whereas, in public initated contacts 63% had been to seek assistance with a whole range of issues, the overwhelming reason for police initated contacts was suspicion that the citizen had committed some offence or crime. During the recall period the survey found 81% of respondents had not had a contact which had been initiated by the police, and of the reported contacts only 3% involved the respondent not being suspected of some offence or crime. The most common reason for being approached by the police was concerned with the use of a motor vehicle. Nearly four times as many citizens had been stopped in connection with a vehicle compared with those who had been stopped whilst on foot, and three times as many had been reported or charged for offences in relation to the use of a motor vehicle compared with other offences.

Although the data did not suggest that the police used the personal categories of the drivers to stop and question suspects, the self-reported offending rates by respondents suggested that the police were not stopping the "right" people, i.e., those committing the most offences. In those cases where the respondents were on foot and had been approached by the police, there was a stronger association between offending rates, by self-report, and the frequency of being stopped. The frequency of being approached by the police whether on foot or in a vehicle was associated with the frequency of alcohol consumption and the number of nights spent out each week. Socio-demographic predictors of the frequency of being approached by the police were age, sex and employment status, with young males and particularly those unemployed being most frequently approached by the police.

Respondents were asked to assess the quality of their personal contacts with the police during the past five years. The first interesting point is a neutral reaction by the majority of the respondents. Sixty-three per cent said that they had been neither annoyed nor pleased by the police contact. Almost twice as many had been pleased (18%) as had been annoyed (10%), and 6% had been both pleased and annoyed. Thus the scale of the annoyance problem is relatively small. Cases of annoyance were more likely to be reported by those who had been approached by the police in relation to some suspected crime or offence, and the largest single source of annoyance was caused by the police officers attitude to the citizen. Another source of annoyance for young people was their assertion that the police used undue force and wrongful arrest or stop procedures. A neutral perception of the police was less likely from men compared with women, younger compared to older people, and unemployed people compared to housewives or the retired. Professional/managerial workers were more likely to be pleased than annoyed with their contacts with the police.

The British Crime Survey used the notions of "politeness, pleasantness, and helpfulness" as the benchmarks of police demeanour. About a quarter of the respondents claimed the police had been impolite in some way. This claim was found to be more likely for males under 25 years of age, the unemployed, members of the ethnic minorities and those living in urban areas. The situation of the contact with the police was also a significant variable. Those who had been stopped by the police on foot or in a vehicle and had been suspected of an offence were more likely to report impoliteness, particularly if they had been stopped more than once and also had been searched. A far greater proportion of respondents (80%) reported having pleasant and helpful contacts with the police, with such responses being more common for middle class respondents, housewives and the retired. The groups less likely to report such experiences were younger, particularly male, residents of the inner city, unemployed and members of ethnic minorities. Southgate and Ekblom (1984) conclude:

"Taken together, these various measures present an overall picture of the state of police-public relations which is largely good, the police being much appreciated for their efficiency, helpfulness and their understanding and discretion. Set against this are the problem areas, with a significant minority of people complaining of misconduct, inefficiency and rudeness by the police". (p. 28)

Ethnic Minorities, Crime and Policing

During the Summer of 1981 research was conducted in the inner city area of Manchester, immediately before and after the disturbances that took place in that city. The report (Tuck & Southgate, 1981) set as one of its objectives an investigation of the contacts between the police and citizens to establish if there were any significant differences in the quality of those contacts between white and non-white citizens. The area surveyed involved both traditional inner city housing and new factory built dwellings on large estates. The survey area contained both West Indians and white people, both of whom shared a very high unemployment level, although the unemployment rate was higher amongst West Indians than amongst white people for men under 55 years of age and for women aged 16-24 years. In fact, one out of every two male West Indians between the age of 16 and 34 were out of work compared with one in five white men in the same age group.

The data from the victim survey in this research established that the crime experiences of both white people and West Indian people were broadly similar and, more importantly in terms of an assessment of police community relations, there were no significant differences in the reporting patterns of either group. West Indians were just as likely to report a crime to the police and were just as likely to be satisfied or dissatisfied with the police response as white people. The overall pattern of contact between the police and West Indians and between the police and whites was remarkably similar. The similarity extended to the occasions when the police stopped, searched, or arrested citizens. In the age group of 16-24, the frequency of being stopped by the police was similar for both groups at 18%. The similarity of this type of contact with the police was repeated for the age group 25-34 with 7% of West Indians and 8% of whites reporting such contacts, but in the older age group of 35-54 years of age, there was a difference reported between the two groups with 5% of West Indians reporting such contacts and only 1% of whites. The data showed that motor vehicle offenses accounted for most of the West Indians who were stopped in this latter age group.

Respondents were asked to give details of the encounters with police. Approximately half of both groups encountered the police as a result of seeking help. Although West Indians were more likely to recall incidents where the police had been "unfriendly", these only represented 18% of the encounters with 65% being assessed as friendly. White people recalled the police as being unfriendly in 9% of the encounters and friendly on 82% of the occasions. When the respondents were asked how the police treated them as "a person", although 70% of West Indians were very or fairly satisfied on this criteria (compared to 82% for whites), 21% were fairly or very dissatisfied (compared with 12% for whites). However, satisfaction with what could be construed as the technical competence of the police was expressed equally by the two groups, 77% and 79% of the West Indians and whites respectively, being very or fairly satisfied with help they receive from the police.

Tuck and Southgate (1981) summarized their findings on the quality of contacts between police and the public as follows:

"Overall, these results cannot be said to support a picture of substantial police discrimination against West Indians, however a striking feature of the findings is the high frequency of stop, search or arrest experience reported to the interviewers by young respondents of either ethnic group. West Indians reported lower rates of 'satisfaction' than whites with the way the police treated them, but the great majority of contacts for both samples were said to be 'friendly' to result in 'satisfaction'. The data do not suggest a community strongly alienated from the local police. Differences of experience by age or by ward within the area were more substantial than ethnic differences." (p. 33)

Police and People in London

Police and people in London was the title of a series of four reports that were commissioned by the Metropolitan Police from the Policy Studies Institute. The research, which was commenced in 1980, was published in four volumes in 1983. Volume 1, a survey of Londoners, described the results of a detailed survey of the citizens of London (Smith, 1983). This report examined the patterns of contact between the police and the citizens.

The survey found that 27% of the respondents had visited a police station in the previous 12 months. Members of the ethnic minorities did not use the police station as a means of gaining assistance as frequently as white people. The data from all respondents showed that 84% of the visits were for matters which did not involve the potential for conflict, for example, to report a crime or collect lost property. On the remaining 16% of the occasions, the persons visiting the police station were suspected of, or were involved in, offences. However, when these latter data were analyzed by ethnic origin, only 15% of whites attended as suspects, but the proportion of West Indians and Asians in this category was 38% and 21%, respectively. When the analysis was restricted to people aged between 15 and 24, 23% of white respondents had this negative contact and 42% of West Indians.

Three quarters of the respondents made favourable comments about the attitude of the police officers towards them on their last visit to the police station. Unfavourable comments were more likely to have been made by younger respondents and West Indians. Those who went to the police station because they were suspected of an offence were more likely to make favourable comments than other respondents. The report concluded that "police officers usually make a good impression on white people at police stations, but less often on Asians and West Indians." (p. 175).

In answer to a general question which asked respondents if they had spoken to a police officer in the past 12 months, 56% gave a positive answer, More than two thirds had had more than two encounters. West Indians reported less encounters than whites (42% and 59% respectively), but the least number of encounters was reported by Asians; only 28% had spoken to a police officer in the past year. The reasons for the encounter were predominantly to request assistance from the police or to offer help; therefore, it was not surprising to see the middle classes reporting more encounters than other groups. Notwithstanding the last observation, unemployed males also reported a high proportion of encounters with the police. Being stopped on the street by the police was only a small proportion of the encounters. Asians had very few encounters with the police and when they did they were rarely in circumstances which would create conflict. The proportion of encounters which were described as "social" were the same for both West Indians and whites.

Although the proportions of encounters where West Indians were suspected of an offence was only a minority of the total, it did represent 28% of the encounters compared with 14% for whites and 12% for Asians. However, when the data for men only are examined, the proportion of West Indians who were encountered as suspects was 48% compared with only 18% for white men. The potential for conflict is also related to age. There is more likelihood of young people being involved in an encounter where they are suspected of an offence. When this is broken down by ethnic origin, it was found that this type of encounter involved 63% of West Indians aged 15-24 who had spoken to the police in the last year compared with only 35% of white men in the same age group. Smith (1983) comments, "while the contacts that most people have with the police are mostly amiable, there are certain small groups whose contact with the police mostly involves conflict; young West Indian men are one example, but there are probably others that cannot be identified from the survey, for example skinheads." (p. 184).

Volume 2, "A group of young black people" (Small, 1983), reports the results of a participant observation study of young black people in London. The significance of this research is more concerned with how it illuminates the attitudes of young black people towards the police as both individuals and as an organization rather than its contribution of direct evidence to police citizen encounters. The descriptions given in Chapter 4 of encounters between police and citizens is based as much on anecdotal material as direct observations. The circumstances of these encounters and the information provided by the individuals creates an impression of a group of people who are somewhat marginal to society and do apparently engage in extralegal activity as a normal part of their everyday life. Thus it is of no real surprise that most of the incidents reported involved individuals being stopped and searched while walking the street or driving their cars. The whole atmosphere created by this chapter is one where young black people consistently have negative encounters with the police with no opportunities being provided where they meet the police in what could be called a positive or constructive encounter. The description of two such encounters experienced by one individual illustrate the conflicts. In the first encounter described by the individual, the police apparently acted in an arbitrary and provoking manner when they insisted on searching the person on his way to work. It is claimed that during this search the police threw the contents of a lunch box on the ground before leaving the subject, having found nothing as a result of the search. On another occasion when this individual was stopped and searched by the police, he reacted in a relatively extreme way by undoing his trousers and allowing them to drop to the ground inviting the police to undertake what he called a thorough search. The police were apparently embarrassed by this response and did not pursue the matter any further, which according to the informant was fortunate because he was carrying in his trouser pocket about 5.00 pounds worth of a controlled drug. In another example, an individual recounts his commission of a crime of robbery accompanied by another black man and the subsequent search and arrest by the police.

In discussing the groups attitude towards the police, Small (1983) notes that it was evident that the police played a significant part in the young people's thoughts and their future expectations of experience in the world. There was no ambiguity in the perceptions of the group toward the police, they unanimously held unfavourable or highly unfavourable attitudes towards the police force, ranging from "deep bitterness and resentment to feelings of hatred and animosity" (p. 109).

The evidence for these extreme views was difficult to determine. Even amongst the group that held these views, only one member claimed that he had ever personally experienced being hit, knocked about or roughly manhandled by police officers. Small said that the attitudes of the remainder of the group appeared to have been produced through hearsay, the press, television and so forth. As a consequence of this stereotype, however, it was claimed that people kept knives and weapons to protect themselves from the threats of police brutality.

The potential problems for police community relations can be assessed from Small's contention that the antagonism felt by young black people towards police is not merely a response to the police either as individuals or as symbolic of a prejudiced white society, but appears to be associated strongly "with a sense of ethnic identity felt by members of the group and their interpretation of the experiences of black people in general when coming into contact with the police." (p. 103).

One interpretation of this observation is that as black people become increasingly frustrated with the opportunities being afforded to them by white society, they respond by exemplifying their ethnic identity. Consequently, the community relations problems for the police may increase independently of any action the police might take.

Summary of Issues

An important conclusion which can be drawn from the data is the differential distribution of encounters between various social groups. The first major dichotomy between police-public experience is defined by the situation in which the encounter takes place. More people initiated contact with the police than are approached by the police. The typical person in a consumer encounter with the police will be a young middle-class male. Where dissatisfaction is expressed, it is likely to be in relation to the officer's attitude to the individual or incident. In police initiated adversarial contacts, the persons involved are more likely to be young, unemployed males from ethnic minorities, particularly West Indians. An additional cause of dissatisfaction for a West Indian was the treatment he or she received as a person. The study which took place in Manchester did not reveal any evidence of discriminating behaviour by police officers; however, the data from young black people in London illustrated the deeply held belief that police officers do routinely discriminate against black people. The evidence in this latter study suggested hatred of the police was part of the fabric of their perceptions of an ethnic identity.

Determinants of Behaviour

It was established from the outset that the purpose of police community relations training was to influence the behaviour of police officers towards citizens in their joint encounters. Even a casual observer would concede that most human behaviour is purposive and not a random response to the environment. In this regard, two major contributors to the research on the relationship between attitudes and social behaviour, Ajzen and Fishbein (1980), have developed a Theory of Reasoned Action. The theory assumes that behaviours are designed to achieve some specific outcome or intention by the actor. The person's intention is a "function of two basic determinants, one based in nature and the other reflecting social influence" (p. 6). Before engaging in the behaviour, the actor evaluates the positive or negative consequences of performing it, resulting in an "attitude towards the behaviour". In simple terms it is the assessment of the individual as to whether the particular behaviour is a good or a bad thing to do. The second determinant of the intention of the person is his or her perception of the social pressures which exist either to perform or not perform the behaviour; for example, if the behaviour is something that "everyone is doing", then it is more likely that the behaviour will be performed than in circumstances where such pressures do not exist. This factor is termed the "subjective norm". Using these two factors, Azjen and Fishbein argue that it is possible to predict social behaviours.

Previous theories have discussed the importance of an individual's attitude towards a particular target or thing. For example, it has been argued that a person's behaviour towards some minority group, such as West Indians, would determine whether they would employ them or not. Azjen and Fishbein argue that this is an inadequate basis on which to predict social behaviour because according to their theory "the degree to which people like or dislike blacks may have little to do with whether or not they hired blacks. Instead this behaviour is assumed to be determined by the person's attitude towards hiring blacks and by his subjective norm" (Azjen & Fishbein, 1980, p. 8). A person who strongly dislikes blacks may nevertheless believe that hiring blacks will lead to more positive than negative consequences. His attitude towards hiring blacks will be positive and he may, therefore, intend to hire blacks and actually do so. This argument is consistent with findings reported by Cruse and Rubin (1973) who found expressions of high levels of prejudice in police officers, but a marked lack of discriminatory behaviour. In these circumstances either the police officers were inhibited by social pressures to behave in a discriminatory fashion or they perceived some negative consequences for behaving in such a manner, for example, through punitive action by the disciplinary procedures of the police force.

Azjen and Fishbein argue that attitudes towards targets, personality traits, and demographic characteristics are of potential importance but do not constitute an integral part of their theory; instead, they are considered external variables. This point is not disputed here, but it is important to note that these external variables make an important contribution to understanding the impact that police community relations training can make on the modification of police officer behaviour.

Social Psychology of the Police

So far, evidence has been presented to outline the circumstances in which police behaviour causes annoyance or offence to citizens. The theory of reasoned action would see such behaviour as an intended consequence on the part of the police officer. This assumption ignores the proposition that encounters with certain people can never be without conflict because of the attitudes of those people. With the exception of the latter issue, psychology can explore the possible causes of police behaviour which are deemed by citizens to be undesirable.

The characteristics of inappropriate police behaviour form a continuum from rudeness to outright hostility and offensiveness. Behaviour at the more acceptable end of the continuum may be simply the result of a lack of commitment to professional behaviour caused by a general cynicism and negative perception of people generally. There is substantial and clear evidence that exposure to police work involves a period of socialization, leading to significant changes in personality measures (Sterling, 1972; Van Maanen, 1975; Butler & Cochrane, 1977; Butler, 1979). These studies have been conducted in the United States and England; the latter study included a comparison of police officers from both countries.

The changes that occur during the socialization process produce police officers with enhanced self assertion, self esteem, and a propensity to view many groups in society more unfavourably (Butler, 1975; Sterling, 1972). It has been argued by Butler (1975) that the development of self assertive personalities with high self esteem and the tendency to see people in a more negative light are two elements of the same process, namely a response to cognitive dissonance. The anticipatory socialization period which recruits undergo before becoming police officers involves a period in which positive occupational images are internalized by the recruits concerning many aspects of police work. The conflicts between these internalized perceptions of police work and the reality of that work have been identified by a number of studies (Niederhoffer, 1967; Skolnick, 1975; Butler, 1979). During this period of "reality shock", police officers are faced with re-adjusting their views of police work, their views of themselves, and, in some contexts, their views of the world in general. People who take an opinion or have beliefs about matters which are central to their working world will have occasions when their beliefs, or actions stemming from them, will be challenged. The more central the belief, the more strongly the challenge will be resisted, and a well documented strategy of resistance is to devalue the status or group making the challenge (Aronson, Turner, & Carlsmith 1963; Cohen, 1959, 1964).

Significant correlations have been found between job satisfaction and cynicism in both English and American police officers (Lester & Butler, 1980). In another American study, police officers who were internally controlled (Rotter, 1966) were found to express higher levels of job satisfaction (Lester & Genz, 1978). This finding was repeated in English police officers (Creek, 1980). In the latter study externally controlled individuals, that is, those who believed their lives were controlled by fate, tended to be aggressive and more dogmatic (as measured by the Eysenck-Wilson's Tough-Tender Minded Personality Test). The study also included measures of performance ratings by sergeants. Overall, externally controlled officers were seen as being poor performers who lacked a knowledge of their beat, did not use their initiative, had poor problem solving capacity, displayed little intelligent behaviour, lacked enthusiasm, were unreliable, and did not get on well with their colleagues. Externally controlled individuals viewed their work as unpleasant and frustrating, whereas internally controlled officers had a higher level of identification with the organization.

These findings have two important implications in the context of community relations training. First, resistance to the challenging communications which community relations training often presents may seriously negate any chances of encouraging appropriate behavior. Second, the development of negative perceptions of people and general cynicism may seriously reduce the officers' capacity to interact harmoniously with many groups of people, but particularly those who are ascribed relatively low status.

The role of job satisfaction is an important element within the psychological orientation of police officers. The membership of police forces by alienated and dissatisfied police officers is a matter of deep concern because at the end of the day the quality of the service given to the community depends on the commitment of individual officers. Alienated and discontented police officers are unlikely to provide the best service.

The evidence from the literature on police socialization attributes rude or off-hand behaviour by police officers to their tendency to view the world cynically, to devalue certain groups in society, and to have assertive personalities which do not inhibit such behaviour. It is not so much that they deliberately intend to be rude, but such behavior is not inhibited by internal values and beliefs. More extreme patterns of behavior may be the result of deliberate intentions to offend or annoy certain individuals. Anti-minority attitudes may be the external variables which, in circumstances not inhibiting offensive behavior, may motivate actions. The rationale of certain aspects of police-community relations training before 1983 were based on the notion of the modification of racially prejudiced attitudes.

An Examination of the Effects of Community Relations Training

In 1980 a project was commenced to examine the impact of community relations training on the attitudes of police recruits (Butler & Tharme, 1981). A second study compared the responses of recruits to those of experienced constables with more than five years police experience. The first study was conducted using 96 police recruits at a police training centre covering the Midlands of England. The study had a longitudinal design, taking data on the recruits first day at the training centre and then 10 weeks later on the completion of their course. As part of a battery of instruments, a small "prejudice scale" and a group perception questionnaire based on the Semantic Differential Technique was designed. The responses to the prejudice scale were moderate on the first test and changed towards more prejudice during training. The perceptions of Asians were relatively neutral on entry, and the changes which occurred during training were minor. The perceptions of West Indians were more unfavourable than Asians on entry and did not change during training. The officers' perceptions of two other groups, Tinkers (groups of people who travel the country in caravans undertaking casual work) and Criminals were substantially more unfavorable than the perception of West Indians, although there was some change towards more favourable perceptions during training. A significant change also took place in their responses to the Internal/External Locus of Control, with the officers showing more inclination to believe in External Locus of Control at the completion of their training.

The result of this study showed that police officers do discriminate between two ethnic minority groups in terms of their perceptions of those groups; and furthermore, what could be termed white minority groups, namely Criminals and Tinkers, were considered far less favourably than black minority groups. However, it does appear that the perceptions of black minority groups are more resistant to change during training than those of white minority groups.

The second study was conducted at the same training centre using the same test instruments and methods after there had been some modification of the training course. In the second study, half the group of 75 recruits were trained under the previous system which had been examined in the first study and the other half of the recruit group were trained under a modified system where more emphasis was placed upon small group learning and greater interaction between staff and recruits (Butler, 1982).

The data for the first test had some similarities with the first study. During training the prejudice scale score declined; the perceptions of West Indians remained static with the exception of the dimension respectful-disrespectful which changed significantly towards disrespectful; and the perception of Asians became more favourable reaching statistical significance of five dimensions. Further evidence was obtained using regression analysis which showed a relationship between the new teaching method and a composite scale of "Asian Prejudice" but no such relationship with the scale "West Indian Prejudice". This result suggested the new teaching method was more likely to change the perception of Asians in a favourable direction. An analysis of variance on the two composite scales showed a significant reduction in "Asian Prejudice" during training, but no change in "West Indian Prejudice".

The comparison group consisted of constables with more than 5 years police experience from a large urban police force. Data were obtained from 72 constables undergoing in-force training. These data were then compared with the data obtained for the police recruits on the first test in the second study. Whilst the experienced officers did not hold extreme views, they were significantly more prejudiced on the measures used than the recruits. The comparisons of the perceptions of recruits and experienced constables showed the two groups had similar perceptions of Asians; the experienced constables saw Asians as more friendly, hardworking and respectful than the recruits. The perceptions of West Indians by the experienced constables were more unfavourable on all dimensions, and for 16 of the 17 dimensions the differences were statistically significant.

Multiple regression analysis using the composite scales "Asian Prejudice" and "West Indian Prejudice" showed that police experience exerts a greater degree of influence on the perceptions of officers in respect to West Indians and less influence with respect to Asians. Further regression analysis showed that the age of officers was a significant influence on the perceptions of Asians, tending to produce more favourable perceptions with age. In respect to the perceptions of West Indians, aging produced more positive perceptions but police experience was a more significant factor in this process.

Conclusions Which can be Drawn from the Studies
(1)   There was no evidence of significant anti-minority perceptions on entry to the police force.
(2)   Police officers do make distinctions between the two ethnic minority groups, West Indians and Asians.
(3)   Other minority groups, not based on race, are seen more unfavourably than racial groups.
(4)   Training did not significantly change perceptions of these racial groups.
(5)   Some changes in perceptions and attitudes can be achieved by training, but these are related to the teaching methods (i.e., small groups and interaction between recruits and instruction) and to Asians and not West Indians.
(6)   Experienced police officers, in comparison with recruits, have more unfavourable perceptions of West Indians, but their perceptions of Asians are very similar, and more favourable on some dimensions, whilst less favourable on others.
(7)   There appears to be some once-and-for-all change in the constables' perceptions of West Indians in an unfavourable direction. Thereafter the perception of West Indians tends to become more favourable.

Police Experience with Citizens
The data cited so far have been concerned with the citizen's perceptions of encounters with the police. There are few observations of the perceptions of police officers of encounters with the public. Southgate (1981) reports data from police officers and observational evidence which shed some light on the other side of this issue. Based on questionnaire data, more police officers reported having experienced difficulties with young West Indians than with young Asians. Almost half of the constables in the survey reported that they had never had a

difficult encounter with an Asian, whereas only 20% made the same observation in relation to West Indians. The difficulties experienced with Asians most frequently related to the complex family and social networks of the Asian community. The most common difficulties experienced in relation to West Indians concerned making enquiries and arrests where officers reported being obstructed and resisted by the individual or by hostile crowds which gathered on the arrival of the police.

A recent study (Butler, 1985) where constables and sergeants were asked to report the frequencies with which they experienced various difficulties in encounters with ethnic minorities showed similar differences between Asians and Caribbean people. Generally, both constables and sergeants reported experiencing difficulties more frequently with Caribbeans compared with Asians. The results indicated that in encounters with Caribbeans, they experienced being obstructed, verbally abused, accused of racial prejudice 'sometimes', and feelings that the citizen did not like them and did not trust them on more than half the encounters.

The need for police officers to maintain control in encounters in the face of challenges to their authority has been discussed. The relevance of this observation is extended when these challenges are interpreted as actual threats to the officers' well being. Muir (1977) showed how perceptions of physical danger act as a catalyst in police-citizen encounters. As the perceived level of danger increases, so police officers are more likely to take steps to protect themselves which may lead to precipitative action by the officer. The alternative, as the officer sees it, is to wait until he has been attacked. Thus, in the face of actual or predicted hostility, an officer will respond in a manner which may be interpreted as unnecessarily hostile by the citizen. The intended consequence of the behaviour, as far as the officer is concerned, is to protect himself; the unintended, but equally real, consequence as far as the citizen is concerned, is resentment of the officer's attitude or actions.

Research by Packham and Barker (1984) found the level of aggressive responses by officers to videotaped vignettes of encounters with citizens was related to the length of experience of the officers. The aggressive content of the verbal responses by police recruits were similar to the responses made by experienced constables, but were less aggressive than the responses made by constables with between one and two years police experience. The degree of aggression of the responses was also associated with the levels of personal confidence about the encounters expressed by the officers. The officers who reported the least confidence were those who would tend to respond in the more aggressive manner.

It is unlikely to be a coincidence that the groups in society which report the greatest frequency of dissatisfaction with police are those who the police see as difficult. Whilst the problem should not be minimized, neither should it be construed as evidence that there is a gulf between the police and the community. The question to be addressed concerns cause and effect. It would be naive to assume that the fault lies entirely with the police, the solution being to increase the amount of training to change the attitudes of police officers. The facts show the complexity of the issues, the causes and possible solutions.

The theory of reasoned action (Ajzen & Fishbein, 1980) argues for an understanding of behaviour in relation to the intentions of the actor.

If this is the case, can it explain why police officers appear to behave in ways which do not apparently meet with universal approval? Two examples can be cited from the literature which indicate behavioural and normative beliefs which would encourage improper police behaviour. The first example is cited by Van Maanen (1978) who describes an encounter between a patrol man and a speeding motorist:

> Police to motorist stopped for speeding:
> "May I see your driving license, please?"
>
> Motorist:
> "Why the hell are you picking on me and not somewhere else looking for some real criminals?"
>
> Policemen:
> "Because you are an asshole, that's why ... but I didn't know that until you opened your mouth."

In this case the police officer's behaviour could be predicted as a response to a challenge to both his authority and professional judgment. The officer had the power to ask the citizen to act in a particular way, namely produce his driving license, but he sought to go further to ensure that the proper balance of respect and status was re-established by belittling the subject.

The second example can be found in an early work on policing. In his examination of violence and the police, Westley (1970) argued that a factor sustaining the undue use of force by police officers on suspected criminals was the police officers' belief, that such methods were accepted as legitimate by the community in cases where serious crimes were being investigated. In short, the behaviour was an intentional means of achieving evidence of a person's involvement in a crime, encouraged by the subjective norm which legitimized the action.

To return to the example of the impolite police officer, such behaviour could be motivated by the behavioural belief that police officers should re-establish their symbolic authority when it is challenged. Such behaviour could also occur when there were no strong attitudes inhibiting the behaviour. As has been described earlier, a cynical view of people is an apparent consequence of a career in law enforcement. Thus, if police officers come to devalue people as 'people', they will be less inhibited towards behaving improperly toward them. Put simply, if a police officer does not care what certain groups of people think about him and the police force, his behavioural intentions are unlikely to encourage him to always act appropriately.

What can Police Community Relations Training Achieve?

The purpose of police community relations training was said to promote socially acceptable behaviour in police officers in their encounters with citizens. Clearly, there are limits as to what can be achieved by training. In principle, training in social skills and professional ethics can create the foundation upon which police officers can base their behaviour. Steps can be taken to alert officers to the 'reality shock' of police work and enable them to recognize the dangers of certain modes of behavioural response to the rigours of police work. Training officers in physical defence techniques could increase levels of confidence in resisting physical attacks.

The major contribution training can make is to raise the officers' levels of consciousness to the need to treat all citizens as people and to be aware of cultural differences which must be observed in encounters. Training should also give the officer confidence in his own professional competence which, in turn, will reduce his anxiety in encounters and thereby enable him to make better decisions.

The Wider Issues - Some Concluding Thoughts

The limits of community relations training are set by society itself and by the police organization. As long as racial prejudice and perceived inequalities exist in society, the police, as the symbolic representatives of the power of society, will continue to be the victim of minority animosity. There is little the police can do about this issue as is illustrated by the data from the young black people in London. Their views of the police in most cases were apparently not based on first-hand experience with the police (Small, 1983). Increasing crime and demands for the police to combat the problem will lead inevitably to more young people, particularly the unemployed and West Indians, (Smith, 1983), being in contact and in conflict situations with the police. Thus there will be an increase in the number of occasions in which these groups will experience adversarial relationships with the police.

The police as an organization carry a responsibility to create the climate in which police community relations can be improved. In the face of increasing demands on the police and either static or decreasing resources, police forces must be realistic about how they will continue to cope with the demand. The soft option may be to ignore the relationship between demand and resources, but experience shows that the quality of police services will decline as officers are forced by circumstances to 'cut corners'. Research has shown that officers who do not feel able to influence their environment become alienated and cynical about their work and about people. No amount of training will encourage an officer to feel professionally committed to work which he and all his colleagues know is below the standard which should be given to the community. Police forces may feel that it is preferable to decide to suspend part of their service which may be seen as peripheral to their main responsibilities, and invest the resources in activities which are seen as priorities by the community. This strategy would indicate to officers that the Force is committed to certain standards of quality and would encourage them to maintain these standards. Therefore, improvements in management training, systems and style must be seen as part of the total approach to police community relations. Recent developments in participative management systems (Butler, 1984) will generate a co-operative and professional climate with the force, encouraging leadership and professional standards.

In conclusion, police forces should recognize the danger of placing total reliance on training as a means of maintaining or improving police community relations. By adopting this notion, the police force will inevitably subsume societal and organizational problems within the individuals who are to receive the training. The bureaucratic ethos of police organizations encourages the sometimes mistaken identification of 'people problems' to the exclusion of 'organizational problems'.

REFERENCES

Ajzen, I., & Fishbein, M. (1980). Understanding attitudes and predicting social behaviour, Englewood Cliffs, NJ: Prentice Hall Inc.

Aronson, E., & Turner, J.A., & Carlsmith, J.M. (1963). Communicator credibility and communication discrepancy as determinants of opinion change. Journal of Abnormal and Social Psychology, 67, 31-36.

Black, D.J., & Reiss, A.J. (1967). Studies in Law Enforcement in Major Metropolitan Areas, Field Survey III, Volume 2, Washington DC: US Government Printing Office.

Butler, A.J.P. (1975). Becoming a Police Officer: A Study of the Psychological Implications of a Career in Law Enforcement. Unpublished Undergraduate Dissertation, Department of Psychology, University of Birmingham.

Butler, A.J.P. (1979). A Study of the Occupational Perceptions of Police Officers. Doctoral Thesis, Faculty of Law, Universty of Birmingham.

Butler, A.J.P. (1982). An examination of the influence of training and work experience on the attitudes and perceptions of police constables. Paper given at the conference on Psychology and Law, Swansea.

Butler, A.J.P. (1984). Police Management. Aldershot: Gower Publishing Co. Ltd.

Butler, A.J.P. (1985). Unpublished research notes, West Midlands Police.

Butler, A.J.P., & Cochrane, R. (1977). An examination of some elements of the personality of police officers and their implications. Journal of Police Science and Administration, 5, 441-450.

Butler, A.J.P., & Tharme, K. (1981). An examination of the effectiveness of community relations training. Unpublished report of West Midlands Police.

Cohen, A.R. (1959). Some Implications of Self Esteem for Social Influence. In C.I. Morland & I.L. Janie (eds.) Personality and persuasibility. New Haven, Conn: Yale University Press.

Cohen, A.R. (1964). Attitude change and social influence. New York: Basic Books Inc.

Creek, D.C. (1980). To determine the main factors which affect the probationary constable's performance during the first nine months in the West Midlands Police Force. Master's Thesis, University of Aston, Birmingham.

Cruse, D., & Rubin, J. (1973). Determinants of police behaviour: A summary. Washington, DC, LEAA, US Government of Justice.

Lester, D., & Butler, A.J.P. (1980). Job satisfaction and cynicism in police: A cross national comparison. Police Studies, 2, No 4, 44-45.

Lester, D., & Genz, J. (1978). Internal-external locus of control, experience as a police officer and job satisfaction in municipal police officers. Journal of Police Science and Administration, 6, 479-481.

Muir, W.K. (1977). Police: Street corner politicians, Chicago: University of Chicago Press.

Niederhoffer, A. (1967). Behind the shield: The police in urban society. New York: Anchor Books.

Packham, R.D., & Barker, C. (1984). Aggressive vs concilitory verbal responses of police officers.

Rotter, J.B. (1966). Generalized expectancies for internal versus external control of reinforcement. Psychological Monographs: General and Applied, 80.

Skolnick, J.H. (1975). Justice without trial: Law enforcement in democratic society. New York: J. Wiley & Sons.

Small, S. (1983). A group of young black people. London: Policy Studies Institute.

Smith, D.J. (1983). _A survey of police officers_. London: Policy Studies Institute.

Southgate, P., & Ekblom, P. (1984). _Contacts between police and public_. London: Home Office Research Unit.

Sterling, J.W. (1972). _Changes in role concepts of police officers_. Gaithersburg Md: International Association of Chiefs of Police.

Tuck, M., & Southgate, P. (1981). _Ethnic minorities, crime and policing_. London: HMSO, Home Office Research and Planning Unit.

Van Maanen, J. (1975). Socialisation: A longitudinal examination of attitudes in a police department. _Administrative Science Quarterly_, _20_, 207-228.

Van Maanen, J. (1978). The Asshole. In Manning, P.K., & Van Maanen, J. (Eds.) _Policing: A view from the streets_. Goodyear Publishing Co.

Westley, W.A. (1970). _Violence and the police_. Cambridge, MA: MIT Press.

THE PUBLIC AND THE POLICE: TRAINING IMPLICATIONS OF THE DEMAND FOR A NEW
MODEL POLICE OFFICER

DONALD G. DUTTON

When Robert Peel presented his "Bill for improving Police in and near
the Metropolis" to the British parliament in 1829, he faced considerable
opposition, based somewhat on fear that the notorious activities of the
pre-Revolutionary French police would be duplicated in England. Indeed,
a parliamentary report in 1818 recommended against the establishment of a
police force, arguing that rational and humane laws, an enlightened
magistracy, and "above all, the moral habits and opinions of the people"
(Reith, 1938) were sufficient to ensure both the maintenance of order and
protection of individual rights.

Peel's strategy for countering such opposition was to present a
modified proposal (he initially wanted a national police force),
buttressed by impressive data on increases in criminal committals, for a
force to preserve the public order. The initial emphasis, therefore, was
on the police force's function of maintaining peace, rather than on its
law enforcement function. To this day, order maintenance and service
functions comprise over 80% of a police officer's time, while law
enforcement duties take up only about 10-15% (Wilson, 1969).

Many writers have noticed the apparent paradox which exists in the
interaction between public and police. While numerous surveys attest to
almost universal satisfaction among members of the public with the
police, the speeches of senior officials decry the deteriorating quality
of the relationship. Morris (1979) contrasted the results of a British
Government survey, in which "83% of those interviewed professed to have
great respect for the police" (Morris, 1979, p. 22) and a subsequent
survey by Belson (1978) which reported 98% of the adults saying they
respected the police, 93% liked them and 90% trusted them, with the
statement of Banton (1964) that since the end of World War II police
forces have feared deteriorating public relations, due, in part, to an
increased public readiness to question authority of any kind.

In the United States, O'Brien (1978) cited Momboise (1967): "That the
police are disliked throughout America there can be no doubt. Many polls
have proven conclusively the existence of that dislike". This, despite a
survey by the National Opinions Research Centre which indicated a
generally high public opinion of the police, a Gallup poll in 1966, and a
Harris poll the following year which showed general public support of the
police (cited in O'Brien, 1978, p. 303).

Cain (1977) said that "policemen themselves combine a paranoia about
loss of public confidence (which has never been substantiated) with a
contradictory belief that the 'mass of decent, respectable people' are
behind them" (p. 158). Koenig (1975) reported that police perceptions of
public respect for them can be remarkably accurate. In a survey of both
public and police opinion he reported that Royal Canadian Mounted Police,

(RCMP), members perceived the general public's evaluation of the RCMP to be slightly more favourable than in fact it was. RCMP perceptions of the public's evaluation of other police forces (highly positive) were also accurate. Morris (1979) argued that it may be helpful to distinguish between police-public attitudes, based on the belief of each group, and police-public relations, which are the outcome of feelings derived from personal encounters or experiences. She argued that while studies may show a high degree of satisfaction with police, there is always a dissatisfied minority which is almost universally made up of individuals who have had frequent contact with the police. The paradox referred to earlier may be explained if we note that these persons will be the police's main basis for perceptions of public attitudes unless they systematically expose themselves to broader samples.

Surveys of General Public Satisfaction

Courtis' (1970) Toronto survey examined the quality of relations between the police and the public and included numerous questions aimed at determining factors which contributed to police-public relations. Courtis' respondents did not have a particularly favourable impression of the quality of relations. When asked about the causes of bad police-public relations, the most frequent responses were the "belligerent/aggressive" behaviour of police, poor publicity, public failure to help police-public relations, and punishment by the police for traffic offences. Remedies mentioned most frequently were increased public and media knowledge of the police, more courteous police behaviour, and the inculcation among the public of respect for the police.

Koenig (1974) surveyed attitudes toward the police among a sample of British Columbia voters. He found that the overall evaluation of police was quite favourable. Just under 95 percent of the public rated their local police as good or very good. Koenig added, though, that individuals had a tendency to believe that other people did not have attitudes as favourable as their own. This shared misunderstanding may account for the decline in favourable evaluations of local police. It may also explain, in part, the underestimation by police of the favour in which the public holds them.

Examination of differences between age groups in their evaluation of police revealed that evaluation became more favourable among older groups. This may be due to an increased likelihood of negative contact with police for younger respondents or to an historical shift in social role expectations, with younger respondents first evidencing that shift. Nevertheless, even among the youngest (19-25 years) group of respondents, about 88 percent gave the police an evaluation of good or very good. Little difference was evident between evaluations by men and women, although women were slightly more favourable.

Koenig also looked at how contact with police affects evaluations. In general, he found that contact with police - as juror, witness, acquaintance of police, or even as receiver of a traffic ticket - had a negligible effect on evaluations. Victimization, however, resulted in less favourable evaluations: what Koenig called "paradoxical" was the finding that "attitudes toward the police are more favourable among those with no need for the police than they are among members of households which have been victimized by crime in the past year. Such a paradox is probably explained by people's unrealistically high expectations of the police" (pp. 69-70).

Individuals may have a generally high regard for police which is maintained in the absence of contact. Victimization, in particular, and contact with police, in general, may demonstrate that there is actually little police can accomplish, and the citizen's and victim's expectations go unfulfilled.

Further analysis of the factors associated with police evaluation and support in B.C. was performed by Thornton (1975). Of greatest importance was the impact of "police experience", a measure of experience or knowledge of police misbehaviour. The more "police experience", the more negative evaluations provided. This should hardly be surprising given the inherent negative bias of the experience measure. The more neutral measure "police contact" (whether respondents had called police, been arrested, or received a traffic ticket in the past twelve months) was not related to ratings of police. Nonetheless, Thornton's analysis underlines the importance of examining experiential factors in addition to demographic factors.

Hylton (1980) examined public attitudes toward crime and the police in Regina, by asking respondents to react to 75 statements about crime and the police. Factor analysis of these statements resulted in them being grouped into seven scales. These were: (1) fear of crime; (2) the seriousness of the crime and measures required to cope with crime; (3) communication with the public; (4) police powers; (5) adequacy of law enforcement; (6) the scope of police services; and (7) police integrity. These factors were examined as to how they related to each other and to the characteristics of respondents, including contact with crime and the police.

Overall, Hylton stated that "the vast majority of Regina citizens have positive opinions about the Regina Police Department." Attitudes were found, though, to depend on contact with police, fear of crime, and victimization, among other factors. For example, the number of times neighbours had been in contact with the police was associated with a negative view of police competence. Similarly, if the respondent had been arrested, he or she was less likely to view the police as competent.

Corrado, Glackman, Roesch, Evans, and Leger (1980) analyzed data collected as part of the Greater Vancouver Victimization Survey, undertaken in 1978. Four of the survey questions assessed whether members of the public felt that their local police had done a good, average or poor job of enforcing laws; promptly responded to calls; were approachable or easy to talk to; and supplied information to the public on ways to reduce crime. The findings replicated previous findings of generally positive public ratings of police: more than half of the respondents assessed the police as having done a good job, particularly with respect to police approachability and law enforcement, while only a small proportion of the sample rated the police as having done a poor job for any item.

In examining the factors associated with evaluations of police, Corrado, et al. found that, although differences in ratings across types of police contact were not substantial, individuals whose last contact with police was as crime victims were more likely to view them in the most positive manner in regard to response and approachability and did not rate police appreciably lower than those with no contact on the other two performance items. In general, individuals whose last contact was for a traffic violation did not rate police as positively as those who participated in crime prevention programs or who were crime witnesses. Corrado et al. found few differences with respect to demographic characteristics.

Studies of public attitudes toward the police have often focused exclusively on demographic variables. Numerous U.S. studies examining race exclusively have yielded inconclusive results. White and Menke (1978) complained of conflicting conclusions, with three images of public opinions of the police resulting - very positive, negative, and ambivalent - and of the methodological limitations of such survey research, specifically the lack of guiding theory.

In a test of the relative explanatory power of demographic variables versus experiential variables, Klein, Webb, and DiSanto (1978) sought to replicate in a Canadian context (Calgary) a study conducted in Seattle by Smith and Hawkins (1973). Klein et al. published the warning that while the dearth of Canadian research into attitudes toward the police results in a reliance on research findings from the United States, Canada has a unique social and cultural history which must be taken into account. This is especially true if one subscribes to the argument that attitudes and behaviours are the result of social and demographic variables. Yet the literature reviewed here, both American and Canadian, supports instead the argument that attitudes toward the police are the result of interaction, contact, and experience with the police, independent of cultural and other demographic differences. Both American and Canadian studies thus contribute to an understanding of the determinants of public attitudes and both point to experience and expectation as more potent explanatory variables rather than demographic differences.

Finally, even if the unique effects of individual difference variables could be determined, they remain something about which little can be done. While it may be of academic interest to know which particular social stratum or neighborhood has especially negative or positive attitudes towards the police, such information does not point immediately to policy. It is not "action research". What is missing is the key set of explanatory variables that describe the nature of citizen-police interaction that brought about the dissatisfaction.

Surveys of Public Satisfaction with Specific Programmes

In recent years police departments themselves have begun to use surveys to measure specific citizen satisfaction with particular programmes initiated by police. This approach seems more productive than broad surveys of general attitudes toward police. Typically, after a new police programme has been in operation for a fixed period of time, citizens are surveyed [for example, through use of "random digit dialing" (Pate, Ferrara, Bowers, & Lorence, 1976; Tuchfaiber, & Klecka, 1976) to estimate the impact of the programme on citizen satisfaction]. Because the programmes involved are relatively specific in nature, more precise profiles of the types of police policy and nature of interaction with police can be drawn. For example, changes in citizen satisfaction (before and after survey measures) occurred for a "Safe Streets Unit" in Dade County Florida (Lougheed, 1973), and in Baltimore, Maryland (Furstenberg & Wellford, 1973). In both cases citizen satisfaction increased and the evaluation of this increase was made via survey.

Surveys of this sort have been instrumental in revealing some police misconceptions about citizen satisfaction. Cirzanckas and Feist (1975), for example, found that while a change in police service did have an appreciable impact on citizen satisfaction, it was more a function of perceptions about the quality of the environment than the extent and level of police service. Ironically, "broken windows" and other signs of neighborhood deterioration also can serve as cues for crimes such as vandalism (Wilson & Kelling, 1982). These authors point out that community disorder (one sign of which is disrepair) is a frequent precursor to crime, because it signals a breakdown in informal community controls. Wilson and Kelling suggest the following:

(1) Police "foot patrols" while ineffective at stopping crime directly, can improve citizen attitudes toward the police.

(2) Police walking the beat had higher morale, greater job satisfaction and a more favourable attitude toward citizens in their neighborhoods than did police in patrol cars.

(3) Police foot patrols heightened a sense of public order, returning police to their role of order maintenance and thereby lowered citizen's fear which stems not only from being victimized by crime but from being harassed by disorderly people.

(4) By re-establishing contact between police and the citizens,
   (a) citizens may have felt that they had an authority to listen to their complaints and anxieties rather than feeling cut off from "faceless officers in patrol cars";
   (b) police would establish open lines of communication into the community and could develop better "distant early warning systems" about potential community problems through utilizing informal community contacts (much of this is lost in car patrols).

Furthermore, Bordua and Tifft (1973) found that citizen satisfaction was more greatly enhanced by a "counselling manner" on the part of police than by "vigorous tactics". In other words, a chief determinant of citizen satisfaction that derives from citizen - police interaction is the citizens' perception that they are being listened to and that the police have a genuine concern about the citizens' problems. One implication of this finding is that citizens may be more satisfied by a police suggestion that they cooperate to prevent recurrences of the event that contributed to the citizen's apprehension rather than the police's charging off to "do something about it". If police are honest and straightforward with citizens about their limitations in dealing with certain kinds of crime, it leads to no decreases in citizen satisfaction (Hahn, 1971b; Sumrall, Roberts, & Farmer, 1982). As it turns out, this finding applies as well to citizen requests for service.

Public Requests for Police Service

Changing public expectations can be reflected in changing requests for service. Douthit (1975), in an historical examination of police roles, stated that the present trend is toward an increased non-enforcement role, as opposed to one aimed primarily at crime control. This contention is shared by many, as we shall see, but Douthit argued that the trend is not new, having developed in the World War I period but replaced in the 1920s and 1930s by a "war on crime" emphasis that discouraged experimentation with new police roles, and by the development of police professionalism measured in terms of efficiency in crime control.

Banton (1964) has said: "the policeman on patrol is primarily a 'peace officer' rather than a 'law officer'. Relatively little time is spent enforcing the law in the sense of arresting offenders; far more is spent 'keeping the peace' by supervising the beat and responding to requests for assistance" (p. 127). Morris (1979) reviewed British studies and concluded that a "relatively small amount of the policeman's working day ...is spent on fighting crime." Pinch and Naylor (1973), for example, found that 59% of calls to police could be defined as service requests and the remaining 41% as requests for law enforcement, with a higher proportion of service calls (75%) in a rural area. Bercal (1970) found that only 16% of all calls to the Detroit police emergency number in 1968 were crime related. Cumming, Cumming and Edell (1965) found that about 60% of calls for service were for support related to personal rather than criminal problems. Lilly (1978) cited numerous other American studies in the 1960s and early 1970s which have found a small proportion of police time devoted to law enforcement. In his own study, Lilly found that 69% of calls to the Newport, Kentucky, police were unrelated to law enforcement. More recently, Levens and Dutton's (1980) classification of requests made to the Vancouver Police during 1975 found that 49.3% of calls (amounting to 52% of police patrol time) were classified as law enforcement, and 46.6% of calls (49.3% of time) were classified as service. Although classification systems may affect the magnitude of these figures ("service" calls may, for instance, result in a charge), it should be clear that public requests are predominantly for social service rather than for law enforcement.

To the extent, then, that public expectations are reflected in the nature of public requests, they represent a real expectation of social service, of policeman as philosopher, guide and friend (Cumming et al., 1965). A growing literature cites the role of the policeman as arbiter in domestic crisis intervention (e.g., Lindman, 1974; Levens & Dutton, 1980). Cumming et al. (1965) have argued that the social service function of police is in conflict with the law enforcement function, on the assumption that it is difficult for a social agent to exercise both support and control at the same time, such that any agent tends, therefore, to specialize in one or the other (see article by Steinhilper in this volume). They argued that the policeman's role is, by definition and by law, explicitly concerned with control—crime prevention and law enforcement—and only latently with support. Thus, when a policeman is called upon for social service, "the balance between support and control has shifted, and he is acting overtly as a supportive agent and only latently in his controlling role. He has, at the same time, changed from a professional to an amateur" (p. 277). Although law enforcement is explicitly the primary police role (Kelling, 1978; Task Force on Policing in Ontario, 1974), social service is most requested and is a function for which police have generally received little training (Levens, 1980). Dutton (1981) noted that in police training, the ratio of community service and order maintenance functions to law enforcement functions is the reverse of that experienced in police activity. McCabe and Sutcliffe (1978) suggested that public expectations of police may not be realized, not because of any lack of concern on the part of police, but because:

the three historic functions of police services, crime prevention and detection, law enforcement...and the easement of annoyance and anxiety, are differing priorities in police organizations...The last...seems to be taken with least seriousness, although in volume it is by far the greatest (pp. 86-87).

Police Response

Policing in North America is primarily reactive in character (Reiss, 1971). "Police departments are organized to respond to citizen requests for service rather than to initiate police intervention" (Shearing, 1972, p. 77). It follows then that because a high proportion of requests are for "social service", a high proportion of police response will be devoted to social service. Wycoff, Susmilch and Eisenbart (1980) reviewed nine studies of police response to calls for service. Categories of citizen requests were (1) information, (2) service, (3) order maintenance, (4) law enforcement, (5) traffic, (6) other. Needless to say, definitions may vary by study and jurisdiction. Also, at the time of dispatch the eventual classification of a request may be unknown. A "domestic disturbance", for example, might be either order maintenance, law enforcement or service depending on what unfolds when the officers attend. Many requests develop in ways that a dispatch code cannot capture.

Wycoff et al. found that police dispatches were primarily for law enforcement calls (30.8%), closely followed by order maintenance (27.4%) and then by service (17.0%) and traffic calls (11.7%). These rank orderings are quite consistent from study to study and lead to the conclusion that about 7 out of 10 dispatches of police cars are not law enforcement related. Of the calls categorized by Bercal (1970), in which 84% were not "crime" related, a police patrol was dispatched in 64% of all calls; about 61% of all dispatches were for non-crime related matters. Shearing (1972) found that of the 47% of calls reporting trouble which were received directly from citizens, 82% resulted in a patrol car being dispatched. Shearing concluded that a dispatch was the normative rule of response. Of the approximately 50% of calls for "personal support" reported by Cumming et al. (1965), a car was sent about three-quarters of the time. Of the 223 domestic disputes identified by Levens and Dutton (1980) in which a police response was requested, it was given in 117 or 53% of the cases. Even when a patrol car was not dispatched, police generally responded by providing advice or referral.

Nonetheless, Kelling and Fogel (1978) said that "in practice an informal priority system operates and that officers tend to emphasize rapid response time for particular kinds of calls, often delaying their responses to others (Pate et al., 1976). This orientation of police toward an emergency response system has the operational consequence of further defining them in terms of crime functions, while downgrading the importance of public service functions" (p. 161).

Kelling (1978) stated that with the development of preventive, automobile-based patrol came the tactic of increasing the rapidity of response time—the theory being that reducing the interval between crime commission and the arrival of police would increase apprehension, deterrence, and citizen satisfaction, and decrease fear. This theory was, apparently, so convincing that response time has itself become an outcome variable, i.e., an indicator of police effectiveness. Yet studies have revealed that it has no effect on apprehension (Bertram & Vargo, 1976) or on citizen satisfaction (Pate et al., 1976). Citizen satisfaction, rather, depends on the callers certainty that police will arrive when they say they will arrive. As Sumrall, Roberts and Farmer (1982) point out "citizens are just as likely to be satisfied by a department which delivers quicker response. What appears to annoy citizens is a failure to fulfill commitments" (op. cit., pg. 34).

Furthermore, the Kansas City study on police response time (Pate et al., 1976) found that the effect of response time on the capacity of the police to deal with crime was negligible primarily because delays by citizens in reporting crimes made the minutes saved by police insignificant. Goldstein (1979) cites the tremendous emphasis given to police response time by U.S. police forces in the 1970s as consistent with the new police emphasis on "vehicle and communications equipment". As Goldstein points out "much less attention was given in this same period to what the officer does in handling the variety of problems he confronts on arriving" (op. cit., p. 237).

Sumrall, Roberts, and Farmer (1982) cite four studies that suggest citizen satisfaction with police response is not adversely affected by "alternative strategies" (to rapid response). These alternative strategies include referral, and delayed response. What is essential is that the communications operator who takes the call conducts the contact with the citizen with skill and honesty. On the basis of this finding, these authors developed Alternative Strategies for Responding to Police Calls for Service, an elaborate coding and priority setting matrix designed to facilitate the separation of calls requiring immediate assistance (i.e., major personal injury – in progress) from those that can wait (i.e., minor property loss – cold).

Public Expectations and the Police Role

The Sumrall et al. (1982) review suggests that the police occasionally misread what the public expects of them. A consistent rapid response to all calls, for example, is not expected. What then, is the public's view of what the police should do? As it turns out, this view is vague and varies from one jurisdiction to the next (Wycoff, 1982). Wycoff concluded that no adequate data existed that compared police and public views of police behaviour.

Wycoff et al. (1980) examined the potential for reconceptualization of the police role. They categorized the concerns which supported the goals and arguments for reconceptualization (which they said were attributable either to a perceived lack of a mandate or to inadequacies or conflicts in present conceptualizations) as "ideological, representing commitment to the importance of certain role functions or commitment to particular styles of policing or policy formulation; pragmatic managerial, representing a concern for operating the agency effectively or efficiently; and psychological, representing concern for the psychological well-being of officers or members of the public". Wycoff (1982) argues that police labels of activities into "order maintenance", "service", etc., obscures the complexity of the problems police handle; and makes alteration of the police role difficult. Goldstein (1979) echoes this belief. More will be said below about how these categories impede problem oriented policing.

Ideological concerns include the debate about what police should do which, according to Shearing and Leon (1977), has become polarized between advocates of "control" versus "support". Shearing and Leon went on to describe the debate over the police role as comprising two major elements: "expectations concerning what policemen should do and a description of what police actually do" (p. 335). There is no debate, according to Shearing and Leon, that police are "traditionally" expected to fight crime, that policemen spend relatively little time fighting crime, and that activities performed by police should be consistent with expectations. The controversy arises over a difference of opinion as to how this consistency is to be achieved. Shearing and Leon's argument is that this debate has been based on what police should do and what they actually do, but has neglected what police can do and have the authority to do. In their analysis Shearing and Leon concluded that the distinction between social service roles or activities and law enforcement roles or activities is confounded and that these can actually be forged into a "topical unity". They implied that what is needed is for police to rediscover this role; that, apparently, being the locus of discontent.

David, Cowan, Renner, and Moore (1976) and Renner, Groves, and Moore (1976) argued that police-community relations are "a process, not a product". They hypothesized that the nature of the police-community relationship is contained in the match between the expectations and behaviour of police and citizens. The evaluation of the relationship by the police is dependent on the extent to which public behaviour matches police expectations and, similarly, public attitudes toward police depend on the match between police behaviour and public expectation. In such an approach, conflicting expectations can be categorized into those which are easily resolvable (where police agree with unmet public expectations) and those for which resolution is more difficult (where police disagree with public expectations). The finding by many writers that survey answers to specific, concrete questions reveal higher rates of dissatisfaction than do answers to very general questions, e.g., your police rather than the police (Courtis, 1970; Kelling et al., 1974; Morris, 1979; Reiss, 1971) may be due to a tendency among respondents to have more stringent and explicit expectations of local police. Similarly, differences in satisfaction between ethnic groups, between victims and non-victims, and between persons who come into more or less frequent contact with the police may result from differing expectations.

Hahn (1971a) said that police officers often consider service functions as inappropriate or demeaning, as an unwarranted interference in their crime control mission. Instead, police should seize the advantages of performing community service activities; calls for such service are likely to originate in segments of the community that tend to be most critical of police behaviour. "By stressing the punitive aspects of their jobs, however, police forces probably have increased their sense of estrangement from the community" (Hahn, p. 28). Morris (1979) described the insistence on public opinion type surveys of public-police relations which demonstrated that most people are satisfied with masking a good deal of hostility, "and even if this represents only minority feelings it is important because it allows the police to 'scapegoat' certain groups in society; they are only 'unloved' by the 'unlovable'. This is, of course, difficult to reconcile with the generally poor self-image that the police appear to hold of themselves, an image which many feel is connected with their isolation from the wider community" (pp. 49-50). Innovations such as team policing or neighbourhood foot patrol programmes promise to reestablish communication and hence reduce isolation. Wilson and Kelling (1982) cited a foot patrol programme in which, while crime rates were not reduced,

> residents of the foot-patrolled neighbourhoods seemed to feel more secure than persons in other areas, tended to believe that crime had been reduced, and seemed to take fewer steps to protect themselves from crime (staying at home with the doors locked, for example). Moreover, citizens in the foot-patrolled areas had a more favourable opinion of the police than did those living elsewhere. And officers walking beats had higher morale, greater job satisfaction, and a more favourable attitude toward citizens in their neighbourhood than did officers assigned to patrol cars ...(p. 29).

Hence, a "side effect" of the foot patrol programme was an opened channel of communication between the police and the public which can serve to synchronize the expectations of both about police behaviour.

The role of public expectations in shaping police policy is an important question, especially during the current economic climate. It is important to know specifically what public expectations are, if they can realistically be met and what information/education programmes should be enacted if they cannot.

Community Policing

As described above, fast response times are not major determinants of public satisfaction with the police. Rather the contributing factors that more consistently re-appear from study to study are the following: quality of the environment (Cirzanckas & Feist, 1975; Wilson & Kelling, 1982), honest communication from police about response options (Sumrall, Roberts, & Farmer, 1982) and a sense that police departments are concerned about local community problems (Alderson, 1979; Reasons & Wirth, 1975). This latter factor is, of course, a two-way street; improved communication between police and community not only improves community satisfaction with police service but informs police about local concerns and improves their ability to respond proactively to those concerns. The price for disregarding effective community policing should by now be obvious; consider, for example, the minority community backlashes against police in the U.S. (Stark, 1972) and England (Alderson, 1979). Not only minority communities react against police indifference, however; vigilante groups are viewed as the result of neighborhood groups reacting to perceived police inefficiency.

One task of police officers and police organizations is to create the structures which will encourage community self-policing. Kelling and Fogel (1978) suggest that citizens are more likely to cooperate when they invoke police presence and have a vested interest in an event's outcome. "When citizens take the initiative, police action is viewed as legitimate and credible. When officers (...especially officers who are strangers to an area) intervene on their own initiative, their intervention is often perceived as illegitimate, intrusive, resented, and on occasion resisted" (p. 169). Assessment of public expectations, realignment of police functions and the development of sound police-community relations can provide the basis for the establishment of cooperative police-community programs.

Wilson and Kelling (1982) argued that a visible, accessible police presence also reinforces the informal control mechanisms of the community itself. Community members are more likely to take responsibility for ensuring that crime is not encouraged—by repairing broken windows and discouraging vagrancy. The police cannot provide a substitute for such informal control but must accommodate it. In a comparison of the effect of citizen behaviours on feelings of control and on fear of crime, Cohn, Kidder and Harvey (1978) found that crime prevention activities (belonging to a community organization that addresses neighbourhood problems related to crime) led to increased feeling of control and decreased crime compared to victimization prevention activities (avoiding dangerous areas, using locks and alarms).

The implication of this latter finding should not be underemphasized. Fear of crime is inversely related to a sense of active control in a community. Any model of police-community cooperation must incorporate this aspect of community requirements. Community relations units are one example of a direct attempt to improve communciation between the police and the community. Unfortunately, this communication may be outward only, not allowing community input, and may present an unrealistic image of the police (Wasson, 1977). Specialist programs aimed at improving two-way communication by designating community relations officers do little to improve the attitudes of and toward the regular police officer (Reasons & Wirth, 1975; Wasson, 1977).

Team policing is also characterizied by a strong emphasis on community relations and by the geographic stabilty of police patrols. The latter is in response to criticisms of preventive patrol, especially automobile-based patrol (Kelling, 1978; Kelling & Vogel, 1978); in order to reduce crime, car patrols were intended to create a feeling of police omnipresence by increasing the area policed. This was supposed to lead to rapid response, increased apprehension, and increased citizen satisfaction. Instead, use of the car discouraged police-citizen interaction (Kelling, 1978).

Team policing has encouraged close interaction between community and police. Geographic stabilty has also facilitated development of relationships between the police and other social agencies as part of the focusing of community resources on crime.

Inter-organizational problems (cf. Parkinson, 1980) may be less jeopardizing than those within the police organization. Kelling (1978) cited an evaluation of team policing in Cincinnati which found, after the first year, increased citizen satisfaction, decreased crime, and continued police enthusiasm. Yet, as of the second year, the team policing project was eventually unsuccessful. Kelling provided two explanations for this. The first was that the first year of improvement was due to the initial enthusiasm of participants with the innovation. The second explanation, which Kelling finds more plausible because Cincinnati's experience followed the pattern of efforts in other cities, was that community policing did not meet the definition many officers and departments have of "real policing". "Special units" such as community policing units are created to satisfy the community demand, but within the police organization they are viewed as an appendage which does not do the real work of the organization (i.e., being "in service", responding to calls). Goldstein (1979) calls this perspective the "means over ends syndrome". That is, that police departments place more emphasis on operations than on the outcome of their efforts.

Bennett-Sandler (1975) has analyzed resistance within police organizations of innovative programmes which are defined as being outside mainstream policing. Dutton (1981) described managerial resistances to such programmes. The conclusion of such analyses is that innovative programmes must be accepted at the middle management and line supervisor level in order to succeed. Getting constables to accept new programmes requires the support of these levels of the police organization. Otherwise the new programme, such as community policing, will not be viewed as legitimate police work, will be designated to a "special group" like a community relations officer and will not be accepted by constables as part of their everyday responsibilities. Consequently, the programme will have only marginal success.

Problem Oriented Policing

Wilson (1973) argues that the basis for police-initiated community

participation should be to appeal to the self-interest of local residents. Borrowing from Saul Alinsky, Wilson proposes the following principles for community based crime prevention:
(1) Identify those individuals who can be recruited as leaders and who are recognized as native leaders in the neighborhood.
(2) Use an approach that speaks to the self interest of the neighborhood.
(3) As many people as possible should be involved in crime prevention efforts.
(4) Citizen capabilities should be matched with self-interest.

Some of the extensions of community input into crime reduction require that police know which community groups may be "crime associated" that is, connected to the crimes in some way other than perpetrator or victim. By knowing this, alternative preventive strategies can be employed. However, this, in turn, may require what Goldstein (1979) refers to as "problem-oriented policing", which he defines as a "systematic process for examining and addressing the problems the public expects them to handle. It requires identifying these problems in more precise terms, researching each problem, documenting the nature of the current police response, assessing its adequacy...engaging in broad exploration of alternatives to present responses, weighing the events of these alternatives, and choosing from among them" (op. cit., p. 236).

Goldstein's argument for the necessity of a more problem oriented approach stems from what he calls the "means over end syndrome"; that modern policing has become "internally efficient" with modern management techniques and technology to improve response times, but the "external efficiency" (the relation of police practice to current community problems) has lagged behind. Administrative competence has not been linked to its effect on community problems.

Dutton (1981) made the same observations concerning police resistances to "crisis intervention" programmes. "The officer defines his job through what he is doing rather than the goal or objective of his work. Hence, sitting in a private home interviewing, mediating or making a referral to a social agency is considered 'social work' not police work, which is seen as being in the cruiser, on patrol, waiting to respond to a crime call" (op. cit. p. 176). Dutton recommended that police recruits discuss their objectives in policing and set priorities as part of the training exercise. The reduction of violent crime and property crime were two priorities with which most recruits agreed. Dutton then asked them to think about the variety of ways these objectives could be achieved. In that particular situation, family crisis intervention, a variety of options existed to decrease repeated violence, and officers were encouraged to view each intervention as a problem solving exercise aimed at choosing the best option to achieve the objective of diminishing repeated violence.

Implications for Training

The role transition suggested by the above review points to a new model police officer who, above all else, has interpersonal communication skills and problem solving skills. Old emphases on "procedure", physical toughness and an uncommunicative and authoritarian demeanour must be altered. Recruitment must not focus so exclusively on young males and training must emphasize the development of communication skills. Human relations training must be given greater prominence and not grudingly tolerated as a useless fad.

Human relations, "crisis intervention" and minority awareness training has been available to a variety of North American police forces for some time (Bayley & Mendelsohn, 1960; Bard, 1970; Dutton, 1981). To a certain extent all three forms of training are necessary for the "new model" police officer, yet in varying degrees all three are resisted by police as irrelevant to the "real business" of police work. Trainers are put into a paradoxical bind in delivering the training: the police recruit is generally good at learning "procedures" yet a procedural approach to interactions with citizens is perceived as stilted and awkward. The type of interpersonal confidence, sensitivity, and spontaneity that would make officers "at ease" in citizen interactions requires relinquishing the "macho" persona that police officers maintain. However, attempts to get police to relinquish this professional persona rarely succeed, especially with aspiring recruits who want to be tougher than the veterans in order to prove themselves. Yet this very persona contributes to communication problems in interviewing rape victims, talking down someone threatening suicide or counselling a battered woman; and police spend more job time in these so-called "order maintenance" and "service" operations than they do making arrests or fighting gun battles (Wycoff et al., 1980).

Morton Bard's early work in training NYPD recruits for crisis intervention went about as far from a cookbook or procedural model as any subsequent training programmes. Bard (1970) used a training model based on the notion that changing officers personal attitudes through group-confrontation induced insights. This approach was later criticized by Liebman and Schwartz (1972) as not being procedural enough so that it would fit into other police training. Here, in a nutshell, is the paradox; human relations training is forced to be "procedural" so it can be assimilated into other training, yet by its very nature the essence of what is being conveyed through human relations training is not "procedural". The program recently introduced at Hendon by the London Metropolitan police (see chapter by Poole in this volume) represents a significant improvement in training, in this regard.

Dutton (1981) listed the resistances that police officers develop to crisis intervention training, and advocated a confrontational model to uncover these resistances and keep them from blocking learning. These resistances included an aversion to dealing with emotionally upset people, a lack of perceived control, an aversion to verbal communication as opposed to action and a tendency to define family conflict as not being police work. This definitional issue reminds one of Goldstein's "means over end" syndrome. If the objective of police work is to decrease violence, effective family dispute intervention is an important place to start since so much violence occurs in families (Straus, Gelles, & Steinmetz, 1980). If verbal skills and interpersonal sensitivity are required for effective intervention, their development should be readily accepted as part of a necessary training curriculum. This, of course, is not the case. It is rare to find any police training curriculum that devotes more than 20% of its time to the development of such skills (Levens, 1980). They simply are not considered by police to be part of what police "do".

This brings us to another problem facing training for an expanded police role: the "socialization" of newly trained recruits by police veterans who advise them to forget what they learned at police college. Hence, even when training has demonstrable short-term effectiveness (as with the program reported by Dutton, 1981), long-term maintenance of training objectives is rare when those objectives are innovative (see Levens & Dutton, 1980). As Bennett—Sandler described, the training must be integrated with overall department philosophy.

Dutton (1981) used confrontation techniques to establish recruits values and objectives in police work. By pointing out discrepancies between a stated objective (such as decreasing violence) and a practice (giving low priority to family crisis calls), he attempted to challenge dogmatic "means over end" approaches to police work and to generate change in new recruits. Such a "value confrontation" technique was originally developed by Rokeach (see, for example, Rokeach, Miller, & Snyder, 1971). Dutton reported short-term success, but eventually the socialization effects described above washed out any change developed (Dutton, 1981; see also Bull, this volume).

Would value confrontation techniques generate improved problem solving skills and less dogmatic response repertoires in experienced officers? Possibly, but civilian trainers have to carefully consider group process issues in attempting such techniques. Specifically, appearing as an outsider who is going to tell the police their business must be avoided. Better techniques involve having subgroups develop lists of possible responses to hypothetical situations and allowing the group to explore their reactions to suggestions which originate with them. Typically this "brainstorming" procedure provides a range of non—dogmatic responses that can serve as a basis for exploration of personal values.

Conclusion

We have reviewed research that indicates (1) that citizen satisfaction with police is based more on personal interaction with police than on "response time" or other performance criteria and (2) that expanded police—community cooperation is necessary. We have argued that this change in role requires a "new model" police officer in whom communication skills, interpersonal sensitivity and problem solving skills are most important. This police officer would be more similar to a good community organizer or effective manager than to an authoritarian "enforcer". This new model requires a change in emphasis where training in the requisite skills is given greater prominence in police curricula. For this to occur, an explicit recognition of these new values must be made by police forces and reward and advancement must be predicated on their demonstration.

REFERENCES

Alderson, J. (1979). Policing freedom. Plymouth: Macdonald & Evans.

Alinsky, S. (1962). Citizen participation and community organization in planning and urban renewal. Chicago: Industrial Areas Foundation.

Banton, M. (1964). The policeman and the community. Tavistock Publications.

Bard, M. (1970). Training police as specialists in family crisis intervention. Washington, DC: Law Enforcement Assistance Administration.

Bayley, D. H., & Mendelsohn, H. (1968). Minorities and the police. New York: MacMillan.

Belson, N. A. (1978). Public and the police. Harper and Row.

Bennett—Sandler, G. (1975). Structuring police organizations to promote crisis management programs. Symposium on Crisis Management and Law Enforcement, Berkeley, CA.

Bertram, D. K., & Vargo, A. (1976). Response time analysis study: Preliminary finding on robbery in Kansas City. The Police Chief, 74-77.

Bercal, T. E. (1970). Calls for police assistance. In H. Haln (Ed.), Police in urban society. Beverly Hills, CA: Sage.

Bordua, D. J., & Tifft, L. L. (1973). Citizen's interviews: Organizational feedback and police community relations decision. In T.J. Sweeney & W. Ellensworth (Eds.), Issues in police patrol. Washington, DC: Police Foundation.

Cain, M. (1977). An ironical departure: The dilemma of contemporay policing. The Yearbook of Social Policy in Britain, 152-163.

Carlson, H. M., & Sutton, M. S. (1979). Some factors in community evaluation of police street performance. American Journal of Community Psychology, 7(6), 583-591.

Cirzanckas, V. I., & Feist, F. (1975). A community's response to police change. Journal of Police Science and Administration 3, 3, 285-291.

Cohn, E. S., Kidder, L. H., & Harvey, J. (1978). Crime prevention vs. victim prevention: The psychology of two different reactions. Victimology, 3, 285-296.

Corrado, R. R., Glackman, W. G., Roesch, R., Evans, J., & Leger, G. (1980). The police and public opinion: An analysis of victimization and attitude data from Greater Vancouver. Unpublished paper.

Courtis, M. C. (1970). Attitudes to crime and the police in Toronto. Toronto: Centre of Criminology, University of Toronto.

Courtis, M. C. (1974). The police and the public. In C. L. Boydell, P.C. Whitehead, & C.F. Grindstaff (Eds.), The administration of criminal justice in Canada. Toronto: Holt, Rinehart and Winston.

Cumming, E., Cumming, I., & Edell, L. (1965). Policeman as philsopher, guide and friend. Social Problems, 12, 276-286.

David, J., Cowan, L., Renner, E., & Moore, T. (1976). Police community relations: A process, not a product. The Police Chief, 16-18.

Douthit, N. (1975). Enforcement and non-enforcement roles in policing: A historical inquiry. Journal of Police Science and Administration, 3(3), 336-345.

Dutton, D. G. (1981). Training police officers to intervene in domestic violence. In R. Stuart (Ed.), Violent behaviour. New York: Brunner/Mazel.

Furstenberg, F. F., & Wellford, C. F. (1973). Calling the police: An evaluation of police service. Law and Society Review, 7, 393-406.

Goldstein, H. (1979, April). Improving policing: A problem oriented approach. Crime and Delinquency, 236-258.

Griffiths, C. T., & Winfree. (1981). Attitudes toward the police. A comparison of Canadian and American adolescents. Paper presented at the American Society of Criminology, Washington, DC.

Hahn, H. (1971a). The public and the police: A theoretial perspective. In H. Hahn (Ed.), Police in urban society (p. 9-33). Beverly Hills, CA: Sage.

Hahn, H. (1971b). Ghetto assessment of police protection and authority. Law and Society Review, 7, 426-444.

Hylton, J. H. (1980). Public attitudes towards crime and the police in a prairie city. Canadian Police College Journal, 4, 243-276.

Kelling, G. (1978, April). Police field services and crime: The presumed effects of a capacity. Crime and Delinquency.

Kelling, G., & Fogel, D. (1978, Spring). The future of policing. In A. Cohn (Ed.), Sage Criminal Justice System Annuals (Vol. 9).

Kelling, G., Pate, T., Dieckman, D., & Brown, C. (1974). The Kansas City Preventive Patrol Experiment. Washington, DC: Police Foundation.

Klein, J. F., Webb, J. R., & DiSanto, J. E. (1978). Experience with the police and attitude towards the police. Canadian Journal of Sociology, 3(4), 79-93.

Koenig, D. J. (1974). British Columbian's attitudes and experiences relevant to the police, law and crime. Victoria: University of Victoria.

Koenig, D. J. (1975). Police perceptions of public respect and extra-legal use of force. Canadian Journal of Sociology, 1, 313-324.

Levens, B. R. (1980). Domestic crisis intervention: A literature review of domestic dispute intervention training programs. In B. R. Levens & D. G. Dutton (Eds.), The social service role of police. Ottawa: Research Division, Solicitor General.

Levens, B. R., & Dutton, D. G. (1980). The social service role of police - domestic crisis intervention. Ottawa: Research Division, Solicitor General.

Liebman, D. A., & Schwartz, J. A. (1972). Police programs in domestic crisis intervention: A review. In J. Snibbe & H. Snibbe (Eds.), The urban policeman in transition. Springfield, IL: Charles Thomas.

Lilly, R. J. (1978). What are the police now doing? Journal of Police Science and Administration, 6, 51-60.

Lindman, R. (1974). Domestic police-citizen encounters. Journal of Police Science and Administration, 2, 22-27.

Lougheed, W. J. (1973). Our safe streets unit. Police Chief, 47, 52.

McCabe, S., & Sutcliffe, F. (1978). Defining crime: A study of police decisions. Oxford University Centre for Criminological Research. Oxford: Basic Blackwell.

Morris, P. (1979). Police work and police community relations in England and Wales. Royal Commission on Criminal Procedure.

O'Brien, J. T. (1978). Public attitudes toward police. Journal of Police Science and Administration, 6, 303-310.

Pate, T., Ferrara, A., Bowers, R. A., & Lorence, J. (1976). Police response time: Its determinants and effects. Washington, DC: Police Foundation.

Parkinson, G. C. (1980). Cooperation between police and social workers: Hidden issues. Social Work, 25, 12-18.

Pinch, M., & Naylor, T. (1973). The police: A social service. New Society, 24, 358-361.

Reasons, C. E., & Wirth, B. A. (1975). Police community relations units: A national survey. Journal of Social Issues, 31, 27-34.

Reiss, A. J. (1971). The police and the public. New Haven, CT: Yale University Press.

Reith, C. (1938). The police idea: Its history and evolution in England in the 18th Century and after. London: Oxford Univerity Press.

Renner, K. E., Groves, T., & Moore, T. (1976). Public expectations of police behaviour. Paper presented at the annual meeting of the Canadian Psychological Association, Toronto.

Rokeach, M., Miller, M. G., & Snyder, J. A. (1971). The value gap between police and policed. Journal of Social Issues, 27(2), 155-171.

Shearing, C. (1972). Dial-a-cop: A study of police mobilization. In R. Aker & Sagarin (Eds.), Crime prevention and social control. Praeger, U.S.

Shearing, C., & Leon, J. (1977). Reconsidering the police roles: A challenge to a challenge of a popular conception. Canadian Journal of Crime and Corrections, 19(4), 331-345.

Singh, A. (1979). Attitudes of Canadians toward crime and punishment. Canadian Journal of Criminology, 21.

Smith, P., & Hawkins, R. (1973). Victimization, types of citizen-police contacts and attitudes toward the police. Law and Society Review, 8, 135-152.

Stark, R. (1972). Police riots. Wadsworth Belmont.

Straus, M., Gelles, R., & Steinmetz, S. (1980). Behind closed doors: Violence in the American family. New York: Doubleday.

Sumrall, R., Roberts, J., & Farmer, M. (1982). Differential police response strategies. Police Executive Research Forum, Washington, DC.

Task Force on Policing in Ontario. (1974). Report to the Solicitor General.

Thornton, L. M. (1975). An analysis of factors associated with police evaluation and support. Canadian Journal of Sociology, 1(3), 325-342.

Tuchfaiber, A. J., & Klecka, W. K. (1976). Random Digit Dialing: Lowering the cost of victimization surveys. Washington, DC: Police Foundation.

Trojanowicz, R., Trojanowicz, J., & Moss, F. (1975). Community based crime prevention. Goodyear: Pacific Palisades.

Walker, D. et al. (1972). Contact and support: An empirical assessment of public attitudes toward the police and the courts. North Carolina Law Review, 51, 43-79.

Wasson, D.K. (1977). Community-based preventive policing: A review. Ottawa: Research Division, Solicitor General.

White, M. F., & Menke, B. A. (1978). A critical analysis of surveys on public opinions toward police agencies. Journal of Police Science and Administration, 6, 204-218.

Wilson, J. Q. (1969, March). What makes a better policeman? Atlantic Monthly.

Wilson, J. Q. (1973). Planning and politics: Citizen participation in urban renewal. In R. L. Warren (Ed.), Perspectives on the American community (2nd ed.). Chicago: Rand McNally.

Wilson, J. Q., & Kelling, G. L. (1982, March). Broken windows. Atlantic Monthly, 29-38.

Winfree, T. L., & Griffiths, C. T. (1982). Adolescent attitudes toward the police. In T. Ferdinand (Ed.), Juvenile delinquency: Little brother grows up. Beverly Hills, CA: Sage.

Wycoff, M. A. (1982). The role of municipal police: Research as prelude to changing it. The Police Foundation.

Wycoff, M. A., Susmilch, C. E., & Eisenbart, P. (1980, November). Reconceptualizing the police role: An examination of theoretical issues, information needs, empirical realities, and the potential for revision. The Police Foundation.

OFFICER-INVOLVED SHOOTINGS: EFFECTS, SUGGESTED PROCEDURES AND TREATMENT

JOHN G. STRATTON

INTRODUCTION

Shooting and killing or wounding another human being can be a traumatic event for a police officer, especially if he/she entered the profession in order to help people. However, there are procedures and professionals available which can enable such officers to feel good about themselves and their work and to continue productively in their careers.

Until Dr. Martin Reiser's pioneering work with the Los Angeles Police Department, which began in 1968, law enforcement agencies provided very little actual assistance for their employees. By 1975, there were still only a few agencies that had implemented a formal psychological counselling service for employees. In Nielson's (1980) examination of the psychological resources available to departments in five states (Colorado, Mississippi, Missouri, North Dakota, and Washington), there were police clinicians in 14.2% of the departments, chaplains in 1.2%, mental-health centers in 4.3% and no services in 80.3% of the departments. Nielson found that the majority of departments tended to be insensitive to officers' needs. In contrast, a survey conducted by the San Francisco Police Department in 1981 found that 65% of California's 48 largest police agencies and sheriffs' departments reported some form of formal psychological counselling services for employees. In a 1982 nationwide survey for the New York City Police Department, it was found that approximately half the 115 responding departments provided in-house services. In short, psychological services for police departments and their employees have mushroomed in recent years. At a national symposium on police psychology sponsored by the Federal Bureau of Investigation in September 1984, there were 166 psychologists who were working directly with law enforcement. There is now a police psychology section in the American Psychological Association.

In the beginning, the general attitude among officers was that only crazy people saw psychologists. Now, many understand the benefits of seeking help with personal or job-related problems. However, this attitude is not wholeheartedly endorsed by all officers. Some feel that they should handle their own problems just as they handle everyone elses' problems in the street. They see themselves as the last line of defense, needing to be stronger than mere humans, and they believe that to seek assistance for emotional/personal problems is a sign of weakness. Unfortunately, such denial turns some officers into pressure cookers. Emotional steam starts to build, and with no method of release, they can explode into inappropriate behavior.

In the Los Angeles County Sheriff's Department, we provide a full range of employee assistance programs involving counselling and training for officers and spouses, consultations to management and peer counselling where people who have experienced certain tragedies are able to help others going through such difficulties. Support groups have been established for widows, alcohol-related problems and officer-involved shootings.

In our programs we encourage people to seek help early. If people realize they are having problems, the sooner they get help, the quicker the recovery. Often they wait too long to seek assistance and may find themselves in deeper trouble. We illustrate the value of counselling by explaining that if people have a physical problem they will think nothing of going to a medical doctor who has a good understanding of how the body works and the best treatment for the ailment. Likewise, for legal problems a lawyer is the one who has the knowledge to give the proper advice. Financial difficulties are often best solved by consultation with an accountant or financial planner. And a travel agent is often beneficial in getting someone to his destination in the quickest and most efficient manner. We can all see the folly of insisting on handling these matters ourselves. However, when it comes to personal/emotional problems, seeing a psychologist trained in human behavior has often been unacceptable to American police--at least in the past. But this situation is changing. A psychologist who has seen numerous officers involved in shootings has a good idea of the various reactions such officers can have. He can help them by sharing this knowledge and by suggesting coping skills they can use to adjust to the possible trauma. It should be noted that police officers in the United States kill about 300 suspects and injure another 300 every year. One hundred officers are killed yearly (although these figures have been decreasing).

OFFICER REACTIONS

Awareness of reactions officers have had to shootings began to emerge at the same time the Post Traumatic Stress Disorder (PTSD) was recognized and accepted as a phenomenon in Vietnam veterans. Initially this knowledge was discussed in anecdotal ways by a few psychologists and described in the literature by Stratton (1983). Just as every Vietnam veteran doesn't experience PTSD, neither do all officers involved in shootings experience traumatic reactions. Our research and clinical experience indicate that approximately 1/3 have minimal or no problems, 1/3 have a moderate range of problems, and 1/3 have serious problems. However, almost all officers return to work and perform effectively again. The intensity of the difficulties is generally related to personality, current life situations, personal history, available support systems, and particular aspects of the incident (closeness to the subject, goriness of the incident, etc.).

The first major study was done by Nielson (1980). Initially, all sheriffs' and police departments in cities of 20,000 or more were sampled in the states of Colorado, Mississippi, North Dakota, Washington and Maryland. Nielson found that 54% of the sheriffs' departments and 88% of the police departments had a written policy regarding the use of deadly force. Nielson also studied the demographics of 63 officers involved in shootings and their reactions. Similar studies were made by Soskis, Soskis, & Campbell (1983) of 14 special agents in the Federal Bureau of Investigation and by Stratton, Parker, & Snibbe (1984) involving 60 Los Angeles County deputy sheriffs. Although each study did not cover all areas in the same manner, Table 1 demonstrates the commonality of reactions of officers involved in shootings.

Table 1
Reactions of Officers Involved in Shootings

	NIELSON	SOSKIS ET AL.	STRATTON ET AL.			
POPULATION	63 POLICE OFFICERS INVOLVED IN SHOOTINGS	14 SPECIAL AGENTS INVOLVED IN 17 SHOOTINGS	60 DEPUTY SHERIFFS INVOLVED IN SHOOTINGS 6 MONTHS TO 3 YRS. PRIOR			
AGE	MAJORITY 29 OR YOUNGER	24-45				
EXPERIENCE	4 YEARS OR LESS PATROL	9 MONTHS TO 15 YEARS	0-5 YEARS 14%	6-10 YEARS 41%		
			11-15 YEARS 37%	16+ 8%		
TIME	79% BETWEEN 8PM-5AM	1:30AM to 11:05PM				
SHOTS FIRED BY OFFICERS	3.7	17 (1) SHOT EACH INCIDENT				
SHOTS FIRED BY SUSPECTS	1.5	14 (1) SHOT BY EACH SUSPECT				
RESULTS		8 KILLED 4 WOUNDED	45% KILLED 55% WOUNDED 9% OFF DUTY			
PRIOR SHOOTINGS			0 32%	1 39%	2 17%	3 8%	4+ 6.6%
LAST SHOOTINGS OCCURRED			1 YR 35%	2 YR 31%	3 YR 29%	4 YR 5%
OTHER OFFICERS			1 53%	2 6%	3 18%	4+ 23%
DURING INCIDENT EMOTIONAL AND PSYCHOLOGICAL REACTION	64% SLOW MOTION 27% AUDITORY BLOCKING 43% TUNNEL VISION	59% SLOW MOTION 65% AUDITORY BLOCKING 53% TUNNEL VISION	79% SLOW MOTION 26% SPEED UP			

	NIELSON	SOSKIS ET AL.	STRATTON ET AL.
EMOTIONAL/ PSYCHOLOGICAL REACTIONS WEEK FOLLOWING SHOOTING	59% THOUGHT INTRUSIONS 52% DEPRESSION 33% ANXIETY, AGITATION 27% SLEEP DISTURBANCES 25% FATIQUE INABILITY TO FOCUS 22% THOUGHTS	47% SLEEP PROBLEMS 41% ANXIETY/TENSION 35% SADNESS CRYING/ DEPRESSION 24% DISTURBING THOUGHTS	37% NO PROBLEMS 63% PROBLEMS 28% ANGER 23% MIXED 18% ELATION 18% CONFUSION 18% ANXIETY 13% DEPRESSION 25% FEAR, WORRY, ANXIETY 7% FEAR OF LAWSUIT 100% FLASHBACKS, RECURRING THOUGHTS 30% AFFECTED GREATLY 33% AFFECTED MODERATELY 35% AFFECTED LITTLE OR NOT AT ALL
FAMILY ASPECTS		59% WIFE WORRIED/ UPSET INCREASE IN INABILITY AT AT HOME AND SUBSEQUENT 33% MARRIAGE PROBLEMS DIVORCED SINCE 6% INCIDENT	76% REACTION FROM SPOUSE OR REATIVES: YES 48% SUPPORTIVE 21% TENSION, FEAR, WORRY 10% GLAD OFFICER NOT HURT 8% AVOIDANCE, DISINTEREST
PEER REACTIONS	41% SUPPORT 41% CURIOSITY 19% AGGRAVATION 7.9% NONE REPORTED	77% SUPPORT 18% CURIOSITY 13% AGGRAVATION 6% NONE REPORTED	
SUPPORT/ TALKED TO MOST	57% PEERS	100% FELLOW AGENTS 53% WIFE/GIRLFRIEND 12% CLERGY 6% OTHER FAMILY 6% SUPERVISOR	98% OTHER DEPUTIES 80% STATION SUPERVISORS 75% STATION BRASS 70% DEPARTMENT BRASS
SOURCES OF AGGRAVATION	42% PRESS COVERAGE UNFAIR 42% THREATS AGAINST SELF/FAMILY 19% FELLOW OFFICERS	PROLONGED NATURE OF INVESTIGATION AND FRAGMENTARY INFORMA- TION (PARAMOUNT) 55% SUPERVISOR'S CONCERN FOR SELF OR POSITION 41% NEWS MEDIA 29% OTHER BUREAU OFFICIALS 12% SUSPECTS' FAMILY AND FRIENDS 6% SUPERVISOR 6% SUSPECTS' ATTORNEYS 6% OTHER AGENTS	47% NEW FEARS OR DOUBTS 30% LEGAL ENTANGLEMENT 30% JOB RELATED 17% DEPT'S REACTIONS

Officers report that during a shooting every sense is heightened and they experience everything in slow motion, like viewing a movie frame by frame. They have reported seeing the bullet leaving the gun or entering the victim's body; seeing the contortions on the the victim's face; watching the body break and bend and palpitate before the final collapse. They hear screams and blood-curdling yells, and they record all of these events vividly in their minds.

Emotional releases sometimes occur immediately. However, often they occur after the fact and away from the police environment because when they're on duty, officers believe they must be in control. Behavioral scientists generally believe that emotional release is better then keeping feelings bottled up and can help to prevent stressful diseases. Yet law enforcement is an occupation which demands that people be objective and unemotionally involved.

Police applicants are often asked if they could shoot and kill another person. Invariably, their response is the same: "I wouldn't like it, but if someone else's life or my life was in jeopardy, I could shoot and kill someone. There are tragedies that occur and that I'll be expected to handle, but that's part of the job, and if you have to do it, it has to be done. I would be able to do it."

If there are strong emotional reactions at the shooting scene, they usually occur when no one is present. However, recurring thoughts or flashbacks occur without exception, and anniversary dates of the incident (or holidays close to it) are often reminders of the event. When officers drive by a location where a shooting occurred, they tend to be reminded of the incident and may even have the same bodily and emotional responses they did at the time of the shooting. Whenever anyone experiences a significant emotional event--whether it is something tragic, like a shooting, or something joyful, like the birth of a child--those impacted do not forget the details or the emotional experiences. Officers have refused to work anniversary dates of traumatic incidents because of the feelings they generate.

A common type of flashback occurs in dreams or nightmares. Dreams can be seen as a way for feelings and thoughts to surface which we can't acknowledge in our waking state and yet which need to be addressed. Issues we cannot handle consciously such as fear, weakness, anger or depression, can often be dealt with in our sleep. Officers have been awakened by their spouses because they are thrashing around, sitting straight up in bed, or yelling profanities and shaking. Others have broken out in sweats ("like having buckets of cold water thrown on me"), and have awakened to find their beds soaked.

Forty-seven percent of the 60 officers we surveyed experienced new fears related mostly to legal entanglements or to job security, with 14% concerned about the department's reactions to them. As our society relies more and more on the courts to settle disputes, the possibility increases of civil suits or of the district attorney filing criminal charges against officers involved in shootings. Being involved in situations where people are alive one minute and dead the next confronts officers directly with the finiteness of life. When their lives are threatened or they've been nearly killed or seriously injured, they may question the way they are leading their lives. Dealing with death has caused significant changes in officers' behavior, thoughts and ideas regarding life and death.

The sheer shock of killing another person, even when seemingly justified, has often led to intense consideration of anyone's right to take another human life. Sometimes an officer wants to know more about the dead suspect's family, his siblings and other aspects of his life, and sometimes the officer feels an increasing sense of guilt depending upon what these private investigations turn up.

When the detectives arrive on a shooting scene, the officer begins recounting what happened, often needing to tell his version over and over. After the initial lengthy interview, which examines every aspect of the incident in detail, the officer is sent home to rest. But he will need to repeat the story many more times. High-ranking department officials must know about the incident, and others may just be curious--a phenomenon which is often perceived negatively by the involved officer.

After the first day or two, the officer is allowed to go home or to an administrative assignment for a few days. He is told to call if he remembers more details. At this point, it is almost impossible for the officer to get the incident out of his mind. Added to this are the other calls he often gets from fellow officers who want a full description of the incident from beginning to end. With all the attention given to them by fellow cops, many officers begin to feel that they are being looked at as heroes. Often their feelings are the exact opposite. They wish they could totally forget the incident. However, as their actions are reviewed by the media, the district attorney, the training staff and others, the process seems to drag on forever.

Often the strongest guilt reactions occur when an officer's partner has been shot, and especially if he has been killed. The surviving officer often feels responsible, believing that if he had taken a different action, been more careful, or said something different, the entire misfortune could have been avoided. Officers risk their lives to protect and cover for one another, and when one dies it is sometimes presumed by the partner to be his fault. Everyone else presumes the surviving officer did his best for his partner, and yet he refuses to relinquish responsibility.

Generally, officers whose partners are killed experience more guilt than from other types of police tragedies. Even worse can be the accidental shooting of one's partner, a fellow officer or an innocent victim. Constant reconstruction of the incident--looking at ways it could have been handled differently--only adds to the guilt and frustration.

RELATED TRAUMAS

The circumstances surrounding serious accidents cause trauma for everyone--victims, witnesses and law enforcement personnel alike. The aftermaths of car and plane crashes, where lives are taken and bodies are mangled, present the officers with formidable tasks which can impact them deeply. Officers who arrive at the scene of a severe incident are confronted with mutilated and distorted bodies: the gore of human tragedy. They are expected to handle this human carnage routinely, providing as much help and assistance as possible. To perform their functions, they suppress their feelings. However, the emotional onslaught may stay with them much longer. Officers working in these incidents have had nightmares and flashbacks. The senses are keenly affected; they see the destruction, smell pungent odors, touch dead bodies, and hear the screams of injured victims. All these sensations and experiences are not quickly, if ever, forgotten.

Officers who investigate or witness bizarre and revolting acts that man has committed upon others don't easily forget either. They may be exposed to the consequences of human destruction and horror: slashed throats, nipples ripped off with pliers, vaginal areas ripped open, or bodies cut in pieces and left in trash bags. Officers are bound to be affected by these sights and often shut off their feelings. They might question their values, the purpose of their work, and the direction society is headed.

Officers experience particular difficulty in incidents related to children. Viewing bruised or abused children or seeing young children injured or killed in traffic accidents often causes officers serious problems, particularly when they have children about the same age. These events can cause officers to question their parental behavior and be over-protective or fearful.

Some of these reactions are similar to those of officers involved in shootings. Other responses are particular to the specific traumatic event, the officer's life situation, his psychological makeup, and his prior experiences. The bottom line is that there are a variety of experiences which can cause officers and their families severe distress and problems. A police department's awareness of possible reactions and the assistance it provides through difficult times can aid greatly in reducing trauma for the officers.

A traumatic incident can bring about a life crisis for some police officers. Crisis theory states that people, whatever their level of psychological health, are for the majority of their existence in a period of equilibrium or homeostasis. When a significant emotional event occurs which has the potential to upset homeostasis, coping mechanisms are set into motion. If these mechanisms are unable to meet the situation, upheaval occurs and there is often a painful period of disequilibrium and disorganization. The person can live with the stressful situation for only a short period of time and must develop some method of adjustment and reintegration.

This reintegration process usually begins immediately or within four to six weeks of the event. The re-establishment of equilibrium may be at the same level or at a higher or lower level of psychological functioning. The emphasis in crisis theory is that the level of equilibrium finally achieved is dependent upon the immediacy of treatment as well as the effectiveness and ability of the people who are intervening. When a traumatic event happens, an officer may start to spin into a period of disruption where he is incapable of handling many aspects of his life with which he had previously coped. The goal in working with the officer should be to at least help him return to the level of equilibrium he had before the crisis and hopefully to guide him toward a healthier level.

When examining the wide range of results that may ensue from the various methods for resolving a crisis, the entire process can be seen in the two characters which make up the Chinese symbol for crisis: danger and opportunity. There is the danger of less healthy psychological and social adjustment, and there is the opportunity for growth in effectively handling the disruption, learning from it, and providing more skills for handling future situations. Anyone the officers comes in contact with, detectives, department officials, psychologists, peers, etc., can have an effect on the level of equilibrium reached.

Departments can establish effective methods to deal with traumatic incidents for officers. But first these departments must recognize and accept that officers have emotional reactions to various aspects of their jobs. This can be accomplished through training at the academy and through the attitudes that supervisors and management take toward their officers. Troubled officers should be encouraged to seek assistance from psychologists familiar with traumatic reactions or from an officer or a group of officers who have experienced similar traumas.

In the case of shootings, there can be victims at both ends of the gun, with the officers often being forced to deal with personal issues that have been focused by the event. Even if they feel prepared for such an occurrence, officers can doubt their courage, strength and fitness. They may fear losing their sanity, and the more they try to avoid the issues confronting them, the more haunted they can become.

DIAGNOSTIC CRITERIA FOR POST-TRAUMATIC STRESS DISORDER (PTSD)

Examining the criteria for PTSD established by the American Psychiatric Association's Diagnostic and Statistical Manual, third edition (DSM III) (1980), it is easy to see that some officers do suffer from the disorder:

(1) Existence of a recognizable stressor that would evoke significant symptoms of distress in almost everyone;

(2) Re-experiencing of the trauma as evidenced by at least one of the following:

    (a) Recurrent and intrusive recollections of the event

    (b) Recurrent dreams of the event

    (c) Sudden acting or feeling as if the traumatic event were reoccurring, because of an association with an environmental or ideational stimulus.

(3) Numbing of responsiveness to or reduced involvement with the external world, beginning some time after the trauma, as shown by at least one of the following:

    (a) Markedly diminished interest in one or more significant activities

    (b) Feeling of detachment or estrangement from others

    (c) Constricted affect.

(4) At least two of the following symptoms that were not present before the trauma:

    (a) Hyper-alertness or exaggerated startle response

    (b) Sleep disturbance

    (c) Guilt about surviving when others have not, or about behavior required for survival

    (d) Memory impairment or trouble concentrating

    (e) Avoidance of activities that arouse recollection of the traumatic event

    (f) Intensification of symptoms by exposure to events that symbolize or resemble the traumatic event.

This syndrome often applies to the officer involved in a shooting. What is important is to assure a professional and sympathetic reaction to the officer's needs. It simply is not true as some have stated that 80% quit within two years after being involved in a shooting; that suicide is common; and that there are three times as many suicides as officers killed in the line of duty. These myths perpetuate a view that officers are unable to handle traumas and are highly suicidal. This view ignores the fact that many officers are minimally affected by such an event and that professional treatment almost always allows officers to return to their prior level of functioning while some gain more insight into themselves, and they work and perform even more effectively. With treatment, officers who experience PTSD generally return to the field and perform well.

TRAINING

During instruction by the academy staff and subsequent field training officers, a recruit's ethical/moral sense is developed along with his attitudes toward the job, the people he encounters on the street, and the dangerousness of his work. This impression formation develops a perceptual set through which the officer sees all of the various events the job entails. It determines how realistically the trainee perceives the situations in which he'll be involved. This process is illustrated in Figure 1. If an officer's perceptual set is distorted, he can overreact and use excessive force or underreact, putting himself in dangerous situations. The goal of all training is to have the circumstances of the event realistically perceived and to select the best approach available for the most beneficial results and least negative consequences for all involved.

PROGRAM COMPONENTS OF TRAINING IN THE USE OF DEADLY FORCE

Particularly in the United States, academy training often emphasizes the violent and dangerous, stressing officer survival techniques, strength and virility, with a non-emotional response viewed as a necessity. Sometimes shootings are presented as heroic acts as the ultimate, the best part of the job, the chance for an officer to really earn the badge. This approach goes along with our intrigue with Western heroes and our admiration of forceful people who act because the end is good even though the means may be objectionable. Such beliefs can be further advanced by attitudes of field training officers and peers toward the use of deadly force.

The police macho image, combined with the need for non-emotional responses and the tendency to seek out violent or dangerous activity, can lead to an inability to express feelings of inadequacy or pain. Emotional responses to traumatic situations are normal and a step toward avoiding stress related diseases. However, officers are often unprepared for their reactions and don't realize that unusual responses are normal. In such situations, it can help for someone to explain the possible reactions of officers involved in shootings, the availability of support, and the rationale for a mandatory nonjudgmental meeting with a psychologist. These actions can reduce concerns about emotional responses, make such feelings more understandable, and promote the view that they are even healthy.

Because the taking of any officer's life is an injustice and devastating to everyone associated with him and law enforcement, heavy emphasis must be placed in training on defense tactics and methods of survival on the job. As a result, trainers often overlook effective communication skills and ways to handle the vast majority of police work--social interactions. Having a commitment to social aspects of police work can enable officers with appropriate communication skills to de-escalate potentially volatile situations, handling them with brains instead of brawn.

We know that if an officer is confident in his ability to defend himself, and if there is no threat to life, he will approach citizens in a relaxed and comfortable manner. There usually will be no need for yelling, bullying or using force when an officer is secure in his physical abilities. Likewise, when officers are skilled in communication, they present the comfortable image needed to interact with the wide range of people they encounter in their duties. Discomfort, fear or anxiety can cause a minor problem to escalate, causing trouble

168

THE OFFICER

PERCEPTUAL SET

Academy Training
Field Training Officer
Peer Influences
Impression Information
Attitudes
Present Life Circumstances
Mood
Values
Sense of Alienation
Information from Roll Call
Information from Radio Call
Knowledge of Circumstances
Risk Involved
Available Alternatives
Immediate Risk of Deadly Force

Personal History
Background Experiences
Education
Individual Personality

FIGURE I

USE OF DEADLY FORCE

If Used:

Highest Degree of Care
and Proficiency
Mental and Physical
Calmness
Determination to Stopping
Life Threat

POSSIBLE
CONSEQUENCES

A. The Officer
  (1) Lifelong psychological trauma
  (2) Severe administrative sanctions
    · Suspension
    · Dismissal
  (3) Severe legal consequences
    · Criminal action in state court
    · Civil action in state court
    · Criminal action in federal
      court
    · Civil action in federal court
    · Even (in the case of an
      injured crime victim) civil
      action for failing to take
      advantage of his authority
      to use deadly force

B. Officer's family and friends
  · Mental strain from "second
    guessing" the decision
  · Trauma from waiting for legal and
    administrative rulings
  · Threat of physical retribution

C. Agency
  · Vicarious liability damage suits
  · Damaged reputation
  · Civil disorders

D. Victim
  · The end of life
  · Crippling damage
  · Serious injury
  · Grave financial loss

E. Victim's family
  · The loss of a loved one
  · The loss of a family provider
  · A drastic change in lifestyle
  · Hatred

for the officer, the citizen and even the department. During training, then, emphasis should be balanced between officer survival, communication techniques, ethics and the law.

An officer's response to deadly force is dependent partly on the attitude and manner in which it is presented. Emphasizing the value of human life and the difficulties involved in moral decisions is important. There is no restitution for taking a human life. When deadly force is used, an officer becomes judge and jury immediately and the repercussions to him/her can last forever.

A training approach endorsing the following principles is encouraged:

(1) When in doubt, don't shoot!

(2) The degree of force used must not greatly exceed the assault (People vs. Shimonaha Cal. App. 117).

(3) Follow the model code on deadly force, which emphasizes that the use of force be justifiable only where the arresting officer believes that:

    (a) the crime for which the arrest is made involved conduct including the use or threatened use of deadly force, or

    (b) there is a substantial risk that the person to be arrested will cause death or serious bodily harm if his apprehension is delayed.

(4) Allow fleeing suspects to escape, rather than injuring innocent victims.

(5) Drive safely and within the speed limits, dependent on congestion and road conditions. The destruction of human life often outweighs the possibility of stopping a criminal.

(6) While off duty, except in immediate life threatening situations, merely observe criminal activity, noting suspects descriptions, license plate numbers, etc., and call the local police as soon as possible. When out of uniform, an officer is not identifiable either by other policemen or by suspects. Overt behavior, unless absolutely necessary, often places officers and innocent bystanders in jeopardy.

A training approach which minimizes the maximum risk (death) increases the chances of seeing events as threatening and causes aggressive behavior. Working from a perspective of "I'd rather be tried by twelve than carried by six" reduces the risk for the individual but can also end in wrongful death and its difficult consequences. Acting on events from a perspective of minimizing the maximum risk causes officers to be proactive, on guard, suspicious and defensive; they will tend to take actions quickly to avoid any personal risk and will fail to develop alternative skills.

While excessive force undermines the ideals of civil society, minimal force undermines officer safety. Therefore it is necessary to draw very careful lines between legitimate and abusive force. Officer survival training should highlight:

(1) Alternative courses of action which lead to the same results without increasing risk to the officer;

(2) Methods that use minimum necessary physical force;

(3) The principle that a capacity for force doesn't mean using it in ordinary occupational routines;

(4) An understanding that use of physical coercion or restraint is rare for all officers and that many never are in a position to have to resort to it.

Training should also include stress-awareness teaching with focus on identified stressors, the effects of stress and especially coping strategies. Emphasis must be placed on physical and emotional fitness, the numerous ways to work through problems, and demonstrations that police work is manageable with the right approach and support. A training brochure ought to explain possible officer reactions, administrative procedures, available peer and professional help, possible reactions of family members and significant others, and suggestions for handling typical problems.

Shooting simulations during training can be very helpful. At Laser Village, the Los Angeles County Sheriff's Department uses lasers rather than bullets to lend a realism to shooting situations far beyond that offered by the traditional firing range. The use of such reality-based training prepares officers for various physical and emotional reactions which can occur in actual situations. All physiological responses (pulse, breathing and sweating) are heightened; all senses are extremely acute and tunnel vision often occurs. After such training, officers are able to discuss their reactions and are informed of additional responses to shootings and the availability of support. Night shooting simulations, which prepare officers for the vast majority of shooting incidents, are beneficial. With some understanding of the perceptual distortions which can occur, officers become more keenly aware of the importance of moving cautiously and of taking a few moments to gain perceptual acuity. Without keen perceptual awareness, the officer's effectiveness is reduced.

The first few moments of a shooting situation are the most critical because the emotional states of the officer and suspect are fragile, leading to the possibility of inappropriate action. When emotions are high, a person's reasoning, judgment and senses are often distorted. This may well account for the fact that the majority of shots fired in field situations miss their objective. Officer's emotions need to be controlled, tempered with good judgment. However, in a few seconds, with awareness of the necessity for emotional control, reasoning and judgment becoming much clearer. Initially emotion is high and reason is low. With awareness and control, these dynamics can become more equal and even reverse themselves--reason now being high and emotion low.

It is of paramount importance that officers should also recognize that their emotional upsets and personal problems can cause them to use excessive force and affect their ability to think clearly. The relationship between emotion and reason is the same whether the emotion be generated by field or personal problems. Not keeping personal emotional control affects officers reasoning and their ability to work effectively.

It should be noted that citizen education can also benefit the officers' role. If citizens can be made aware of basic police procedures through meetings, for example, conducted by neighborhood watch groups, this understanding could benefit citizens and police alike. The public should know why officers are cautious when they pull over an automobile, enter a house or arrive at a street scene, and why various reactions by citizens cause police to be even more on guard. Appropriate behavior by citizens which would reduce problems for them and officers should be demonstrated and explained.

The importance of training, supervision and special weapons teams is dramatized by the lower justifiable homicide rates in departments that:
(1) Spend a greater number of hours on non-shooting issues (legal, moral, policy aspects) than on firearms training;
(2) Provide in-service crisis intervention training;
(3) Have a high supervisor to officer ratio (greater than 1/10);

(4) Provide tactical guidance and manpower support;
(5) Use special Weapons units to confront armed, fortified criminals, thereby decreasing the number of shooting incidents.

The value of Special Weapons Teams (S.W.T.) to the Los Angeles County Sheriff's Department, the community it serves and suspects is clearly evident in Table 2.

Table 2
Los Angeles County Sheriff's Department
Special Weapons Team Statistics 1971 - July 1985

```
1,022 DEPLOYMENTS
   20 (2%) SHOOTING INCIDENTS
    7 (.7%) SUSPECTS DIED
    6 (.6%) SUSPECTS INJURED
    7 (.7%) MISSED
1,265 ARRESTS OF DANGEROUS FELONS
```

During the 1,022 deployments, one officer has been killed and no innocent citizens have died. During 64 hostage situations only one victim has been killed by the suspect after S.W.T. was deployed. All other victims were rescued by S.W.T. and hostage negotiators. Currently Los Angeles County Sheriff's Department Special Weapons Teams average 100 call-outs or warrant services a year, providing the safest law enforcement in the most volatile and dangerous situations.

DEADLY-FORCE POLICY ISSUES
   Caution must be the cornerstone of any use-of-force policy, often more restrictive than the law. The fleeing-felon rule guided shootings for most of this century. The guidelines were developed in England (where most felons were punished by death), and they were simple: Shoot if you have no other means to apprehend the suspect or if your life or someone else's life is in danger, a stricture which could be loosely interpreted. For example, having or using cocaine is a felony, yet the danger to the officer may be minimal. If the suspect attempts to flee, in years past he could have been shot. However, in America in the 1980s there are few death sentences given by the court and fewer carried out. Stricter standards have been adopted by the police resulting in a slight annual decrease in the number of deaths to citizens and officers the last five years.
   Law enforcement almost always finds itself in a double bind. Most citizens want aggressive law enforcement because of an increasing fear of crime. However, they also have some apprehension about their protectors and want to limit their discretionary power, including the use of force. A model policy on the use of deadly force has been developed by the International Association of Chiefs of Police (Matulia, 1985) due to the extreme diversity of policies by departments throughout the Country. The idea is to promote uniformity. The Supreme Court has quoted and referred to this policy, suggesting it be adopted by all American police agencies (Garner vs. Tennessee). The Model Penal Code philosophy is to ignore the technical classification of a crime as a felony or misdemeanor and to focus instead on a balance of interests--the need to apprehend suspects, preserve the safety of citizens and the arresting officers and the value of human life.

Recommended Policy for Officers Involved in Shootings

The following policy guidelines demonstrate support and concern about officer's welfare:

(1) After the shooting scene is secured, personnel should be physically and mentally well-cared for.

(2) A good friend or an officer previously involved in a shooting and trained as a peer counselor should be assigned to the involved officer, not necessarily to talk about the incident but rather to take care of the officer's needs and be a friend.

(3) The officer should be provided a brochure explaining possible reactions, administrative procedures, legal aspects and peer and professional help available.

(4) The officer should be allowed to immediately contact his family to explain that he is okay, but that he will be at the station for some time to complete the investigation.

(5) Spouses should also be provided with a brochure which includes suggestions for what role the family can play, and which lists available peer and professional help. All questions the spouse has should be answered.

(6) If the officer's weapon is taken for investigative purposes, another weapon should be provided.

(7) If possible, have an officer who has been involved in a prior shooting conduct the investigation.

(8) Officers need to know their legal rights and liabilities and have legal counsel, if it's desired.

(9) It can aid in the officer's adjustment if the person in charge contacts the officer and the family in a supportive way and offers assistance.

Following are supportive reactions from administrators that officers have found helpful:

"He communicated a personal friendly approach and good concern for how I felt. He understood the situation."

"I was told as long as I felt in my mind and in my heart that I had made the right decision, then I had nothing to fear. Those words were what I needed at the time."

"He sat us down and told us he would help in any way, any time. I felt he could."

Conversely, officers often perceive a lack of management support, as illustrated by the following comments:

"The department was more concerned with protecting their image than protecting its officer."

"I was treated like a suspect during the investigation of the incident."

"The way it was handled afterward was more harmful than the shooting itself."

"They acted like I provoked the shooting. I felt alienated."

The F.B.I. policy of not releasing names is helpful to officers involved in shootings because of community reactions and possible threats. If information has to be released, it should be only the officers' names. A brief memo or teletype highlighting the pertinent facts should be promulgated to inform department members and control rumors.

Within five days of an incident, contact should be made with a psychologist who has experience working with officers involved in shootings. Providing support, sharing reactions of others, and offering services to the family allows for ventilation without jeopardy. Officers should be encouraged to discuss shootings with their children to the level of their comprehension, explaining their feelings and the necessity for their actions. After an incident children can sense something is wrong and may take responsibility for family problems. It is awkward for everyone when children find out at school rather than from their parents. Some children know about these incidents for years but are uncomfortable talking about them, thus maintaining undue concerns and operating under misinformation or misunderstanding.

The officer should work on an inside assignment for five days to be available for further questioning or just to take a break. This provides him with a safe law-enforcement environment and support of peers and friends. These comments from officers testify to the advantages of such a policy: "It felt good not to be placed in the breach for awhile"; "My adrenalin was flowing for the next three days. I felt the R & R inside was needed"; "I might hesitate to use force initially if I went right back out onto the street."

Within 30 days, officers should be given three days administrative leave to take care of things they were unable to attend to because of the disruption, and to provide them with the opportunity to spend some comfortable time with their families.

Officers should not be assigned to duties likely to bring armed confrontation after involvement in two or three shootings. Shooting incidents and life-threatening situations often challenge the sense of security and basic trust of the strongest and best adjusted-person. Officers are extremely sensitive to how the organization supports or withholds support. Prolonged investigations and fragmentary information are major sources of stress for officers causing anxiety and feelings of abandonment. Perceptions that produce statements such as "I worried a lot about the investigation" and "They treated me like a suspect and tried to avoid me" demonstrate officers' concerns. Every effort should be made to facilitate and expedite the investigation. The officer should be kept verbally informed and written communication to him should be clear and concise.

EMOTIONAL DEBRIEFING GUIDELINES FOR OFFICER INVOLVED SHOOTINGS

The process of seeing officers after they have been involved in shootings should not be an evaluation to determine their psychological fitness or their ability to work in the field. Rather the process should allow them to discuss their emotional reactions and concerns in a nonjudgmental and supportive way with recommendations give for handling any troubling reactions. This is referred to as an emotional debriefing, and these are the suggested procedures:
(1) Explain that the policy of an emotional debriefing has been developed after studying various reactions of officers involved in shootings. Explain that these officers have seen the benefits of consulting with a psychologist and have agreed that the stigma of seeing a professional would be removed by making it a departmental policy.
(2) Describe your research and experience in working with officers involved in shootings, in order that the subject understands your knowledge of commonalities; differences in officer reactions.
(3) Make clear that your meeting and any subsequent meetings are confidential. Explain that this process is not an investigation, but rather an avenue for the subject to discuss his feelings, thoughts and concerns in a helpful, non-accusatory way.

(4) Allow the officer to freely discuss the incident and the circumstances surrounding it. During this discussion explain perceptual distortions involving the speeding up or slowing down of time; auditory effects, and tunnel vision. Have the officer describe his reactions related to these occurrences.

(5) Discuss the phenomena of flashbacks and the replaying the shooting as if on a video tape recorder. Ask if this is happening to the officer and explore his thoughts and feelings when they come up. Explain to him that he will never forget the incident but that its impact on him will probably diminish over time.

(6) Explore how the officer is handling any problems with sleeping, eating, fitness, concentration or other aspects of daily life.

(7) Explore the reactions of spouse, children, parents, fellow officers, supervisors, administrators, neighbors, media and others. The officer's feelings about the victim should also be examined.

(8) Discuss any new feelings, thoughts, reactions, fears, anxieties or concerns that have come up as a result of being involved in a life-and-death situation.

(9) Explore feelings about returning to the field and concerns about job performance. It is valuable to point out that research indicates officers who are involved in shootings have more of a tendency to react quickly in future incidents and may be involved in subsequent shootings. This certainly doesn't mean they shouldn't shoot, but rather should be aware of this phenomenon, not take unnecessary risks, practice officer-survival techniques and monitor whether they are over-interpreting the dangerousness of future situations.

(10) Have them discuss their overall feelings about the incident and refer them to other officers who have been involved in shootings and who would be willing to talk about their reactions.

REFERENCES

Matulia, K. (1980). Diagnostic and Statistical Manual, Third Edition. American Psychiatric Association.

Nielsen, E. (1980, December). Salt Lake City Police Department: Deadly Force Policy--Shooting and Post-Shooting Reactions. Salt Lake City: Salt Lake City Police Department.

Soskis, D.A., Soskis, C.W., & Cambel, J.H. (1983). An analysis of the effects of post shooting trauma on special agents of the Federal Bureau of Investigation. Unpublished manuscript, FBI.

Stratton, J.C. (1983). Traumatic incidents and the police. Police Stress, 6(1), 4-7.

Stratton, J.G., Parker, D.A., & Snibbe, J.R. (1984). Post traumatic stress: Study of police officers involved in shootings. Psychological Reports, 55, 127-131.

POLICE AND THE MENTALLY DISORDERED[1]

JOHN MONAHAN and BRIAN MONAHAN

Nowhere are the controversies that can arise when police deal with mentally disordered persons more tragically evident than in a recent New York City case of Mrs. Eleanor Bumpurs (Raab, 1985). Mrs. Bumpurs was a 67-year-old mentally disordered black woman who lived alone in a public housing project in the Bronx. Her rent was $89 a month and she had not paid it for 5 months. A New York City marshall went to the apartment to evict Mrs. Bumpurs for failing to pay her rent, but she refused to let him in and made threats through the locked door. The next day, October 29, 1984, the Emergency Service Unit of the New York City Police Department was notified of the threats. Six Emergency Service Unit officers went to Mrs. Bumpurs' apartment to evict her. They punched out the lock and went into the apartment carrying plastic shields designed to protect them against blows and knife thrusts and also carrying a "restraining bar," which is a U-shaped bar attached to a long handle that is used to pin a person against a wall.

The officers tried to pin Mrs. Bumpurs, who was 5 feet 8 inches tall and weighed close to 300 pounds, with the restraining bar. In the process, she grabbed a kitchen knife and thrust it at an officer, hitting the plastic shield. When she raised the knife a second time, another officer shot her twice in the chest with a shotgun.

The next day Mrs. Bumpurs daughter claimed that her mother had been murdered by the police: "Shot guns are for elephant hunting, not for an old woman who is terrified by people breaking into her apartment. They were there to kill her, not to subdue her." Two days later, New York City Police Commissioner Benjamin Ward ordered a major revision in the rules for handling emotionally disturbed people. Ward said: "Modified procedure will require whenever an emotionally disturbed person believed to be armed or violent can be contained to the extent that the person poses no immediate threat or danger to any person, no further action will be taken until the Precinct Commander or Duty Captain arrives and evaluates the situation."

The New York City Housing Authority, which was responsible for the apartment complex, responded to Mrs. Bumpurs' death by demoting several officials whom they said should not have tried to have Mrs. Bumpurs evicted. A psychiatrist, who was a consultant to the Housing Authority and who had examined Mrs. Bumpurs in her apartment four days before the eviction, concluding at that time that Mrs. Bumpurs was psychotic but not dangerous, was dismissed.

---

[1]We would like to thank Dr. Linda Teplin and Dr. John Stratton for their help in locating material used in this chapter.

One month after the shooting, the New York City Police Chief called a press conference to unveil a new talking robot that could shoot mace at mentally disordered people who needed to be restrained. The Chief said that if the robot had been sent in to deal with Mrs. Bumpurs, the robot might have been able to subdue her without exposing any police officers to injury. The Chief also said that he was studying the possibility of whether all 240 police officers in the Emergency Service Unit should undergo psychological testing to determine whether they were emotionally suitable for handling tense situations involving the mentally disordered. The Chief imposed a policy whereby every time police officers have to remove a mentally disordered person from a dwelling, they must be accompanied by a psychologist or a social worker.

The psychiatrist who had interviewed Mrs. Bumpurs shortly before her death called his own press conference on December 2, 1984, to state that the reason he did not have Mrs. Bumpurs committed to a mental hospital was that he did not believe at that time that she was imminently dangerous to others, and therefore she did not qualify for involuntary commitment under New York's narrow commitment law. He said that calling the police to have Mrs. Bumpurs evicted was "the best way I know within the law for getting this woman to a hospital for evaluation and treatment" (Raab, 1985).

A Bronx grand jury began investigating Mrs. Bumpurs' death in early December 1984. The New York City Police Officers' union, the 18,000 member Patrolman's Benevolent Association, began taking out 30,000 worth of ads on radio stations and in newspapers to defend the officers' conduct. The following radio announcement is representative: "This 300 pound woman suddenly charged one of the officers with a 12-inch butcher knife, striking his shield with such force that it bent the tip of the steel blade. It was as she was striking again that the shots were fired. It happened so quickly they had no chance to subdue her -- no chance."

Several weeks after the grand jury began its investigation, the family of Mrs. Bumpurs filed a $10 million wrongful death suit against the City of New York and the City Housing Authority.

On New Year's Eve, 1984, the Bumpurs' story moved from the back of the second section of the New York Times to the front page. On that day, police officer Steven Sullivan, the officer who had fired the two shotgun blasts that killed Mrs. Bumpurs, was indicted by the Bronx grand jury for manslaughter. Bronx District Attorney, Mario Merola, stated that the fact that Officer Sullivan fired two shots and not just one was relevant in the grand jury's determination. Mr. Merola described the indictment as "an agonizing, difficult, and possible problem." He chided the Housing Authority for failing to provide Mrs. Bumpurs with psychiatric assistance that might have averted the eviction procedures. In response to a question about the Police Commissioner's statement that Officer Sullivan had complied with departmental guidelines at the time of the shooting, Mr. Merola said, "Hitler's people also followed guidelines. You can't just follow orders blindly and escape your individual responsibility."

Four days after officer Sullivan's indictment, all 250 officers in the Emergency Service Unit of the New York City Police Department demanded transfers to protest the indictment. The Patrolman's Benevolent Association instructed all officers in the city to refrain from using force with mentally disordered persons unless an Assistant District Attorney was physically present on the scene to authorize in writing that the officers would not be indicted for their actions. The head of the union stated that "primarily we feel that Commissioner Ward's guidelines have exposed us to undue danger and we are not going to tolerate it."

On February 7, 1985, fully 10,000 of New York City's 18,000 police officers took the unheard step of protesting outside the State Supreme Court in the Bronx against the indictment of Officer Sullivan. The officers chanted that "Merola must go," and referred to the District Attorney as "Ayatola Merola."

On April 12, 1985, a New York State judge ruled that the evidence in the Bumpurs case was legally insufficient to indict Officer Sullivan for manslaughter or any other offense (Raab, 1985). After the ruling, Officer Sullivan was asked whether, under similar circumstances, he would shoot again. "Yes, I would," he replied.

The District Attorney immediately announced that he would appeal the judge's dismissal of the indictment. It will be years before the civil suit filed by Mrs. Bumpurs' family is heard in the courts. Relations between the Police Department and the black community, between the Police Department and the District Attorney's office, and between the police officers and the Police Commissioner are still severely strained.

Handling mentally disordered people in the community has always been a necessary but undesirable part of police work around the world. It is a necessary part because disturbed people are often disturbing to those around them. Psychiatrists, like other doctors, no longer make house calls, and the police officer is often the only person available to restore order. It is an undesirable part of police work because disturbed people are often disturbing to the police officer as well. It is frequently unclear whether the individual is "bad" and should be taken to jail, or "mad" and should be taken to the hospital, or simply "odd" and should be sent on his or her way. No matter what the officer does, there are those who will criticize his or her actions, and there is usually very little in the way of departmental policy or the officer's personal experience that provide clear guidance about what should be done.

In the past several years, there has been a great deal of research and policy activity in the United States on the issue of crime and mental disorder, in general, and the police and the mentally disordered, in particular. In this chapter, we review five of the most important topics in the area: The first topic has to do with the generic question of crime and mental disorder: Are they related? The second has to do with how frequently the police encounter mentally disordered people: Are these interactions increasing? The third topic concerns what police officers do when they encounter someone they think may be mentally disordered: How do they decide what course of action to take? The fourth topic deals with mentally disordered people after they have been processed by the police: How are they handled by the mental health and criminal justice systems? Finally, the policy recommendations that have recently been issued by the American Bar Association on how police should deal with mentally disordered people that they encounter will be analyzed. The research discussed here deals exclusively with the relations between the police and the mentally disordered in the urban American context. There are reasons to believe that it may be generalizable to other urban cultures (see Manning, 1984).

The Relationship Between Crime and Mental Disorder

The belief that mental disorder and crime are closely linked has always been part of the popular culture. Brydall, writing in 1700, said that "mad men" were committed to mental hospitals in England "not only to look that they do not mischief to themselves, but also that they be not destructive to others" (quoted in Dershowitz, 1974). After Daniel McNaughten was acquitted by reason of insanity in 1843, The Times of London published the following ditty on its editorial page: "Ye people of England exhalt and be glad, for you're now at the mercy of the merciless mad" (quoted in Monahan, 1981).

Before the American Revolution, Benjamin Franklin, one of the founding fathers of the United States, argued before the Assembly of the Colony of Pennsylvania that a hospital should be built to take care of disordered people for humanitarian reasons. He got nowhere. He then argued that mentally disordered people "are a terror to their neighbors, who are daily apprehensive of the violences they commit." In response to this argument, the money for the hospital was immediately forthcoming (quoted in Monahan & Geis, 1976).

More recently there have been several hundred research studies on the relationship between crime and mental disorder. These studies have been reviewed by Monahan and Steadman (1983). They found that the factors that are associated with crime among mentally disordered people appear to be the same as the factors that are associated with crime among any other group in American society: age, gender, race, social class, and prior history of criminality. Likewise, the factors that are associated with mental disorder among criminal offenders appear to be the same as those that are associated with mental disorder in other groups in the American population: age, social class, and history of previous disorder. Much of the relationship between crime and mental disorder found in the research appears related to these demographic factors. The lowest social class groups in the American population, for example, have by far the highest rates of both crime and mental disorder. In other words, crime rates are no higher among mentally disordered people than they are among non-mentally disordered people with similar demographic characteristics. And the rates of mental disorder among groups of criminals are no higher than among groups of non-criminals who have the same demographic characteristics. Unfortunately, this point is more interesting from an academic perspective than from the point of view of policy making. In the real world of police work, one does not have to be concerned about why there is a relationship between crime and mental disorder, only that such a relationship exists. One of America's less illustrious former governor's once said that what prisons need is a better class of offenders. He did not say how this could be achieved.

It is important to note that the research deals with groups of offenders and groups of mental patients. It is statistical research. It does not deal with individual offenders and individual mentally disordered people. It seems obvious that in individual cases mental disorder can have an effect upon someone's propensity to crime. Daniel McNaughten's delusion in 1843 that the Queen of England and the Pope were conspiring to kill him was no doubt related to his attempt on the life of the Prime Minister. On the other hand, being mentally disordered can sometimes reduce a person's likelihood of committing crime, as would be the case with catatonic rapists or depressed Mafia hit men.

Whatever the precise causal pattern, it is clear from the data that in the world in which police officers work and in which third variables such as social class are conspicuously left "uncontrolled," there is a substantial relationship between crime and mental disorder.

The Frequency of Police Encounters with the Mentally Disordered

It is widely believed that there are now many more mentally disordered persons at liberty in the United States than there have been in the past. Three reasons are commonly given to explain this observation (Teplin, 1983). First, the drastic deinstitutionalization of mental hospitals in the United States over the past thirty years has dumped many former mental patients back into the community where they are supposed to receive local care, usually outpatient care. Second, the recent cutbacks in social services, including mental health services, across the United States has meant that "local care" usually means "no care." And third, in the guise of protecting people's civil rights, there has been a substantial narrowing of the legal standards for involuntary mental hospitalization. The standards for involuntary hospitalization in most American states are no longer that the person be mentally ill and in need of treatment. Rather, the individual has to be seriously mentally disordered and dangerous to others or suicidal. In other words, the laws in many American states are written so that it is more difficult to commit disordered people, and there are few hospital beds left to put them in even if they could be legally committed.

If it is true that there are now more mental patients at liberty in the community, then it should not be surprising that there would now be more interactions between the mentally disordered people and the police.

It is impossible to do good research on whether or not any of these claims are true. No one collected the necessary data before the laws were changed, before mental hospitals were deinstitutionalized, and before local budgets were cut. All we can do is look at the frequency of police interactions with mentally disordered people now and make estimates about whether these frequencies are higher or lower than in the past. Certainly, the best American study in this area was the one published by Linda Teplin (1984). Teplin wanted to find out how often police officers dealt with mentally disordered people and whether they were more likely to arrest someone who was mentally disordered than someone who was not mentally disordered. She and a staff of five graduate students, working in a large American city, spent 2,200 hours over a fourteen month period accompanying police officers on their rounds. Two hundred and eighty three officers were involved. Each time the police officer had an encounter with a citizen, the research worker noted the kind of interaction that it was and whether the person exhibited symptoms of mental disorder, such as confusion, paranoia, or bizarre behavior. She obtained data on 2,555 citizens who were encountered by the police. This is a rate of approximately one person for every hour that the researchers were with the police. She excluded any public service encounters (such as asking the police officer for directions) and any encounters related to traffic offenses (such as giving speeders a ticket), and she also excluded anyone who was not suspected of some kind of wrongdoing (for example, she did not analyze whether a witness to a crime was disordered). This left slightly over 500 people in her study. The researchers judgment was that 30 of these 500 people were mentally disordered. This is six percent of the sample. Interestingly, when the police officers were asked after the interaction whether they thought the person was disordered, the police officers thought that only 15 of the 30 people were disordered. In other words, the police officers thought that three percent of the people they suspected of having committed a crime were mentally disordered, while the graduate students in psychology thought that the rate was twice as high.

Whether the "true" current rate at which police encounter mentally disordered persons as suspects of crime is 6 percent or 3 percent, and whether this represents an increased or a constant portion of police work, it is clear, as Teplin (1984, p. 801) has stated, that "police officers must receive adequate training in recognizing and handling the mentally ill, such that persons who are more disordered than disorderly may be handled humanely and channelled through the most appropriate system" (see also Teplin, 1985).

Police Decision-Making Regarding Mentally Disordered People

When police officers do encounter a person they perceive as mentally disordered, how do they decide what to do with him or her? There are several American studies on this topic. Matthews suggests that police may commit a disordered person to a hospital rather than make an arrest "because of the trouble such persons may cause when placed behind bars, because police officers, like citizens generally, balk when obviously sick people are denied medical care, and because the critical decision about hospitalization is merely temporarily postponed [by arrest]" (1970, p. 293).

According to Bittner (1967) the five types of cases in which police will file a petition for commitment to a hospital rather than make an arrest or take no action, are: (1) when the person has attempted suicide; (2) when signs of serious mental disorder are accompanied by distortions in appearance (e.g., nudity, bizarre posturing); (3) when the person appears to be in an agitated and possibly violent state; (4) when the person is gravely disoriented and creating a public nuisance; and (5) when requested to commit by someone in an "instrumental relationship" to the person (e.g., an employer or a physician). Bittner concluded that "the general impression one gets from observing the police is that, except for cases of suicide attempts, the decision to take someone to the hospital is based on overwhelmingly conclusive evidence of illness" (p. 285).

Schag (1977) reported that most police-initiated commitments to mental hospitals were precipitated by an overt act or threat of harm to oneself or others, or a significant omission in person care. Like Bittner, he found that an act of self-injury was a _prima facie_ justification for commitment. In those cases in which an overt act or threat was not present, factors such as bizarre conduct, creation of a public nuisance, and presence of a psychiatric history were invoked by police in initiating commitment.

In a study by Monahan, Caldeira and Friedlander (1979), 100 police officers from a large suburban county in California were interviewed at the county jail, after that had just "booked" a suspect, and 50 were interviewed at the county medical center's psychiatric ward after they had civilly committed a patient. Only cases involving public drunkenness were excluded. The officers were asked questions about the mental illness and "dangerousness" of the people involved, and why they processed them as they did.

The police, not surprisingly, believed that all of the people that they brought to the hospital were mentally ill, (although only about one-third of them were believed to be "severely" mentally ill.) In contrast, only about one-third of the people brought to the jail were believed to be mentally ill, and most of these were only "somewhat" mentally ill.

In terms of "dangerousness" to others, the groups were approximately the same: about half of each group were believed likely to physically assault someone. In terms of danger to themselves, however, the groups were markedly different. Fully 82% of the hospital group were believed to be suicidal, while only 4% of the jail group were believed to be suicidal.

The acts or threats precipitating a police perception of dangerousness to others did indeed appear "dangerous." In 65% of the cases they involved an assault with fists, knives, guns, or other objects (e.g., furniture, dogs). One person threatened arson; one left his car running in the fast lane of a freeway. In 19% of the cases they involved assaults on property such as "kicking the seats and dashboard of a bus," "tearing up an apartment," and "shooting out the street lights." The only case of violence to animals was a man who crushed a small bird in his hand. One person began "prowling" the residence of strangers while they were home. In the majority of cases in which the victim or potential victim could be identified, he or she was a family member.

Likewise, in those cases in which an act or threat precipitated a perception of dangerousness to self, the acts and threats appeared substantial. In 30% of these cases, a direct verbal threat of suicide was made, and in 70% an overt attempt at suicide was committed, including overdosing on medication (22%), wandering in traffic (22%), and a variety of other acts (e.g., jumping out a window, setting one's house on fire, biting one's arms, head banging).

Officers at the jail who reported a person to be at least "somewhat" mentally ill and also a danger to others or themselves were asked why they chose to arrest rather than to commit the persons, since the officers appeared to have that legal option. Of the 50 cases, 15 cases (30%) fell within this technically committable category. In two-thirds of these cases, the officers stated that the person's mental illness was not sufficiently severe, or dangerousness not sufficiently demonstrated, to have the commitment sustained by the hospital staff. Other reasons for choosing not to commit a technically committable person were variations on the theme that "it's not our job to commit," and a desire to preserve the criminal charges against the person with the question of mental illness being deferred for judicial determination. As one officer stated, "If I took him to the hospital, they would just give him his medication and he'd be on his way. Then how would justice be served?" Another officer observed, "If a guy commits a crime and he comes here [to jail] first, then the courts can decide if he's insane or not. It's a legal term. If we took him to the hospital first, then the case is blown."

Likewise, in 30% of the commitment cases the police believed that they technically could have made an arrest rather then initiated commitment. The charges on which these persons could have been arrested covered a wide range from disturbing the peace, trespassing, public intoxication, and indecent exposure to assault with a deadly weapon (40% of the potential charges), burglary, and arson.

In only 14% of the total commitment cases, however, did the responsible police officer seriously consider making an arrest. That is, in less than half the cases in which arrest was a legal option was it a seriously weighed course of action. Further, the commitment law in California provides for the police officer, if he or she chooses, to be notified before any person held in emergency commitment is released to the community, so that the officer can file criminal charges. In only 3 cases (6% of the total number of commitments and 20% of the cases that were legally susceptible to arrest) did the officer check the box on the commitment form requesting such notification. Two of these cases involved the most serious precipitating events ("set fire to her house" and "went up to the roof of his house with shotgun and fired two rounds of ammunition"), and the other was a man "standing on a corner screaming for no apparent reason" who had many outstanding traffic warrants.

The reasons given by the police officers for choosing not to arrest those individuals susceptible to a legal arrest were evenly divided between variations of "no intent or motivation to commit a crime" due to mental illness--a form of "presumptive insanity defense"--and variations of "in need of help not incarceration."

The authors of this study were led to the conclusion that, "[w]hile it is not in the nature of empirical research to resolve conflicts of social values, it would appear from these data that rather than arresting those they should commit, or committing those they should arrest, the police do a surprisingly accurate job of triage along the dimensions dictated by official public policy" (Monahan, et al., 1979, p. 517).

Interactions Between the Mental Health and Criminal Justice Systems

In addition to the questions of whether there is any relationship between crime and mental disorder, how often the police encounter the mentally disordered, and how the police deal with those mentally disordered people they do encounter, one can also consider what happens to mentally disordered people after they have been processed by the police.

The specific question that immediately arises in this context is whether the drastic increase in the American prison population in recent years has been the result of the equally drastic decrease in the population of state mental hospitals. Between 1968 and 1978, for example, the population of state mental hospitals fell by 64 percent, and the population of state prisons rose by 65 percent. The hypothesis that has been advanced by some is that people released from mental hospitals are quickly violating the law in the community, and shortly thereafter wind up in state prisons.

However, Steadman, Monahan, Duffee, Hartstone, and Robbins (1985) found that between 1968 and 1978--years in which the population of state mental hospitals fell by two-thirds--the proportion of men with a history of mental hospitalization who were admitted to state prisons only increased from 7.9 percent to 10.4 percent. Indeed, in three of the six states in the study, the percentage of male prisoners with a history of mental hospitalization actually decreased over the period. The deinstitutionalization of state mental hospitals, therefore, does not seem to have been a major factor in the recent drastic increase in the U.S. prison population.

From the opposite perspective--crimes committed by the mentally disordered--there is a great deal of research on the arrest rates of persons who have been treated for mental disorder in a state hospital. In terms of the arrest rate subsequent to hospitalization, every study performed before 1965 has found that rate to be lower than that for the general population, while every study performed in more recent years has found it to be substantially higher.

Steadman and Cocozza (1978) have explained this shift in terms of changes in the arrest rates of mental patients prior to hospitalization. Patients released from New York State mental hospitals in 1975, for example, had arrest rates for violent crimes substantially higher than those of the general population (12.03 per 1,000 for ex-patients compared with 3.62 per 1,000 for the general population). Yet for patients who had no arrest record at the time they were hospitalized, the arrest rates subsequent to hospitalization were actually lower (2.21 per 1,000) than those of the general population. It is only patients who had a history of prior arrests--particularly multiple prior arrests--who had above-average rates of offending when they left the hospital (e.g., 60.46 per 1,000 for ex-patients with 2 or more prior arrests).

  This is consistent with the well-known criminological finding that persons who have been arrested in the past tend to be arrested in the future. Mental hospitalization in itself, therefore, does not seem to affect arrest rates, independent of the effect of past criminality (and social class). The substantial increase in arrest rates for released mental patients after 1965 is attributable to a steady increase in the percentage of mental patients with a history of arrest prior to hospitalization. Further studies showed that, by 1978, 55 percent of all males admitted to mental hospitals had a prior arrest record (Steadman et al., 1985).

  The most obvious form of interaction between the mental health and the criminal justice systems occurs in the context of people who are legally adjudicated as "mentally disordered offenders." "Mentally disordered offenders" in the United States is an umbrella term, covering four legal categories: (1) persons judged incompetent to stand trial, (2) those found not guilty by reason of insanity, (3) mentally disordered sex offenders, and (4) individuals transferred from prison to a mental hospital (Monahan & Steadman, 1983). The number of persons in each category admitted to a mental hospital in the U.S. in 1978, and the number residing in institutions on any given day in that year, are shown in Table 1.

  Given that 278,141 persons resided in United States prisons and 158,394 in United States jails on any given day in 1978 (Weis & Kenny, 1980), "mentally disordered offenders" constituted only 3.2 percent of the institutionalized offender population. The President's Commission on Mental Health (1980) reported the resident population of state and county mental hospitals to be 191,391 in 1975 (the most recent year for which data were available). Mentally disordered offenders, therefore, composed 7.3 percent of the institutionalized mentally disordered population. The authors compared these admission figures to previously existing ones and concluded that admission rates for mentally disordered offenders in the U.S. have been fairly constant for the past decade.

Table 1
Legal Status of Mentally Disordered Offenders in U.S. Facilities, 1978*

	Admissions	Census
Incompetent to stand trial	6,420	3,400
Not guilty by reason of insanity	1,625	3.140
Mentally disordered sex offenders	1,203	2,442
Mental ill inmates: in external units	5,648	2,684
Mental ill inmates: in prison units	5,247	2,474
Totals	20,143	14,140

*from Steadman, Monahan, Hartstone, Davis, and Robbins (1982).

The Regulation of Police Handling of the Mentally Disordered

Since 1981, the American Bar Association has been involved in drafting model standards for all areas of interaction between the criminal justice and mental health systems. Working for three years, and with ample support from the MacArthur Foundation, 79 lawyers, psychiatrists, psychologists, police officers, and others hammered out scores of standards that each of the American states can adopt as legislation. On August 7, 1984, after 50 meetings, the standards were formally adopted by the American Bar Association. While many of the standards deal with issues such as competence to stand trial and the insanity defense, nine of them are addressed to the police. They can be summarized as follows:

The first standard (7-2.1) limits the kind of mentally ill and mentally retarded people a police officer may take into custody in an emergency. Only people who are dangerous to themselves or others, or who are so gravely disabled that they cannot provide themselves with such basic necessities as food, clothing and shelter qualify. It also specifies that this custody should be imposed for only one purpose: to provide transportation to a facility where evaluation or treatment will be provided. So a homeless mentally retarded person in danger of starvation or frostbite, or a mentally ill person threatening to jump from a roof, could both be taken to a hospital for a civil commitment evaluation under this standard.

The second standard (7-2.2), simply stresses the value of having the police and mental health professionals agree on what the proper procedures for handling mentally ill and mentally retarded people should be. It attempts to rectify the situation, unfortunately common in the United States, of the police bringing someone to a mental health facility and the staff refusing to admit the person even for evaluation. Such situations engender bitterness on the part of the police and lead officers to take mentally ill people to jail where they at least can be assured of admission.

The third standard (7-2.3) reflects a preference for voluntary over involuntary custody procedures in order to minimize the infringements on the liberty of the mentally ill. If an informal disposition, such as driving the person home, where there is someone to care for him or her, will handle the emergency, that is to be preferred.

The fourth standard (7-2.4) specifies that police should use only the minimum amount of force necessary to protect the mentally ill or mentally retarded person--or anyone else--from bodily harm. Where it is feasible, bringing along a mental health professional to assist in taking custody of the person should be considered.

The fifth standard (7-2.5) addresses the problem of what to do when someone appears both to be mentally disordered and to have committed a criminal act. Here, the police officer is faced with the choice of arresting the person or taking him or her to the hospital. The answer given by the Standard is that if the criminal behavior is "minor," the person should be taken to the hospital, but where a felony--such as murder, rape or robbery--has been committed, the person should be arrested. After effecting the arrest, however, the police officer should make sure that steps are taken to obtain evaluation and treatment for the disordered felon. The reason that the officer should record in writing the reasons that he or she thinks the person is disordered is to create a record in case the issues of incompetence to stand trial or insanity later arise in the case.

The sixth standard (7-2.6) focuses on the issue providing treatment to jail inmates. Jail officers should be trained to recognize signs of mental disorder, and especially of suicide potential, and to report these whenever observed. A professional evaluation is called for when a jail inmate appears to be disordered, and if any treatment is indicated, it should be provided, even if this means transferring the prisoner to a civil hospital if that is the only place where the appropriate treatment is available.

The seventh standard (7-2.7) states that a court order should be obtained before a jail inmate is subjected to involuntary treatment. The only exception to obtaining a court order for involuntary treatment is for emergency situations when serious injury to the inmate or someone else is likely. Whenever treatment is at issue, both the prosecuting and defense attorneys must be informed.

The eighth standard (7-2.8) addresses the issue of training the police to deal with disordered persons. Both police academy as well as in-service courses, preferably taught by mental health professionals, are specified. Knowledge of how to handle disordered persons should be included on police promotion examinations.

The final standard (7-2.9) deals with the records that the police should keep on those mentally ill or mentally retarded people they come into contact with whom they do not charge with a crime. These records should be filed separately from arrest records, and they generally should be treated as confidential.

These proposals were only recently adopted. Concerted efforts are now underway to have them enacted into law in each of the 50 states in the United States. There is no doubt that these standards are the major developments in this area in the United States in the past several decades and will have an enormous impact in the future.

For the purposes of this chapter, the most relevant standard is the eighth one, which concerns police training in dealing with the mentally disordered. While some material on this topic exists (e.g., Reiser, 1974; Haley & Moushigian, 1974; Mohr & Steblein, 1976; Nemetz, 1977), it tends heavily toward the anecdotal and is now seriously dated. In our view, the development and field testing of a comprehensive set of training materials to prepare the police for their inevitable interactions with disordered persons is the single highest priority in the area.

REFERENCES

Bittner, E. (1967). Police discretion in emergency apprehension of mentally ill persons. Social Problems, 14, 278-292.

Dershowitz, A. (1974). The origins of preventive confinement in Anglo-American law. Part I: The English experience. University of Cincinnati Law Review, 43, 1-60.

Haley, E., & Moushigian, C. (1974). Mental health services in a law enforcement setting. Journal of California Law Enforcement, 8, 184-190.

Manning, P. (1984). Police classification and the mentally ill. In L. Teplin (Ed.), Mental health and criminal justice (pp. 177-198). Beverly Hills: Sage.

Matthews, A. (1970). Observations on police policy and procedure for emergency detention of the mentally ill. Journal of Criminal Law, Criminology, and Police Science, 61, 283-295.

Mohr, W., & Steblein, J. (1976). Mental health workshops for law enforcement. FBI Law Enforcement Bulletin, 45, 3-8.

Monahan, J. (1981). Predicting violent behavior. Beverly Hills: Sage.

Monahan, J., & Geis, G. (1976). Controlling "dangerous" people. Annals of the American Academy of Political and Social Science, 423, 142-151.

Monahan, J., & Steadman, H. (1983). Crime and mental disorder: An epidemiological approach. In Morris, N. & Tonry, M. (Eds.), Crime and justice: A review of research, Vol. 3 (pp. 145-189). Chicago: University of Chicago Press.

Monahan, J., & Steadman, H. (Eds.). (1983). Mentally disordered offenders: Perspectives from law and social science. New York: Plenum.

Monahan, J., Caldeira, C., & Friedlander, H. (1979). Police and the mentally ill: A comparison of committed and arrested persons. International Journal of Law and Psychiatry, 2, 509- 518.

Nemetz, W. (1977). Crisis intervention. Police Chief, 44, 16-70.

President's Commission on Mental Health, Report to the President. (1980). Washington, D.C.: U.S. Government Printing Office.

Raab, S. (1985). State judge dismisses indictment of officer in the Bumpurs killing. New York Times, April 13, p.1.

Reiser, M. (1974). Mental health in police work and training. Police Chief, 41, 51-52.

Schag, D. (1977). Predicting dangerousness: An analysis of procedures in a mental health center and two police agencies. Unpublished doctoral dissertation, University of California, Santa Cruz.

Schuerman, L., & Kobrin, S. (1984). Exposure of community mental health clients to the criminal justice system: client/criminal or patient/prisoner. In L. Teplin (Ed.), Mental health and criminal justice (87-118). Beverly Hills: Sage.

Steadman, H., & Cocozza, J. (1978). Psychiatry, dangerousness and the repetitively violent offender. Journal of Criminal Law and Criminology, 69, 226-231.

Steadman, H., Monahan, J., Duffee, B., Hartstone, E., & Robbins, P. (1985). The impact of state hospital deinstitutionalization on United States prison populations, 1968-1978. Journal of Criminal Law and Criminology, 75, 474-490.

Steadman, H., Monahan, J., Hartstone, E., Davis, S., and Robbins, P. (1982). Mentally disordered offenders: A national survey of patients and facilities. Law and Human Behavior, 6, 31-38.

Teplin, L. (1985). The criminality of the mentally ill: A dangerous misconception. American Journal of Psychiatry, 142, 593-599.

Teplin, L. (1984). Criminalizing mental disorder: The comparative arrest rate of the mentally ill. American Psychologist, 39, 794-803.

Teplin, L. (Ed.). (1984). Mental health and criminal justice. Beverly Hills: Sage.

Teplin, L. (1983). The criminalization of the mentally ill: Speculation in search of data. Psychological Bulletin, 94, 54-67.

Weis, J., & Kenny, J. (1980). Crime and criminals in the United States, In E. Bittner & S. Messinger (Eds.), Criminology review yearbook, Vol. 2. Beverly Hills: Sage.

CRIMINAL PSYCHOPATHS

ROBERT D. HARE

It is ironic that those who have the most direct contact with psychopaths---family, relatives, friends, employers, and front-line members of social agencies and the criminal justice system, including the police---are the ones least likely to have formal exposure to the clinical concept of psychopathy and to the associated research literature. Police officers, for example, have frequent encounters with psychopaths, and although they may have a good intuitive understanding of human behavior and an ability to size up people accurately, they will often find these encounters to be perplexing, frustrating, and threatening. For these reasons, and also because of the relative ease with which many psychopaths are able to flout moral, ethical, and legal conventions, it is important that police know as much about them as possible. This chapter provides an overview of the sort of material that might be covered in police training programs.

The individuals to be described present a formidable challenge to the criminal justice system. They are responsible for a considerable amount of personal and social distress, but because of their ability to manipulate others and to use the law to their own advantage, their extensive criminal activities are probably underrepresented in crime statistics. In spite of this, the number of charges and convictions they do receive is disproportionately large.

Psychopaths are considered sane by most legal and psychiatric criteria, yet they are capable of behavior so callous and grossly antisocial that it is easy to conclude that "they must be crazy." Considerations of this sort led Cleckley (1976) to suggest that their surface manifestations of clinical normality may mask a profound underlying pathology. The nature of this pathology, or even whether it exists, is as yet unclear. What is certain, however, is that psychopaths are responsible for an inordinate amount of physical, emotional, and social harm. We also know that their asocial and antisocial behavior and attitudes emerge at an early age and persist throughout much of the lifespan. There is a temporal consistency to the behavior of criminal psychopaths that makes it generally more predictable than is the behavior of most other criminals.

I should note here that not all psychopaths are criminals in the legal sense of the term. Many manage to avoid incarceration or even formal contact with the criminal justice system because of family background, influence and support of family and friends, extraordinary personal charm, or an ability to operate on the shady side of the law or to exploit the weaknesses of the legal system. Nevertheless, there is no reason to assume that the core personality structure of these individuals is fundamentally different from that of psychopaths who are convicted of breaking the law. The specific behaviors associated with this core

personality structure are no doubt influenced by the socioeconomic milieu
in which the individual develops. Like other criminals, the psychopaths
who end up in prison tend to come primarily from the lower socioeconomic
levels in which social, financial, and educational opportunities are
severely limited.

It is beyond the scope of this chapter to discuss the various
sociological, psychological, and biological theories of psychopath (see
Hare, 1970; Hare and Schalling, 1978; McCord and McCord, 1964; Raine, in
press; Smith, 1978; Venables, in press; Weiss, in press). For present
purposes it is perhaps sufficient to note that there is little convincing
evidence that the core features of psychopathy are related to
socioeconomic factors or to family dynamics. On the other hand, there is
the increasing possibility that genetic and constitutional factors
contribute to psychopathy and to a spectrum of other disorders, including
alcoholism, schizophrenia, and persistent criminality (see Mednick's
chapter, this volume).

Most of the material presented below is based on research with men
incarcerated in Canadian prisons. There has been very little research
with female psychopaths, but there is no reason to assume that they
differ in any fundamental way from male psychopaths.

Following a clinical description, I will present recent data on the
assessment of psychopathy, the criminal history of male psychopaths,
their use of violence, and their behavior after conditional release from
prison.

CLINICAL DESCRIPTIONS OF THE PSYCHOPATH

The concept of psychopathy has a long and sometimes confusing history
(see Cleckley, 1976; Craft, 1965; Maughs, 1941; McCord and McCord, 1964;
Pichot, 1978; Weiss, in press). This confusion has resulted in the
emergence of a number of terms used to describe much the same underlying
disorder: moral insanity, constitutional psychopathic inferiority,
psychopathic personality, sociopathy, psychopathy, and antisocial
personality, to name only a few. The problem is compounded by the
tendency for some commentators to use these terms, especially
psychopathy, in a variety of ways that are inconsistent with the original
intent. For example, psychopathy is sometimes used (carelessly) as a
synonym for criminality, or as a "wastebasket" category for antisocial
patients who do not fit into other psychiatric categories. Some
commentators have argued that psychopathy, as a clinical entity, does not
exist, because the defining traits are not actually present in any one
individual. However, this argument owes much to armchair reasoning and
to biases against the use of typologies to pigeon-hole people. There is
ample empirical evidence that the traits purporting to define the
construct of psychopathy do in fact form a meaningful cluster, and that
the cluster is valid, clinically useful, and amenable to reliable
measurement (e.g., Blackburn, 1973; Hare, 1985a; Hare and Cox, 1978;
Quay, 1964; Schalling, 1978).

Clinical Features

The richly detailed clinical profiles provided in the five editions of
Cleckley's The Mask of Sanity form the basis for much of the North
American research on psychopathy. Cleckley (1976) describes the
psychopath as an individual whose asocial and antisocial behavior is not
readily understood in terms of psychosis, neurosis, or mental deficiency.
The most salient characteristics of the psychopath include:

unreliability; insincerity; pathological lying and deception; egocentricity; poor judgment; impulsivity; a lack of remorse, guilt, or shame; an inability to experience empathy or concern for others, and to maintain warm, affectional attachments; an impersonal and poorly integrated sex life; and an unstable life-plan with no long-term plans or commitments. Other clinical descriptions of the psychopath are in basic agreement with the picture provided by Cleckley (see Hare and Cox, 1978; Weiss, in press). For example, Buss (1966) describes psychopathy in terms of thrill-seeking, disregard for societal conventions, inability to control impulses or to delay gratification, rejection of authority and discipline, poor judgment about behavior but good judgment about abstract matters, failure to alter punished behavior, pathological lying, persistent asocial and antisocial behavior, and a fundamental incapacity for love, genuine friendship, guilt, or shame. McCord and McCord (1964) portray the psychopath as an impulsive, aggressive individual who is driven by primitive desires and an exaggerated craving for excitement, and who is capable of the most appalling behavior without any signs of genuine guilt or remorse.

ASSESSMENT OF PSYCHOPATHY

The procedures used to make a diagnosis of psychopathy include global clinical impressions, self-report inventories, rating scales, and checklists (see Hare and Cox, 1978). The assessment procedures used in our research on criminal psychopathy are described below. For comparison purposes several other popular procedures are also described.

Rating Scales

We have devoted a considerable amount of research effort to the development of a reliable and valid procedure for the assessment of psychopathy in forensic populations. In the 1960s we used what amounted to a 3-point rating scale to classify prison inmates as psychopaths (P), mixed (M), and nonpsychopaths (NP) according to the extent to which their characteristics and behavior over a long period were consistent with Cleckley's (1976) conception of psychopathy. This 3-point scale was later replaced by a 7-point rating scale. In each case the ratings were based on interview and case-history data. Although these ratings were reliable and valid (see Hare and Cox, 1978), the raters had to be experienced in working with prison inmates, familiar with the Cleckley conception of psychopathy, and able to integrate large amounts of data into a single score. Moreover, other investigators were sometimes uncertain about how we arrived at a particular rating.

Psychopathy Checklist

In 1978 we began a project to determine whether we could make the nature of our global rating procedure more explicit. The result was a checklist of 22 items (Hare, 1980). The psychometric properties of the checklist and its relationship to other assessment procedures have been described elsewhere (Hare, 1980, 1985a, 1985c; Kosson, Nichols, and Newman, 1985; Raine, 1985; Schroeder, Schroeder, and Hare, 1983). The checklist is highly reliable. For example, a recent analysis of data from 301 inmates in 5 studies obtained alpha coefficients (a measure of internal consistency) of .82 to .92, interrater reliabilities of .84 to .93, and an overall generalizability coefficient of .90 (Schroeder et al., 1983).

We have recently made several minor changes in the checklist. Two items have been deleted and several others have been changed slightly. The items and scoring procedures are described in more detail than they were before, and some difficulties and apparent inconsistencies in the scoring criteria have been removed. The result of these revisions is the 20-item Psychopathy Checklist (Hare, 1985b). The two scales are substantively identical and they classify individuals in the same way. Early indications are that the revision is at least as reliable as the original scale.

The items in the Psychopathy Checklist are presented in Table 1. A complete description of the items and the procedures for scoring them are available on request. Satisfactory completion of the checklist requires a semi-structured interview (about 2 hours long) and access to reasonably detailed files and case-history information. Each item is scored on a 3-point scale (0, 1, 2) according to the extent to which it applies to a given individual. The total score can range from 0 to 40. We generally have two investigators independently complete the checklist for each individual; their scores are then averaged for subsequent use.

Table 1

Items in the Revised Psychopathy Checklist

---

1. Glibness/superficial charm
2. Grandiose sense of self-worth
3. Need for stimulation/proneness to boredom
4. Pathological lying
5. Conning/manipulative
6. Lack of remorse or guilt
7. Shallow affect
8. Callous/lack of empathy
9. Parasitic lifestyle
10. Poor behavioral controls
11. Promiscuous sexual behavior
12. Early behavior problems
13. Lack of realistic, long-term plans
14. Impulsivity
15. Irresponsibility
16. Failure to accept responsibility for own actions
17. Many short-term marital relationships
18. Juvenile delinquency
19. Revocation of conditional release
20. Criminal versatility

From Hare (1985b).

DSM-III

Many of the clinical characteristics of the psychopath are reflected in the description of Antisocial Personality Disorder (APD) listed in the 3rd edition of the American Psychiatric Association's (1980) Diagnostic and Statistical Manual of Mental Disorders (DSM-III). However, the criteria for a DSM-III diagnosis of APD place too much emphasis on evidence of antisocial and criminal behaviors (some of them trivial) and not enough on the personality traits that are responsible for these behaviors. As a result, DSM-III is not only over-inclusive (too many criminals fit the criteria for APD) but also creates difficulties for those attempting to identify individuals who may fit the classic picture of psychopathy but who manage to avoid early, frequent, or formal contact with the criminal justice system. As Millon (1981) put it, DSM-III "fails to recognize that the same fundamental personality structure...is often displayed in ways that are not socially disreputable, irresponsible, or illegal" (p. 185).

Self-report Inventories

Many clinicians rely heavily on self-report inventories for personality assessments and diagnoses. Two of the more popular inventories used in the diagnosis of psychopathy are the Minnesota Multiphasic Personality Inventory (MMPI; Dahlstrom and Welsh, 1960), and the Socialization (So) scale from the California Psychological Inventory (Gough, 1969). MMPI diagnoses are often based on a particular profile of scores on standard MMPI validity and clinical scales. For example, elevated scores on scale 4, Psychopathic Deviate (Pd), and scale 9, Hypomania (Ma), along with certain other cookbook conditions, are supposedly indicative of psychopathy. The So scale is based on Gough's (1948) role-taking theory of psychopathy, and measures a range of behavior from asocial to social, as well as the extent to which values are internalized. In some cases the MMPI and the So scale are used in conjunction with other assessment procedures.

Self-report inventories have several advantages: they are easy to administer and to score, the client does all the work, the procedures are objective, interpretations can be automated, and so on. However, these advantages are offset by a lack of demonstrated validity. There is little evidence that self-report inventories purporting to measure psychopathy in criminal populations actually do so with any real degree of accuracy or practical usefulness. This should not surprise anyone. Criminals in general, and psychopaths in particular, are often test-wise and unwilling to disclose anything of significance about themselves uness it is in their interest to do so. In many cases it is the criminal and not the clinician who is in control of the testing session.

Comparison of Assessment Procedures

Because clinicians and researchers use a variety of procedures for the diagnosis of psychopathy, we might expect that these procedures would be conceptually and empirically related to one another. Unfortunately, this is not the case (Hare, 1985a; Hundleby and Ross, 1977; Ross and Hundleby, 1973). The study by Hare (1985a) compared a variety of assessment procedures that had been used with 274 male prison inmates. These procedures, described above, included the 22-item psychopathy checklist, the 7-point rating scale, DSM-III diagnosis of APD, the MMPI, the So scale, and an experimental self-report psychopathy (SRP) scale based on the psychopathy checklist. In addition, two composite scales used by several investigators were derived from the MMPI. These composite scales were the sum of the Pd and Ma scores (Pd + Ma), and the Pd score minus the So score (Pd - So).

Table 2 presents the correlations among measures (above the diagonal) and the kappa coefficients of agreement between extreme groups (below the diagonal). In computing kappa, each distribution of assessment scores was first divided into approximate thirds to form groups representing low, medium, and high psychopathy. The extreme groups from one distribution were compared with the corresponding groups from another distribution. The kappa coefficients represent the proportion of joint decisions (about group assignment made by any two assessment procedures) that are in agreement beyond chance (Fleiss, 1981). Both the correlations and the kappa coefficients clearly indicate that the greatest diagnostic agreement was among the clinical-behavioral measures, and that agreement between the clinical-behavioral and self-report measurement domains was poor.

Table 2

Correlations Between Psychopathy Assessment Procedures (Above Diagonal) and Kappa Coefficients of Agreement Between High and Low Psychopathy Groups (Below Diagonal)

Variable	1	2	3[a]	4	5	6	7	8[b]	9[b]
1. Rating	.	.80	.57	.28	.21	.22	-.29	.27	.36
2. Checklist	.93	.	.67	.38	.26	.27	-.32	.35	.33
3. DSM-III[a]	.71	.79	.	.35	.29	.21	-.37	.33	.44
4. SRP	.31	.42	.44	.	.26	.36	-.53	.40	.49
5. Pd	.16	.27	.37	.36	.	.14	-.34	--	--
6. Ma	.26	.42	.18	.40	.15	.	-.31	--	.27
7. So	.41	.42	.46	.52	.44	.44	.	-.42	--
8. Pd + Ma[b]	.31	.46	.36	.52	--	--	.53	.	--
9. Pd - So[b]	.40	.37	.56	.54	--	.29	--	--	.

Note. Adapted from Hare (1985a). DSM-III = 3rd edition of Diagnostic and statistical manual of mental disorders (APA, 1980); SRP = Self-report psychopathy scale; Pd = MMPI Psychopathic Deviate scale; Ma = MMPI Hypomania scale; So = Socialization scale.

[a]Correlations involving DSM-III (0 versus 2 diagnoses of APD) are point-biserial.

[b]Correlations and kappa coefficients between composite measures and their components are omitted.

Additional analyses evaluated several standard cookbook procedures for identifying psychopaths on the basis of MMPI profile type. None of these procedures was very successful in picking out inmates that were considered to be psychopaths according to the clinical-behavioral procedures. Somewhat better results were obtained when the 13 basic MMPI validity and clinical scales were entered into a discriminant analysis and used to classify inmates into high and low psychopathy groups formed on the basis of clinical-behavioral measures. For example, a linear combination of the 13 MMPI scales was able to correctly classify 72.9% of the inmates into the low and high psychopathy checklist groups. However, the kappa coefficient for agreement between predicted and actual group membership was only .45.

In evaluating these results it might be argued that clinical-behavioral and self-report procedures tap different aspects of the psychopathy construct, and that each is important in its own way. Nonetheless, my confidence in the inherent superiority of clinical-behavioral procedures is strengthened by clear evidence (some of it reviewed below) that they are related, in the predicted direction, to a variety of demographic and behavioral variables. In contrast, self-report inventories, including the MMPI, typically are only weakly related to relevant behavioral and demographic ariables (e.g., Carbonell, Moorhead, and Megargee, 1984).

PSYCHOPATHY AND CRIME

The incidence of psychopathy in prisons varies according to the criteria used for its diagnosis and the type of prison involved. A reasonable estimate is that between 15 and 25 percent of incarcerated males would meet relatively stringent criteria for psychopathy. Whatever the incidence, there is no doubt that psychopaths commit a disproportionate number of crimes. A recent analysis (Hare and Jutai, 1983) of the criminal records of inmates in Canadian federal medium and maximum security institutions who volunteered to take part in one of our research projects between 1964 and 1975 illustrates this point. The criminal records were obtained from the RCMP Fingerprint Service (FPS) files, which contained a listing of charges, convictions, and dispositions from the first appearance in adult court until December 31, 1975. The inmates were placed into three groups--psychopaths (P), mixed (M), and nonpsychopaths (NP)--according to how well they fit the Cleckley criteria for psychopathy (see Hare and Jutai, 1983 for details). The data from Groups P (N = 97) and NP (N = 96) are presented here. The mean number of charges for crimes committed (per year free) by each group during the analysis period (which averaged 11.2 years) is presented in Table 3. It is clear that Group P received many more charges than did Group NP.

Table 3

Mean Number of Criminal Charges Per Year Free

Type of Offence	Group P (N = 97)	Group NP (N = 96)	p^a
Theft, possession, B & E	2.44	1.16	< .001
Robbery	.26	.04	< .01
Fraud, forgery, etc.	.92	.69	< .10
Murder, attempted murder	.02	.01	--
Assault	.27	.10	< .05
Possession of weapon	.22	.06	< .05
Driving	.17	.19	--
Narcotics	.21	.52	< .01
Escapes	.21	.09	< .05
Miscellaneous	.34	.40	--
Total Charges	5.06	3.25	< .001
(Violent)	.91	.27	< .05
(Nonviolent)	4.15	2.98	< .001

Note. From Hare and Jutai (1983). P = psychopaths; NP = nonpsychopaths.

[a]Based on two-tailed t test.

Some other data are of interest here. The mean age of first appearance in adult court was 18.1 for Group P and 20.0 for Group NP (p < .01). Almost 40% of the inmates in Group P first appeared before age 17 whereas only 19% of those in Group NP did so. The inmates in Group P were twice as likely to have used an alias when arrested than were those in Group NP. And in spite of their generally poorer record, the inmates in Group P received more paroles than did those in Group NP.

Similar results have recently been obtained by Wong (1985). He selected a random sample consisting of 15% of the male inmate population of eight Canadian federal prisons. There were 315 inmates in the sample, 24, 179, and 112 from minimum, medium, and maximum security institutions respectively. The 22-item psychopathy checklist (Hare, 1980) was completed for each inmate, using only case-history information (an interview was not held). The interrater reliability was .85. The distribution of checklist scores was used to select two extreme groups of inmates, one with scores of 30 or above (psychopaths, Group P; N = 52)) and the other with scores of 20 or below (nonpsychopaths, Group NP; N = 68). The two groups were approximately the same age (M = 32.2 and 31.7 for Groups NP and P respectively). Criminal history data were obtained from the National Parole Board files; only convictions were used in comparing the two groups. Reports of offences committed while in prison were obtained from institutional files. A summary of Wong's findings is presented in Table 4. It is clear that the inmates in Group P (psychopaths) began their criminal careers at an early age and that they committed many more offences than did those in Group L. In spite of a generally atrocious record, both in and out of prison, the inmates in Group H were just as likely to receive a parole as were those in Group L.

Table 4

Comparison of Criminal Groups on Offence Variables

Variable	NP	P	p
Age of first offence	24.1	17.8	< .001
Total number of offences	6.8	25.0	< .001
Mean number of offences per year free	2.0	4.4	< .002
Number of known aliases	0.1	0.3	< .04
Age of first substance abuse	14.6	13.8	ns
Time incarcerated (years)	2.6	7.4	< .001
Total number of institutional offences	0.7	6.4	< .001
Mean rating of violence[a]	0.8	1.5	< .002
Mean rating of threat[a]	0.6	1.1	< .001

Note. From Wong (1985). P = psychopaths; NP = nonpsychopaths.
[a]3-point scale (0, 1, 2).

Violent and Aggressive Behavior

Considering their nature, it is hardly surprising that psychopaths commit more crimes and are more recidivistic than are other offender groups (Hare, 1981; Quinsey, Warneford, Pruesse, and Link, 1975). They are also capable of considerable violence and aggression (Hare, 1981; Hare and McPherson, 1984; Kozol, Boucher, and Garofalo, 1972; also see Tables 3 and 4 above). Some serial murderers, contract killers, mercenaries, armed robbers, and kidnappers are psychopaths in the classic sense.

Several recent analyses of the relationship between psychopathy and violence are available. In one paper (Hare, 1981), case-history data from 243 male inmates were used to make tabulations of convictions for various kinds of violent crime, as well as assessments of aggressive and violent behavior. The inmates were divided into three groups on the basis of ratings on the 7-point psychopathy scale described above. Group P (psychopaths) consisted of 75 inmates with a mean rating of 6-7, and Group NP (nonpsychopaths) consisted of 104 inmates with a mean rating of 1-3.5. The remaining 64 inmates constituted Group M. The percentage of inmates in each group that engaged in various types of violent and aggressive behavior is presented in Table 5. It is clear that Group P was generally more violent and aggressive than was either of the other groups. Only 3% of the inmates in Group P, compared with 22% in Group M and 25% in Group NP, did not have at least one formal conviction for a violent crime.

Table 5

Percentage of Inmates in Each Group That Engaged in Various Types of
Violent and Aggressive Behavior

Activity	P (N=104)	M (N=64)	NP (N=75)	p^a
Convictions				
Murder or manslaughter	4	4	4	--
Armed robbery	19	8	9	< .05
Robbery	20	16	16	--
Assault	24	14	7	< .01
Forcible seizure	9	0	1	< .01
Rape	4	0	1	--
Behavior				
Use of gun	11	4	1	< .01
Use of other weapon	7	0	3	--
Fights	56	46	20	< .001
Aggressive homosexuality	6	6	0	< .01

Note. From Hare (1981). P = psychopaths; M = mixed; NP =
nonpsychopaths.

[a]Based on chi square (P versus NP).

A study by Hare and McPherson (1984) provides a detailed analysis of
the relationship between psychopathy and violence from age 16 to 30.   Two
investigators used interview and case-history information to complete the
22-item psychopathy checklist for 227 male inmates of a federal medium
security institution.   The distribution of checklist scores was divided
into approximate thirds to produce Group P (psychopaths; N = 73), Group M
(mixed; N = 75), and Group NP (nonpsychopaths; N= 79).   Data on
convictions for violent crimes and on violent and aggressive behaviors
were obtained from RCMP FPS files, institutional records, and transcripts
of interviews.   The data were coded for the 14-year period from age 16 to
30.   The mean number of convictions for violent crimes committed during
each year that an inmate was not in prison or custody is presented in
Table 6.   A multivariate analysis of variance (MANOVA) indicated that
the overall difference between groups was highly significant, $F(16,434)$ =
2.91, p < .001.   The results of post hoc univariate analyses of variance
(ANOVA) are summarized in the right-hand column of Table 6.   It is clear
that the inmates in Group P received many more convictions for violent
crimes between the ages of 16 and 30 than did those in the other groups.
Although only about 32% of the inmates were in Group P, they received 60%
of the total convictions, whereas Group NP, with 35% of the inmates,
received only 17% of the convictions.   A second analysis revealed that
84.9% of the inmates in Group P, 64.0% of those in Group M, and 54.4% of
those in Group NP were convicted of at least one violent crime during the
analysis period.

Besides information on formal convictions the institutional files
contained entries on weapon use and aggressive behaviors, both in and out
of prison.   The percentage of inmates in each group that possessed,
threatened with, or actually used a weapon at least once during the
analysis period is presented in Table 7.   The psychopaths (Group P) were
clearly much more likely to make some use of a weapon than were the other
inmates.

The percentage of inmates that displayed violent and aggressive
behaviors while in prison is summarized in Table 8.   The results are
consistent with Millon's comment that many psychopaths "have an irascible

temper that flares quickly into argument and attack, as evidenced in
frequent verbally abusive and physically cruel behaviors" (1981, p. 182).

Table 6

Mean Number of Convictions Per Inmate For Violent Crimes Committed
During Each Year Not in Prison

Crime category	Group			p^a
	P	M	NP	
Murder	.078	.014	.019	--
Possession of weapon	.090	.053	.024	< .005
Robbery	.377	.017	.117	< .10
Assault	.239	.069	.037	< .001
Kidnapping	.057	.006	.001	< .001
Rape	.061	.017	.007	--
Vandalism	.041	.007	.006	< .005
Fighting	.058	.017	.002	< .05
Total convictions per year free[b]	1.001	.362	.269	< .001

Note. From Hare and McPherson (1984). The analysis period was age 16
to 30. P = psychopaths; M = mixed; NP = nonpsychopaths.

[a]Based on post hoc univariate analysis of variance following a
significant MANOVA.

[b]Total convictions for all crimes of violence (per inmate); $F(2,224)$ =
12.49. In a post hoc test, Group P differed from Groups M and NP.

Table 7

Percentage of Inmates in Each Group That Engaged in Weapon Use

Weapon use	Group			p^a
	P	M	NP	
Possession	28.8	16.0	15.2	< .05
Threaten with	42.5	29.3	15.2	< .001
Actual use	24.7	10.7	11.4	< .01
Any use of weapons	49.3	33.3	21.5	< .001

Note. From Hare and McPherson (1984). The analysis period was age 16
to 30. P = psychopaths; M = mixed; NP = nonpsychopaths.

[a]Based on Bartholomew's test for ordered proportions (Fleiss, 1981).

Table 8

Percentage of Inmates In Each Group That Displayed Violent and
Aggressive Behavior in Prison

| Behavior | r^a | Group | | | $\underline{p}^b$ |
		P	M	NP	
Attempted suicide	.85	19.2	10.7	15.4	--
Self-mutilation	.80	6.8	4.0	3.8	--
Verbal abuse	.62	24.7	9.3	2.6	< .001
Verbal threats	.58	26.0	9.3	2.6	< .001
Easily annoyed or irritated	.71	45.2	28.0	10.3	< .001
Belligerent	.64	46.6	21.3	3.8	< .001
Aggressive homosexuality	.74	6.8	8.0	2.6	--
Fighting	.59	50.7	29.3	26.9	< .001
Any of above	.85	86.3	80.0	55.1	< .001

Note. From Hare and McPherson (1984). The analysis period was age 16
to 30. P = psychopaths; M = mixed; NP = nonpsychopaths.

[a]Interrater reliability for a sample of 69 inmates.

[b]Based on Bartholomew's test for ordered proportions (Fleiss, 1981).

THE CRIMINAL HISTORY OF PSYCHOPATHS

Thus far I have presented data on the criminal activities of
psychopaths without consideration of the changes that might occur over
time. Robins (1966) has suggested that although psychopaths may become
less antisocial after age 30, they often continue to be somewhat
disagreeable individuals. Similarly, part of the clinical folklore is
that psychopaths "burn out" or at least become less blatantly antisocial
around age 30 or 35.

We now have a considerable amount of empirical data on the criminal
behavior of well-defined groups of psychopaths over a 30 year span from
age 16 to 45 (Hare, McPherson, and Wong, 1985). The data were obtained
from 521 male criminals first assessed for psychopathy (as subjects in
one of our psychophysiological research projects) sometime between 1964
and 1982. They had originally been classified as psychopaths, mixed, or
nonpsychopaths, according to how well they fit the Cleckley conception of
psychopathy. In this paper criminals classified as mixed or
nonpsychopaths were combined into one group (Group NP) for comparison
with the psychopaths (Group P). The RCMP FPS files were used to tabulate
charges and convictions for criminal offences; these were broken down
into 5-year periods from age 16 until the end of the analysis period,
October 31, 1982.

The data presented here are both retrospective (the period from age 16
to the age of a given subject when the psychopathy assessment was made)
and prospective (the period from the time of the assessment until October
31, 1982). The data within each period were positively skewed, and for
this reason they were subjected to square-root transformation for
presentation here. Because there were differences in the age at which
the subjects were first studied, and because they were first studied
anywhere from 1964 to 1982, the numbers in each group for whom data were
available decreased across age periods. The number in each of the six
periods respectively was as follows: Group P (204, 187, 127, 87, 60, 35);

Group NP (317, 281, 193, 134, 87, 46). Two sets of data are presented, the first using all subjects available in each period, and the second using the same subjects throughout the entire analysis interval (16-45).

Figure 1 shows the conviction rate (per year free) of Groups P and NP as a function of age; the data from all subjects are included. Psychopaths (P) received many more convictions than did the other criminals (NP) until at least age 35, whereupon the difference decreased dramatically. It is important to note, however, that both groups continued to engage in a considerable amount of criminal activity until at least age 45, the end of the analysis period. The persistence of criminal behavior in some individuals is evident in Figure 2, which depicts the percentage of criminals in each group that received at least one conviction (left side of figure), and at least three convictions (right side of figure), during each period; again, the data from all subjects were included. In spite of the sharp decrease with age in the percentage of psychopaths convicted of a crime, more than half still received at least one conviction between age 41 and 45, and over 20% received at least three convictions during this period.

The preceding analyses were performed on data from different numbers of criminals in each period. This procedure provides a composite picture of criminal history which, although useful, is subject to distortion by sampling error in each period. Perhaps a more accurate representation of year-by-year changes is obtained by following the same individuals over time. At the end of the current analysis period 35 psychopaths (P) and 46 nonpsychopaths (NP) were at least 45 years old. Their conviction rate (per year free) over the 30-year period from age 16 to age 45 is presented in Figure 3.

Figure 4 shows the percentage of criminals in each group that received at least one conviction (left side of figure) and at least three convictions (right side of figure) in each period. Convictions received by Group P reached a maximum around age 30, somewhat later than suggested by the composites in Figures 1 and 2. Moreover, the decline in Group P's convictions after age 30 was not as rapid as was that depicted in the composite figures. In evaluating these two sets of results, I might note that in the first two periods of the composite analyses Group P contained many young criminals with unusually high conviction rates. Their data inflated the values for the 16-20 and 21-25 periods. I suspect that as we follow the progress of these criminals they will show the same pattern of illegal activity as that represented in Figures 3 and 4: an increase in convictions until age 30 or 35, followed by a gradual decrease over the next 10 or 15 years.

Although I have presented data on criminal convictions, essentially the same group trends were obtained with criminal charges as the dependent variable. There were no systematic age-related differences between groups in the type of crimes committed or in the degree of violence involved.

If criminal psychopaths "burn out" they apparently do so somewhat later than do other criminals. Actually, burn-out is probably not the correct term here; it has connotations of being worn out mentally and physically that may not apply to psychopaths. The truth is, we do not really know why their mean conviction rate, previously very high, decreases relative to that of other criminals by age 40 or so. Some of our current research is directed at this question. Meanwhile, it is important not to lose sight of the fact that more than half of the criminals in our study continued to be convicted of crimes after age 40.

Figure 1. Mean number of convictions per year free (square-root) transformation) received by psychopaths (P) and nonpsychopaths (NP) in each age period. The number of criminals in each of the six periods was as follow: Group P (204, 187, 127, 87, 60, 35); Group NP (317, 281, 193, 134, 87, 46). From Hare et al. (1985).

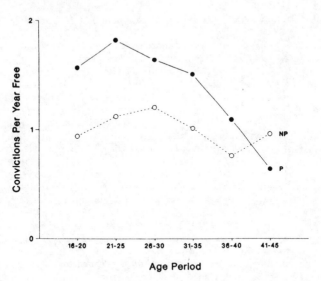

Figure 2. Percentage of psychopaths (P) and nonpsychopaths (NP) with one or more convictions (left side) and three or more convictions (right side) in each age period. The number of criminals in each period was as follows: Group P (204, 187, 127, 87, 60, 35); Group NP (317, 281, 193, 134, 87, 46). From Hare et al. (1985).

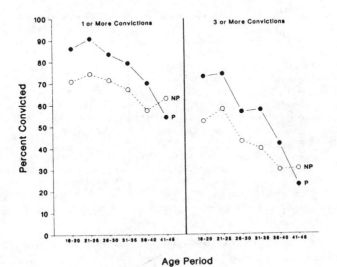

<u>Figure 3</u>
Mean number of convictions per year free (square-root) transformation)
received by the same 35 psychopaths (P) and 46 nonpsychopaths (NP) over a
30-year period from age 16 to 45. From Hare et al. (1985).

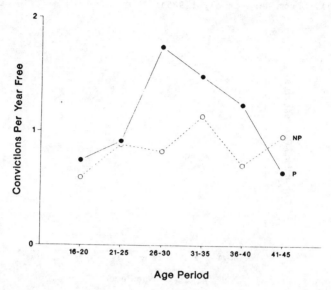

<u>Figure 4</u>
Percentage of 35 psychopaths (P) and 46 nonpsychoaths (NP) with one or
more convictions (left side) and three or more convictions (right side)
over a 30-year period from age 16 to 45. From Hare et al. (1985).

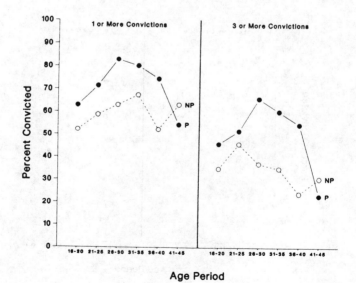

PSYCHOPATHY AND CONDITIONAL RELEASE

In a previous section I noted that psychopaths are at least as successful in obtaining parole as are other criminals. This may seem puzzling to some, given that when applying for parole they may already have a long criminal record, including previous violations of the conditions of parole, probation, bail, and temporary absence. However, as anyone who has had to deal with psychopaths can attest, they can be extremely manipulative, deceptive, and convincing (see Items 1, 4, and 5 of the Psychopathy Checklist in Table 1). They may be very skilled in manipulating the justice system, in soliciting community support, and in using facilities and programs that give the appearance of a sincere concern for rehabilitation, including educational upgrading, drug and alcohol programs, religious and quasi-religious organizations, and fashionable movements and groups with a pseudo-scientific, mystical, or pop-psychology flavor.

Although psychopaths are often successful in obtaining parole and other forms of conditional release, a recent study by Kropp, Hart, and Hare (1985) clearly demonstrates that they seldom satisfy the conditions attached to their release from custody. Our sample consisted of 105 male criminals released from a medium security prison, 38 on parole and 67 on mandatory supervision (release after serving two-thirds of the sentence). Two investigators independently completed the 22-item psychopathy checklist for each inmate prior to his release. Neither the checklist scores nor any other information obtained as part of the inmate's involvement in our research was available to those responsible for making decisions about conditional release. The distribution of checklist scores was divided into approximate thirds to produce Group P (psychopaths; N = 37), Group M (mixed; N = 34), and Group NP (nonpsychopaths; N = 34). Through the cooperation of the National Parole Service of Canada we were able to chart each criminal's progress for at least one year following his release.

Table 9 shows the percentage of criminals in each group that had a conditional release suspended or revoked before the end of the analysis period. As a group, the criminals on parole generally did better than did those on mandatory supervision, a common finding (the former are carefully selected whereas the latter are not). As predicted, Group P performed much worse than did Group NP, particularly on parole. The parolees in Group P were five times more likely to have their parole suspended, and four times more likely to have it revoked, than were those in Group NP.

The data in Table 9 tell us only that psychopaths are much more likely than are other criminals to violate the conditions of their release sometime within the analysis period. Survival analysis permits estimates to be made of the time before the occurrence of a violation. For this particular analysis the parole and mandatory supervision data were pooled (as conditional release). The survival curves for time to suspension and revocation of conditional release are plotted in Figures 5 and 6 respectively. The curves represent estimates of the proportion of criminals in each group that will survive (that is, will not have received a suspension or revocation of conditional release) as a function of time after release from prison. Figure 5 indicates that about 78% of the criminals in Group P, 57% in Group M, and 30% in Group NP will have their conditional release suspended within the first year. Only about 10% of those in Group P, compared with almost 70% of those in Group NP, will last three years before suspension. Figure 6 shows that about 58%

of those in Group P, 52% in Group M, and only 23% of Group NP, will have their conditional release revoked within the first year. The probability of survival beyond three years is good for Group NP and extremely poor for Group P.

Table 9

Percentage of Criminals In Each Group That Had Conditional Release Suspended or Revoked

Group	Percent Suspended	Percent Revoked
	Parole	
P	83.3	50.0
M	42.9	28.6
NP	16.7	12.5
Total	32.4	21.6
	Mandatory Supervision	
P	80.6	67.7
M	63.0	51.9
NP	60.0	50.0
Total	70.6	58.8

Note. From Kropp et al. (1985). P = psychopaths; M = mixed; NP = nonpsychopaths.

   Additional analyses compared the psychopathy checklist with several actuarial procedures commonly used to predict the parole outcome. The following 13 background variables were included in one set of analyses: age, education, socioeconomic status, employment history, age of first arrest, marital status, type of offence, degree of violence, length of sentence, drug and alcohol use, previous time served, and institutional behavior. We also computed a Revised Salient Factor Score (SFS 81) for each individual. A SFS is derived from six demographic variables; these scores are used by the U.S. Parole Service in making decisions about parole (Hoffman, 1983). A series of discriminant analyses was performed in which the predictive power of the 13 background variables and the 6 SFS variables or subscores was compared with that of the 22 items in the psychopathy checklist. The results are summarized in Table 10. The checklist items by themselves did a much better job of predicting suspension of conditional release than did either the background variables or the SFS subscores. These 22 items were able to predict suspensions with 81% accuracy, with reasonable false positive and false negative rates; the kappa coefficient of .60 indicates that, with chance excluded, there was 60% agreement between predicted and actual outcome. Note that combining the checklist items with the SFS subscores did not improve on the accuracy of prediction obtained with the checklist items alone.

<u>Figure 5</u>
Survival curves for time to suspension of conditional release from prison. The curves show the estimated proportion of each group still surviving (conditional release not suspended) as a function of time after release. P = psychopaths ($\underline{N}$ = 37); M = mixed ($\underline{N}$ = 34); NP = nonpsychopaths ($\underline{N}$ = 34). From Kropp et al. (1985).

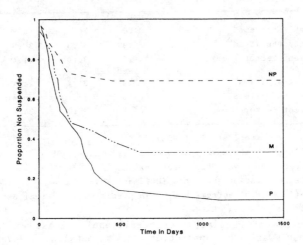

<u>Figure 6</u>
Survival curves for time to revocation of conditional release from prison. The curves show the estimated proportion of each group still surviving (conditional release not revoked) as a function of time after release. P = psychopaths ($\underline{N}$ = 37); M = mixed ($\underline{N}$ = 34); NP = nonpsychopaths ($\underline{N}$ = 34). From Kropp et al. (1985).

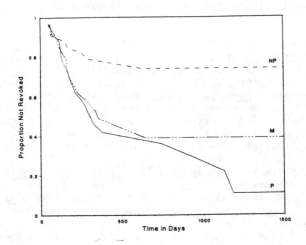

Table 10

Comparison of Procedures For Prediction of Outcome on Conditional
Release

Variables	Percent Correct	Percent False +	Percent False −	Kappa[d]
	Suspension			
Checklist items[a]	81.0	21.4	14.3	.60
Background items[b]	68.4	33.3	26.9	.33
Salient Factor items[c]	69.5	30.0	31.4	.36
	Revocation			
Checklist items[a]	72.4	31.4	24.1	.45
Background items[b]	63.3	38.7	35.8	.23
Salient Factor items[c]	66.7	36.7	30.4	.33

Note. From Kropp et al. (1985).

[a]22 items in the psychopathy checklist (Hare, 1980).

[b]13 background variables; see text.

[c]6 Salient Factor subscores (Hoffman, 1983).

[d]Coefficient of agreement between predicted and actual outcome.

The prediction of revocation of conditional release was generally less
accurate than was the prediction of suspension. Nevertheless, the
checklist items were still better than were the actuarial methods,
although the difference was not as large as it was for suspension. The
most accurate predictions occurred when the checklist items were
supplemented with the SFS subscores.

These results provide strong evidence for the predictive validity of
the psychopathy checklist. They also indicate that psychopaths, as
defined here, are not good candidates for conditional release. Research
currently in progress should determine whether or not their performance
on conditional release improves as they become older.

REFERENCES
American Psychiatric Association. (1980). Diagnostic and statistical
manual of mental disorders (3rd ed.). Washington, DC: Author.
Blackburn, R. (1973). An empirical classification of psychopathic
   personality. British Journal of Psychiatry, 127, 456-460.
Buss, A. (1966). Psychopathology. New York: Wiley.
Carbonell, J. L., Moorhead, K. M., & Megargee, E. I. (1984). Predicting
   prison adjustment with structured personality inventories. Journal of
   Consulting and Clinical Psychology, 52, 280-294.
Cleckley, H. (1976). The mask of sanity (5th ed.). St. Louis, MO:
   Mosby.
Craft, M. J. (1965). Ten studies into psychopathic personality.
   Bristol: John Wright.
Dahlstrom, W. G., & Welsh, G. S. (1960). An MMPI handbook: A guide to
   use in clinical practice and research. Minneapolis: University of
   Minnesota Press.
Fleiss, J. L. (1981). Statistical methods for rates and proportions.
   New York: Wiley.

Gough, H. G. (1948). A sociological theory of psychopathy. American Journal of Sociology, 53, 356-366.

Gough, H. G. (1969). Manual for the California Psychological Inventory. Palo Alto: Consulting Psychologists Press.

Hare, R. D. (1970). Psychopathy: Theory and research. New York: Wiley.

Hare, R. D. (1980). A research scale for the assessment of psychopathy in criminal populations. Personality and Individual Differences, 1, 111-119.

Hare, R. D. (1981). Psychopathy and violence. In J. R. Hayes, T. K. Roberts, & K. S. Solway (Eds.), Violence and the violent individual (pp. 53-74). New York: Spectrum.

Hare, R. D. (1985a). Comparison of procedures for the assessment of psychopathy. Journal of Consulting and Clinical Psychology, 53, 7-16.

Hare, R. D. (1985b). The Psychopathy Checklist. Unpublished manuscript, University of British Columbia, Vancouver, Canada.

Hare, R. D. (1985c). A checklist for the assessment of psychopathy in criminal populations. In M. H. Ben-Aron, S. J. Hucker, & C. D. Webster (Eds.), Clinical criminology. Toronto: M and M Graphics, in press.

Hare, R. D., & Cox, D. N. (1978). Clinical and empirical conceptions of psychopathy, and the selection of subjects for research. In R. D. Hare & D. Schalling (Eds.), Psychopathic behavior: Approaches to research (pp. 1-27). Chichester, England: Wiley.

Hare, R. D., & Jutai, J. W. (1983). Criminal history of the male psychopath. In K. T. Van Dusen & S. A. Mednick (Eds.), Prospective studies of crime and delinquency (pp. 225-236). Boston: Kluwer-Nijhoff.

Hare, R. D., & McPherson, L. M. (1984). Violent and aggressive behavior by criminal psychopaths. International Journal of Law and Psychiatry, 7, 35-50.

Hare, R. D., McPherson, L. M., & Wong, S. (1985). A longitudinal study of criminal psychopaths. Manuscript in preparation.

Hare, R. D., & Schalling, D. (Eds.). (1978). Psychopathic behavior: Approaches to research. Chichester, England: Wiley.

Hoffman, P. B. (1983). Screening for risk: A revised Salient Factor Score (SFS 81). Journal of Criminal Justice, 11, 539-547.

Hundleby, J. D., & Ross, B. E. (1977). A comparison of questionnaire measures of psychopathy. Journal of Consulting and Clinical Psychology, 45, 702-703.

Kosson, D. S., Nichols, S., & Newman, J. P. (1985). Assessment of psychopathy in a United States prison using Hare's twenty-two item checklist. Unpublished manuscript, University of Wisconsin, Madison, Wisconsin.

Kozol, H., Boucher, R. J., & Garofalo, R. F. (1972). The diagnosis and treatment of dangerousness. Crime and Delinquency, 18, 371-392.

Kropp, R., Hart, S., & Hare, R. D. (1985). Psychopathy and performance on conditional release from prison. Manuscript in preparation.

McCord, W., & McCord, J. (1964). The psychopath: An essay on the criminal mind. Princeton, NJ: Van Nostrand.

Maughs, S. B. (1941). Concept of psychopathy and psychopathic personality: Its evolution and historical development. Journal of Criminal Psychopathology, 2, 329-356.

Millon, T. (1981). Disorders of personality: DSM-III: Axis II. New York, Wiley.

Pichot, P. (1978). Psychopathic behavior: An historical review. In R. D. Hare & D. Schalling (Eds.), Psychopathic behavior: Approaches to research (pp. 55-70). Chichester, England, Wiley.

Quay, H. C. (1964). Personality dimensions in delinquent males as inferred from factor analysis of behavior ratings. Journal of Research in Crime and Delinquency, 1, 33-37.

Quinsey, V., L., Warneford, A., Pruesse, M., & Link, N. (1975). Released Oak Ridge patients: A follow-up study of review board discharges. British Journal of Criminology, 15, 264-270.

Raine, A. (1985). A psychometric assessment of Hare's checklist for psychopathy on an English prison population. British Journal of Clinical Psychology, 24, 247-248.

Raine, A. (in press). Antisocial behavior and social psychophysiology. In H. Wagner (Ed.), Bodily changes and social behavior: Theory and experiment in social psychophysiology. London: Wiley.

Robins, L. N. (1966). Deviant children grown up. Baltimore: Williams & Wilkins.

Ross, B. E., & Hundleby, J. D. (1973). Comparison of measures of psychopathy on a prison sample (summary). Proceedings of the 81st Annual Convention of the American Psychological Association, 8, 533-534.

Schalling, D. (1978). Psychopathy-related personality variables and the psychophysiology of socialization. In R. D. Hare & D. Schalling (Eds.), Psychopathic behavior: Approaches to research (pp. 85-106). Chicester, England: Wiley.

Schroeder, M. L., Schroeder, K. G., & Hare, R. D. (1983). Generalizability of a checklist for assessment of psychopathy. Journal of Consulting and Clinical Psychology, 51, 511-516.

Siddle, D. A., & Trasler, G. B. (1981). The psychophysiology of psychopathic behavior. In M. J. Christie & P. G. Mellet (Eds.), Foundations of psychosomatics. London: Wiley.

Smith, R. J. (1978). The psychopath in society. New York: Academic Press.

Venables, P. H. (in press). Autonomic nervous system factors in criminal behavior. In S. A. Mednick & T. Moffit (Eds.), Biology and crime. Cambridge: Cambridge University Press.

Weiss, J. M. A. (in press). The nature of psychopathy. Directions in Psychiatry.

Wong, S. (1985). The criminal and institutional behaviors of psychopaths. Program User Report, Ministry of the Solicitor General of Canada, Ottawa, Canada.

THE INHERITANCE OF HUMAN DEVIANCE: ANTI-GENETIC BIAS AND THE FACTS

SARNOFF A. MEDNICK

INTRODUCTION

Many social scientists have a negative bias in their perceptions and judgments concerning biological (especially genetic) factors influencing human behavior. In fact, attitudes concerning biology are highly politicized so that an agency of the Department of Justice (Office of Juvenile Justice and Delinquency Prevention) in a recent program announcement (Federal Register, 1985) indicated that the "office is legislatively restricted from conducting research involving any biomedical experimentation on individuals" (Section 261 (d) JJD PAct). To the extent that any biological factors are etiologically related to delinquent or criminal behavior, this law (which makes it illegal for research to be supported), serves neither the interests of the delinquents, his/her victims, or society. A law, such as this, which restricts free inquiry is simply pernicious; it calls to mind laws concerning scientific inquiry in certain, now-defunct, totalitarian states.

Nowhere is this negative bias more marked than in consideration of the role of heritable factors in the causes of criminal behavior. When I talk to concerned individuals about their fears in this matter, three themes emerge:
(1) The mystical "bad seed" notion
(2) Genetic determinism
(3) The hopeless untreatability of genetic deficit.

The "Bad Seed"

This notion suggests that some infants are born with "criminality" genes which will inevitably lead the innocent child to a life of crime and imprisonment. But this concept is nonsensical. We do not inherit anything like "criminality". We inherit predispositions to eye color, height etc., that is we inherit physiological and biochemical potentialities. If some of these physiological characteristics interact with a powerful environment to predispose this child to antisocial acts, then s/he will have an increased probability to engage in criminal behavior. But this same physiological characteristic may interact with a more favorable environment to produce a more positive outcome.

For example, when we study delinquents, criminals, and psychopaths in the lab we find them to be emotionally unresponsive and relatively fearless. One can imagine that this could be a valued characteristic for an individual who tends (uninvited) to walk around at night in other people's homes. But this same physiological characteristic of emotional unresponsiveness might be a part of "The Right Stuff" in a successful test pilot or astronaut or deep sea diver. Perhaps what matters is his family rearing experience and perhaps other personal characteristics. What is inherited is not a BAD SEED but some subtle physiological trait which the family and society will shape.

Genetic Determinism

Now perhaps we can more easily see the inappropriateness of the fear of what is called genetic determinism. The first genetic study of criminal behavior was entitled "Crime as destiny". Lange (1929) stated that if you had the "crime gene" you were destined inexorably to become a criminal. As we have just noted, the same physiological characteristics may "hurl one down into the mud! or up among the stars!" Rostand (1972, p. 86). It depends very much on the environment. The inheritance of physiological characteristics is no more deterministic than being born into a family with inconsistent disciplinary practices.

Untreatability

In the same vein, some individuals fear that accepting genetic factors as playing any role in crime may lead to a pessimistic abandonment of treatment of offenders. The same prejudice once existed among scientists studying the origins of schizophrenia. At a professional meeting some years ago, I shared the podium with an eminent psychiatrist. In passing, during my talk, I noted that all reasonable workers in the field would bow to the accumulated evidence and acknowledge that genetic factors play some role in the etiology of schizophrenia. The eminent psychiatrist leaped to his feet and shouted that it wasn't true; and even if it were true he would never admit it since that would lead to a pessimistic attitude towards treatment. A similar stance is taken by some workers in the field of criminal justice. They fear that if a partial genetic etiology is found, public policy might turn towards a "lock 'em up and throw away the key" mentality. They feel that if the "cause" is environmental then retraining is more likely to be successful and treatment professionals will be more optimistic. (It has even been suggested that I suppress findings on genetic reseach in criminology). I hesitate to accept this rationale for several reasons:

(1) Concerning the suggestion that I suppress these findings, I must refuse. Attempts to control or limit scientific inquiry have in any case ultimately proven to be fruitless. Even highly centralized and controlled governments have not been completely successful in blotting out the spirit of free inquiry.

(2) Even with current environmental assumptions, our treatments for offenders can hardly be described as exceptionally effective, nor are treatment professionals overly optimistic. It seems possible that a more complete understanding of the causes of criminal behavior (including biological factors) would hasten improvement of our methods of treatment of offenders.

(3) Understanding of the interaction of genetic and environmental factors in the causes of crime must inevitably lead to improvement of treatment and prevention. Consider phenylketonuria, a condition which caused a sizable percentage of mental deficiency until its genetic/environmental etiology was detected. These children are born with an inherited intolerance for substances present in certain common foods. After birth, as they are exposed to these substances in their everyday diets, they gradually sink into severe mental retardation. The genetic contribution to the condition was discovered in the thirties; the nature of the biological deficit was found in the fifties. Now newborns

are routinely tested for this condition. A diet excluding the dangerous substances means a relatively normal life for many of these children. In this paragraph I have simplified the complex problems involved in the treatment and prevention of phenylketonuria; the issues involved in the treatment and prevention of criminal behavior will almost certainly prove to be even more complex. But despite this, it should be clear that partial genetic causation need not imply pessimism regarding treatment or prevention. Quite the contrary!

(4) There is a fear among some that if a partial biological etiology for criminal behavior were found, the treatments implied involve radical medical intervention including psychotropic drugs, or even psychosurgery. This is simply not true. The treatments implied need not be medical or even biological. Baker and (B.) Mednick (1984) point out that "a number of environmental mediators have been shown to actually protect the biologically at-risk child against long-term deviant or less-than-optimal outcomes. Some of the mediators identified were high SES, low levels of family conflict, availability of counseling and remedial assistance..." (p. 144). Baker and Mednick cite an extensive literature which clearly indicates that long-term negative outcomes for children suffering a variety of biological deficits may be totally or largely prevented by appropriate environmental intervention. Much of the research they cite pertains to perinatal injuries and consequent childhood cognitive deficit. To prevent cognitive deficits in children with biological damage, very early intervention is most successful. But for the treatment or prevention of delinquency and criminal activities, our research suggests that stabilizing rearing conditions in early adolescence would produce optimal results. We found that children with certain biological deficits had an increased likelihood to become involved in delinquent acts. More careful examination revealed that if the adolescent period was spent in a stable family, the biological predisposition did not result in delinquency outcomes. It was only in unstable family circumstances during early adolescence that the biological factors seemed to be criminogenic. (Unstable family circumstances in this case refers to large numbers of changes in the adult constellations in the household). These results imply devoting societal resources to help stabilize family conditions of early delinquents. The state cannot easily put itself in the business of policing marriages; but some potentially viable alternatives might exist. Ideas we have been considering include offering pay to appropriate unemployed or part-time employed individuals to develop and maintain stabilizing relationships with adolescents with biological predispositions. Such individuals might be women without occupational training whose children are grown, or active, interested retired couples. The important point is that the evidence indicates that biological deficits can be compensated by appropriate environmental intervention.

Current State of the Evidence for Biological Factors

I have described emotional and political motives for social science's failure to embrace enthusiastically the role of biological factors in the causes of criminal behavior, but there has also been a rational reason. This was simply that the evidence for the influence of genetic variables was weak. Below I summarize this older evidence and present more recent research which strongly supports the hypothesis of the influence of genetic factors in the etiology of criminal behavior.

Recently (Christiansen, 1977a), has reported on the criminal behavior of a total population of 3,586 twin pairs from a well defined area of Denmark. He expressed his results in terms of concordance. Twins are concordant for crime if they have both committed criminal acts. He found 52% of the twins concordant for criminal behavior for (male-male) identical twin pairs, and 22% concordance for (male-male) fraternal twin pairs. This result suggests that identical twins inherit some biological characteristic (or characteristics) which increases their common risk of being registered for criminal behavior.

It has been pointed out, however, that identical twins are treated more alike than are fraternal twins (Christiansen, 1977b). Thus, their greater similarity in criminal behavior may be partly related to their shared experience. This has produced hesitation in the full acceptance of the genetic implications of twin research. The study of adoptions better separates environmental and genetic effects; if convicted adoptees have disproportionately high numbers of convicted biological fathers (given appropriate controls), this would suggest the influence of a genetic factor in criminal behavior. This conclusion is especially supported by the fact that almost none of the adoptees know their biological parents (Teasdale & Sorensen, in preparation); the adoptee often does not even realize he has been adopted.

Two U.S. adoption studies have reported highly suggestive results. Crowe (1975) finds an increased rate of criminality in 37 Iowan adoptees with criminal biological mothers. Cadoret (1978) reports on 246 Iowans adopted at birth. Reports of antisocial behavior in these 246 adoptees are significantly related to antisocial behavior in the biological parents. In a study of Swedish adoptees Bohman, Cloninger, Sigvardsson and von Knorring (1982) report that criminal behavior in the biological parents is significantly related to criminal behavior in the adoptees. This relationship holds only for property crimes. Thus we have three investigations from two different national settings which report that sons of criminals are more likely to engage in criminal behavior than sons of law abiding parents even though the sons were adopted away by strangers at-or near birth. It seems clear that the criminal biological parents transmitted some biological characteristic to their sons which increased the likelihood that the sons would become involved in criminal activities.

The present study is based on a register of all 14,427 non-familial adoptions in Denmark in the years 1924-1947. This register was established at the Psykologisk Institut in Copenhagen by a group of American and Danish investigators (Kety, Rosenthal, Wender, & Schulsinger, 1968). The register includes information on the adoptee and his/her adoptive biological parents. We hypothesized that registered criminality in the biological parents would be associated with an increased risk of registered criminal behavior.

PROCEDURES

Information on all non-familial adoptions in the Kingdom of Denmark between 1924 and 1947 (N = 14,427) was obtained from records at the Ministry of Justice. The distribution of adoptions by sex of adoptee for 5-year periods appears in Table 1. Note the increase in adoptions with increasing populations, especially during the war years, and the larger number of females adopted.

Table 1
Number of Adoptions in Five Year Periods

Years	Male	Female	Totals
1924-1928	578	1051	1629
1929-1933	730	1056	1786
1934-1938	832	1092	1924
1939-1943	1650	1731	3381
1944-1947 (4 years)	2890	2782	5672
Year uncertain	20	15	35
Totals	6700	7727	14427

Criminality data
   Court convictions were utilized as an index of criminal involvement.
"The reliability and validity of the Danish record keeping system are
almost beyond criticism. The criminal registry office in Denmark is
probably the most thorough, comprehensive and accurate in the Western
World" (Wolfgang, 1977). Minors (below 15 years of age) cannot receive
court convictions. Court convictions information is maintained by the
chief of the police district in which an individual is born. The court
record (Strafferegister) contains information on the date of the
conviction, the paragraphs of the law violated, and the sanction. To
access these records it is necessary to know the place of birth. When
subjects' conviction records could not be checked it was usually because
of lack of information or ambiguity regarding their date and/or place of
birth. The court record was obtained for all of the subjects for whom
date and place of birth were available (N = 65,516).
   Information was first recorded from the adoption files of the Ministry
of Justice. In these adoption files, birth place was then available for
the biological and adoptive parents but not for the adoptee; birthplace
for the adoptees was obtained from the Central Persons Register or the
local Population Registers. The Central Persons Register was established
in 1968; adoptees who died or emigrated before 1968 were thus excluded
from the study. There were some difficulties in these searches. The
criminal records of persons who have died or have reached the age of 80
are sometimes removed from the registers and archived in the Central
Police Office in Copenhagen. Thus, if an individual had a court
conviction but had died before our search began, his record might have
been transferred from the local police district to the Copenhagen Central
Police Office. There the record would be maintained in a death
register. In view of this the entire population (adoptees and parents)
was checked in the death register. If an adoptee had died or emigrated
before the age of 30, the adoptee and parents were dropped from the study
since he had not gone through his entire risk period for criminal
conviction. A small section of Denmark in southern Jutland belonged to
Germany until 1920. If an individual from this area was registered for
criminality before 1920 but not after 1920, his record was lost to this
study.
   For each individual we coded the following information: sex, date of
birth, address, occupation, place of birth, and size of the community

into which the child was adopted. The subjects' occupations permitted us
to code socioeconomic status (Svalastoga, 1959). For the adoptees we
also coded marital status in 1976.

Not Fully Identified Cases

It will be recalled that in order to check the court register it was
necessary to have name, date, and place of birth. A considerable number
of cases were lost to this investigation for the following reasons:
(1) Lack of record of place and/or date of birth;
(2) In Denmark the biological mother is required by law to name the
    biological father. In some few cases she refused, was unsure or
    named more than one possible father. These cases were dropped from
    the population;
(3) For 397 of the adoptive parents, the child was adopted to a single
    woman. This was due either to the adoptive father's death just
    before the formal adoption or to adoption by a single woman (not
    common in this era);
(4) Because of extra difficulties involved in checking the criminal
    registers before 1910, individuals who were born before January 1885
    were excluded from the study.

In the case of exclusion of an adoptee for any of the above reasons the
entire adoptive family was dropped. If a parent was excluded, the
remaining subjects were retained for analysis. Table 2 presents the
number of fully identified individuals in each of the subject categories.

Table 2
Conviction Rates of Completely Identified Members of the Adoptee Families

Family Member	Number Identified	Number Not Identified	Number of Criminal Law Court Convictions			
			None	One	Two	More than two
Male Adoptees	6129	571	.841	.088	.029	.040
Female Adoptees	7065	662	.972	.020	.005	.003
Adoptive Fathers	13918	509	.938	.046	.008	.008
Adoptive Mothers	14267	160	.981	.015	.002	.002
Biological Fathers	10604	3823	.714	.129	.056	.102
Biological Mothers	12300	2127	.911	.064	.012	.013

RESULTS

The data to be reported will consist of convictions for violation of
the Danish Criminal Code (Straffeloven). The levels of court convictions
for each of the members of the adoption family is given in Table 2. the
biological fathers and the male adoptee conviction rates are considerably
higher than the rates for the adoptive father. The adoptive father is a
bit below the rate (8%) for men of this age group, in this time period
(Hurwitz & Christiansen, 1971). Note also that most of the adoptive
father convictions are attributable to one-time offenders. The male
adoptees and the biological fathers are more heavily recidivistic.

The rates of conviction for the women are considerably lower and there
is considerably less recidivism. The biological mothers and female
adoptees evidence higher levels of court convictions than the adoptive
mothers. The adoptive mothers are just below the population average for

women of this age range and time period, 2.2%. The individuals who gave up their children for adoption, and their biological offspring evidence higher rates of court convictions than the general population and the adoptive parents.

In light of current adoption practices one might be surprised that adoptive parents with court convictions were permitted to adopt. It should be recalled, however, that many of these adoptions took place during the Great Depression and the World War II years. It was more difficult to find willing adoptive homes in these periods owing partly to the relative unavailability of adoptive parents and to the additional numbers of adoptees available. Adoptive parents were accepted if they had a 5-year crime-free period before the adoption.

In most of the analyses which follow, we will consider the relationship between parents' criminal convictions and criminal convictions in the adoptees. If either mother or father (biological and/or adoptive) have received a criminal law conviction, the parents for that adoptee will be considered criminal. In view of the low level of convictions among the female adoptees, analyses will concentrate on the criminal behavior of the male adoptees.

Types of Crimes

Of the adoptive parents, 5.50% were convicted for property crimes; 1.05% committed violent acts; 0.54% were convicted for sexual offenses. For the biological parents, 28.12% are responsible for property crimes; 6.51% committed violent crimes, 3.81% committed sexual offenses. Individuals could be registered for more than one type of crime.

Genetic and Environmental Influences

Because of the size of the population, it is possible to segregate subgroups of adoptees who have combinations of convicted and non-convicted biological and adoptive parents. Table 3 presents four such groups. As can be seen in the lower right hand cell, if neither the biological nor adoptive parents are convicted, 13.5% of their sons are convicted. If the adoptive parents are convicted and the biological parents are not convicted this figure rises to only 14.7%. Note that 20.0% of the sons are convicted if the adoptive parents are not convicted and the biological parents are convicted. If both the biological and adoptive parents are convicted we observe the highest level of conviction in the sons, 24.5%. The comparison analogous to the cross-fostering paradigm favors a partial genetic etiology assumption. We must caution, however, that simply knowing that an adoptive parent has been convicted of a crime does not tell us how criminogenic the adoptee's environment has been. (Recall the preponderance of one-time offenders in the adoptive parents and the adoption agency's condition that the adoptive parents may not have a conviction for the five years preceeding the adoption.) On the other hand, at conception, the genetic influence of the biological father is already complete. Thus this analysis does not yield a fair comparison between environmental and genetic influences included in the Table. But this initial analysis does indicate that sons with a convicted, biological parent have an elevated probability of being convicted. This suggests that some biological characteristic is transmitted from the criminal biological parent which increases the son's risk of obtaining a court conviction for a criminal law offense.

Table 3

"Cross Fostering" Analysis: Percent of Adoptive Sons Who Have Been
Convicted of Criminal Law Offenses

	Are Biological Parents Convicted?	
	Yes	No
Are Adoptive Parents Convicted?		
Yes	24.5%	14.7%
	(of 143)	(of 204)
No	20.0%	13.5%
	(of 1226)	(of 2492)

Note: The numbers in parentheses are the total Ns for each cell.

  The adoptive parents have a low frequency of court convictions. In
order to simplify interpretation of the relationships reported below, we
will exclude cases with adoptive parent criminality. (Analyses completed
which did include adoptive parent criminality did not alter the nature of
the findings to be reported.)
  Figure 1 presents the relationship between convictions in the sons and
degree of recidivism in the biological parent. The relationship is
positive and relatively monotonic (with the scales utilized on the X and
Y axes). Note also that the relationship is highly significant for
property crimes and not statistically significant for violent crimes.

Figure 1

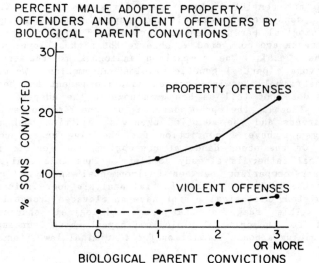

PERCENT MALE ADOPTEE PROPERTY
OFFENDERS AND VIOLENT OFFENDERS BY
BIOLOGICAL PARENT CONVICTIONS

The Chronic Offender
    The chronic offender is infrequent but commits a markedly
disproportionate number of criminal offenses (see chapter by Hare in this
volume). This extremely high rate of offending suggested the hypothesis
that perhaps genetic predisposition may play an important role in these
cases. We examined the relationship between convictions of the chronic
adoptee offender and his biological parents.
    In an important U.S. birth cohort study (Wolfgang, Figlio, & Sellin,
1972), the chronic offender was defined as one who had been arrested five
or more times; these chronic offenders comprised 6% of the males and had
committed 52% of the offenses. In our adoption cohort we have recorded
court convictions rather than arrest data. If we select as chronic
offenders those with three or more court convictions this includes 4.09%
of the male adoptees. This small group of recidivists accounts for 69.4%
of all the court convictions for all the male adoptees. This is a high
concentration of crime in a very small fraction of the cohort.
    Table 4 shows how the chronic offenders, the other offenders (one or
two convictions) and the non-offenders are distributed as a function of
level of crime in the biological parents. As can be seen, the proportion
of chronic adoptee offenders increases as a function of level of
recidivism in the biological parents.

Table 4
Proportion of Chronic Offenders, Other Offenders and Non-offenders in
Male Adoptees as a function of Convictions in the Biological Parents

Number of Male Adoptee Convictions	Number of Biological Parent Convictions			
	0	1	2	3 or more
Non-offenders (no convictions)	.87	.84	.80	.75
Other offenders (1 or 2 convictions)	.10	.12	.15	.17
Chronic offenders (3 or more convictions)	.03	.04	.05	.09
Number of adoptees	2492	547	233	419

Note: Table excludes cases in which adoptive parents have been
       convicted of criminal law violation.

    Another way of expressing this concentration of crime is to point out
that the chronic male adoptee offenders with biological parents with
three or more offenses number only 37. They comprise one percent of the
3,691 male adoptees in Table 5; they are responsible, however, for 30% of
the male adoptee convictions. We should also note that the mean number
of convictions for the chronic adoptee offenders increases sharply as a
function of biological parent recidivism. The biological parents with 0,
1, 2, or 3 or more convictions have male adoptees averaging, .30, .41,

.48, and .70 convictions, respectively.

We have presented evidence that there is an association between biological parents' convictions and the convictions of their adopted sons. The relationship seems stronger for chronic offenders. The sons of chronic offenders account for a disproportionate amount of the convictions in the cohort.

Sibling Analyses

There are a number of instances in which a biological mother and/or biological father contributed more than one of their children to this population. These offspring are, of course, full and half-siblings; they are sometimes placed in different adoptive homes. We would predict that the separated full siblings should show more concordance for criminal convictions than the separated half-siblings. Both of these groups should show more concordance than two randomly selected, unrelated, separately-reared male adoptees.

The probability of any one male adoptee being convicted is .159, the probability of drawing a pair of unrelated, separated male adoptees with at least one having a conviction is .293. The probability that both of the pair have been convicted is .025. Thus pairwise concordance for unrelated separated male adoptees is 8.5%. This can be seen as a baseline. There were 126 male-male half-sibling pairs placed in separate adoptive homes. Of these, 31 pairs had at least one member of the sibship convicted; of these 31 pairs, four pairs were concordant for convictions. This yields a concordance rate for half-siblings of 12.9%. There were 40 male-male full sibling pairs placed in different adoptive homes. Of these, 15 pairs had at least one member of the sibship convicted; of these 15 pairs, three pairs were concordant for convictions. This yields a concordance rate for full siblings of 20%. These numbers are very small, but the results are in the predicted direction. As the degree of genetic relationship increases, the level of concordance increases.

We also considered the level of concordance of the siblings pairs whose biological father was a criminal. (He had at least one conviction.) Of 98 fathers with at least one pair of male-male, separated, adopted siblings, 45 had received at least one conviction (it should be noted that this is a significantly higher rate of convictions (45.9%) than the conviction rate (28.6%) for the total population of biological fathers, $\chi^2(1) = 14.6$, $\underline{p} < 0.01$).

We combined full-and-half sibling pairs (because of the small numbers and since the siblings shared criminal biological fathers). Of the 45 sibling pairs, 13 have at least one member with a conviction; of these 13, four pairs were concordant for convictions. This yields a concordance rate of 30.8%. Table 5 presents a summary of these sibling analyses. These pairwise concordance rates may be compared with the male-male rates for twins from a population twin study; Christiansen (1977a) reports 36% pairwise concordance for identical twins and a 13% rate for fraternal twins.

Table 5

Concordance for Criminal Law Convictions in Male Siblings Placed in Separate Adoptive Homes

Degree of genetic relationship	Percent Pairwise Concordance
Unrelated raised apart	2.5
Half siblings raised apart	12.9
Full siblings raised apart	20.0
Half and full siblings raised apart; criminal father	30.8
Unrelated "siblings" raised together in adoptive home	8.5

While these numbers are very small, they represent all of the cases, as defined, in a total cohort of adoptions. The results suggest that a number of these separated, adopted siblings inherited some characteristic which predisposed them both to being convicted for criminal behavior. As would be expected, in those instances in which the biological father is criminal, the effect is enhanced.

Specificity of Genetic Relationship

Earlier, I mentioned a study of a small sample of adoptees (Crowe, 1975). He reports the impression that there was some similarity in the types of crimes of the biological mother and the adoptees. This suggests specific genetic predispositions for different types of crimes. In order to explore this possibility, we examined the rates of violent crimes in the adoptees as a function of violent crime in the biological parents. We completed similar analyses for property crimes. We also examined more specific types of crimes (theft, fraud, assault, etc.) for similarity in the biological parent and the adoptee.

If the genetic predisposition was specific for type of crime these "specificity" analyses should have resulted in our observing a closer relationship between adoptee and biological parent levels of conviction for each of these types of crime. The best predictor of each type of adoptee crime, however, was number of biological parent convictions rather than type of biological parent offense. This suggests that the biological predisposition which the adoptee inherits must be of a general nature helping to determine degree of law abidance. It is also possible that the data of this study was too gross to detect a specificity relationship. This may require careful coding of details of the criminal behavior. This was not possible in this study.

Sex Differences

As may be seen in Table 2, convictions of females for criminal law violations are very infrequent. It may be speculated that those women who do exhibit a level of criminal behavior which prompts a court conviction must have an especially severe predisposition for such behavior. Criminal involvement in many men, on the other hand, may tend to be more socially or environmentally inspired. These statements suggest the hypothesis that convictions in the biological mother will be better related to the adoptees' conviction than criminal behavior in the biological father.

In every analysis we conducted, the relationship between biological mother conviction and adoptee conviction is significantly stronger than the relationship between biological father convictions and adoptee convictions. In comparison to the biological fathers, convictions in the biological mothers is more closely related to convictions in the daughters. This result is statistically significant, but the relatively low frequency of female convictions causes us to interpret these findings with caution.

Historical Period

The period of these adoptions (1924-1967) spans some rather important historical changes in Denmark. These changes include a world war, the Great Depression and industrialization. It is conceivable that the influence of genetic factors might be affected by these social upheavals. It is also possible that changes in level or type of crime across these years might influence the relationships observed. Analyses conducted for the entire population were repeated for each of the 5-year periods. The results were virtually identical for all of the periods and virtually identical to the analyses of the total sample. The social changes across these years did not interact with the relationships between biological parent and adoptee crime.

Controlling Genetic Influence in Examining Environmental Effects

In many social science investigations genetic characteristics are not considered. In some analyses this may contribute error; sometimes omission may lead to incomplete conclusions. For example, separation from a father is associated with increased levels of delinquency in a son. This has been interpreted as a result of failure of identification or lack of consistent discipline. As we can see from Table 2, some fathers who permit themselves to be separated from their child tend to have relatively high levels of criminal convictions. The higher levels of delinquency found for separated children might be partially due to genetic transmission of criminogenic predispositional characteristics from antisocial fathers. If this genetic variance were partially accounted for, the environmental hypotheses could be more precisely tested. We have utilized such partial genetic control better to study an important criminologic variable, social status. In a study by Van Dusen, Mednick, Gabrielli, and Hutchings (1983), we separated the variance ascribable to "genetic" social class and "rearing" social class. We examined adoptee convictions as a joint function of biological parents' social class and adoptive parents' social class. The result may be seen in Table 6. It is clear from inspection of Table 6 that male adoptee convictions vary both as a function of genetic and environmental social class; log-linear analyses reveal that both effects are statistically significant. While the genetic effect is of interest we wish to emphasize that to our knowledge, this is the first controlled demonstration that environmental aspects of social class life influence the social class-crime relationship. This finding suggests that regardless of genetic background improved social conditions are likely to lead to reductions in criminal behavior.

Table 6
Percent Male Adoptees with Criminal Convictions as a Function of Adoptive
and Biological Parents' SES

| Adoptive Parents' SES | Biological Parents' SES | | | Total |
	High	Middle	Low	
High	9.30	11.52	12.98	11.58
	(441)	(903)	(775)	(2099)
Middle	13.44	15.29	16.86	15.62
	(320)	(870)	(795)	(1985)
Low	13.81	17.25	18.04	17.19
	(210)	(568)	(787)	(1565)
Total	11.64	14.31	16.00	14.55
	(971)	(2341)	(2337)	(5649)

Note: Tabled values are percent adoptees with criminal convictions.
       Numbers in parentheses are cell total Ns.

Table 6 is of interest in another regard. Careful inspection reveals a
correlation between adoptive parent SES and biological parent SES. This
represents the attempt by the adoptive agency to match certain
characteristics of the two sets of parents. This was done in order to
increase the likelihood that the adoptee would fit into the adoptive
home. In terms of the adoption research design this correlation is
undesirable since it reduces the independence of the genetic rearing and
environment influences on the adoptee. Since social class is not
independent of convictions (Table 6) it is conceivable that the
relationship between biological parent and adoptee convictions may be, in
part, mediated by social class. Inspection of Table 6 reveals, however,
that the relationship between biological parent and adoptee criminal
convictions exists at each level of adoptive parent social class. In
addition, we have conducted stepwise multiple regression analyses which
varied the order of entry of biologial parent convictions and SES and
adoptive parents convictions and SES. These analyses indicate that
independent of SES, biological parent convictions are significantly
related to adoptee convictions.

METHODOLOGICAL ISSUES
Subjects Not Fully Identified
If we are to generalize from the results of this study, it is useful to
consider what biases may be introduced by loss of subjects in specific
analyses. Table 2 indicates the total number of subjects who could not
be fully identified (name, birthday, and birthplace). We should note
that for most cases which were not fully identified we know the name,
occupation, birthdate and other facts concerning the lost subject; in
almost all cases a subject could not be checked in the court conviction
register because we were not certain of the subjects' place of birth.
Another item often lacking was date of birth.
The information is relatively complete for the adoptive parents. On
the other hand, 26.5% of the biological fathers and 14.7% of the
biological mothers are not fully identified. These differences probably

reflect the relative importance of the adoptive and biological parents to the adoption agency. The agency's chief concern was with the placement and welfare of the adoptee. After the adoption, they had less reason to be concerned with the biological parents.

The most general characteristic of those not fully identified is that they tend slightly to come from areas outside of Copenhagen. Perhaps the urban adoption offices were more thorough in their recording procedures. The differences are very small. The sons of the biological fathers not fully identified evidence a rate of 10.3% criminal law convictions; the identified biological fathers' sons have criminal law convictions in 11.4% of the cases. In cases in which the biological mother is not fully identified, slightly fewer of the sons evidence criminal law convictions (9.6%). The adoptees who were not fully identified have biological mothers and biological fathers with slightly higher SES than those who were fully identified. Their rearing (adoptive) homes were of almost identical SES.

Our consideration of the characteristics of those not fully identified does not suggest that their inclusion would have altered the nature of the results presented above. Perhaps the most critical facts in this judgment are that the adopted-away sons of parents not fully identified, have levels of criminal law convictions and rearing social status which are approximately the same as for the sons of those parents fully identified. The differences which are observed are small; it is difficult to formulate any manner in which the lost subjects might have an impact on the relationships reported.

Transfer History

Most of these adoptions were the result of pregnancies of unwed women. The adoptive agency had a policy of removing the newborn from the biological mother and either immediately placing it in a previously arranged adoptive home (25.3% of the adoptions) or placing the infants in orphanages from which they were available for adoption. Of those placed in orphanages, 50.6% were placed with an adoptive family in the first year; 12.8% were placed with an adoptive family in the second year of life and 11.3% were placed after the age of two.

Within each of these age-of-transfer groups, analyses were conducted to see whether the biological parents' convictions were related to male adoptee conviction. Similar significant positive relationships were observed at each transfer age. Age of transfer did not interact with genetic influence so as to alter significantly the relationships observed with the full population. It should be noted that there was a statistically significant tendency for high levels of adoptee criminality to be associated with more time spent in the orphanage awaiting adoption. This effect was true for males only.

The operational definition of criminal behavior in this study included only court convictions for criminal law offenses. (We completed an analysis of police arrest data using a subsample of this adoption cohort and obtained highly similar results, Hutchings and Mednick, 1977.) Use of the conviction definition has some advantages. We are relatively certain the individual actually committed the offense recorded. Court convictions imply a high threshold for inclusion; minor offenses are less likely to result in court conviction. There are also disadvantages. The subjects' behavior goes through several screening points. Someone must make a complaint to the police or the police must happen on the scene of the crime. The police must decide a crime has been committed and apprehend the culprit. The prosecuting attorney must decide that the evidence is sufficient to warrant a court trial. The court must then find the culprit guilty. There are decision points all along the way which may act to exclude individuals who have actually committed offenses against the criminal code. Such individuals might then end up among our control subjects (assuming they do not also commit offenses for which they are convicted). In this case they add error to the analyses. Data comparing self-reports of crimes and official records of crimes suggest, however, that while only a fraction of crimes committed by an individual are noted by the police, those who "self-report" more crimes have more crimes recorded in the official registers. Those offenders who are not found in the official registers have typically committed very few and very minor offenses (Christie, Andenaes, & Skerbaekk, 1965).

Labelling of the Adoptee

The advantage of the adoption method is the good separation of genetic and rearing contributions to the adoptee's development. But the adoptions were not arranged as controlled experiments. The adoption agency's prime concern was the welfare of the adoptee and his adoptive parents. Prospective adoptive parents were routinely informed about criminal convictions in the biological parents. This could result in the labelling of the adoptee; this in turn might affect the likelihood that the adoptee would commit criminal acts. Thus, the convictions of the biological parents might conceivably have had an environmental impact on the adoptee via the reactions of the adoptive parents.

We examined one hypothesis which explored this possibility. If the biological parents suffered a criminal conviction before the adoption, it is likely that the adoptive parents were so informed; if the biological parents' first conviction occurred after the adoption, the adoptive parents could not have been informed. Of the convicted biological parents, 37% had their first conviction before the adoption took place. In these cases, the adoptive parents were likely to be informed regarding this criminal record. In 63% of the cases the first conviction occurred after the adoption; in these cases the conviction information could not have been transmitted to the adoptive parents. For all the convicted biological parents, the probability of a conviction in their adopted son is 15.9%. In cases in which the biological parent was first convicted before adoption, 15.6% of the male adoptees were convicted. In the cases in which the biological parent was convicted after the adoption, 16.1% of the male adoptees were convicted.

In the case of the female adoptees, these figures are 4% and 4%. These analyses utilized convictions. In a previous analysis with a large sub-sample of this population, a very similar result was obtained by studying the effect of timing of the initial arrest of the biological father (Hutchings & Mednick, 1977). Additional analyses by type or severity of crime could detect no effect of the adoptive parents being informed of the convictions of the biological parents. The fact that the adoptive parents were informed regarding the biological parents' convictions did not alter the likelihood that the adoptive son would be convicted. This result should not be interpreted as suggesting that labelling (as defined) had no effect on the adoptees' lives. It did not, however, affect the probability of the adoptee experiencing a conviction for a criminal act.

Denmark as a Research Site

This project has been completed in Denmark; on most crime-related social dimensions Denmark must rank among the most homogenous of the Western nations. This fact may have implications for the interpretation of this study. An environment with low variability permits better expression of existing genetic tendencies in individuals living in that environment. This factor probably magnifies the expression of any genetic influence. At the same time, however, the Danish population probably has less genetic variability than some Western nations; this, of course, would serve to minimize the expression of genetic influence in research conducted in Denmark. It is very likely impossible to balance these two considerations quantitatively. We are reassured regarding the generality of our findings by similar results in adoption studies in Sweden and Iowa (Crowe, 1975; Cadoret, 1978; Bohman, Cloninger, Sigvardsson, & von Knorring, 1982).

SUMMARY AND CONCLUSIONS

In a total population of adoptions we have noted a relationship between biological parent criminal convictions and criminal convictions in their adoptive children. The relationship is particularly strong for chronic adoptee and biological parent offenders. No evidence was found that indicated that type of biological parent convictions was related to type of adoptee conviction. A number of potentially confounding variables were considered; none of these proved sufficient to explain the genetic relationship. We conclude that some factor is transmitted by convicted parents which increases the likelihood that their children will be convicted for criminal law offenses. This is especially true for the chronic offender. Since the factor transmitted must be biological this implies that biological factors are involved in the etiology of at least some criminal behavior.

Biological factors and their interaction with social variables may make useful contributions to our understanding of the causes of criminal behavior.

REFERENCES

Baker, R. L., & Mednick, B. (1984). Influences on human development: A longitudinal perspective. Boston: Kluwer Nijhoff Press.

Bohman, M., Cloninger, C., Sigvardsson, S., & von Knorring, A. L. (1982). Predisposition to petty criminality in Swedish adoptees: Genetic and environmental heterogeneity. Archives of General Psychiatry, 39, 11, 1233-1241.

Cadoret, R. J. (1978). Psychopathy in adopted away offspring of biological parents with antisocial behavior. Archives of General Psychiatry, 35, 176-184.

Christiansen, K. O. (1977a). A review of studies of criminality among twins. In S. A. Mednick & K. O. Christiansen (Eds.), Biosocial bases of criminal behavior. New York: Gardner Press.

Christiansen, K. O. (1977b). A preliminary study of criminality among twins. In S. A. Mednick & K. O. Christiansen (Eds.), Biosocial bases of criminal behavior. New York: Gardner Press.

Christie, N., Andenaes, J., & Skerbaekk, S. (1965). A study of self-reported crime. Scandinavian Studies in Criminology, 1, 86-116.

Crowe, R. (1975). Adoptive study of psychopathy: Preliminary results from arrest records and psychiatric hospital records. In R. Fieve, D. Roentha., & H. Brill (Eds.), Genetic research in psychiatry. Baltimore: Johns Hopkins University Press.

Farrington, D. (1984). Delinquency from 10 to 15. In K.T. Van Dusen, & S.A. Medinick (Eds.), Prospective studies of crime and delinquency. Hingham, MA: Kluwer-Nijhoff.

Hurwitz, S., & Christiansen, K. O. (1971). Kriminologi. Copenhagen: Glydendal.

Hutchings, B., & Mednick, S. A. (1977). Registered criminality in the adoptive and biological parents of registered male criminal adoptees. In S. A. Mednick & K. O. Christiansen (Eds.), Biosocial .bases of criminal behavior. New York: Gardner Press.

Kety, S. S., Rosenthal, D., Wender, Ph. H., & Schulsinger, F. (1968). The types and prevalence of mental illness in the biological adoptive families of adopted schizophrenics. In D. Rosenthal & S. S. Kety (Eds.), The transmission of schizophrenia. Oxford: Pergamon.

Lange, J. (1929). Verbrechen als schisksal. Leipzig: Georg Thieme. (English edition, London: Unwin Brahers, 1931.)

Rostand, E. (1972). Cyrano de bergerac. New York: Signet.

Svalastoga, K. (1959). Prestige, class and mobility. Gyldendal: Copenhagan, Denmark.

Teasdale, T. W., & Sorensen, T. The Copenhagan Adoption Register: A note concerning adoptees' knowledge of their biological parents.

Van Dusen, K., Mednick, S. A., Gabrielli, W. F., & Hutchings, B. (1983). Social class and crime in an adoption cohort. Journal of Criminal Law and Criminology, 74, 1, 249-269.

Wolfgang, M. E. (1977). Forward (Quote). In S. A. Mednick & K. O. Christiansen (Eds.), Biosocial bases of criminal behavior. New York: Gardner Press.

Wolfgang, M. E., Figlio, R. M., & Sellin, T. (1972). Delinquency in a birth cohort. University of Chicago Press.

MEANINGFUL RESEARCH IN THE POLICE CONTEXT

JOHN C. YUILLE

I considered titling this chapter "The Confessions of a Disillusioned Academic", since it would accurately describe the path which brought me to the work reported here. I have been an experimental psychologist for over two decades, with most of my work focused on human attention and memory. My career began with excitement about the promise of experimental psychology to provide insights about the nature of the human mind. However, the longer I engaged in the laboratory research enterprise, the more my disenchantment grew. During the past few years, I have become convinced that the laboratory has limited value to the student of human nature (a conclusion that I elaborate in this chapter). I remain convinced that careful, systematic research is still a useful approach to the study of mental processes, however, the research must be done in real contexts (that is, in the contexts one wishes to know about, not the artificial context of the laboratory). It was the search for meaningful contexts to study human memory and cognition that led me to the investigation of eyewitnesses and victims of crime. The current status of this research is summarized in this chapter.

The Role of Research

The raison d'etre of the academic psychologist is research – exploring issues, causes, and phenomena through the medium of systematic investigation. Research is a broad term, encompassing a range of methodologies from laboratory experiments through field research to archival studies. Psychologists have some powerful tools at their disposal: sophisticated questionnaires and testing procedures, complex statistical methods, and the logic of experimental design. With these tools the psychologist can make a variety of useful contributions to police work by providing the police with knowledge of the causes of crime, recognition of criminal behaviors, prevention of crime, methods of dealing with domestic crises, ways of handling hostage incidents, and so on.

However, research is not without its limitations and problems. I consider the greatest problem facing psychological research its emphasis and dependency upon laboratory experiments and a laboratory style of research thinking. I begin with the presentation and defense of the assertion that laboratory research is often useless and sometimes dangerous to psychology and to police concerns. After reviewing some examples, I outline one alternative to the laboratory approach. Finally, I conclude with some proposals for carrying out meaningful psychological research in the context of police training.

Psychological Research Does Not Belong in the Laboratory

The purpose of research is the generation of knowledge. Systematic research is the preferred method of knowledge generation because it allows evaluation of alternative interpretations of the results. We feel that we understand something best when we can explain its cause. Thus, research is generally aimed at teasing out the causes of a phenomenon. The most effective way to establish causality is through control of all of the factors operating in a situation. Thus, researchers prefer the laboratory as the venue for research. In the context of the laboratory, most factors are under the control of the researcher and the relative contributions of variables to any phenomenon can be determined. This is the basic philosophy which has created and maintained laboratory research. This philosophy has been supported by fundamental discoveries in physics, chemistry, medicine, and biology. Understandably, psychologists, seeking major discoveries about human behavior, have been attracted to the same research location. The precision and control which the laboratory affords have become the interdependent goals of most psychologists. This has been a serious mistake, it has led psychology astray, and it has resulted in a discipline characterized by fads and fashions and little substance. The purpose of this chapter is not to provide the reader with an elaborate defense of this condemnation of laboratory based research in psychology, this defense has been elaborated elsewhere (Corteen & Yuille, 1985; Yuille, 1986). However, it is necessary to provide a brief examination of the rejection of laboratory work before I can elaborate the alternative of meaningful psychological research with police.

The training that most psychologists receive leads them to perceive laboratory research as an unqualified good. Given that the rules of good experimental design are followed, and that the dependent and independent variables are operationally defined, an experiment, it is believed, will yield replicable knowledge. The resulting data will at least contribute to the data base of the field, and, in addition, the observations may bear upon some theoretical issue. The problem is that while the laboratory observations are replicable, they are generally useless, and potentially destructive. The data base to which experiments contribute is a house of cards, enjoying a precarious existence until the changing winds of fad bring about its collapse. The theories which develop from these data are equally transient and, most important to the present thesis, irrelevant outside of the laboratory.

Any of the hundreds of topics of laboratory research could serve to support this dismissal of the relevance of much of laboratory research (it should be noted that for some aspects of psychology, e.g., sensory processes, the laboratory is an appropriate context for research), but it is appropriate for this context to choose examples of forensic relevance. Consider the following example: many citizens have become concerned about the widespread availability of sexually explicit films, photographs, magazines, etc. Many of these materials present women in a degrading fashion, and combine sex and violence in a disturbing manner. Critics of these materials quite correctly question their role in a society sensitive to violence against women. Some opponents of the availability of these materials argue further that the materials contribute to sexual and violent attacks on women. I am not concerned here with the pros and cons of this argument, but rather with an example of the pointlessness of laboratory based psychological research. Obviously psychologists should contribute to this issue. Indeed some have through useful field research (see Dutton, this volume). But some believe that laboratory research has made a contribution. In particular, opponents of pornography often cite the research of Edward Donnerstein and of Neil Malamuth, which they believe shows that exposure to sexually explicit materials leads people to treat women violently. Donnerstein (1980) studied male college student volunteers. He tried to make them angry, and then instructed them to deliver an electric shock to a woman in a different room. The shock was only simulated, but the men didn't know that. The volunteers who previously saw a violent, erotic film gave a higher shock than those who had seen a non-violent erotic film. Malamuth (1981) reported that men who indicate on a questionnaire that violent pornography is arousing will also state that they might commit rape if they were guaranteed that they would not be caught.

Administering shocks in a laboratory or completing questionnaires have nothing, prima facie, to do with violence against women. Even the most ardent believer ought to be hard pressed to demonstrate the relevance of this kind of research to the pornography/violence issue. Malamuth admitted that the application of his findings to this issue would be "pure speculation" (Malamuth, 1981). The problem is that this example is typical. An important issue is addressed by a laboratory study which trivializes the issue. In order to control all of the factors involved, psychologists have to change the problem so much that it bears no relationship to the original question. In their search for precision, psychologists have created an artificial world, the laboratory, in which they can manipulate people in an infinitude of ways. Although recorded with precision, the behavior that is observed has no relevance to any other context. The laboratory is a peculiar world under the control of the experimenter. A clever researcher, by selecting the appropriate behavioral measures, by controlling the information supplied to the subject, by employing the right context can support any reasonable hypothesis about human behavior. If he or she hypothesizes that violent pornography enduces violent behavior, an artificial context can be created to support that hypothesis. If the belief is that pornography doesn't affect behavior, that hypothesis can also be supported. This is the basic reason that laboratory experiments are useless: the knowledge they produce reflects the control the experimenter has exercised and the malleability of human behavior. I am not suggesting that researchers are consciously manipulating these factors. The investigators are also victims of the myth that the laboratory produces useful knowledge. It is the perpetuation of this myth that always results in conflicting and confusing results emerging in any area of laboratory investigation. There is no reason to assume that laboratory research tells us anything about extra-laboratory human behavior.

The lure of the laboratory is understandable. As noted earlier, it has proved of great value in the study of natural phenomena in the physical world. But the physical world is not informationally sensitive and people are. Gravity operates in the same fashion whether studied in the laboratory or out. In contrast, our behavior is dramatically affected by the context in which we find ourselves. Certainly there are aspects of human psychology which are immune to context effects. For example, some components of sensory processes are context independent, and are therefore appropriate for laboratory study. But all of the higher psychological processes (e.g., memory, attention, thinking) are very context dependent. Probably every issue of concern to the criminal justice system involves a level of complexity and context dependence which renders the laboratory a useless context for their investigation.

I noted earlier that the laboratory is not only the wrong place to be doing psychological research; its use is also potentially destructive. This latter effect results from the tremendous control inherent in the experimental method. Any research paradigm begins with an interesting, and often socially important, question. For example, does pornography affect violence? As noted earlier, this original question is distorted by the researcher to fit the needs of the laboratory. Then, a set of research findings is reported, and a new research fad becomes established. Many other researchers then join the band wagon and a flurry of experimental activity ensues. At first, studies appear confirming the phenomenon and a theoretical interpretation is elaborated. Then someone reports an inconsistent result, and the experimental work now enters a new phase. Contradictory findings are published and the interpretation of the phenomenon becomes clouded and confused. Inertia sets in, and many experimenters abandon the phenomenon, often preferring some new, more promising fad. The research area dies. The problem is that no accumulation of knowledge has occurred, since each fad operates in relative isolation. Perhaps the greatest casualty in this process is the original question. A phenomenon that had interest and potential importance was abandoned, destroyed as a viable focus for the discipline. This is the destructive nature of a laboratory based psychology.

In the police context, the problems associated with laboratory research create another danger. Eager to find solutions to forensic problems, police will usually accept the assistance of an expert who claims to have relevant knowledge.

Experimental psychologists have claimed, on the basis of their laboratory investigations, to have knowledge of relevance to police work. Given the weaknesses of laboratory research such claims have not always been valid. The danger of the application of incorrect or misleading knowledge is obvious.

Laboratory Eyewitness Research

This strong condemnation of laboratory research needs further support, and I turn to an example of forensic relevance: eyewitness testimony. During the past decade a "new" area of interest to psychologists has been eyewitness testimony. Eyewitness testimony is the single most important source of information in the investigation of crime. A 1975 study by the Rand Corporation concluded that the most important determinant of whether a case will be solved is the information supplied by the witness or victim of the crime. Obviously, the more we know about eyewitness behavior the better. A number of researchers have responded to the need for such information in the criminal justice system by conducting eyewitness research. I will attempt to demonstrate that the laboratory research on eyewitnesses is of indeterminate relevance.

Before pursuing this I should note that the current eyewitness research activity is the second incarnation of this fad. It enjoyed its first life at the turn of the century. That fad originated in France and Germany, and became known by its German name, Aussage (meaning oral testimony). Like all research fads, Aussage research declined, assisted in this case by the devastating effect of the First World War on German psychology in general. Aussage research did have a brief life in the United States but it succumbed to the developing hegemony of the behaviorist revolution. As a result, with a few exceptions, psychologists ignored eyewitnesses until 15 years ago. The reason for noting this earlier fad is that contemporary researchers have paid little attention to the Aussage work, although the parallels between the current work and that of eighty years ago are many (Cutshall, 1985). This is an example of the non-cumulative nature of psychological research. In any case, it is the more recent research that I wish to examine in the context of the shortcomings of laboratory research.

Eyewitness research reappeared in the late 1960s and early 1970s to address two needs. Some researchers wanted more complex situations in which to study human memory (in particular, the work of Loftus, 1979). Academics had been studying memory for almost one hundred years. The methods that they had employed largely constituted having people learn lists of nonsense syllables or pairs of words. By the late 1960s they had begun to realize that these materials were not suited to the task of exploring the complexities of memory. One consequence of this realization was a search for more complex materials to have people learn. Observing a crime or accident seemed to fit the need for complexity, and some psychologists began to study eyewitness recall and identification.

The second motive for renewed eyewitness research was a concern for reform in the criminal justice system (see in particular, Buckhout, 1974). These researchers perceived the justice system as giving too much weight to eyewitness identification and testimony, and they sought empirical support for the fallibility of human memory. Whether motivated by theoretical or practical concerns, eyewitness research has become popular, and has produced an extensive literature in the past fifteen years (for summaries see Lloyd-Bostock & Clifford, 1983; Loftus, 1979; Yarmey, 1979).

What does the typical eyewitness study look like? A group of volunteers witnesses an event. They are almost always undergraduate students serving as research subjects for credit or experience. A survey of 41 published papers during the years 1974 to 1983 revealed that 92.7% of the studies employed college students. The event may be recorded and presented via slides, video, or film, or the event may be a staged live sequence involving actors. In the survey noted above, 58.9% of the experiments employed recorded events. Often the witnesses are aware that they will be tested about the event, this is certainly true when the event is recorded, and may or may not be true when the event is live. Sometimes psychologists go to considerable efforts to deceive the experimental witnesses about the true purpose of the experiment. The event is usually an automobile accident or a theft.

After the witnesses have seen the event they are usually interviewed about what they saw. In the interests of experimental control and precision, this interview typically takes the form of a short answer or multiple choice questionnaire. After completing the questionnaire, witnesses will often be asked if they can select the "thief" from a photo-spread. They will be asked to indicate the confidence of their choice, usually by providing a rating on a seven-point scale. Typically the entire procedure from event through recall to identification takes place in less than one hour, although longer retention times are occasionally investigated.

The image that has emerged from this work is a very negative one. Witnesses are found to have poor memories, poor ability to identify, and a likelihood to misidentify. Their memories are reported as fallible, malleable, and subject to the effects of misleading and suggestive questions. Many of the researchers have made it clear that the results of these experimental studies are applicable to police work. Several texts have appeared in the last seven years, and in each case the authors have sounded notes of caution about the acceptability of eyewitness testimony given the performance of people in the laboratory research context. Yet other than stressing the weaknesses of eyewitness accounts, there is no unanimity concerning the factors which affect eyewitness behavior. Whether one examines stress, cross-racial issues, the effects of time, or other factors, the experimental literature reveals a confusing picture (Cutshall, 1985).

I would suggest to you that this whole enterprise may be a waste of time, and a danger for law enforcement personnel to take with anything other than a grain of salt. Laboratory based eyewitness research is rife with problems. For example, the presentation medium has a variety of effects on eyewitness recall. Yuille & Cutshall (1985) found qualitative differences in recall about the same event depending whether witnesses viewed it live or via videotape. Even live staged events must be viewed with suspicion. Wells (1978) has noted that researchers could choose an actor to play a thief who has no outstanding features, making identification more difficult than is true for most real-life eyewitness situations. Also, the memory measure used in research can affect the outcome. Lipton (1977) reported an accuracy rate of 83% when open-ended questions were employed compared with only 56% in response to multiple choice questions. And this was for witnesses who had viewed the same event. Most important are the social dynamics which operate in experiments as opposed to those affecting real-life witnesses. Undergraduate volunteers are willing to answer questions. Why shouldn't they? Their answers have no consequence, it is not as if they are in a court of law. They will select someone from a line-up or photo-spread, since the selection is unimportant (see Wells, 1978). In a field study, Brigham, Maass, Snyder, & Spaulding (1982) asked 73 convenience store clerks to identify a customer from photographic line-ups. The overall accuracy rate was 46.8%, but for those clerks who agreed to swear in court to their identification the accuracy rate was 85%. In real-life situations there is a selection process which makes eyewitness behavior very different from the way college students act in laboratories.

In short, it is an interesting and challenging game which psychologists play in their laboratories but it is often irrelevant. The only way we can learn about eyewitness behavior is to study real witnesses to real crimes. Of course we may learn as a result that some of the laboratory findings were applicable to the real world. But only real world data will tell us this. I suggest that this is a general conclusion that all people involved in the criminal justice system should draw. Laboratory research should be ignored unless there exists strong evidence to show its applicability outside of the context in which it was collected. The researcher is obliged to show the value of his/her work by direct evidence before any attention should be given to it. Fortunately, some field investigations of eyewitnesses have been conducted, so a more useful picture of eyewitness behavior can be drawn.

Ride-along Research

For the past two years, I have been conducting research with the Royal Canadian Mounted Police (R.C.M.P.) and with the Vancouver Police. While the R.C.M.P. serve the functions of a federal police force in Canada, they serve other police roles as well. In those provinces and municipalities which elect not to train their own police forces, the R.C.M.P. play a kind of rent-a-cop function. The municipality hires constables and officers from the R.C.M.P. on a contractual basis, and that group becomes the civic police force. To date, I have been working with two such forces, one in Burnaby and the other in Surrey. Burnaby and Surrey are suburban communities which are part of the greater metropolitan Vancouver area. I have also been doing work with the Vancouver police, who patrol the central urban area of Vancouver. This is a separate force and not part of the R.C.M.P. The Vancouver police are trained at the British Columbia Police Academy. The academy is part of the Justice Institute of British Columbia which is concerned with training in all occupations that serve a law enforcement function. The Justice Institute has five training divisions: one is concerned with corrections, parole, probation, and prison officials; a second with emergency health teams; a third with fire service; a fourth with officers of the court; and the fifth is the police academy. These divisions share common facilities and have some budget overlap but are otherwise autonomous. All non-R.C.M.Police in British Columbia are trained at the academy. As a part-time instructor there I teach a course on the psychology of eyewitness testimony.

The general purpose of my eyewitness research has been to develop a comprehensive picture of the behavior of witnesses in real life situations. The work I am going to review has been carried out with the able assistance of Doreen Kum, Judith Cutshall, and Brenda Gillstrom, among others. Our procedure has consisted of three phases. In the first phase we ride along with officers on patrol to learn about the procedures they use when interviewing eyewitnesses. All police patrols in the areas in which we have been working involve automobiles. These ride-alongs involve one of us accompanying an officer for several full shifts. A sampling of several officers is made in each jurisdiction in which we work. When an officer answers a call which involves interviewing witnesses, we sit in on the interview (with the permission of the witness), making any notes or observations we deem relevant.

Our conclusions from this phase of our work are easy to summarize. Generally, the experienced police that we have observed do an excellent job in interviewing witnesses. The interview procedure that they should follow is to ask the witness to describe the event in his or her own words. The officer makes a verbatim written record of that account, mentally noting any inconsistencies or important gaps during the course of the account. When the witness is finished, the officer asks if there are any other details that were left out of the account. After they have been noted, the officer may then ask some specific questions. It is here that great care must be taken. Questions must never be leading or deal with aspects of the event which were ignored by the witness during the event. At this vulnerable stage immediately after the event, there is the potential of ruining the value of the witness by suggesting things that he or she didn't observe. Even a casual suggestion can permanently destroy the capacity of the witness to distinguish suggestion from actual memory of the event.

When the investigating officer is asking specific questions, several concerns must be maintained. First, the officer should keep in mind the perspective of the witness, and not ask questions about aspects of the event which the witness could not or did not observe. Willing witnesses will unconsciously fabricate details to appear co-operative and capable. Once they have done so they may not be able to distinguish their fabrications from their memories. Second, it is important to keep in mind the poor judgment abilities of most people. Estimates of height, weight, age, distance, and speed are generally inaccurate. Our research suggests that a witness has about a 50/50 chance of making a correct numerical estimate of this kind. The officer should ascertain if the witness has any special training or experience which would allow such estimates. If the witness has no such experience these judgments should be made on relative grounds only. Thus, height might be estimated relative to the officer or to some environmental feature.

Once the interview is concluded, the witness reads the verbatim record of the interview, makes any additions, deletions, or corrections, and signs the record as a true statement of his or her account. The officer should then note any information he or she needs to subsequently reconstruct the event. In addition to the obvious record of time and place, a note about the weather and visibility is important. Any observations about the mental and physical condition of the witness should also be recorded.

Interview Training

I have reviewed the interview process in some detail because I believe that there exists a training problem in this area. In interviews with a number of police officers (for details see Yuille, 1984) many have expressed dissatisfaction with their training in note-taking and interviewing procedures. They found that they had to learn by trial and error, and that, on occasion, cases were dismissed in court because of problems with their notes. Furthermore, I have been a consultant in a number of cases where police interviewing procedures violated those that I outlined above, and witness' accounts were permanently distorted as a consequence. It appears that the major problem in training is a lack of specification of the reasons for using certain interview techniques and avoiding others. Trainees are not informed of the psychological dynamics which operate when a witness is reconstructing an event. This is an area in which psychologists can be useful, they can supply those training police with an understanding of the underlying psychological mechanisms of perception, attention, and memory which influence eyewitness accounts. If one understands the selective nature of attention, the relationship between memory and attention, and the reconstructive nature of memory, the interview procedure that I outlined becomes mandatory. The course which I offer at the British Columbia Police Academy is intended to provide this kind of background information.

Archival Research

The second phase of our investigations has involved police file research. We have been using the extensive information in police files to ascertain the profiles of witnesses to various crimes. We begin by determining the incidence of different types of crimes in the community, and then try to assess the demographics of witnesses to those crimes. For example, one part of our research has been concerned with witnesses to major crimes of violence. Such crimes include homicides, robberies, and assaults. The data in the Table 1 provide some comparative figures of the incidence of such crimes in Canada, in British Columbia, and in Burnaby, one of the communities in which we have been working. Nationally, violent crimes constitute less than six percent of the total number of reported crimes. In Burnaby, a relatively peaceful community, they are less than two percent of the reported crimes. However, the pattern of distribution of these crimes is the same in Burnaby as it is nationally. Less than one percent of these crimes involve homicide, and the majority (over 80%) are assaults.

Table 1
Summary of Crime Statistics

	Canada 1981	British Columbia 1981	Burnaby 1981
Total Reported Crimes	2,850,059	413,349	81,930
Crimes of Violence	162,228	29,160	1,109
	(5.69%)	(7.05%)	(1.35%)
Homicides	1,547	228	8
	(.95%)	(.78%)	(.72%)
Robberies	26,292	3,102	164
	(16.21%)	(10.64%)	(14.79%)
Assaults	134,389	25,830	937
	(82.84%)	(88.58%)	(84.49%)

Once the base rate data have been obtained, we proceed to examine a sample of files for each type of crime. For example, we examined six of the eight homicides which occurred in 1983 in Burnaby. There were a total of 21 witnesses, 16 to one murder, four to a second, and one to a third. Three of the homicides had no witnesses. Twenty of the 21 witnesses knew the victim, 17 knew the assailant. In these cases at least, eyewitness identification was not usually an issue. I should note that because of Canada's relatively strict gun control laws, homicides are rarely committed during a robbery. Consequently, murder is usually committed during the course of a family dispute or similar altercation. If there are witnesses, they typically know one or both individuals. We are not aware of any particular pattern in the type of witness who sees a murder but fortunately the small number of such incidents has made searching for such a pattern difficult. A distribution of the ages of the 21 witnesses is provided in Table 2.

Table 2
Age Distribution of Witnesses and Victims of Sample Crimes in Burnaby, B.C.

Age Range	Homicides	Robberies	Non-Sexual Assault	Sexual Assault
< 15		4	33	18
16 - 25	4	72	123	15
26 - 35	11	19	96	9
36 - 45	4	22	49	2
46 - 55	1	21	27	1
56 - 65		6	8	
> 65		4	4	
Not Available	1	7	16	

We examined the records of 75 robberies in Burnaby (45% of the total number which occurred in 1983). There were 85 victims and 70 witnesses of these events. In 40 of the cases there was only one witness, the victim. Thirty-one cases involved an additional one to four witnesses, and in only four cases were there more than four witnesses plus the victim. Thus, the typical pattern is for there to be only one witness, the victim, and in fewer cases non-victim observers. Of the 70 non-victim witnesses in our sample, 27 (38.6%) knew the victim, no one knew the thief. The type of witness researched in the laboratory is parallel to these non-victim witnesses. While they constitute a minority of witnesses of crimes, they are nonetheless important in the investigative process, particularly with respect to identification evidence. I provide a more in-depth look at this type of witness later. No particular pattern emerges concerning the demographics of robbery victims or witnesses. The age distribution of these witnesses is found in Table 2.

We examined the files of 274 assaults (29% of the total occurring in 1983). Of these, 229 (83.6%) were non-sexual assaults involving 243 victims and 113 eyewitnesses. In 159 (69.4%) of these cases the only witness or witnesses were victims. In 35 instances there was one non-victim witness, and in another 35 cases from two to nine additional witnesses. Clearly, multiple witnesses to any type of crime are rare. Most of the time the only witness was the victim. In the case of the non-sexual assaults the witnesses usually knew the assailant (70.3% of the time). Reflecting the fact that violence is over-represented among males in their late teens and early twenties, the victims and witnesses of these crimes tend to be young and male. The age distribution of witnesses to non-sexual assaults is shown in Table 2.

This survey concluded with 45 cases of sexual assault, which involved 45 victims and 3 eyewitnesses, the latter in only two of the cases. Twenty of the victims previously knew their attacker, 25 did not, and none of the eyewitnesses knew the assailant. The victims and witnesses were generally female and young. The age distribution is found in Table 2.

Witnesses of a violent crime are generally also the victims of the crime. While a few laboratory studies have attempted to make the subjects victims (e.g., Hosch & Cooper, 1982) this has been rare. The ethical restrictions which operate in the lab context make it unlikely that this typical witness can ever be the focus of laboratory investigations. Since we presume that the stress of being victimized affects the person's perception and memory of the event, we must rely on field research with actual victims to learn about their eyewitness abilities. We currently are conducting such research. However, since the focus of this chapter is on laboratory studies of witnesses, I should like to describe the outcome of one of our studies which is more comparable to the laboratory witness. We selected an incident which involved a number of non-victim witnesses, the kind who are most typically the focus of experimental study.

Interviewing Witnesses of a Crime

The third phase of our research on witnesses has involved interviewing the witnesses of actual crimes. In an initial attempt to compare witnesses who observed the same crime, we have been searching for cases which involve multiple witnesses. We realize that these cases are not representative, but they provide the most cost efficient place for us to begin. Another consideration that affects our choice of cases is that there must be sufficient forensic evidence (or a confession) to permit a reconstruction of the basic facts of the event. Furthermore, the case must be closed either because prosecution was inappropriate or because the prosecution has been completed. When such a case is found, we make verbatim copies of the eyewitness accounts provided to the investigating police. We also contact the eyewitnesses to determine if they are willing to be interviewed by us. If the person agrees we conduct an interview concerning the event they witnessed. During the interview we follow police interview procedures, as I outlined earlier. Once the event has been described, we may request additional information from the witness that is of theoretical interest to memory researchers but of little or no forensic value. In some instances we ask for an identification from a photo-spread, and we sometimes try to mislead witnesses during our questioning.

Following this procedure, we end up with a minimum of two accounts from each witness. The first is the account provided to the police during the investigation of the crime. There may be more than one such eyewitness account, but generally there is only one. The second account is the one we obtain in our interview. We subject both accounts provided by each witness to a detailed analysis. This involves rewriting each account to a standard declarative sentence format. This removes idiosyncracies of speech and descriptive style. We have found that this rewriting can be done with a high degree of reliability. The rewritten account is then partitioned into distinct units of information. Generally these units are of two types: verb and adverb phrases referring to action details; and noun and adjective phrases for descriptive details. Each detail is scored as correct, incorrect, or unclassifiable, using the available forensic information, the eyewitness accounts, our own inspection of the scene of the event, and the constraints of logic. We are then in a position to evaluate the performance of each eyewitness, and to examine the type and source of errors they make. An example of this work follows.

Twenty-one people witnessed a shooting incident in Burnaby in 1983 (for details of this study see Yuille & Cutshall, 1986). Twenty of these witnesses were non-victims, and only three of them knew the victim. Thus, most of the witnesses were independent. The incident resulted from an attempted robbery of a gun store on a bright spring afternoon. The thief had entered the store, tied up the store owner, and stolen money and a box of hand guns. The store owner freed himself, picked up a revolver, and went outside, expecting to record the thief's license number. However, the thief had not entered his car. In a face-to-face encounter in the street, separated by about six feet, the thief fired two shots, critically wounding the store owner. After a momentary pause, the store owner fired all six shots from his revolver. The thief was killed whereas the store owner recovered from his serious injuries. Witnesses had viewed the event from several vantage points along the street, from adjacent buildings, and from passing cars.

Thirteen of the 21 witnesses agreed to a research interview, and we conducted them four to five months after the event. We analyzed the eyewitness accounts and were able to classify roughly 95% of their details as correct or incorrect. Table 3 provides a quantitative summary of the accounts. The variability among witnesses reflects the amount of the event that each witness had seen. The greater number of details in the research interview reflects the fact that we asked many more questions. It turns out that the witnesses can be separated into two distinct groups: central and peripheral. The former witnessed the event at a close range and supplied both the police and us with about twice as many details as the peripheral witnesses.

Table 3
Quantitative Summary of Witness' Accounts to Shooting Incident

| | Number of Reported Details | | |
	Police Interview		Research Interview
Action Details	392	(60.35%)	551.5 (52.20%)
Person Descriptions	180	(27.71%)	267 (25.27%)
Object Descriptions	77.5	(11.93%)	238 (22.53%)
Total Details	649.5		1056.5

Our primary concern was with the accuracy of the eyewitness accounts. Unlike the typical performance of laboratory witnesses, Table 4 shows that these eyewitness accounts were quite accurate. Concerning the action details of the event the witnesses were roughly 82% accurate. Similarly, in their descriptions of objects (such as the thief's car) accuracy was between 85% and 90%. The descriptions of people were less accurate but still impressive in the 70% to 75% range. Note that there was little change in accuracy over the five month delay between the original police interview and our research interview. Also, the central and peripheral witnesses did not differ in accuracy, indicating that accuracy was not related to the number of details which the witnesses reported.

Table 4
Percent Correct Accuracy of Classifiable Details

| Type of Detail | Police Interview | | | Research Interview | | |
	Range	Mean	Median	Range	Mean	Median
Action	40-98	81.90	81.82	47-100	81.90	83.33
People Descriptions	33-100	75.57	73.33	47-90	72.74	75.68
Object Descriptions	50-100	88.53	100	60-100	85.45	89.74
Subtotal of Descriptions	62-100	82.03	83.56	64-96	78.97	77.78
Total Details	59-96	82.14	81.82	54-95	80.63	82.93

The results of this investigation bear little relationship to the pattern one would expect from laboratory research. People were more accurate and showed less loss over time than the experimental literature suggests. This is not to say that there are not problems associated with eyewitness memory. There clearly are a variety of factors which can have a negative effect on eyewitness recall. The point is that the only way for us to learn about the factors affecting eyewitness performance is to study real eyewitnesses.

Although errors were few in this case, it is none the less of interest to note their nature. Figure 1 displays the distribution of errors in the two interviews. Two-thirds of the action errors were found in the accounts of only three of the witnesses. Two of them, teen-age males, reported that physical contact had occurred between the thief and the gun store owner. The sharp angle from which these witnesses had viewed the event had distorted their view, and collapsed the distance between the thief and the shop owner. This is an example of why it is important to determine perspective when evaluating eyewitness evidence.

Figure 1
Error Analysis of Witness' Accounts to Shooting Incident

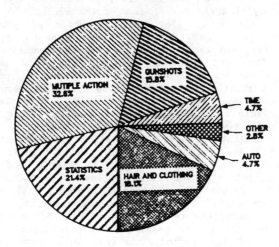

POLICE INTERVIEW
TOTAL OF 107.5 ERRORS

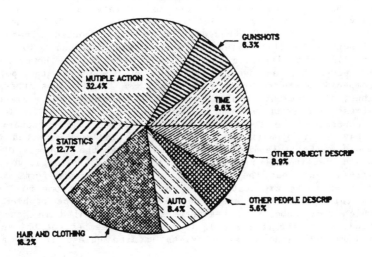

RESEARCH INTERVIEW
TOTAL OF 198.5 ERRORS

Only one witness correctly reported the pattern of shots. For most of the witnesses the first two shots went unattended, although the sound may have oriented them for the second volley. Thus, most witnesses reported hearing five or six shots. Errors of time and date were common in our research interview. Ten of the witnesses could not tell us the exact month of the incident, and only three of these were correct about the day of the week. Note that the inability to remember the date had no effect on the accuracy of their description of the event.

Turning to the errors in the description of people, 23 incorrect estimates of age, height, and weight were given to the police (out of 46 such estimates), and 25 of the 49 estimates given in our interviews were incorrect. Thus, in spite of generally accurate descriptions of the event, the witnesses had about a 50-50 chance of providing a correct descriptive statistic. I should note that we were generous in our scoring of these estimates, allowing a range around the correct values to be correct. This finding reinforces the concern about the procedure for obtaining such estimates from witnesses.

One final result to note is the consistent pattern we find of errors in color memory. The color of clothing in particular seems to be very difficult for people to retain. An article of clothing described as yellow to the police becomes blue in the research interview. Colors do not seem to be systematically retained in memory.

Following procedures used in laboratory research, we tried to mislead the witnesses during our research interview. For example, we asked them if they noticed the broken headlight. Laboratory research has suggested that the use of the definite article will increase acquiescence in witnesses. Our attempts to mislead witnesses were totally unsuccessful. In response to misleading questions the witnesses either said that they did not know or corrected us concerning the misleading implication. In this instance, at least, this field study failed to confirm laboratory expectations.

The final aspect of the results which I will note concerns the effects of stress on eyewitness performance. The experimental literature is confused in this regard but some (Loftus, 1979) have concluded that stress is likely to have a negative effect on eyewitness performance. We could only indirectly infer stress in this case by asking witnesses to rate how stressed they felt, and to indicate any stress related responses they had, like lack of sleep, nightmares, etc. We found five witnesses had been severely stressed, and eight reported minor or no stress effects. In this situation stress was confounded with how centrally involved the witnesses had been with the event. However, the stressed witnesses had an overall accuracy of 93.36% in the police interview compared to an accuracy rate of 75.13% for the non-stressed witnesses. Thus, the present results offer no confirmation of a negative effect of stress on eyewitness memory.

Laboratory investigations have led to certain expectations about the behavior of eyewitnesses. For example, it was expected that witnesses would be fallible in their testimony, that the accuracy of their reports would decline with time, that they would be negatively affected by stress, and that they would be misled by certain forms of questioning. Each of these expectations may be fulfilled in some real situations but in this particular case none of them were. The problem is the haste which some laboratory researchers have exhibited in generalizing their findings to the real world. I trust that members of the criminal justice system will ignore psychologists' advice unless it has a sound (i.e.,

non-laboratory) basis. In fact, an appropriate evaluation was provided
by a British Royal Commission which investigated problems related to
eyewitness testimony. The Devlin (1976) report concluded:

> It has been represented to us that a gap exists between
> academic research into the powers of the human mind and the
> practical requirements of courts of law and the stage seems
> not yet to have been reached at which the conclusions of
> psychological research are sufficiently widely accepted or
> tailored to the needs of the judicial process to become the
> basis for procedural change (p. 73).

Clearly, it is my contention that the conclusions of psychological
research will remain valueless to the criminal justice system until we
abandon our experimental methodolatry. Our aspiration to attain the
precision of physics is futile, instead we must concentrate our efforts
on the development of new methods and on the improvement of applied
technologies. The eyewitness study that I just outlined is an example.
We have demonstrated that an eyewitness account can be reliably scored,
and given a meaningful interpretation. This study is only a beginning
but it demonstrates that a combination of archival and field research can
yield data which are meaningful to psychologists and useful to the
criminal justice system.

Meaningful Research

The final section of this chapter is devoted to specific proposals for
effective and meaningful psychological research. First, I offer some
guidelines to police in evaluating research proposals. Finally, I
conclude with an outline of a procedure which serves both police training
and research goals.

When co-operating in a research program the first concern of police
officials should be the meaningfulness of the proposed project. That is,
the project should bear upon issues which are of interest and concern in
the criminal justice system. I do not mean by this that research should
be screened to protect the status quo. Nor am I proposing that research
must be atheoretical. Often psychologists can serve the useful function
for the police of an outsider able to perceive the conceptual forest
rather than be preoccupied with the day to day trees of police work.
Police forces, like all organizations, need examination, evaluation,
change, and improvement. But the research enterprise will only work when
a spirit of mutual co-operation exists between police force and
researcher. The need for co-operation points to a central issue in
applied research, the value laden nature of the research enterprise. The
laboratory psychologist can entertain the illusion that research is value
free. This assumption is false, but it cannot even be entertained in the
applied context. Every study has a purpose, or multiple purposes, and
co-operation is only possible if both police and researchers understand
each others goals. Consequently, the investigator must make every effort
to explicate those purposes. I am not naive in expecting that we are
always, or even regularly, capable of specifying the motivations behind
our investigations. But we must make an effort to explain why we have
selected a problem for study. Why are certain behaviors being recorded
and others ignored? What do we hope to learn from the research?
Questions like these must be raised and at least an attempt made to
answer them before the research proceeds. If not, serious problems may
result. For example, two years ago the Vancouver police agreed to
co-operate in a study conducted by some members of the Criminology

Programme at Simon Fraser University. The focus of the study was the use of firearms by the members of the police force. Since such co-operative efforts had proved fruitful in the past, the Vancouver force agreed to participate in the research. In the end, it was apparent that some of the researchers held strong beliefs that police are too eager to use firearms. The results of the study appear (at the very least from the perspective of the Vancouver police) to be biased to support that 'conclusion. For example, the researchers relied on unsubstantiated newspaper accounts and selected conclusions from coroner's reports. Names of individual officers were published in the research report, a clear violation of the fundamental protection of confidentiality in research. Questionable methods were used to obtain information from police officers. After the publication of the conclusions of this study the Vancouver police were hesitant to co-operate in future research. With some justification they perceived research as a value justification process rather than a knowledge generation one. If the investigators had made their values clear at the start, at the very least there would have been less misunderstanding between them and the police. More positively, a sharing of views might have led to a more valuable study.

I think the following guidelines would prove useful for police forces when evaluating research proposals:

(1) The police force should establish a central individual or office which is responsible for co-ordinating all research. Obviously, budgetary constraints are paramount, however, if an officer can be committed, fully or in part, to this work, that person should be familiar with research procedures, instruments, and research personnel in the community. If needed, researchers might assist the police officer in developing a familiarity with research issues and techniques.

(2) The research officer should control all access to police personnel. Knowing who is working with whom will facilitate communication while maintaining security. This would also promote communication between the police involved in the research and the police research officer.

(3) All research should be conducted with the informed consent of the personnel involved. Again, this will facilitate communication, and assure that all of the police involved understand the purpose of the project. As part of this communication process, a form of feedback should be established in advance to assure that all personnel are informed of the outcome of the study.

(4) The researcher should supply a detailed research proposal, including a statement of purposes, and copies of all instruments and questionnaires to be employed. The proposal must include a statement of all extra-police sources of information to be used in the project.

(5) If the project is approved, the police must retain the right to terminate it, with cause. Such termination must be accompanied by a justification, and suggestions about how the project could be resumed.

(6) The police research officer should be guaranteed an opportunity to review any report that comes out of the research before it is submitted for publication. This suggestion is not intended to give the police veto powers concerning publication. Rather the intention is to allow feedback from the police about any controversial aspects of the study. This would also allow the police a chance to prepare a response to the report if one was felt necessary.

(7) Proposals for solutions to any problems that are discovered by the research should be included in any research report. In short, criticism

should be constructive.

I shift to an example of how psychological research and police training can be combined. I noted much earlier that eyewitness testimony is the single most important information in the solution of crime. As far as courts are concerned, one type of witness is more consistently involved in trials than any other, the police officer. Regardless of the role of other witnesses in a case, the investigating officers will always be called to report on their attendance at the incident, and to make an identification of the accused. Since the trial is typically months after the event, and sometimes years later, the ability of the officer to accurately reconstruct the incident is critical. The officer must depend on notes to aid this reconstruction. As I mentioned at the start of my talk, training in note taking is often inadequate. However, it is possible to provide a good training in note taking and, at the same time, use the training procedure to provide useful research data relevant to eyewitness memory issues.

What follows is a training module which is currently being implemented at the British Columbia Police Academy. Within a few weeks of arriving at the academy, police trainees will be exposed to a simulated crime. The simulation will be either a domestic event, or a theft. The content of the simulation can be accommodated to fit any other training needs at that stage of the recruits training. At the end of the event, a few of the recruits will be interviewed by the training personnel. Some of the interviews will demonstrate how not to interview witnesses. Thus, the interview will include leading questions, too extensive questioning, etc. Other recruit witnesses will be interviewed correctly. The training personnel will provide the psychological justification for avoiding particular interview pitfalls.

All of the recruits will be expected to make notes of the interviews. At a later date, they will be asked to provide a written reconstruction of the event, based upon their notes. The reconstructions can then be criticized to demonstrate inadequacies in the notes. This procedure will be repeated throughout the course of training, providing a trial-and-error learning experience for the trainees.

In the process of taking notes and reconstructing the simulations, the recruits will provide a great deal of information of interest to the student of memory. For example, we intend to manipulate the availability of notes during event reconstruction to determine their memorial function. Clearly, this situation meets both police training goals and the interests of the researcher. The theoretical goals of the psychologist can be pursued, and the close liaison of researcher and police trainer assures a constant evaluation of the effectiveness of the training program. Further, the research has been designed with an awareness of the training needs and goals of the police.

Conclusions

The enthusiasm of many experimental psychologists for their methodology is understandable. If human behavior was causally determined in a context free fashion the laboratory would have provided us with a capacity to control and predict our behavior. But we are not the predictable machines some researchers believe us to be. Trying to force us into that mold has proved fruitless. However, the experimental enterprise has been of use. The technology and sophistication in observation procedures which have developed during the past decades can be applied to field research. It is now possible to conduct useful, complex research within an appropriate context. The only problem is overcoming the reticence of psychologists to leave their laboratories.

Police organizations may play a role in affecting the attitudes of psychologists. It is likely that police psychologists will constitute a rapidly growing contingent during the next decade. As this volume demonstrates, the field is new and will provide a variety of opportunities for clinical, training, and research activities. Police will play a central role in determining the type of psychologist that emerges in police work. Programmes to train police psychologists are just beginning to appear. Whether the police psychologist of the future is stamped from the experimental mold or from an alternative mold is yet to be determined. I hope that the training of psychologists in the future will include:

(1) The selection of police psychology candidates who have some "street" experience as well as the requisite analytic and intellectual skills;

(2) An emphasis in training on field work and the application of knowledge in the appropriate contexts;

(3) An appreciation for the needs of the individual (as opposed to a fictitious average) in the context of police work;

(4) Encouraging the psychologist to resist the temptation to distort psychological tools to suit the political needs of police organizations (this is particularly likely in the area of selection).

The training of police officers is changing, the training of police psychologists is just beginning, and the need for research of relevance to both types of training is great. These needs are interdependent and co-operation between police and psychologists is the most important determinant in meeting these needs. The NATO conference and this volume demonstrate that such co-operation is possible.

REFERENCES

Brigham, J.C., Maass, A., Snyder, L.D., & Spaulding, K. (1982). Accuracy of eyewitness identifications in a field setting. Journal of Personality and Social Psychology, 42, 673-681.

Buckhout, R. (1974). Eyewitness testimony. Scientific American, 231(6), 23-31.

Corteen, R., & Yuille, J.C. (1985). The study of human cognition: The failure of experimentation and a proposed alternative. Unpublished paper, University of British Columbia.

Cutshall, J.L. (1985). Eyewitness characteristics and memory: An in situ analysis. Master's thesis, University of British Columbia.

Devlin, Lord Patrick. (1976). Report to the Secretary of State for the Home Department of the Departmental Committee on evidence of identification in criminal cases. Her Majesty's Stationery Office, London.

Donnerstein. (1980). Aggressive erotica and violence against women. Journal of Personality and Social Psychology, 39(2), 269-277.

Hosch, H.M., & Cooper, D.S. (1980). Victimization and self-monitoring as determinants of eyewitness accuracy. Unpublished manuscript, University of Texas at El Paso.

Lipton, J.P. (1977). On the psychology of eyewitness testimony. Journal of Applied Psychology, 62, 90-93.

Lloyd-Bostock, S., & Clifford, B.R. (Eds). (1983). Evaluating witness evidence. New York: Wiley.

Loftus, E.F. (1979). Eyewitness testimony. Cambridge, MA: Harvard University Press.

Malamuth, N.M. (1981). Rape fantasies as a function of exposure to violent sexual stimuli. Archives of Sexual Behavior, 10(1), 33-47.

Rand Corporation. (1975). The criminal investigation process. V.1-3, R-1776-DOJ, R-1777-DOJ.

Wells, G.L. (1978). Applied eyewitness-testimony research: System variables and estimator variables. Journal of Personality and Social Psychology, 36, 1546-1557.

Yarmey, A.D. (1979). The Psychology of eyewitness testimony. New York: The Free Press.

Yuille, J.C. (1984). Research and teaching with police: A Canadian example. International Review of Applied Psychology, 33, 5-23.

Yuille, J.C. (1986). On the futility of a purely experimental psychology of cognition: Imagery as a case study. In D.F. Marks (Ed.), Theories of Image Formation. New York: Brandon House.

Yuille, J.C., & Cutshall, J.L. (1985). Live vs. video events in eyewitness research. Unpublished manuscript, University of British Columbia.

Yuille, J.C., & Cutshall, J.L. (1986). A case study of eyewitness memory of a crime. Journal of Applied Psychology, in press.

SECTION II
DELEGATES' PAPERS

PSYCHOLOGICAL STANDARDS RESEARCH FOR CALIFORNIA LAW ENFORCEMENT OFFICERS

GEORGE E. HARGRAVE

A two-year research program has provided the basis for the psychological suitability standard recently adopted by the California Commission on Peace Officer Standards and Training. Overall, the project consisted of three major components: (1) The development of a psychological skills analysis; (2) a predictive academy study, which related psychological test data obtained on cadets in training to various later performance variables; and (3) an incumbent officer study which examined predictive relationships between pre-employment test scores and subsequent job performance measures.

PSYCHOLOGICAL SKILLS ANALYSIS

Two statewide surveys were conducted in which systematic samples of law enforcement supervisors rated descriptions of behavior on frequency of occurrence among peace officers and estimated the impact of the described behavior upon officers' job performance. The first survey examined abnormal behaviors, with the descriptions reflecting behaviors of psychodiagnostic categories from the Diagnostic and Statistical Manual of Mental Disorders, 3rd Edition (DSM III). One hundred and nine such descriptors were rated by 100 supervisors. The results of this survey indicated that there was a perceived low frequency of behaviors associated with diagnosable psychopathology among law enforcement officers. The ratings of impairment for behaviors associated with diagnostic categories were, as expected, assessed as moderately to profoundly detrimental to job performance.

Those areas of psychopathology rated as having the most severe impairment upon job performance involved different mental and emotional dimensions. One thing the areas seemingly shared was a core of unpredictability due either to an inability to accurately perceive situations and respond appropriately, as in the case of thought disorders, or due to an inability to exercise self control as in the case of impulse, borderline, psychosexual, and affective disorders. Those categories rated as having "moderate" impairment were those which are typically seen as having somewhat less impact in most life spheres (e.g., compulsivity).

The second survey was designed to assess a wider range of personality and behavioral dimensions than those presented in the survey of abnormal behavior. Interpretation sources for tests typically used in screening were reviewed, and fourteen global areas were labeled as achievement, flexibility, sensitivity, maturity, intellectual functioning, somatic concerns, mood, social adjustment, anxiety, emotional control, dominance, ethics, impression formation, and liberal/conservative attitudes. Six behavioral descriptors were then written for each of the 14 areas which expressed testable dimensions and were sufficiently broad to enable most individuals to be classified into one of the descriptors. The survey was, as before, administered to a statewide systematic sample of 141 law enforcement supervisors who rated the described behaviors on estimated impact upon job performance. The results indicated exceptional consistency in the supervisors' ratings of the survey behaviors, with no statistically significant variability occurring even as a function of size or type of agency. Further, the results enabled the development of quantified descriptions of desirable and undesirable attributes based upon how such dimensions were expected to impact upon job performance. The combined data from the two surveys were used to identify scales and scale levels on the Minnesota Multiphasic Personality Inventory (MMPI) and the California Psychological Inventory (CPI) which corresponded to the rated survey descriptors. This enabled the rated behaviors to be translated into psychological test profile information which was hypothetically related to job performance as a peace officer.

ACADEMY STUDY

This research component was designed to address two major methodological problems which have impaired validation research in the psychological screening of peace officers; these are the inability to assess performance of individuals who are disqualified by testing, and the lack of criterion measures which relate directly to mental/emotional functioning. This component of the research was designed to address the first problem by testing entry-level individuals who had been selected for law enforcement academy training with screening procedures which did not include psychological testing. Assuming that other such selection procedures (e.g., reading and writing tests, background investigation, oral board interview) do not fully duplicate the information provided by psychological tests, this would allow the tracking of individuals who would have been disqualified on the basis of psychological testing through academy and field training, during which time their performance could be assessed. To address the second problem, these individuals would be rated on factors of emotional suitability for law enforcement work with a behavioral rating scale (BRS) designed specifically as a criterion for this research.

Cadets (N=742) from selected academies throughout the state were administered the MMPI, CPI, and a research test on the first day of training. (Only the results of the first two tests will be reported here.) These subjects were subsequently followed through the academy training, field performance, and onto the job. Numerous criterion measures were selected including training attrition, BRS ratings by training officers and peers, and academy and field performance.

Two approaches were used to relate predictor (test scales) and criterion variables. The first of these was a "clinical analysis," in which three psychologists participated in a prediction of training performance. MMPI and CPI profiles were interpreted on the basis of the survey data from the psychological skills analysis, and predictions were made for the criteria of academy attrition and low instructor or peer ratings of emotional suitability. Subsequent analyses of the criterion data indicated that, on the basis of either the MMPI or the CPI, clinicians accurately classified approximately 70% of the subjects. Inter-rater reliability and validity were both statistically significant. The second approach statistically related test scales to the various criterion measures. Although numerous relationships were found, the most useful results to emerge were scales which differentiated between cadets who attrited versus those who did not and between cadets with high BRS ratings versus those with low ratings. In the former case, elevations on MMPI scales F, 1(Hs), 2(D), 7(Pt), O, A, Ca, and Pr and low scores on MMPI scales Es, Do, and St were significantly (p<.002) associated with attrition. Likewise, low scores on CPI scales Sp, Ie, In, and Lead were comparably significant predictors of attrition. Low ratings of emotional suitability were associated with an elevation on MMPI scale O (Si) and low scores on MMPI scales Do and St (p<.002).

INCUMBENT OFFICER STUDY

This component of the project was conducted to replicate other research and to examine whether predictive relationships could be identified between test and performance data, given the range restriction problems inherent in this type of study. (Since officers with deviant test profiles had not been hired, only the test data from "normal" officers could be related to job performance.) A sample of 328 officers with approximately three years on the job was systematically selected from five of the larger police and sheriffs' departments in the state. Every officer in the sample had received pre-employment psychological testing which, in turn, had been used as a component of the selection process. Test and criterion data were obtained on each officer from appropriate files. Both types of data varied widely from agency to agency; consequently, complete and comparable data sets were difficult to obtain. The two tests with sufficient sample sizes for analysis consisted of the MMPI and the Edwards Personal Preference Schedule (EPPS). The performance criteria from personnel records which existed with both sufficient quantity and consistency were academy and field training data, supervisors' evaluations, and disciplinary actions. Although several statistically significant relationships were found between psychological test scales and various performance measures, this report focused upon those criteria deemed most important; these were supervisors' performance ratings and disciplinary actions. Both the MMPI and the EPPS predicted performance ratings. Four MMPI scales, 1(Hs), 8(Sc), R, and Ca, had statistically significant inverse relationships with performance, and scales 2(D) and Cn both had significant direct relationships with this criterion. Scale Dom of the EPPS had a strong direct relationship with supervisors' ratings, and Ord had a significant, but weaker inverse relationship with this criterion. No scales on the MMPI, CPI or EPPS significantly predicted disciplinary actions.

DISCUSSION

In general, the description of an effective officer to emerge from these data was that of a dominant, calm, goal-oriented, out-going, socially assertive, clear-thinking individual who had few somatic or psychological concerns and who maintained excellent emotional control. Any psychological difficulties associated with overt anxiety, misperceiving situations, poor impulse control, lack of assertiveness or withdrawal were consistently viewed as seriously interfering with job performance. The elements of this description do not, of course, differ much from those associated with the "police personality" described by numerous authors in the literature.

ASSESSMENT STRATEGY FOR SPECIAL UNIT ASSIGNMENTS: AN ALTERNATIVE TO PSYCHOLOGICAL TESTS

ELLEN M. SCRIVNER

A number of studies have evaluated the use of psychological tests to select law enforcement personnel (Hargrave & Berner, 1984; Hogan & Kurtines, 1975; Shusman, Inwald, & Landa, 1984; Spielberger, 1979). Study findings demonstrate variable success for entry level selection and many law enforcement agencies now employ these tests as standard recruit selection tools. The perception of success attributed to psychological tests by law enforcement has fostered new requests to employ these tests in mid-career selection decisions. This practice is becoming especially prevalent in the selection of personnel for sensitive special unit assignments, such as emergency operation teams (Reiser, 1982). At first glance, the use of tests in this manner may appear to be a legitimate function, since the emotional stability of special unit personnel is critical to successful job performance. Decidedly different issues emerge, however, when selecting inexperienced police recruits and when evaluating experienced officers with a history of job related behaviors. In fact, to employ psychological tests with experienced officers may represent a practice of doubtful efficacy and also raises a host of ethical and legal issues.

Police psychologists then are faced with a dilemma: law enforcement needs to employ effective personnel methods to staff these critical positions; yet, mid-career selection decisions must be guided by parameters that are different from entry level selection. This paper presents an assessment strategy that may facilitate the resolution of this dilemma. It was developed in response to requests for assessments of candidates for a special operations team in a mid-size, suburban police jurisdiction. The candidates for evaluation would be experienced police officers, with varying degrees of effectiveness, who had histories of job behavior, or track records, that might well contradict findings on psychological tests. Hence, it was determined that any assessment strategy developed to screen candidates for the team should include an assessment of patrol behaviors that would document and evaluate prior work behavior. This approach was based on the premise that the best predictor of future behavior is past behavior.

To meet this objective a patrol behavior check list was developed to be used as a supplement in the evaluation of candidates (supplement to other department criteria). It was proposed that candidates could be rated on this check list either by supervisors, field training officers or peers, but preferably by someone who had familiarity and access to a consistent sample of the candidate's work behavior. Because of a specific behavioral focus, the check list would differ from general performance appraisal evaluations. Furthermore, it was believed that the completed ratings might contribute to an understanding of the general personality characteristics that would be relative to appropriate or inappropriate performance in this assignment.

Method Used to Develop Check List

A critical incident methodology (Flanagan, 1954) was employed with the 20 male officers who staffed the current team (SMES). Initially, the team members met with the psychologist in small groups (n=5). The overall screening objective was explained to each group and anyone who did not wish to take part in the exercise was assured that they could terminate their participation without consequence. All officers agreed to participate. Their motivation appeared to be enhanced by the knowledge that they would be assisting in developing an instrument to select officers with whom they would be working in critical circumstances. The team members were able to articulate both the positive and negative characteristics that they felt were necessary to effective team performance. They particularly focused on issues relative to safety, reliability, and integrity of team function.

Each group of five officers then met in three hour workshops. Their first task was to generate independently ten patrol behaviors that they had personally observed in other officers during the course of their own patrol activity. Five of the behaviors were to define observed patrol behaviors that, in their opinion, would be detrimental to the functioning of a special operations team; the other five behaviors were to define positive behaviors or assets. It was specified that they were to use statements that depicted behaviors they had actually observed, rather than behavioral characteristics, such as, "the officer acted immature." They were also told to frame their responses as sentences with active verbs. For example, "Officer X responded to a burglary and did ...." Finally, they were told to elect behaviors on the basis of frequency, criticality and importance to performing the patrol function, rather than using obscure instances that might occur only under special circumstances. Several examples were discussed with the group before they described these behaviors on 3" x 5" cards.

In the second phase of the workshop, the fifty patrol behaviors generated by each group were discussed by the group and only those items that achieved consensual agreement were considered for inclusion in the final product. Overall, 200 behaviors were developed across the four groups and consensual agreement was reached on 43 patrol behaviors. One hundred fifty-seven behaviors could not be included because they were germane only to a certain jurisdiction, reflected individual supervisory styles, or were not considered as critical to the patrol function.

The 43 selected behaviors (see Table 1) were then categorized into four classes: general complaint behavior; arrest behavior; communication behavior; and general law enforcement behavior. These four classes of behaviors were then compiled into the check list and a frequency of occurrence rating, anchored from 1 to 4, accompanied each statement. These ratings were as follows:

(1) A rating of 1 signified that the behavior was never observed in patrol.
(2) A rating of 2 signified that the behavior was observed but on an infrequent basis such as once or twice in a career.
(3) A rating of 3 signified behavior that was observed more regularly, about once in every six complaints.
(4) A rating of 4 signified behavior that could generally be expected from the officer.

Table 1
Examples of Patrol Behavior Check List
(Behaviors classified as positive (+) or negative (-))

CATEGORIES OF PATROL BEHAVIOR

Complaint Behavior
+ Before entering complaint area, checks to make sure it is secure.

+ Provides dispatcher with correct information about location.

- Approaches complaint in casual manner, ie. coffee cup in hand.

- Proceeds to handle complaint before fully assessing situation.

Arrest Behavior
- Positions self so that firearms are readily available to suspect.

(Only negative behaviors identified)
- Strikes a handcuffed subject.

- Stands back and observes while another officer engages in a struggle.

- Doesn't call for assistance when effecting group arrests.

Communication Behavior
+ Listens to others, avoids interruptions, and allows subject to finish sentences.

+ Is able to talk subject into surrendering weapon.

- Argues with subject in an arrest process.

- Shows agitated response to heated verbal exchange, ie, spits on sidewalk, strikes cruiser.

General Law Enforcement
+ Is reliable as a back-up unit and responds immediately.

+ Is able to accept and follow orders.

- Demonstrates a preoccupation with taking lives by talking a lot about it.

- As back-up officer, attempts to take charge of situation.

BEHAVIORS ARE TO BE RATED ACCORDING TO FREQUENCY ON A SCALE OF 1 TO 4
1) Behavior never observed in patrol.
2) Behavior observed on infrequent basis (once or twice in career).
3) Behavior observed more regularly (at least one in six complaints).
4) Behavior generally expected from the officer on patrol (usual behavior).

These ratings were necessary to define a consistent behavioral sample for all candidates rated on the check list. The ideal ratings would be 4's on all positive statements and 1's on all negative statements with the reverse for inappropriate candidates. Each statement was also weighted to account for an unequal distribution of positive and negative statements. The check list was developed in this manner so that factor analytic solutions could be applied to the subsequent ratings to determine the underlying structure of the data set. This method would also enable subsequent predictive validation analysis.

Proposed Use of the Check List

Two different models were proposed for using the check list in the selection process. The first model would use the selection panel to collect ratings on individual candidates from the multiple raters who have the most frequent contact with the candidate's work behavior. Multiple raters were suggested to overcome squad rivalry affecting ratings, and because the different categories of behaviors on the check list might require more than one observer to obtain the most consistent sample of a candidate's work performance. The advantages of this model include the collection of quantifiable information that can be submitted to subsequent statistical analysis; the documentation of job related behavior to substantiate select and non-select decisions; and the provision of job related feedback to candidates who are non-selected. In the latter instance, the non-select candidate could then be apprised of the specific behavior that needs to be corrected. This feedback focuses on behavior and avoids global evaluative statements such as "poor judgment" or "immature".

The second model uses the check list as the basis for a structured interview. The selection panel would fill out the check list while interviewing supervisors and peers and would direct interview questions to the specific behavioral areas. This approach circumvents hesitancy by peers or supervisors to commit, in writing, explicit information that might affect someone's career. It also avoids problems with traditional rating errors, and the verbal exchange might facilitate more disclosure of more accurate information. Furthermore, quantifiable data can still be collected; but this model is more subject to challenges of subjective or biased evaluations. In either case, both models provide specific job-related decisions and, as such, represent viable alternatives to psychological tests for mid-career assessments.

Conclusions

In conclusion, a behavioral-based assessment strategy has been presented that will enable law enforcement to select experienced officers into sensitive special unit assignments. The methodology used to develop a patrol behavior check list is explained and two different models for using the check list have been detailed. The behaviors, themselves, reflect certain personal characteristics which, in this instance, would have been inappropriate to functioning on a special operations team. This methodology, however, can be adapted to other types of assignments.

This type of assessment strategy provides an alternative to psychological testing for mid-career selection decisions and is free of the criticisms surrounding the practices of collecting psychological test data on officers who have a history of job related behavior. This history, when documented, may be a more reliable and consistent account of an officer's personal characteristics then would a pattern of scales on psychological tests. In this regard, the method developed and its proposed use, facilitates the resolution of the dilemma initially posed. Psychologists can assist law enforcement to collect the information they need to staff their critical positions, and can do so in a manner that is compatible with legal, ethical, and professional standards. The selection decisions can be better defended because of their job-relatedness. Most important, officers who are not selected receive realistic and practical information that is relative to their own behavior rather than to global, abstract labels. Hence, the officers are in a position to remediate patrol behaviors so as to become viable candidates in the future. This assessment strategy can be a useful personnel management tool which benefits both the law enforcement agency and the individual employee.

REFERENCES

Flanagan, J. C. (1954). The critical incident technique. Psychological Bulletin, 51, 327-358.

Hargrave, G. E., & Berner, J. G. (1984). POST psychological screening manual. California Commission on Peace Officers Standards and Training.

Hogan, R., & Kurtines, W. (1975). Personalogical correlates of police effectiveness. Journal of Psychology, 91, 289-291.

Mills, C. J., & Bohannon, W. E. (1980). Personality characteristics of effective state police officers. Journal of Applied Psychology, 65, 680-684.

Reiser, M. (1982). Police psychology: Collected papers. California: LEHI.

Shusman, E., Inwald, R. E., & Landa, B. (1984). Correction officer job performance as predicted by the IPI and MMPI. Criminal Justice and Behavior, 11(3), 302-329.

Spielberger, C. (1979). Police selection and evaluation. New York: Praeger.

MUNICIPAL POLICE EVALUATION: PSYCHOMETRIC VERSUS BEHAVIOURAL ASSESSMENT

P. SERRANO, L. GARCIA-SEVILLA, J.L. PEREZ, M. PINA, AND J.R. RUIZ

INTRODUCTION

Modern society demands and expects from police, in an ever increasing manner, a multiplicity of services and related skills from knowing medical first aid techniques, to self-defense or sports-like automobile driving. Many of these skills constitute in themselves the foundations of apparently incompatible professions. In other words, society expects a good police officer to be a sort of "social athlete" with the rank of champion in many events, which raises the costs of training recruits as well as maintaining police structure. It is for such a reason that there is a need to improve the systems of selection for police recruits, with the aim in mind of increasing the output of such an expensive system. On the other hand, the selection of police recruits is a question that poses multiple difficulties and appears, therefore, as very attractive to behaviour researchers, not only due to the complexity of the topic, but also because of its limited scientific tradition (Chenoweth, 1961). These aspects are applicable equally to the selection of police recruits as well as to the assessment of duty policemen if a better working position, job promotion, specialized training, etc., are being considered for him/her.

Psychometric tests are widely used in many areas of psychology and they show themselves to be reliable and valid. However, in the case of evaluation and selection of police, little is known about the validity of the criteria of the various parameters in selection. Because of that, a very clear tendency in the progressive utilization of policemen's behavioural assessment can be detected (Bull, Bustin, Evans, & Gahagan, 1983), despite the fact that behavioural assessment as such implies the possibility of problems within the structure of the police (Von Behren, 1976), and is very influenced by environmental and interpersonal factors (Grey & Kipnis, 1976). Furthermore, behavioural assessment is a more expensive procedure than the use of standardized psychometric tests which can be easily applied to a large number of candidates or duty policemen.

The purpose of our study was the comparison between behavioural assessment and the psychometric assessment in the case of duty policemen, taking as subjects the entire staff of the Municipal Police Corps of a Catalan city. The city holds a population of about three-hundred thousand inhabitants, half of whom are immigrants from economically depressed areas of Spain. The abnormal physical and human growth of this city is connected to the industrial and urban boom that originated in the country since the late 1950s. Needless to say, the city in which our subjects perform their duty is far from an ideal social setting, if we consider its chaotic urban layout, absence of adequate public and social services, high unemployment rate, etc. Until recently, the municipal police profession had very low social recognition in the country. In this city, specifically, the job of municipal policeman was basically filled by Castilian-(or, as it is more usually termed in English, Spanish) speaking immigrants. More recently their bilingual sons (Strubell, 1982) and those of natives of the area are entering the force. The re-establishment of democracy in Spain has permitted the official use of the Catalan and the Spanish languages in Catalonia.

Despite the fact that under Spanish legislation municipal police have the same rank as any of the other police corps, in real practice, reflecting the low social prestige it has traditionally enjoyed, its main function has been traffic regulation. However, as a result of the transition into democracy and modern society, there has been a reevaluation of this corps; resulting, among other things, in an increased interest on the part of the municipal police hierarchy to expand the service, as well as to update the force and provide a more sophisticated system of selection. This paper is basically intended as another step in the improvement of a profession, the municipal police, that very much needs objective and reliable evaluating systems.

METHOD
Subjects
There were 195 on duty municipal police officers, 30 of whom were women, who participated in our study. Four corporals and two sergeants were used as raters because of their thorough knowledge of the ratees. The raters were trained beforehand so they could perform the evaluation.

Procedure
Behavioural assessment. One hundred and forty-seven items were produced by seven professors and managers of the Municipal Police Academy of the City of Barcelona in describing the ideal officer. These items were reduced to 78 after discarding repetitious and ambiguous ones. Such reduction was made by two successive teams of six independent judges. An effort was made so that every item would not have the same response direction. The items were converted into 10 cm Visual Analogue Scales (VAS) through which the supervisor raters evaluated all the staff they knew well. In this manner, each policeman was evaluated by a maximum of 6 supervisors and a minimum of 2, with a mode of 4 raters to every ratee. The score on each VAS of each ratee was the mean of his/her ratings.

Psychometric assessment. Three months before the behavioural assessment, the entire staff was explored by means of a battery composed by personality inventories, intelligence tests and perceptual motor laboratory tests developed or administered by the Institut de Psicotècnia de Catalunya. Personality inventories were the Spanish versions (Seisdedos et al., 1982, 1983) of Cattell's Sixteen Personality Factors (16 PF) and of the Minnesota Multiphasic Personality Inventory (MMPI). Intelligence tests were Raven's Standard Progressive Matrices and the Spanish version (Alvarez, 1976) of Lorge-Thorndike's tests. Laboratory tests were Witmer's Cylinder Test, Toulouse-Piéron's "Test de barrage" (5 trials of 20 seconds), a sort of Memory-for-Designs test (Ballvé), a performance test (5 trials of 20 seconds) of visual manual coordination (the "palogràfic" test), and a Choice Reaction Time test (Marti) in which the subject must respond with the four extremities (5 series of 5 trials).

Analysis. The two sets of data were submitted to two independent factorial analyses using a principal factor analysis with Varimax rotation (Nie, Hull, Jenkins, Steinbrenner, & Bent, 1975). Further, one regression factor score for each analysis was computed and their correlations were calculated (Nie et al., 1975).

RESULTS
Behavioural assessment

Prior to factorial analysis, 28 VAS (those which showed greater variability intra-subject than inter-subject) were eliminated. Table 1 shows the Varimax-rotated factor (Kaiser normalization) loadings for the VAS.

Factor I can be interpreted as Good Policeman. It loads substantially on the ability to transmit orders to make decisions, to observe and retain details related to one's job, to verbally express oneself well, to know how to write reports, to show the wish to exceed oneself professionally, to fine correctly, to solve work-related problems, and to know how to act with authority.

Factor II can be interpreted as Bad Policeman, because it refers to the policeman who argues with fellow citizens, does not show good manners, shows unnecessarily ostentatious authority, is not respectful, and is not in favour of warning before sanctioning.

Factor III reflects the Good Bureaucrat, because he/she collaborates with his/her supervisors; he/she does not have to be cautioned; his/her supervisors are satisfied with his/her work; and he/she is a good worker. He/she differs from the Good Policeman in that he/she has fewer physical and verbal aptitudes, as well as fewer observational and decision-making skills, though he/she is more punctual and disciplined. In regard to the linguistic use, the Good Bureaucrat would use Spanish, still predominant at local administrative level, while the Good Policeman would utilize Catalan.

Factor IV, or Physical Capacity, loads on physical endurance, agility, fitness, strength, physical health and good physique, in this order. The Good Policeman is seen as agile and in shape, the Bad Policeman and the Good Bureaucrat do not show any kind of outstanding physical capacity.

Factor V can be named Traffic Warden because of its important loadings on knowledge of the city, mechanical skill, traffic regulation, and ability to perform small mechanical repairs.

Factor VI can be interpreted as Bad Demeanor because it loads on abuse from alcohol, abuse of his/her position, disregard for overall neatness of uniform, lack of concern for the public property (equipment) he/she uses at work, and undue use of weapons.

Factor VII, or Good Demeanor, loads on punctuality, correct physical appearance (uniform), acceptance of orders, and respectful.

Psychometric assessment

Table 2 shows the Varimax-rotated factor (Kaiser normalization) loadings for the psychometric battery.

Factor I can be interpreted as the general factor of Intelligence because its larger loadings are on verbal as well as on non-verbal intelligence tests.

Factor II or Mental Disorder loads on the MMPI neurotic and psychotic scales as well on MMPI's F (Infrequency) scale.

Factor III can be named Manual Dexterity because it loads on the "palogràfic" test and, on a lower degree, on Toulouse-Piéron's test.

Factor IV, or Complex Reaction Time, loads fundamentally on the Choice Reaction Timne test and also significantly on Witmer's test.

Table 1
Varimax-rotated Factor Pattern (N=195) of VAS

VAS	I	II	III	IV	V	VI	VII
1. Knows how to make decisions	88	01	20	16	17	03	03
2. Uncollaborative with fellow officers	-30	54	-61	-07	12	-06	11
3. Acts with authority	77	17	32	12	37	-05	-04
4. Utilizes Catalan language	23	-05	-38	-16	-18	02	18
5. Transmits orders orally	91	-00	09	20	08	-09	01
6. Good partner	49	-51	54	22	-00	-02	01
7. Does not solve problems	-72	03	-37	-08	-16	02	24
8. Physical strength	39	21	15	76	16	02	03
9. Regulates traffic	21	25	09	03	68	-10	19
10. Cultural level	66	-22	-19	39	-48	-08	01
11. Fines correctly	77	-08	28	19	27	-10	-04
12. Is not discreet	-14	74	-34	12	02	19	29
13. Punctual	-09	-11	59	01	33	-18	43
14. Uses acquired knowledge	75	-21	44	24	09	-12	03
15. Knows the city	04	27	11	-30	77	05	22
16. Good assessment of situations	79	-33	25	17	04	-04	07
17. Good observer	83	-06	18	22	04	05	10
18. Accepts orders	01	-67	52	-08	03	03	34
19. Abuses of his position	01	32	-44	-17	25	49	15
20. Verbal expression	82	-24	-06	30	-05	-06	07
21. Slow worker	-65	-21	-44	-30	-13	-07	16
22. Physical health	46	02	05	75	-10	-11	04
23. Respectful	11	-81	32	04	-02	-12	29
24. Argues with fellow-citizens	01	86	-23	-02	15	08	05
25. Physical agility	52	03	12	77	-07	-04	-08
26. Concerned about his work	50	-28	68	12	13	-09	23
27. Has to be cautioned	-18	42	-77	08	-02	14	11
28. Good driver	45	12	02	45	57	12	-18
29. Warns before sanctioning	04	-82	-20	-01	-21	03	15
30. Mechanical Aptitude	04	10	03	19	76	20	-17
31. Does not wish to exceed himself	-76	06	-38	-31	13	13	05
32. Does not like the job	47	-13	67	16	22	-04	20
33. Does not care for public property	-03	23	-58	14	05	36	02
34. Good worker	54	-06	71	19	13	-04	14
35. Remembers details	81	-12	13	30	-09	-02	00
36. Without social prejudices	48	-07	-14	43	-51	10	10
37. Avoids difficult missions	-50	-00	-65	-29	-13	-05	17
38. Supervisors are satisfied with him	49	-27	72	16	10	-11	11
39. Kind	31	-77	24	11	-07	02	32
40. Good physique	29	-18	01	73	06	-10	08
41. Correctly uniformed	-24	40	-78	02	04	05	00
42. Uses weapon unjustifiably	28	-12	42	24	19	-42	34
43. Uncollaborative with supervisors	10	68	-01	15	07	36	36
44. Writing Ability	77	-00	02	29	-06	07	10
45. Unnecessary ostentatious authority	02	83	-06	09	19	27	16
46. Bad manners	-12	84	-29	-05	10	01	-01
47. Physical endurance	45	11	14	83	03	01	-01
48. Abuses from alcohol	-10	30	-19	-12	09	67	-06
49. Transmits written orders	85	-15	-05	27	-17	-03	09
50. Physical fitness	50	-00	17	76	-05	-06	-00
Percentage variance	39.7	17.2	9.9	4.3	3.2	2.6	2.1

Decimal points omitted.

Table 2

TESTS		I	II	III	IV	V	VI	VII	VIII	IX	X	XI
A	16PF	03	-01	09	03	-05	68	07	13	08	19	-08
B	16PF	71	-08	18	-22	11	07	-00	10	09	09	02
C	16PF	40	-41	18	03	18	40	-24	05	13	27	25
E	16PF	08	04	07	-17	10	42	11	-15	08	-06	56
F	16PF	38	-10	17	-11	10	65	-19	03	12	-09	08
G	16PF	13	06	01	-04	06	18	-06	05	81	02	-01
H	16PF	21	-18	12	-01	09	70	33	03	23	-00	20
I	16PF	-12	01	10	-02	-02	05	03	83	01	-08	-08
L	16PF	-06	42	03	07	-15	13	11	03	09	-44	32
M	16PF	32	-03	14	-01	-07	37	03	32	01	20	13
N	16PF	-03	08	-03	04	01	-19	17	47	42	11	-01
O	16PF	-26	32	-16	04	01	-02	63	13	-14	08	-01
Q$_1$	16PF	24	-04	06	-08	11	-00	-09	-10	02	02	76
Q$_2$	16PF	-14	08	-11	-00	-15	-45	09	41	13	02	50
Q$_3$	16PF	10	-13	03	01	-02	12	-06	02	80	15	11
Q$_4$	16PF	-19	51	-13	-11	-11	-32	35	13	-18	-29	07
L	MMPI	-09	01	06	13	04	16	-09	01	26	75	05
F	MMPI	-26	73	-07	14	-08	-08	02	-03	-08	-12	04
K	MMPI	34	-15	09	-07	20	33	-60	15	02	41	05
Hs	MMPI	-46	65	-19	17	-17	-20	-08	06	-03	-01	-10
D	MMPI	-11	66	-13	02	-12	-21	-05	24	12	31	-10
Hy	MMPI	02	48	-05	03	01	12	-66	22	-06	33	-06
Pd	MMPI	-21	78	-15	02	05	-01	-25	-01	-01	-01	09
Mf	MMPI	12	28	04	-04	07	17	-29	67	-01	08	-08
Pa	MMPI	-18	55	-09	06	-03	12	-05	08	-08	30	-06
Pt	MMPI	-30	73	-10	09	-21	-24	28	07	-04	-15	-09
Sc	MMPI	-44	74	-10	14	-17	-21	16	03	-04	-10	-01
Ma	MMPI	-00	63	10	01	04	30	21	-04	08	-19	09
Si	MMPI	-29	56	-16	09	-11	-49	28	17	11	18	-02
Raven		53	-20	19	-12	44	12	-06	-03	28	-10	-04
V I	L-T	75	-14	19	-28	16	12	18	02	09	-02	01
V II	L-T	80	-16	16	-25	06	04	-05	-03	03	-04	14
V III	L-T	77	-20	10	-19	21	09	-03	-12	07	-07	04
V IV	L-T	76	-16	24	-18	21	13	-17	-01	-02	02	06
V V	L-T	74	-22	16	-23	23	08	-14	-06	03	03	02
NV I	L-T	79	-25	19	-17	22	13	-12	-04	01	-00	09
NV II	L-T	78	-27	19	-18	23	11	-10	-08	04	-01	04
NV III	L-T	81	-25	14	-17	23	10	-18	-02	01	-02	03
Witmer		-27	07	01	40	-05	21	05	32	07	01	-01
T - P 1		46	-04	32	-06	64	13	-10	-06	02	-05	-05
T - P 2		26	-06	25	-10	81	07	-10	-01	02	-03	-04
T - P 3		22	-07	17	-04	85	02	-10	00	04	10	07
T - P 4		24	-11	16	-07	85	-04	02	04	-07	04	05
T - P 5		17	-08	18	-06	78	03	18	-04	00	07	08
Mem-for-Des		41	-29	-15	05	40	-01	-24	01	24	-17	05
Palogràfic 1		21	-11	89	-00	18	06	-04	03	-02	00	02
Palogràfic 2		23	-10	93	-02	15	09	-03	05	-01	01	05
Palogràfic 3		21	-08	92	-04	22	09	-05	03	02	03	03
Palogràfic 4		25	-10	90	-04	21	12	-04	04	04	-01	03
Palogràfic 5		26	-13	86	-05	23	11	-03	01	06	03	-01
CRT 1		-13	06	-06	88	-14	-01	04	-02	01	06	02
CRT 2		-25	04	01	87	01	-04	-03	-02	03	-00	-10
CRT 3		-25	05	-03	88	-02	-02	01	-04	-01	-02	-01
CRT 4		19	05	-06	90	-05	-06	01	02	-08	04	-03
CRT 5		-26	12	01	84	-06	-02	01	-02	02	04	-07
Percentage variance		31.3	8.2	7.3	6.1	4.4	3.7	3.5	3.1	2.4	2.2	1.8

Decimal points omitted

Factor V can be interpreted as Visual Short-Term Memory because of its important loadings on Toulouse-Piéron's test, and its significant loadings on Raven's test and on the Memory-for-Designs test.

Factor VI, or Extraversion, loads fundamentally on the H (Parmia), A (Affectia) and F (Surgency) scales of the 16PF and also negatively on the Si (Social introversion) scale of the MMPI.

Factor VII can be interpreted as Psychic (versus Somatic) Anxiety because it loads positively on the O (Guilt proneness) scale of the 16PF and negatively on the Hy (Conversion hysteria) scale of the MMPI, a scale reflecting somatic manifestations of anxiety (Corah, 1964).

Factor VIII or Sensibility loads on the 16PF I (Premsia) scale and on the MMPI Mf (Masculinity-femininity) scale.

Factor IX can be named Rigidity because of its important loadings on the 16PF G (Superego) and Q3 (Self-sentiment) scales and, on a lower degree, on N (Shrewdness) scale.

Factor X or Social Conformity fundamentally loads on the MMPI L (Lie) scale and significantly on the MMPI K (Correction) and the 16PF L (Protension) cales.

Factor XI can be interpreted as Autonomy because of its loadings on Q1 (Radicalism), E (Dominance) and Q2 (Self-sufficiency) scales of the 16 PF.

Factorial Correlations

Table 3 shows the correlations between the factors of both factorial analyses.

Intelligence correlates positively as much with Good Policeman as with Good Bureaucrat, on a lower degree with Traffic Warden, negatively with Bad Demeanor, and on a lower degree with Physical Capacity and Bad Policeman.

Mental Disorder correlates positively with Bad Demeanor, and negatively and on a lower degree with Good Bureaucrat. Manual Dexterity shows a converse pattern: positively correlating with Bad Demeanor and negatively with Good Bureaucrat.

Good Policeman, Good Bureaucrat and Bad Policeman, in this order, show lower Complex Reaction Time. Visual Short-Term Memory only correlates with Good Bureaucrat.

Extraversion correlates positively with Good Policeman and negatively with Bad Demeanor, and Psychic Anxiety correlates positively with Bad Policeman and Bad Demeanor, thus configuring Good Policeman as an Extraverted-Stable, Bad Policeman as a Neurotic, and Bad Demeanor as Neurotic Introversion.

Sensibility distinguishes Traffic Warden from Bad Demeanor, the latter with less Sensibility. Rididity correlates positively with Bad Demeanor and on a lower degree with Good Policeman, following Social Conformity the previous same pattern: correlating negatively with Good Policeman and on a lower degree with Bad Demeanor. Autonomy only correlates with Bad Policeman.

Good Policeman stands out because of its Intelligence, fast Complex Reaction Time and Extraversion. However it has about 4.6% of factorial (IX, X) communality with Bad Demeanor because of its Rigidity and Social Unconformity.

Bad Policeman although it is fast in Complex Reaction Time, does not show neither Intelligence nor Extraversion but Psychic Anxiety. Moreover, it is the only one showing Autonomy.

Good Bureacrat stands out because of its clerk skills (Intelligence, Visual Short-Term Memory and Manual Dexterity) and its good Mental

Table 3

	GOOD POLICEMAN	BAD POLICEMAN	GOOD BUREAUCRAT	PHYSICAL CAPACITY	TRAFFIC REGULATION	BAD DEMEANOR	DEMEANOR
INTELLIGENCE	4437***	-1285*	3492***	-1932**	2038**	-2829***	-0814
MENTAL DISORDER	-0535	0347	-1615**	0791	0112	2216***	0053
MANUAL DEXTERITY	0925	-0778	1352*	-0073	-0111	-2128***	0000
COMPLEX RT	-1980**	-1269*	-1790**	0439	0619	0000	0561
VISUAL SHORT-TERM MEMORY	1005	0509	2622***	-0706	-0081	0017	0189
EXTRAVERSION	1764**	0053	0858	0920	0787	-1835**	-0252
PSYCHIC ANXIETY	-0027	2237***	-0882	0932	0612	1888**	-0919
SENSIBILITY	-0927	-0602	-0814	0292	2016**	-2115**	-0747
RIGIDITY	1686**	0418	0314	-0262	-0280	2237***	-0106
SOCIAL CONFORMITY	-1644**	-0484	0456	0574	-0307	-1561*	0467
AUTONOMY	1147	1809**	0740	-0846	-0778	-0160	0619

Decimal points omitted.

*p < 0.05   **p < 0.01   ***p < 0.001

Adjustment. Moreover, it is fast in Complex Reaction Time almost as much as Good Policeman, but is not Extraverted. On the other hand, Good Bureaucrat has about 46.8% of factorial (I, II, III) communality with the converse of Bad Demeanor, that is, Good Bureaucrat is a "well done!" person with Visual Short-Term Memory and fast Complex Reaction Time.

Physical Capacity only associates with lower Intelligence. Traffic Warden associates with Intelligence and Sensibility.

Bad Demeanor stands out because of its Mental Disorder. It has not the Intelligence and Extraversion of Good Policeman but its Rigidity and Social Uncomformity. Moreover, Bad Demeanor has neither the Manual Dexterity of Good Bureaucrat nor the Sensibility of Traffic Warden. On the other hand, Good Demeanor shows no correlation with any psychometric factor.

DISCUSSION

Through the application of VAS we have arrived at factors similar to those obtained by Landy, Farr, Saal, and Freytag (1976), who used behaviourally anchored rating scales, though ours is a simpler method which corroborates Bull's et al. (1983) suggestion that it is not the most complex rating method that produces the best results. The main difference between our results and those of Landy et al. (1976) lies in the way of obtaining factors; ours were obtained through orthogonal rotation and theirs through oblique rotation. Thus, they get a clearer description since the policeman's skills must be necessarily related among themselves. On the other hand, we obtain greater independence on the factorial measures, since our goal is to correlate them in the purest possible way with the psychometric battery. Moreover, our results differ from those of Landy et al. (1976) in regard to the population studied. Their subjects were full street policemen, ours a kind of "police embryo", dealing fundamentally with traffic regulation and being excessively bureaucratized, which, in fact, would explain the Traffic Warden and the Good Bureaucrat factors. It is possible to explain the appearance of the Physical Capacity factor on the basis of the general belief among municipal police higher ranks of the importance of the policemen's physical aptitude for a good professional performance. Such belief manifests itself in the rejection of the physically weaker policewoman (Charles, 1982), a belief that is not confirmed in the present study since physical capacities relate only moderately to the Good Policeman (Table 1).

With respect to the analysis of psychometric tests, it is important to underline the appearance of the Extraversion factor (Table 2). Gudjonsson and Adlam (1983) concluded that the most remarkable characteristic in the case of British police recruits is their high Extraversion. The present results support their finding (Table 3). It is also of interest to note the independent factors, Extraversion and Psychic Anxiety, or Neuroticism, which support the factorial structure of personality (Eysenck & Eysenck, 1985), and allowed us to simply evaluate it by means of dimensional tests, like the Eysenck Personality Questionnaire.

The orthogonality of our rotation impeded a stronger prediction between VAS and psychometric battery, although this makes the relationships which we did find more relevant. We are not surprised about the lack of prediction from the MMPI scales (Table 3), since the policeman characteristics are trait-like, of personality, not state-like, as psychopathology is. Thus Schoenfeld, Kobos and Phinney (1980) did not find any relationship between the MMPI and the candidates for law enforcement selected through interviews. Bernstein, Schoenfeld, and Costello (1982) had to use sophisticated statistics in order to find some relationship; and Bernstein (1980) found that the majority of the members of a security guard company had elevations on Ma and/or Pd, which could indicate more an effect of self-selection of psychopathic personalities towards this job than the ideal policeman's profile. However, the MMPI's Mf (Sensibility) and Si (Extraversion) scales, which are not pathological, have shown some implication in our study (Good Policeman and Traffic Warden), and these scales evaluate personality individual differences instead of psychopathological states. The MMPI would be useful to discard persons with Mental Disorder from among those applying for the position of policeman or among duty policemen (Bad Demeanor), but it would not be useful for the selection of a type of person for police work, since the MMPI, despite of its name, was conceived for the evaluation of pathological states not personality (Hathaway, 1965).

Excluding specific typologies (Table 1) of the atypical police population we studied, and considering that complex reaction time is a product of intelligent behaviour, our results indicate that the intelligence variable is the major one in defining the policeman. In this manner the good policeman would be fundamentally a stable, intelligent person with just a drop of rigidity and social nonconformity, dedicated to a social kind of work, hence the importance of Extraversion.

REFERENCES

Alvarez, A. (1976). Tests de inteligencia de Lorge-Thorndike.
Madrid: Espasa-Calpe.

Bernstein, I. H. (1980). Security guards' MMPI profiles: Some
normative data. Journal of Personality Assessment, 44, 377.

Bernstein, I. H., Schoenfeld, L. S., & Costello, R. M. (1982).
Truncated component regression, multicollinearity and the MMPI's use in
a police officer selection setting. Multivariate Behavior Research,
17, 99.

Bull, R., Bustin, B., Evans, P., & Gahagan, D. (1983). Psychology for
police officers. Chichester: Wiley.

Charles, M. T. (1982). Women in policing: The physical aspect.
Journal of Political and Scientific Ad., 10, 194.

Chenoweth, J. H. (1961). Situational tests--a new attempt at assessing
police candidates. Journal of Criminal Law, Criminology and Police
Science, 52, 232-238.

Corah, N. L. (1964). Neuroticism and extraversion in the MMPI:
Empirical validation and exploration. British Journal of Social and
Clinical Psychology, 3, 168-174.

Eysenck, H. J. (1982). A model for intelligence. Berlin: Springer-
Verlag.

Eysenck, H. J., & Eysenck, M. W. (1985). Personality and individual
differences. New York: Plenum Press.

Grey, R. J., & Kipnis, D. (1976). Untangling the performance appraisal
dilemma: The influence of perceived organizational context on
evaluative processes. Journal of Applied Psychology, 61, 329-335.

Gudjonsson, G. H., Adlam, K. R. C. (1983). Personality patterns of
British police officers. Personality and Individual Differences, 4,
507-512.

Hathaway, S. R. (1965). Personality inventories. In B. B. Wolman (Ed.),
Handbook of Clinical Psychology. New York: McGraw Hill.

Landy, F. J., Farr, J. L., Saal, F. E., Freytag, W. R. (1976).
Behaviorally anchored scales for rating the performance of police
officers. Journal of Applied Psychology, 61, 750-758.

Nie, N. H., Hull, C. H., Jenkins, J. G., Steinbrenner, K., & Bent, O. H.
(1975). Statistical package for the social sciences. New York:
McGraw-Hill.

Schoenfeld, L. S., Kobos, J. C., & Phinney, I. R. (1980). Screening
police applicants: A study of reliability with the MMPI. Psychological
Reports, 47, 419.

Seisdedos, N., & Cordero, A. (1983). Questionario de personalidad MMPI.
Madrid, TEA.

Seisdedos, N., Cordero, A., Gonzalez, M., & Cruz, M. V. (1982). 16 PF,
cuestionario de personalidad. Madrid: TEA.

Strubell, M. (1982). Catalan sociolinguistics: A brief review of
research. International Journal of Social Language, 38, 70-84.

Von Behren, G. E. (1976, April). Police Service by objectives: A
performance evaluation plan. The Police Chief, 12-13.

POLICE SELECTION AND TRAINING IN WEST GERMANY

KNUD BUCHMANN and REINHOLD KORBMACHER

SELECTION METHODS IN WEST GERMANY

Selection methods in West Germany can be demonstrated by the example of the country of North Rhine-Westphalia. Selection takes place in four stages:
(1) Advertising and professional offers
(2) Selective procedure in a more restricted sense
(3) Training process including examinations
(4) Qualification on the job and promotion.

Advertising and Professional Offers

Years ago the advertising campaigns for the police were similar to those for washing powder. Attractive posters and papers represented the police service as an extremely desirable job. An unrealistic job image was created which led to disappointment, frustration, performance refusal and dismissals during the training period. Today the police offers a more realistic picture of itself. The aim of advertising is nowadays to win applicants who identify themselves with the police, but who also judge their chances in this profession in a realistic way. It is no longer necessary to do expensive advertising. As a result of unemployment there are always enough applications, so that we can select the best, according to the demand for recruits.

The applicants come from all social classes and generally represent a true image of the structure of our population. The main motive for application is the desire for security in a social situation of high unemployment. Policemen are civil servants and have a secure job for their lifetime. Every year there are 8-10,000 young people who express their interest in the police service by applying for this profession. In their absence a pre-selection, based on the application documents, takes place, checking general health, reputation, and school-leaving certificates. Last year 4,600 applicants were pre-selected in this way, and they were then invited to the selective procedure.

Selective Procedure in a more Restricted Sense

The applicants are invited to a two-day selective procedure, consisting of a test of mental aptitude, a medical pre-test, a personal interview, a main medical test, and a sports test. After each of these tests, a number of applicants are eliminated. The test of mental aptitude, in written form, serves to check the suitability for training as well as for the police service. This test was developed by Prof. Brengelmann of the Max-Planck-Institute for Psychiatry and Psychology in Munich, and it was introduced in 1983. First, general intelligence is tested by elements of the I-S-T (Intelligence Structure Test). The items refer to arithmetical problems, logical thinking, speech command, fluency of words and ideas and space conception. Then concentration and memory are tested. Errors have to be detected in number sequences and the details from six descriptions of persons and four outlined scenes of a crime have to be reproduced. In a so-called enumeration test, details relating to a general subject have to be found in order to test creativity; for example, name all the fluids you know. Then speech command is tested by retelling an oral presentation and by a dictation. Finally, with the help of 80 selected items, the personality is tested by way of self-appreciation. This test relates to self-conduct, self-confidence, self-assertion as well as to stability and stress resistance in general and specific situations.

The preliminary medical pre-test includes weight, height, the locomotor system, and the like. The psychological and medical tests complete the first day.

In regard to the qualifications of the examiners, they are all selected and specifically trained police officers, who undergo frequently repeated exercises in self-control in order to obtain greater objectivity with the tests.

On the second day, the remaining applicants are invited to a personal interview. The applicant speaks about a topical subject of his own choice. Thus he gets into conversation with the examiner. He can speak about his attitudes and his motives for his application. In this way, the examiner gets an impression of the candidate's personality and appearance. Then the main medical test takes place. Fitness for the police service must be tested in a very thorough and specific manner. The internal tests are especially important.

Finally, there is the sports test. The applicant has to complete a number of exercises and demonstrate his readiness for physical exertion. The test consists of five exercises: the triple jump without running up, a relay run (4 x 18 m), a 2,000 meter run, swimming, and chin-ups (women are exempt from the latter). With the completion of this test, the selective procedure is over.

Last year 4,600 applicants took part in this procedure. Eight hundred were selected for engagement: among these were 100 women (we are very satisfied with their training and service).

The number of employees depends on the level of minimum requirements as well as on the demand for recruits. Thus the minimum level can be raised if the demand grows less. In any case, the best are employed according to the demand. In the last few years the engagements have shifted more and more in favour of higher school education.

Training Process Including Examinations

All selected and employed recruits start their career in the so-called middle service. They have to complete a training period of 3 1/2 years. Here they must learn how to react to danger to public security and order. They have to do many physical exercises and a number of examinations. In this aspect the whole training program is also a selection tool (8% - 12% of the recruits are eliminated during the training period and by the final examination). The remaining recruits are on duty in the middle service. Most of them (about 80 per cent) remain on this level.

Qualification on Job and Promotion

Those who are efficient on the job can reach the so-called elevated service as police officers. During three years they have to study law, police strategies, leadership on a middle level and social sciences at the so-called Fachhochschule, and they have to pass a final examination. This means a further selection. About 15 per cent of all policemen are on this second level of police career.

The uppermost level of police career is the so-called higher service, which can be reached by two years of training at the Police Leadership Academy in Münster. There is a final examination, too. Only a small percentage of all policemen (about 1 or 2 per cent) can reach this level of upper leadership. So the whole training and service system can be considered as a frequently repeated process of selection. All policemen take part in a uniform career. That means every police officer or leader started his career as a policeman who did his duty in the streets for several years. We think this encourages an efficient performance of police duties.

TRAINING EXPERIENCED POLICE OFFICERS

There are five tasks psychologists perform in the German police:
(1) teaching and training, including motivation for personal growth;
(2) helping in operational decisions (i.e., taking hostages);
(3) research: for example, analysis of handwriting or finding reasons for corruptability or evaluating deviant behavior;
(4) developing and employing selection techniques for police, especially for higher police officers;
(5) helping officers with personal conflicts or when problems develop through their job.

When a young policeman begins his career in Germany, he does not learn anything about psychology. Perhaps one of his instructors has learned something about stress and some other topics, and may try to teach, usually in an amateurish fashion (often with the understanding of a layman), something about the topic. After their first course of instruction (about two years), the young policemen do their duties at the districts (precincts). As we have a very young police force in Germany, it's not very easy to find superiors who are skilled enough to be really good instructors, because the good ones leave the "street-work". To advance their career, qualified officers try to complete a further education course leading to a special matriculation, and they are not available as instructors.

Those who remain subordinate officers subsequently have some hours of psychology during advanced training courses on special problems. While it's true to note that they learn psychology, as most of them say themselves, it is always too little. Further, colleagues working as psychologists have to do "everything" (i.e., all five tasks noted above). In any event, below is presented a brief outline of the kind of psychological training currently provided.

At the Police Academies (for training of two to three years) we find two hours per week of psychology and two hours of sociology for about 40 weeks a year. We try to teach the basic conceptions and fundamental ideas of human emotions and behavior, and we try to blend this with the practical knowledge of the students. In a very brief form these are the themes we are working with:
- the brain and nervous system
- perception, retention and recognition (including eyewitness memory), and reasoning

- emotions, aggression, anxiety and motivation (including sources of frustration for the policeman)
- psychopathology and abnormality (neurosis, psychosis, suicide, and addiction to alcohol and drugs)
- behavior of people in groups and crowds including the formation of panic at police controlled events (accidents, catastrophes), and disaster control
- taking hostages and kidnapping
- dealing with illegal house occupants
- minority groups.

In addition to the above, we try to train our students about stress and conflict-management as well as stress-inoculation, progressive relaxation, and autogenic training. A considerable amount of time is devoted to training in better communication skills, since 60% - 80% of their leadership role will be talking and dealing with people. Our students know about using machines or weapons; they know a lot about the relevant laws; but they don't know how to handle their own problems or problems in administration (or dealing with the Civil Service).

It is also very important to help these police-officers (they are about 25-27 years old) develop insights about their personalities. It is the desire of our government that the police have high moral standards, and psychologists can help them in this pursuit. Further, it is necessary that the police are democratic in their views. They want to be democratic, but they are not always treated democratically in their own hierarchy. There is not yet a long tradition of democracy in the German police.

Another disturbing problem relates to the problem of limited personnel. There are not very many psychologists in the German police force (between two and seven per state, with a total of about fifty for the Federal Republic of Germany). Since the cooperation between psychologists and police is just now starting (it dates back only a couple of years), there is, first of all, no basis for effective teamwork. Secondly, it is very difficult to have small training groups. It's not very valuable to talk about communication strategies in front of a group of 20 or 30 police officers. They should have more opportunities to practice or exercise with video cameras, role-plays and so on.

Although good relations with police officers are important, we should not identify too closely with them. Social scientists must maintain some distance from the day to day work of the police. That doesn't mean that we shouldn't have our hearts in our work, but we are not police officers and our perspective must be different. Perhaps our role, in part, should be something like the conscience of policing. Whatever our role, we psychologists have to apply our services to the difficult aspects of police work.

Some special methods we use in training communication and conflict-management will now be outlined. It's necessary to note, however, that we don't only want the officers to use methods and techniques, they must also share the right attitudes. Using the basic elements of transactional analysis, we encourage the police officer to accept the other person (burgler, dealer, criminal, murderer, etc.) as a human being while not accepting criminal activity. We try to train the police in verbal and non-verbal reversibility; even in the context of interrogation (as far as it is wise or at least efficient). They learn to be good, understanding listeners; it is often not useful to only hear words - it is better to understand what the person meant with his words, or even with the things he did not say. If it is useful (i.e., in human relations in the department), the police should practice feedback techniques (because there is no social learning without feedback). And if it is meaningful and sensible, the police officers should show their genuine feelings. We try to teach our students what it means to practice a non-directive communication (analog to Carl Rogers client-centered therapy). We use this way of talking with kidnappers, with colleagues in a conflict, or with their relatives.

On the intellectual side, police officers learn to analyze a conflict in which they are involved. If they are able to realize the structure of a conflict, they are less likely to make it worse (see Stratton in this volume). We teach them competence in finding out on which level the problems are located: the factual-intellectual level, the social-emotional level, or the level of standards of values.

Since it is useless to argue on different levels, we are sure that we don't always reach that goal not even at the latest state of training. We are not always successful ourselves in practising what we preach. So we try to teach them using methods of conflict management without setting unrealistic expectations.

A related problem to conflict management is the issue of stress. It's not possible to avoid stress in the job of a policeman, but he has to work toward avoiding unhealthy consequences. We try to teach them what we call "restructuring of cognitions". We have a lot of unconscious wishes, we learned things in early childhood which are no longer useful today; and we develop mental tensions if people or things are not as we think they should be. Wrong thoughts make sickness and for mental hygiene it's inefficient to have stress. Therefore, we try to help the police see themselves and our world realistically. That is difficult as we all know, but it's always worth trying. They can learn to change their perception, to find their real needs, to know their ideologies, and to have realistic expectations. We try to give them something they can use for self-education, both individually and in their families.

RESIGNATION DURING POLICE TRAINING IN BRITAIN

N.G. FIELDING and J.L. FIELDING

Premature resignation, or "wastage", has always been a concern of the police. During the sixties and seventies, pay levels in the police declined sharply in relation to comparable occupations, and wastage rates were high. High unemployment in the eighties paradoxically "improved" wastage rates and allowed police management a greater measure of selectivity at recruitment and during the "probationary" period before recruits were offered a permanent job. Even so, unemployment was hardly an unalloyed "good" for the police, particularly as the research force was in a mining area whose response to unemployment and the very long miners strike of 1984/5 created fresh public order problems. This stimulated a keen interest in the force in factors associated with resignation. With 22% of our sample resigning during training, the matter plainly bore investigation.

The research was sited at the Derbyshire Police Training Establishment in the English Midlands where four intakes of recruits formed the core sample. The total sample was 125, comprising 115 men and 10 women. The mean age was 25. The bulk of recruits were drawn from semi-skilled and skilled manual occupations. The level of educational attainment was low, with nearly half having minimum school-leaving qualifications. Quantitative data were from 3 survey questionnaires administered at induction, 12 and 24 month stages. One questionnaire examined attitudes to policing as a job, the second included rating exercises concerning priorities in police work and the third comprised items to be ranked on Likert scales concerning attitudes to crime, law enforcement and social issues. Qualitative data were from interviews with a subsample of recruits at similar intervals to the administration of the questionnaire.

Elsewhere we report that youth was associated with resignation, as was low education (Fielding & Fielding, 1985). Because cadets are necessarily young they also pose a risk of wastage, as did recruits from professional and intermediate occupational backgrounds. The "least" risk were recruits from a skilled non-manual occupation. The same level of resignation applied to former students as to former cadets. The implication is that the similarity indicates an age effect rather than an effect of previous police experience.

Studies of anticipatory socialization show that potential incumbents prospectively imagine the demands of the job and rehearse their practice of it (Thornton & Nardi, 1975). Their reference groups embrace both imaginary groups as in mass media portrayals of the police, and actual police contacts. Reference groups transmit such information as perceived status, future role expectations, police-related self conceptions, and attitudes and values which enhance an acceptance of the police as an occupation (Merton and Rossi, 1968). Such influences can be important in initiating a process of re-evaluation of self-identity. Facilitators or retardants of the process include the amount of time spent in anticipatory socialization and the accuracy of the transmitted information (Thornton & Nardi, 1975), but one also needs to take into account prior experience of a similar occupation, such as work as a military policeman or welfare claims investigator.

Research on attitude shift in occupations suggests that the effect of such factors is short-lived and confined to the early stages of the career, particularly in the case of policing (van Maanen, 1975). Rather than their background, the chief influence on recruits appears to be their exposure to police work and the culture generated by police to cope with it. Sparger and Giacopassi (1983) suggest that resignation is related to the stresses of the job and is an implicitly cumulative process. It is unlikely that one especially stressful event will "cause" resignation. Rather, when stress variables operate they are likely to be viewed as pernicious sources of dissatisfaction whose effects are continuous and accumulate over time. Since the effects of stress are relatively constant and become apparent to the novice shortly after joining (van Maanen, 1975), the logic is that a "triggering mechanism" operates which "alerts the officer to the reality of his particular situation, to the likelihood that significant job factors will change, and which accounts for an officer finally deciding he should change occupations" (Sparger & Giacopassi, 1983, p.109). This process can be related to the distinction between idealistic and instrumental orientations to occupations, a difference suggested by a study of job commitment and job satisfaction amongst students in medical school (Becker, Geer, Hughes & Strauss, 1961). Instrumental views pertain to the extrinsic aspects of the job, such as pay, status, or security, whereas non-instrumental views refer to intrinsic aspects, such as its interest or social utility. We have already suggested that the "occupational culture" generated by police is an important influence on occupational socialization. Salaman (1975) developed a theory of occupational community to account for situations where work and non-work worlds are closely interdependent. He suggested the police formed an extreme case. They tend to regard themselves as being of higher social status than the general community, as is apparent in their preoccupation with presenting policing as a profession. Linked to this is social marginality - members have to rely on internal validation because they are very often rejected by outsiders. Second, occupational exclusiveness is influential, arising from the isolation of police from other occupations, both for legal reasons such as rules of association and discipline codes, and for structural reasons like shift work and police housing. Salaman suggested police would be especially prone to emphasize the positive moral nature of their work rather than an instrumental orientation to it.

An empirical study by Reiner (1978) pursued these arguments exploring the orientation to work of police constables and showed that intrinsic, non-instrumental aspects of the work, such as performing a public service, attract the would-be recruit, rather than extrinsic instrumental satisfactions such as high pay. He also looked at the other aspect of the "occupational community", that of occupational exclusiveness, especially the relationship between the work of police and their private life. Part of his investigation used the five statements in Table 1 in conjunction with interviews. Reiner found that while all constables felt that work affected their private life, they varied in their acceptance of the intrusion. We used Reiner's instrument to further investigate this "variation in acceptance", and also to examine temporal shifts in attitude. The indications from the literature were that we should pick up variations in attitude over time. The appeal of Reiner's five statements was that instead of statements of general attitudes they were clearly focussed on the job of policing itself, and reflected instrumental/idealistic orientations in terms that would be appropriate at any time in a police career.

Table 1
Frequencies of Agreement

	Induction % agree		Year 1 % agree		Year 2 % agree	
	NR*	R*	NR	R	NR	R
	N=93	N=28	N=91	N=12	N=79	N=2
1. The police constable should not let his work interfere with his private life.	52	57	60.4	83.3	68	100
2. The police constable should never stop being a police constable.	60	50	53.8	41.7	44	100
3. The police constable is obliged to perform his duty even if it involves overtime or other interference with his private life.	95	93	84.6	66.7	92	100
4. When it really comes down to it, police work is just like any other job.	4	3.6	14.3	33.3	11	0
5. The police constable should only be concerned to do what he must to earn a living.	1	0	5.5	16.7	1	0

*NR: non-resigners
*R: resigners

In our initial analysis frequencies of agreement were computed; these results appear in Table 1. There are two notable points here. One is the change over time and the second is the difference between resigners and non-resigners. Considering change over time, in both resigners and non-resigners there is a steady increase in agreement that police officers should not let their work interfere with their private life and also that police work is just like any other job. Similarly, there is increasing agreement that police officers should only do what they must to earn a living. There is decreasing agreement that a police officer should never stop being a police officer. These responses are all consistent with the idea that, over time, the recruits come to see the police role in a more pragmatic, realistic way. They become more instrumental in their attitude toward the job, beginning to see police work as more like a job than a calling.

The importance of this movement was highlighted by our awareness of the highly "idealistic" reasons for joining cited by recruits. The data here were gained independently of. our research by a requirement of the force that applicants write an essay on why they wished to join. A total of 80 of these were available to us. It will not surprise anyone who has conducted admissions interviews that the more self-less "reasons", such as an urge to help people, considerably exceeded the citation of instrumental reasons, like job security and pay. Even the rather scarce references to job security were balanced by allusion to other, more "worthy" goals. Thus, "I wish to be a police officer because I want a varied working life, a secure future and a job which is useful to the community. The police force also offers job satisfaction and good promotion prospects" (2:9). Ideas concerning a sense of duty, wishing to be of service, helping people and working with people were most used by applicants. Interestingly, relatively few references were made to crime fighting, and those that were emphasized either cooperative notions of crime control, such as "explaining" the law to those who might be unsure if they had committed an offence (!), or the suggestion that, by the applicants' leading an exemplary life, a good model would be held up to those tempted by crime. However, by the time recruits had been in the force a year our interviews revealed declining emphasis on qualities of service and a corresponding internalization of a "lie low, don't make waves" philosophy amenable with an instrumentalist emphasis. Thus there was a plain enough change over time, with a trend to increasing instrumentalism according to both the quantitative and qualitative data.

Table 2
Profiles of Views with Frequencies 3/8 2%

Profile* 12345 (statement No. see Table 1)	Induction	Year 1	Year 2
00000	33.9	20.4	14.1
10000	18.2	18.4	19.2
01000	10.4	13.6	10.3
00010	–	–	5.1
11000	27.3	15.5	39.7
10100	–	5.8	–
10010	2.5	–	–
11100	–	4.9	–
11010	–	5.8	–
11110	–	–	2.6

*Coding for statements 2 and 3 are inverted. Therefore agreement with 1, 4 and 5 and disagreement with 2 and 3 scored a 11111 profile – an expression of high instrumentality towards the police role.

As to our interest in differences between resigners and non-resigners, we found no clear distinctions at induction, but by year one differences did become apparent. This emerged when we examined patterns of response. If recruit A was in favor of statement one, we wanted to know if he would also be in favor of statement two, and so on. This required inverting the coding of certain statements to clarify the reference to instrumentality. The profiles of response are presented in Table 2. Even without reading the figures, one can see the general pattern: profiles clustered in the top and right-hand side of the table, but not on the bottom left. Of course, this depends not only on the arrangement of the items within an individual profile but also on the order of the profiles in the list. The items within a profile were ordered such that those easiest to pass (i.e., agree with - statements 1, 4, 5; and disagree with - statements 2, 3) were placed nearer the left hand side of the profile.

Having satisfied the criteria of a Guttman scale, scores could be calculated for each recruit where greater numbers of items passed indicated greater instrumentality. Table 3 shows the distribution of scores of resigning and non-resigning recruits in each year. No recruit scored a maximum of 5. One can see there are differences between resigners and non-resigners, especially in year one. The non-resigners' modal frequency quite clearly shifts towards greater instrumentality with time, there being a modal frequency of 0 at induction, 1 at year one, and 2 at year two. While the non-resigners also shifted toward greater instrumentality, this was not to the same extent as the resigners. The resigners displayed a bimodal distribution. At induction, peak frequencies occurred at 0 and 2, and by year one they appeared between 1 and 2, and 4. This bimodal response suggested that they fell into two groups - those with instrumentality scores that matched the non-resigners at induction, and those whose scores were higher. Clearly, factors other than instrumentality are also involved in the resignation decision.

Table 3
Instrumentalism Scores

Instrumentalism	Induction		Year 1		Year 2	
	Non-Res %	Resigners %	Non-Res %	Resigners %	Non-Res %	Resigners %
LOW	N=93	N=28	N=91	N=12	N=76	N=2
0	33.3	35.7	22.0	8.3	14.1	0.0
1	33.3	17.9	35.2	25.0	34.2	100.0
2	32.3	39.3	25.3	25.0	44.7	0.0
3	1.1	7.1	14.3	16.7	3.9	0.0
4	0.0	0.0	3.3	25.0	2.6	0.0
HIGH						

Another approach to the data was to calculate the mean scores for each time and for resigners and non-resigners, as shown in Table 4, where the resigners are further sub-divided by length of service before resignation. It is interesting that the score of those who resign in the first year is not significantly different from the non-resigners mean score. In fact, the mean score of those who resign after 25 months service is the highest. Instrumental views at induction are not an indicator of early resignation, but high instrumentality here presages later resignation. Instrumentalism scores at induction do not offer any indication of early resignation because the questionnaire was administered during the first week of training before any real job experience. However, a year later, when experience may have provoked conflict with original job conceptions, there were striking differences between resigner and non-resigner scores.

A further means of characterizing groups of non-resigners and resigners, and subgroups of the latter, was by expressed attitudes on the survey questionnaire. When a factor analysis was carried out, the differences in response between resigners and non-resigners on the questions concerning crime were particularly suggestive.

Table 4
Instrumentalism Score Means

| | Resigners | | | Non-resigners |
| | Months in service | | | |
	1-12	13-24	25+	
Induction	N=13 1.077	N=11 1.182	N=4 1.5	N=93 1.12
Year 1	–	N=8 2.38	N=3 2.33	N=91 1.42
Year 2	–	–		N=76 1.46

Factor Analysis
Responses to the (30) attitude-toward-crime statements were scored by Likert-type scales. Many of the items were selected from the questionnaire devised in Hogarth's (1971) study of the sentencing behavior of magistrates. They afford a means of identifying several different orientations towards crime comprising consistent responses on clustered groups of items. After our factor analysis, three factors emerged, and they closely matched three of the five factors found by Hogarth.

The first factor corresponded to the scale Hogarth termed "Justice", which included items relating to the concept of equity and "just desserts". It concerned the idea that "crime" should be punished and that the punishment should be in proportion to the crime; for example, "Criminals are being mollycoddled by the correctional agencies". The items are offence-oriented rather than offender-oriented. This factor accounted for 40% of the total variance in response in the overall sample. The second factor corresponded to the factor Hogarth called "punishment corrects" or, more conventionally, individual deterrence. It addresses the idea that offenders deserve and need punishment, in order to prevent them from committing further crime. An example (with negative weighting) is "Our present treatment of criminals is too harsh". Here punishment is directed to the offender rather than the offence. It accounted for 9% of the variance. The third factor, Hogarth's "social defence", or general deterrence, includes items directed at potential offenders. Items included "Most people are deterred by the threat of a heavy penalty". This factor accounted for 6% of the variance.

There was a tangible difference between resigners and non-resigners on one of the three "crime" factors (see Table 5). On factor 2, the resigners scored a statistically-significant greater mean on the individual deterrence scale, suggesting a stronger belief in punishing the criminal at any cost, even corporal and capital punishment (Table 6). The resigners were significantly more punitive in their inclination towards offenders, and also show a trend towards a lesser concern with achieving fairness in assessing punishment in close regard to the offence itself (factor 1). On general deterrence the two groups show near-identical responses.

Table 5
Factor Scores

Factors	Resigners N=12	Non-resigners N=84	T-value	Sig.
Justice	0.271	0.316	-0.23	.82
Individual deterrence	0.65	0.122	2.19	0.03
Social defence	0.1	0.11	-0.05	0.96

The most consistent emphasis in the interview responses of resigners pertinent to these issues was their negative assessment of non-custodial alternatives to imprisonment, such as probation. There was majority support for capital punishment, and some support for corporal punishment. The more rigid proponents of capital punishment tended to combine reference to deterrence with practical experience they thought was relevant. An ex-soldier rejected the idea of capital punishment only for those who murdered police officers. "Not necessarily a policeman, they should bring the death penalty back in general. Only because its like why we have an atomic bomb. I've no intention of using it, I hope to God no one in this country has. It's a deterrent, that's all" (3: 5,4).

Strong supporters of capital punishment link their stance to other matters of penal philosophy, as the comment suggests. Relating interview responses to the attitude questions relevant to punishment over time enabled us to recognize views which were consistently held. A recruit who reported spending many hours discussing capital punishment, and supported the death penalty, had moved more firmly to support during his first year in the force. "It should be there as a deterrent, despite what people say. You can't say it won't be a deterrent unless they bring it back and see if it is. As far as I'm concerned if there's a hundred men and only one thinks 'I'm not doing that if I'm going to get topped' it's doing its job" (10:2,11). His reasoning had not changed since induction.

Those who were concerned about individual as opposed to general deterrence emphasized the need for tough, punitive reaction to crime. One resigner replied to a question about delinquency that "they all ought to be sent away....They ought to fine them more heavily or send them away. I'm sure when they see how they're treated they wouldn't do it again. It's not strict enough" (4:2,3); and another insisted that "for violence there should be some kind of corporal punishment. Sentences are not really long enough....If a person is involved with violence...then the punishment should be violent" (5:1,5). The resigners were particularly vehement about the matter, with non-resigners more equivocal, a fair number being opposed to capital and corporal punishment and more inclined to speak of matching offender characteristics to the punishment tariff. The resigners saw this as soft. An indicative comment was "trouble is, these days it's all human rights....You can't do anything" (2:2,4). A comparison of resigners' and non-resigners' responses to the items on the questionnaire concerning these issues was therefore made, and a scale comprising these responses is shown in Table 6. The resigners did hold harsher views on these matters; the difference on attitudes to corporal punishment, capital punishment and non-custodial alternatives was statistically significant. This led us to subdivide factor analysis scores to determine whether age or previous occupation was the principal determinant of overall attitude towards the notion of individual deterrence. It emerged that age was critical in distinguishing resigners on this factor. "Young" resigners had a mean score of .81 on this factor (ex-civilians scored .92 and ex-military .37), while the group of resigners over 25, all of whom were ex-military, scored .16. This sub-division in the resigners group proved analytically important. Youth appears to be an index of punitive views on individual deterrence across the board. Of the non-resigners, young recruits had a mean score of .18 and the over 25's of .03.

Table 6
Corporal and Capital Punishment Score*

	Resigners N=12	Non-resigners N=90
Mean score	22.58	19.66**

*Items included in the scale:
1. Probation should only be given to first offenders.
2. The strap should be used more often with young offenders.
3. Capital punishment should remain completely abolished (invert coding).
4. Capital punishment is a deterrent to murder.
5. Our present treatment of criminals is too harsh (invert coding).

**Significant at the 2% level.

Discriminant Analysis
Further indications of the nature of differences among the recruits arose when the (16) items concerning attitudes towards policing were entered into a discriminant analysis in order to isolate variables which discriminated resigners from non-resigners and to predict likely

resigners. The SPSS discriminant analysis entered each item in step-wise fashion until Rao's V criterion for inclusion was not met. In this way seven of the original 16 items were included. First was the statement that the "Police Federation should be more closely consulted in regulating working conditions"; resigners more strongly agreed with this. Second was the item that the "Police in Britain should be equipped with guns", with which the resigners less strongly disagreed. The third statement was that "A policeman's behavior off the job must be exemplary", with which the resigners less strongly agreed. Fourth was "The average PC (police constable) has to spend too much time on paperwork; it should be streamlined and cut down", with which the resigners more strongly agreed. The fifth item suggested that "The media have conducted a vendetta against the police and this accounts for much contemporary suspicion of the police"; the resigners agreed with this less strongly. Sixth was the statement that "The only person who really understands being on the beat is another PC", with which the resigners agreed more strongly. The final item stated "The police should play a bigger part in politics"; the resigners less strongly disagreed with this. Table 7 shows the predictive adequacy of the discriminant analysis.

Table 7
Discriminant Analysis

	Total n	Predicted Resigners	Predicted Non-Resigners
Resigners	10	8	2
Non-resigners	90	13	77

% of 'grouped' cases correctly identified: 85%

These responses suggest that resigners preserve an "employees" perspective, comparing policing with other occupations, and discounting some of the stock reasons with which police tend to insulate themselves from unfavorable characteristics of the occupation. They wished for greater consultation of the Police Federation, the representative body for the ranks, and were more dissatisfied with paperwork. The resigners also appear to be more dissatisfied with the social isolation of the job and with the public image of the police (that is, they were less impressed by the argument that suspicion of the police was the result of a media conspiracy). The "employees" perspective could plausibly be shared by the two subgroups of resigners; the "youth" because their qualifications and low "stake" encourage them to consider what policing has to offer them as a job and the ex-soldiers because long experience with the military sensitizes them to negative aspects of the ranks' status in hierarchical organizations. These results are consistent with the "instrumentalism" data. It will be recalled that we approached these data by examining the score means, and we also divided resigners into groups according to length of service (i.e., their point of resignation). This gave rise to the interesting finding that even those who did not resign until some point in year two had a significantly higher year one score than non-resigners. It appears that those who eventually resigned in year two may become more "instrumental", and arguably less "committed" to the police role, in the first year. It seems that "commitment" is important to establish in the first year.

The one index of job satisfaction that could bind both young, inexperienced recruits and those with a military background during training and early service is the "social" quality of the occupation, initially manifest in the intake groups with whom recruits underwent initial training. The peer group is particularly important because of the formation of strong bonds during socialization to the police role noted by previous research. We noted that the highest percentage of resignation was from the smallest intake group, who also had the longest period of service before resignation. From cross-tabulation against former occupation it emerged that this intake group also contained the highest percentage of cadet resigners. It did not include any former soldiers among resigners; in the other intakes, they were the most likely to resign. All the resigners from this group were "young", i.e., 16-24, and all the resigners were relatively highly-educated. The group was not only small but unusually homogeneous. Group dynamics may amplify the salience of one person's decision to resign in a small group. The possibility of a "peer group" effect is further implied by the finding that by year one, resigners were emphasizing "good workmates" as the second most important index of job satisfaction.

In terms of job satisfaction criteria, those who resigned chiefly differed from those who did not by the emphasis they put on having good companions at work. At induction "interest and variety" was chosen by most resigners and non-resigners, followed by "a sense of performing a public service", then "good pay" and, fourth, "good workmates". However, at year one, while most resigners still considered "interest and variety" most important, "good workmates" had become second most important, and "good pay" was least important. The profile for non-resigners did not change at all.

The interviews also pointed in this direction. A recruit who described himself as having a lot of friends "outside" mentioned that his friends thought he would back out before starting the training and were taking a keen interest in his progress. He also commented, in discussing violence at football games, that "they can very often get arrested for doing nothing, which I've seen done....I do feel sometimes they're (the police) a bit heavy-handed, in that they can cause a lot of the trouble themselves" (5:3,5). One of the ex-cadets claimed his best friends were outside the force and stressed the role of family friends in prompting him to become a cadet; he also alluded to thinking "have I made the right decision?" frequently during the "classroom" segment of training (5:1). A recruit who had been working in a "dead-end" post as a civilian in police administration spoke at induction of having to sever links with former friends. "I've got lots of young friends who like the life a bit and really I've got to forget them....I suppose I'll have to adapt myself to a lot of police friends" (5:4,1). He hoped that no "me and them thing" would cloud relations with his civilian friends, many of whom were unemployed. After 12 months he emphasized friendship ties with other police--"we all seem to stick together...work together and play together"--but complained that everything changed each time he had a new posting.

A recruit whose father and grandfather's police service had influenced his decision to join as a cadet also emphasized social isolation at these two stages. At induction he felt "it may have an effect on where you go on your own time, which is one of the reasons I was thinking about the job, that was one of the disadvantages" (6:1,1). Of his civilian friends, "nobody turned enemy" and he believed they accepted that nowadays "its just a job". After 12 months he stated he had no friends outside the police, emphasized the comradeship of the shift, but spoke of the disruption of friendship by the shift system (12:1). He also complained of rumor and gossip in the organization, the way that his reputation for shyness as a cadet had preceded him, the fact that his father being in the same force seemed to encourage people to pre-judge him, and that he had been reprimanded over "some nightlife" which was taken as a sign of failing commitment. "I've thought about making it a career. When I think of it as 30 years it sounds like a lot to me...but I could retire at 48....It doesn't seem so bad" (ibid).

Resigners were more likely to state they would consider the police ranks having stronger negotiating rights with the employer; the exceptions to this were the resigners from a military background. This group also put less emphasis on the "social" aspect of the job, noting that during training "I haven't got time for friendships, it would be an inconvenience" or "every time I meet somebody in 'civvy' street I must question their motives for relating to me" (3:5) or that mobility in the Army taught them to do without intense friendships and that their spouses were unconcerned about the effect on their social life as they were used to insults as the partner of a military policeman (2:2). The "military" resigners tended toward expressions of intolerance of the inexperience and youth of many police constables, were hostile to female constables, and much more likely to express suspicion of ethnic minorities than other resigners, who were unusually inclined to "defend" racial minorities and acknowledge the police had problems in dealing with them. The qualitative data again suggest the division of resigners into two groups: former military personnel bearing relatively embittered attitudes to crime and punishment and younger recruits concerned at the social isolation of the job. Both groups express traces of instrumentalist orientations to the occupation.

There were two distinct groups within the overall pool of resigners; those who were young and relatively well-educated, and those who were above the average age whose previous occupation was military service. This was consistent with the idea that the mechanism triggering resignation is contingent on opportunities of alternative employment; for the first group, their qualifications act as a positive career contingency, enabling them to try something new while their stake in the police occupation is low. For ex-soldiers, a negative career contingency may account for their departure; their "attitudes" may be thought unsuitable, or police service may not be what they anticipated.

This research poses some clear questions for police recruitment, selection and training. The first is a matter of resources; police must decide how tolerant of wastage they are prepared to be. If it is thought desirable to bring about a closer convergence between recruitment and training, the police must determine how much to formalize selection criteria. The evidence is that in the UK this is ad hoc and variable (Hanley, 1979), yet the present research suggests that it is possible to anticipate safe, and unsafe, bets. Here, several things could be done. It is feasible to train recruit selectors, and at least one official body has called for the involvement of experts from other organizations in selection panels (Manolias, 1983). It is also possible to convey to potential recruits a realistic profile of the working situation of police, including their social position. A more drastic measure would be

284

to screen potential recruits so as to discourage those associated with high risk of resignation. Police might opt for quotas for recruits having a particular profile. Finally, the present evidence suggests the need for professional career counselling during training and early service.

REFERENCES

Becker, H. S., Geer, B., Hughes, E. C., & Strauss, A. L. (1961). Boys in white: Student culture in medical school. Chicago: University of Chicago Press.

Fielding, N. G., & Fielding, J. L. (1985). May the force be without you: A study of resignation during British police training. Journal of Police Science and Administration, in press.

Hanley, J. (1979). The rhetoric of police recruit selections. Unpublished MSc thesis, University of York.

Hogarth, J. (1971). Sentencing as a human process. Toronto: Toronto University Press.

Manolias, M. (1983). A preliminary study of stress in the Police Service. Home Office Scientific Research and Development Branch Human Factors Group, HMSO.

Merton, R., & Rossi, A. (1968). Contributions to the theory of reference group behavior. In H. Hyman & E. Singer (Eds.), Readings in reference group theory and research (pp. 28-68). New York: Free Press.

Reiner, R. (1978). The blue-coated worker. Cambridge: Cambridge University Press.

Salaman, G. (1975). Occupations, community and consciousness. In M. Bulmer (Ed.), Working class images of society (pp. 219-36). London: Routledge and Kegan Paul.

Sparger, J., & Giacopassi, D. (1983). Copping out: Why police leave the force. In R. Bennett (Ed.), Police at work. New York: Sage.

Thornton, R., & Nardi, P. (1975). The dynamics of role acquisition. American Journal of Sociology, 80, 870-85.

van Maanen, J. (1975). Police socialization: A longitudinal examination of job attitudes in an urban police department. Administration Science Quarterly, 20, 207-27.

LEADERSHIP TRAINING AND AN INTEGRATED INTRODUCTION TO PSYCHOLOGY FOR POLICE OFFICERS[1]

GERHARD STEINER

POLICE IN SWITZERLAND

This first section gives the reader a brief introduction to the peculiarities of police organization in Switzerland. Police organization follows the general lines of the federalistic structure of the country, according to its constitution.

Different Types of Police Forces

Swiss police may be divided into two different types: the Police Forces of the cantons (states) and the communities and the Federal Police. The majority of police officers in Switzerland are members of the Cantonal or Communal Police Forces. According to the Swiss Constitution, policing is part of the autonomy of each of the 26 cantons (states). Thus, each canton has its own police force (so-called police corps). These forces differ from each other in size, organizational structure, formation and training and also in their appearance (different uniforms). Within the cantons and besides the Cantonal Police Forces, there are police corps in all cities and communities with an organizational autonomy. They are, of course, integrated into a network of cooperation within communal as well as cantonal policing. Cantonal Police Forces fulfill all policing tasks (traffic regulation, security, crime, etc.); whereas, in general, the cities' or communities' police corps concentrate on traffic, security and trade and do not deal with crime affairs by themselves; in general, they lack the specialists necessary for this kind of task. The cities of Zürich and Bern are exceptions in this concern: both of them do have a criminal police force. Reflecting cantonal autonomy, it is difficult to give a precise description of the whole Swiss police system; what is mentioned in this first section has to be taken as the description of an "average" Swiss police corps.

The Federal Police Force (less than 50 police officers) deals exclusively with criminal acts that are under control of the federal law such as espionage or explosive crime. There is a tight cooperation with cantonal police forces. The Federal Police Force is comparable to the United States FBI as far as tasks and responsibilities are concerned. There is also a Swiss Army Police Force, but this is not part of the Swiss civil police organization; it is a part of the army. Police officers from cantonal or communal police forces serve also as army police officers. Switzerland has a so-called milice-system army, i.e., every male citizen is for a certain period of time, about 50 weeks in total, distributed over the years from 20 to 50, an active member of the army with his complete equipment at home. Thus, the army reflects the whole male Swiss population. The Army Police Force is, therefore, responsible for managing military traffic, personal security for army members, in short, for all police activities within the army organization.

Selection of Police Recruits
The opening of a police recruit school is advertised in local and regional newspapers. Male applicants over 20 years of age are required to have achieved: (1) their primary professional education (i.e., a craftsman apprenticeship as a carpenter, a plumber, a baker, etc., or a clerk, only exceptionally with a degree from senior high school, the so-called "Maturität"); (2) their basic military training (17 weeks of military recruit service); and (3) to be of good health (both physical and psychological). Female applicants (a very low percentage) fulfill requirements (1) and (3) only. Selection is by testing and/or interviewing according to the practice in the several cantons or cities.

Police Recruit Schools - Curriculum
Police recruit schools have an average duration of 12 months; participants are fully paid on a level somewhat below that of a young constable after recruit school. The school provides full-time training. There is, however, one remarkable exception referring to the basic formation of constables. Some cantons in the French speaking part of Switzerland have introduced a police apprenticeship of 3 years duration, analogous to any other kind of apprenticeship. The police apprenticeship comes closer to a clerk's or businessman's apprenticeship than to a craftsman's. Police apprenticeship is not the usual case in Switzerland, however.

The main topics of the recruits' training (12 months) are as follows (this, again, is a "Swiss average", also the number of lessons is provided in brackets):

General Education (Total: 290)
- Language (High German; people speak exclusively their local dialects in everyday use) (75)
- Typewriting (also useful on computer keyboards) (65)
- Political Science (including local history) (105)
- Psychology (45)

Law (Total: 320)
- Introduction to law, administered law (25)
- Highway and traffic law (120)
- Work and business law (40)
- Police Service law (25)
- Criminal or penal law (85)
- Civil law (25)

Policing (Total: 465)
- General training: Weapon activities (160)
                    radio technique and skills (20)
                    traffic controlling (20)
                    first aid (55)
                    knowledge of cars, driving technique (30)
                    general protocol writing skills (45)
- Traffic policing: accident activities (drawing and writing specific
                    protocols, interviewing, etc.) (105)
- Criminal policing (more specialized training is given only after
                    recruit schools) (30)

Cooperation with Different Organizations (130)

Physical Education (Total: 245)
  - Gymnastics (60)
  - Swimming (60)
  - Boxing and Judo (100)
  - Orienteering (25)

Although each police force in Switzerland has its own training program for police recruits, differences in the curricula are rather small. Some cantons have even fully coordinated the content of their curricula. When the final examinations are passed, the young constable is integrated into a section where he serves in all activities under the supervision of a subofficer (a sergeant) for about one year.

Continuing Training and Promotion

All Swiss police forces give their police officers a continuing education of approximately 1 week a year. Training focuses mainly on changes in traffic situations (of longer duration), in traffic or other kind of law or in equipment and its use.

One special 3-day course that has been introduced in several cantonal as well as communal police forces is concerned with how to cope with people in everyday situations. The course is an adaptation of a transactional analysis based education, originally elaborated for United Airlines, years ago. The rights for executing these courses are at the SPIN (Swiss Police Institute at Neuchatel). The SPIN has trained the trainers for the single police forces, thus, there are no psychologists, but well trained police officers who teach their corps mates.

Special training courses (e.g., in leadership) are also offered by SPIN. Several cantonal police forces send their future non-commissioned officers to a leadership seminar of 2 weeks duration at the SPIN, usually before their promotion (as part of a personnel development program). Some police forces have, in addition, their own promotion courses (of 1 week duration on the average) that the constable has to attend before promotion.

Promotion levels are appointee, corporal, sergeant I (Wachtmeister), sergeant II (Feldweibel), sergeant III (Adjutant). In some cantons promotion is automatic after a certain number of years for every level; in other cantons promotion follows the merits (qualifications) of the respective police officer. But the rules about how many pre-promotion training courses have to be attended, or how many years of service are required differ from one canton to another.

A FRAMEWORK FOR LEADERSHIP TRAINING
The Participants

This section focuses on a police corps of a mid-size, industrialized city in the eastern part of Switzerland: St. Gallen (capital of the canton of St. Gallen with approximately 75,000 inhabitants). The city police corps (152 police officers) is closely cooperating in case of need with the larger police force of the whole canton of St. Gallen.

Leadership training was organized for police officers on the three sergeant levels (see above). All of the participants looked back on more than one decade of police activities, some of them on almost two decades. Besides their basic leadership training at the SPIN (many years ago) they had specific leadership skills. Thus, many of them had a typical need of catching up both certain skills and knowledge in leadership problem solving. The average age of the training participants was 44 years.

Some of them were the chiefs of important sections, others were their substitutes (seconds in command), others were the responsible officers for certain parts of recruit training. All of them were to be located, therefore, on a relatively high level of responsibility in regard to city policing. Their position put them onto a level of leadership that I assess as the most important: they are the closest collaborators of the supervisor lieutenants and the superintendent on the one hand; on the other hand, they have direct access to their subordinated police officers and by these to the public. They have both a direct and an indirect influence on the working climate in the interior as well as on the image of the police corps in the public. Participation in the leadership training seminar (3 full days) was by invitation, basically not forced by any kind of a command. Some of the possible participants resisted heavily against participation. The participants of the first two courses were excited by their experiences in leadership training and made a whispering campaign in its favor. After the third course, most of the formerly reluctant sergeants complained for not being invited to such a leadership course so that a fourth one had to be organized.

The courses took place outside the city in a guesthouse in the mountains, thus providing three days and two nights in a totally isolated but socially fully active group.

The primary intention of the superintendent of the St. Gallen city police corps was to provide some personal security and social support to his higher subofficers in coping with leadership stress by the kind of training to be described below as well as in solving several long lasting interpersonal problems (conflicts or non-optimal management).

The first leadership seminar was a true pilot study; the following ones were slight modifications of it. Our report refers to the current (final) version.

Prejudices Against Psychology and Psychologists

Most of the participants in our training showed scepticism towards psychology as a scientific area or towards people representing it. Usually, they did not discriminate psychiatrists from psychologists, and scepticism stemmed from bad experiences with some psychiatric or psychological service (i.e., in the school area or even from hearsay). Also, the training was announced by the superintendent's office as a course involving individual activities that were not described precisely, and some uncertainty or even fear in the participants may have played a role in their response: the fear of possibly being exposed to critique so that the personality would be affected or even "denuded".

Rich Leadership Experiences and "Naive Theories"

All the police officers who were invited to the training course had an experience in leadership of several years (up to 10 or more). Some of them were undoubtedly skillful leaders. But on the whole, leadership as an ability was never a subject of formal reasoning, and most leadership behavior was not executed with high consciousness. Police officers develop "naive theories" (in the sense of the theory of a naive psychology by Heider, 1958) that can easily be taken as a starting point for theoretical considerations of what is going on in leading other people (collaborators). One of the important tasks of the trainer was, thus, to systematize the participants' naive theories of leadership, to elaborate and to utilize them.

Leadership Within a Given Hierarchy

One outstanding characteristic of the situation is the fact that all leaders within this particular police corps stem from the same population of police officers, i.e., all of the promoted officers have been members of the same corps from the very beginning of their police career. Thus, everyone knows everyone else in the corps, and everyone knows exactly the functions as well as the role expectations for everyone else. The possible advantage of this fact is that individual adaptations to new leaders (after their promotion) take place rather quickly since everybody already knows the persons or rather the personalities of the promoted colleagues; but this fact may also become a disadvantage just because everybody knows everybody, including the knowledge about the weaknesses of promoted leaders.

LEADERSHIP TRAINING AND AN INTEGRATED PSYCHOLOGY
Goals

The main goals of the training course were: (1) explaining what leadership means; (2) examining the crucial processes in leadership, i.e., what stimulations lead to what responses in leadership situations; (3) practicing the most important leadership skills and acquiring some security in their execution; (4) designing an individual program for progress in leadership during the forthcoming 4-6 months after the course; and (5) preparing to discuss leadership problems more frankly with colleagues.

Establishing a Climate of Trust and Learning Readiness

From the beginning we felt quite clearly that the trainer had first of all to be accepted by the participants. He was the first and main agent to reduce the participants scepticism. To attain this goal an introductory circle was of great help: The trainer introduced himself as a person (not as a university professor) with whom they will share three days of their lives. The participants learned about his age, his family background, his wife and children, their social situation, his professional career as well as his hobbies. After this, each participant did the same for the whole circle (8 participants). This introductory circle showed that the participants did not know each other very well; many of them learned about completely unknown qualities of their corps mates--a rather astonishing fact. As many police officers admitted later, this circle was an ice-breaker for them; they felt comfortable in the group and felt well accepted by the trainer who joined the group as an outsider. After having explained the goals of the course, the trainer asked the participants to help him formulate some rules for the three days so that they would have the feeling of being challenged instead of being bored. The following was the result (with slight modifications in the wording for each of the courses):
(1) I will not hesitate to ask questions whenever something is unclear.
(2) I will let everybody know whenever something makes me nervous or angry (e.g., smoking).
(3) I will tell the trainer frankly whenever I feel bored or disinterested about learning.
(4) I will always have the opportunity to ask for a practical exercise since I want to do not only to talk.

(5) I may bring my own experiences, questions, uncertainties, and
    problems into the discussion at any time it seems reasonable to do so.
    These rules were read again after every half day in order to be
modified or to test whether or not they were being followed.

A First Approach to Leadership Problems: Detection of Emotions

Training began by coping with everyday stress situations: being under
time pressure for getting a ticket and standing in a long line in front
of a ticket counter, saying "no" in special situations, complaining
because of bad food in a restaurant, etc.

Participants received postcards with typed, short problem situations
they had to play; 3 or 4 of them received the same problem. Within
blocks of 20-25 minutes, each participant played his ascribed role, the
other ones being partners or opponents (so-called "downers"). The scenes
were recorded on TV and played back, since the first task was to find out
whether some of the role players were successful in asserting themselves
and why. The most striking fact with almost all players was the high
percentage of use of physical power, of aggressive discussions, or at
least of useless long verbal debates.

Successful sequences were played back more than once to urge the
participants to look for particular behavior patterns. Careful help in
focussing attention on crucial segments of the scenes by the trainer was
highly necessary. As was intended, it was found that the expression and
formulation of bad feelings about a certain situation was more successful
than a mere intellectual debate. (Some of the scenes, however, were
characterized by definitely good feelings such as satisfaction or
pleasure.) In several cases, the trainer played a particular role again,
stressing or slightly exaggerating the crucial part of a sequence to draw
attention to emotions.

To recognize emotions and to name them was extremely difficult for
almost all participants. Nevertheless, they succeeded in finding a whole
list of them that are felt or experienced more or less explicitly in
everyday situations; among them were:

dissatisfaction	satisfaction
displeasure	pleasure
dismay	euphoria
disappointment	sadness, depression
aversion	sympathy
fear	affection
anger	love
guilt	good luck
anxiety	happiness
envy	disgust
shame	hate
annoyance	grief
sadness, depression	

The list of emotions was written down for further use, i.e., to judge
which ones appear in leadership situations.

The first series of role play reported here had an important effect
concerning learning readiness. Everybody played several roles without
being exposed as a police officer's personality, since the problems were
everyday problems and happened to everybody; and therefore, even a
failure (e.g., in complaining in a restaurant) did not lead to a feeling
of weakness or incompetence. The role play even had a relaxing effect
(laughter) and, by this, brought an overall mood of the security of not

being criticized or attacked or ridiculed as a person.

One important question remained to be answered, however. What have all these everyday problems to do with leadership? A discussion circle produced the following answers:

(1) One is not leading another person but one tries to have a certain influence on others.

(2) One wants to assert oneself.

(3) One tries to persuade another person or a group of persons.

(4) One wants to have success.

(5) It is crucial how you say things to others.

(6) One has a certain goal.

(7) One sometimes has the same bad feelings as in leadership situations.

(8) One has the tendency just as in leadership situations to hesitate or to withdraw in order to avoid a confrontation.

Within this first training block there was no attempt made to change or modify systematically any behavior; thus, there were no special reinforcement trials but there was a systematic exchange of roles. Whenever time allowed, each participant had played both roles within a certain topic (e.g., the restaurant waiter and the guest as well).

It might be mentioned here that developmental psychology has done much research in role-taking development (e.g., Flavell, Botkin, Fry, Wright, & Jarvis, 1968). They have shown that role-taking skills develop during the elementary school grades. With police officers who have to learn role-taking to become better leaders, we do not face the problem of competence deficits. Rather, there are strong situational factors and emotions that inhibit adequate role-taking and, accordingly, affect the appropriate behavior in particular situations. Several inappropriate (e.g., aggressive) behaviors have to be inhibited in favor of more appropriate ones, and this should be possible even under heavy stress.

The roles that were played, in the very first series as well as in the forthcoming ones during the course, were discussed. Discussions neither establish nor consolidate the to-be-learned-behavior, but they may contribute to an enlargement or modification (up-dating) of the cognitive representation of the whole social situation and, by this, to the formation of active behavior-guiding (or behavior-monitoring) cognitions. Sometimes, it is the important task of an experienced and skilled psychologist-trainer to take part in the role play and to show suitable primary reactions, thus to act as a model, or to induce primary responses in the play mate (the to-be-trained police officer) that can be reinforced in an adequate way.

Developing the Content of the Training Curriculum: Formulating True "Critical Incidents in Leadership"

In my view, one of the most important points concerning police officers' training is to come as close as possible to the real or true problems or difficulties they are experiencing in their daily activities. To use a metaphor, it seems crucial to me to "pick up" the trainees at the point where they are. By doing so, we avoid confronting them with topics or exercises that are merely academic, not relevant at all to them; topics that do not involve them as personalities and about which they are not motivated to learn. Motivation for learning as well as modifying their own behavior has to start from their own experiences-- probably more typically from their own incapabilities or failures.

Working in small groups (two officers in each), the participants were required to reflect on their work of the previous 3 or 4 weeks in order

to recollect leadership situations about which they had a bad feeling or
had felt unsuccessful. Police officers were matched according to the
similarities in their functions (e.g., both working in the security
section) in order to concentrate on more or less common "critical
incidents". Every group was expected to contribute 2-3 critical
incidents. They should, furthermore, prepare one of these for role play,
i.e., think about the context of the event, about the roles and the
respective responses of the partners. The participants were informed by
the trainer about the importance of this part of work within the course:
their situations or problems would be the "material" for the forthcoming
two days of training. As could be expected, all groups did an excellent
job; they were most interested to get their real problems solved. The
main categories for critical leadership incidents (in all courses) were:

(1) Disobedience or refusing an order or sulking in an inappropriate
    situation by a subordinated collaborator
(2) Dissatisfactory work, mostly written work (e.g., protocols); not
    fulfilling the duties correctly
(3) Lack of discipline (cleanness, completeness of equipment, being on
    time, etc.)
(4) Interpersonal quarrels, provocations or frictions
(5) Problems of a police officer with one of his supervisors
(6) Some very special individual problems (but interesting enough for the
    whole group).

The concrete topics were presented by the groups to the plenary
circle. Similar problems were pooled and all critical incidents were put
into a rank order according to which single training blocks were
planned. Each participant had the right to play and to have at least one
of his own problems (critical incidents) discussed.

Training Blocks

According to the rating of the participants, the first leadership
situation was presented in a role play by the respective group. Officer
A played his own role whereas officer B (his teammate in the small group)
played the partner, with the help of others, if necessary. After the
whole sequence was recorded, which lasted between 1 and 3 minutes, it was
played back from the recorder. The first discussion focussed, on the one
hand, on the description of the behavior of the two (or more) role
players and their feelings, and assessment of the whole situation as they
had presented it. On the other hand, the situation was briefly analyzed
to find out the individual intentions or needs of the individuals
involved (the leader and his "downer"). At this point, a first
theoretical contribution by the trainer was inserted, as a first part of
the integrated introduction to psychology: the hierarchy of needs
according to Maslow (e.g., 1954, 1967), but in an applied form, tailored
for the police officers' comprehension. After this, the role play was
repeated with exchanged roles to teach role taking, changing viewpoints,
seeing the social world from the opposite side, i.e., from that of the
partner. Playing this sequence back from the TV-recorder often showed
the leader-in-training the different position of his partner which he had
never considered before in such a conscious way. Many police officers
who had this experience for the first time (either by themselves or by
observing others) had the explicit desire to repeat the whole role play,
trying to do a better job. Of course, they do not always succeed at
first stroke but much of their behavior will change and can be reinforced
while the scene is played back again. Reinforcement comes from the

teammates and from the trainer as well.

Often, police officers are not successful in their behavior, above all in what they say in the critical incident situation. They are lacking the adequate words or the verbal fluency necessary for coping efficiently with the situation. To enhance learning in this concern, there are several possibilities, two of which have proved a success: (1) A police officer who is not directly involved in the problem may play his version of the leader's verbal behavior, or the trainer plays the respective role; (2) In a situation that can be seen as very important in a general sense for all participants, everybody is asked to write down either what he would do or, even more important, what he would say in this situation. This forces all participants to decide for themselves a specific version so that for each of them an alternative behavior can be role played, played back from the TV-recorder, and then discussed. Officer A, upon whom we focus, is then observing the alternatives offered by some of his teammates. This allows him to cope--internally--with his role, his behavior and his future possibilities. Having seen 2 or 3 possible solutions played by others, including the trainer, he himself might try again--most of the time with considerable success. In a rare case of severe lack of verbal fluency (eloquency), a special pairwise training with another police officer with whom he is well acquainted, or with the trainer, may be helpful. Such training must take place in a fully trustful context; it should, furthermore, be carefully prepared with the trainer talking to the trainee, explaining the importance of eloquent behavior, as well as the practical goal of a possible training procedure strictly avoiding a feeling of a particularly heavy incompetence in the trainee. Often the suggestion to go through this kind of situation mentally in order to be prepared whenever a similar case might occur leads the officer to actively enhance his particular verbal or communication skills. Police officers have a strong bias towards asking the trainer to give them a set of recipes for coping with certain situations. I have never agreed with this request since recipes include the danger of rigid use. What is required with well trained police officers is the flexible use of behavior patterns in critical incident situations. A successful procedure to teach at least a certain flexibility was the following one: When officer A has played a good role, has made progress in coping with a certain situation, and has been reinforced for it; the trainer may play again with him, slightly changing some aspects of the situation or of the sequence of events. The changes must not be too big, just such that an adaptation of A's behavior is within his ability, i.e., within his just elaborated repertoire of coping behavior.

Role play can be very fatiguing for the actors since they are both physically and psychologically fully involved. Therefore, the exchange of roles is an important means to prevent people from stress in role play. But there is also a high risk for the spectators to become tired. Here also, changing roles in a relatively vivid manner may prevent the whole training from being either too hard, or, even worse, boring. Furthermore, there is the possibility of relaxing people by offering some interesting, theoretically oriented information from psychology that fits into the actual training situation.

Table 1
Maslow for Police Officers

V Need for self-actualization

Promotion; being responsible, being fully challenged by everyday tasks; feeling of deep job satisfaction; persuaded that one has the best job.

IV Need for being a valuable person

Experiencing acceptance, appreciation and praise for successful work with difficult tasks or in critical situations; feeling accepted as a leader; experience of being trusted by others (asked for advice), of being popular, of being an expert in regard to particular skills and abilities.

III Need for social acceptance

The feeling of being accepted by the working group (the shift section), including immediate supervisors as well as subordinate officers; exchange of practical help and social support among teammates; experience of sympathy and affection.

II Need for security

Not so much need for social-material security (salary, social security etc.) since this is well established nowadays, but rather physical security during work, security with equipment, trust in functioning of weapons; furthermore, the need for predictability of events while at work, i.e., minimal discrepancies between expectations and real facts during service, both in the interior of the corps and in the exterior (street work), certain invariances in all the usual everyday activities.

I Physiological needs

The particular work schedules of police officers (e.g. night shifts) lead to particular elementary needs such as the need for sleep or, at least, relaxation (the latter is the strongest when hard activities are required just before the end of the shift when all expectations focus on stress reduction, on having a meal); the need for being with his spouse or more generally the family, for being at home; the need for feeling healthy, physically well in shape and psychically stress-proof to, at least, a certain degree.

Table 2
Application of Maslow's Pyramid of Needs to the Chief-Substitute-Relation

---

V Need for self-actualization

Self-actualization is, at least in part, reached when the substitute replaces successfully his supervisor in absence of the latter; repeated success may lead to further promotion up to a limit defined by individual characteristics.

IV Need for being a valuable person

Need for appreciation and overt expression of praise, also publicly (e.g. vis-à-vis the whole section). Good supervisors do introduce their substitutes to all know-how and information necessary for leadership; they reduce their information advantage in favor of an optimal functioning of cooperation.

III Need for social acceptance

Acceptance by the supervisor is best recognized if the substitute is asked to take a certain limited responsibility on his own (without direct supervision or support) with the expectation of an unbiased technical critique.

II Need for security

Predictability of the supervisor's reactions; need for reinforcements, feedback (blame as well as praise), and appreciation from the boss to ensure certain skills and behavior; avoidance of unjustified (mood dependent) harsh critique. In the case of more than one substitute, equal treatment and use of all substitutes by the supervisor.

I Physiological needs

Need for activation, i.e., feeling of being useful; feeling of being stress-proof, physically as well as psychically, therefore, the boss must not do everything himself.

THE INTEGRATED INTRODUCTION TO PSYCHOLOGY, OR INTERSPERSING THEORETICAL ASPECTS OF PSYCHOLOGY
   Not only for relaxation, but primarily for instructional reasons, several topics from psychology are taught to the police officers during the training. The timing of their introduction is chosen according to the needs of the trainees and the knowledge of the trainer. The following list gives examples of topics that have been elaborated according to the actual needs of the participants or to the necessities of the situation:
(1) Maslow's pyramid of needs, which was adapted to the professional situation of police officers, particularly to the special relations between supervisors and their (one or several) substitutes (seconds in command), is shown in Table 1. As a first example, Table 2 shows the

summary of the trainer's contribution that was elaborated with the participants during a guided discussion session. Some of our preliminary (and not always very successful) training work with police officers revealed one special leadership problem: the interpersonal relations between a supervisor and his immediate substitute(s), the second(s) in command, and their mutual needs. Several failures in policing activities showed that the chief did not use the abilities of his substitute in an optimal or, at least, an adequate manner. For this reason it seemed appropriate to examine the special needs of substitutes towards their bosses, to involve these problems in role plays and to sum up the acquired knowledge about some characteristic needs of both members of the dyad.

(2) Why certain behavior patterns of recently promoted leaders are inappropriate; cues for sensing a bad leadership climate.

(3) The hidden role of emotions in leadership; leadership messages to express emotions, to state the desire for behavior change and to open the door for doing so (adapted from Gordon, 1977).

(4) Awareness that conflicts are normal; self-reinforcement for coping with conflicts and not postponing confrontations.

(5) What "stress" means.

(6) Frustration – what is it really, and what are the reactions to it?

(7) Hopeless cases in leadership? Motivating weak collaborators and planning specially tailored programs. At this point a second extensive example of a trainer's theoretical contribution might be added: The use of individually tailored objectives in special instruction or the art of setting reachable goals for so-called hopeless cases.

One leadership problem that had been recognized early, even before starting these seminars, was dealing with "hopeless cases", i.e., with subordinated collaborators (sometimes even police officers with many years of policing experience) who were either not able or not willing to change a certain behavior, especially in regard to enhancing a certain skill required in their policing activities. Typical cases were, among others, a lack of exactitude in filling in forms about people involved in a traffic accident and a lack of accuracy in taking photographs of an accident situation. The stated "hopelessness" referred to the fact that the leader (e.g., the sergeant who was responsible for managing the particular traffic accident event) had already explained many times to his collaborator how he wanted the things to be done, but it did not work. The collaborator was even reluctant and expressed feelings of being annoyed or even tormented.

This part of instruction focused on motivation (achievement motivation), primarily on defining short learning sequences with partial goals, and on reinforcement (including feedback) strategies for the leader. To this end, the following steps can be elaborated: Taking for granted that the collaborator wants to do a good job but is technically unable to fulfill the particular requirements, there is a gap in the learning process somewhere between the original formation and the actual situation of today. Therefore, the police officer has to catch up on something he has missed at earlier occasions. The unskilled police officer must, first of all, realize that the missing skills do not signify a deficit in his personality but in his skills, just something he has to focus on now. He must also be reassured that he has another chance to learn.

Some of the missing skills mentioned above are indeed complex behavior patterns. Thus, they cannot be formed (or shaped) within one trial, i.e., the goal of mastering the particular skill is too distant to be reached in one step. The distance to the goal has to be cut up into several pieces, into several partial goals. Leadership consists now in describing the objectives (the goals in near distance) and in elaborating the appropriate procedure to get there.

The intention of the leader must be manyfold: (1) to secure that his collaborator develops a feeling of trust towards him; (2) to reach consent that special training is not only necesssary but reasonable; and (3) to involve the subordinated police officer in planning, as well as in evaluating, his own learning progress. Such a procedure would be a micro-level-management by objectives, consisting of an individually tailored learning schedule, and would enforce a future self-monitoring of behavior in the trained police officer.

This kind of leadership activity is individual work, individual personnel development. It needs careful preparation, analysis of individual prerequisites and time planning. The single steps require, moreover, careful feedback and reinforcement to the learner so that he can, by himself, assess his activities and his progress or success.

An introduction to reinforcement techniques might be given here. Different kinds of possible reinforcements (such as tokens or just verbal-social ones) are discussed. Effects of punishments are also mentioned, above all, what punishments look like; that is, that they are not physical in kind but are mainly verbal or facial expressions which are aversive. Trainees have to learn about the timing of reinforcements as well as about different qualities of reinforcement. One main point is the knowledge that sooner or later external reinforcement for the trainee has to be turned into self-reinforcement of the trainee to make him independent in assessing the quality of his activities (see Bandura, 1975). Often, it is necessary to create simulated situations for the formation of skills. The proof of having made progress in learning can be given in the real life situations only in a typically irregular time sequence. The leader has to take into account the difference between simulation and real events in assessing his trainees's achievement.

This kind of leadership is not a weak one (i.e., training of "softies"), but can be arranged to be very difficult by forcing the trainee to reach intermediary goals with high precision or completeness or whatever is taken as the criterion and by giving very precise feedback according to adequate but high expectations. The central idea for the leader has to be: Everything can be learned when the learning conditions are prepared adequately and the learner is allowed to spend enough time on the task.

LEARNING TO UTILIZE LEARNED BEHAVIOR IN LEADERSHIP SITUATIONS
Individual Planning of Further Steps

Almost two days are dedicated to playing roles in critical incidents, interrupted by the trainer's theoretical contributions, by discussions of individual problems close to the played critical incidents, by sports activities, and by informal evening circles (with Swiss Jass play, i.e., a special kind of card play, and with singing and discussions). Every training block is summarized by the participants as well as the trainer in regard to the learned information and the newly acquired behavior skills. Before closing the course, every officer is required to think about his forthcoming work, the very special situations he will encounter when he is back from the training holidays; and he will write down one or two important situations or leadership tasks with which he will cope in the near future in a more skilled manner, according to what he has learned in the course. He is told that the whole group will meet again in about 5 or 6 months to listen to each of the group account for his leadership endeavors during the past weeks.

Evaluation of Progress

After about 6 months a follow-up session (half a day) takes place to evaluate the midterm effects of the training course as well as the individual experiences with what has been learned. The starting point in the follow-up course is always one of the sequences (video-play-back) from the training course in order to bring the police officers back to one of those situations. Recently experienced problems or difficulties in leadership are now discussed and taken into another training of the same kind as in the first course. Some theoretical topics may be repeated, but rather briefly unless there is a special need for a more extensive treatment. In order to evaluate the training, we abstained strictly from formal testing of our participants. This would have shed a strange light on all that had been done in both the first course and the follow-up. Evaluation of the training was exclusively by informal, spontaneous comments of the participants, either written or additionally, in some cases, by calling them to get some more detailed information.

The rank order of the statements about the training (frequency of statements) was as follows: (1) greater ability to cope with difficult partners; (2) enhanced ability to cope with difficult situations; (3) a better understanding of how theoretical psychology (specific knowledge) can help in everyday situations (including in private situations and family problems); (4) excellent comradeship and a strong feeling to form a group during the course (as the basis for later discussing leadership problems); (5) being much more aware of both problems and possible solutions (including the acquired knowledge of how to communicate better across the whole hierarchy); (6) greater ease in expressing feelings (of discontent, disappointment, anger, satisfaction); (7) awareness that training has to be continued individually, including the knowledge for some of the participants of still lacking verbal fluency in very difficult encounters with downers.

Introducing Newcomers

Every second year, the young policemen (after their recruit school) are integrated into the city's police corps. This is, in my view, a special opportunity for planning and implementing particular leadership measures. Leaders have to take into account what is going on when new collaborators enter the field. When a whole entity is changed at some place, the structure of the whole will change. What do these changes mean in the concrete situation? There will be new social connections, new groupings; the communication network will be different from the one before.

Supervisors can, above all, plan preventions by asking questions of the following kind: What leadership difficulties can be expected according to the experiences in former years (identification of difficulties or troubles) and how can they be prevented? Especially, what has to be expected from the "old" police officers in the corps or in the particular single section? In what respect are they expected to be models for the young constables? Questions like these have to be discussed by the supervisors and their directly subordinated leaders. We did not do this in our training courses but encouraged the trainees to do it on their own.

REFERENCES

Bandura, A. (1975). Social learning theory. Englewood Cliffs, NJ: Prentice-Hall.

Flavell, J. H., Botkin, P. T., Fry, C. L., Wright, J. W., & Jarvis, P. E. (1968). The development of role-taking and communication skills in children. New York: Wiley.

Gordon, T. (1977). Leader effectiveness training. New York: P. H. Weyden.

Heider, F. (1958). The psychology of interpersonal relations. New York: Wiley.

Maslow, A. H. (1954). Motivation and personality. New York: Harper & Row.

Maslow, A. H. (1967). Self-actualization and beyond. In: J.F.T. Bugental (Ed.), Challenges of humanistic psychology. New York: McGraw-Hill.

FOOTNOTE

[1] I would like to thank Dr. Robert Heuss, Hubert Schlegel, mag. oec., and Günther Thierstein from both the City Police Forces of Basel and St. Gallen for their information and helpful comments on an earlier version of this paper, respectively.

HELPING YOUNG POLICEMEN COPE WITH STRESS AND MANAGE CONFLICT SITUATIONS

FRANK M. STEIN

CONFLICT AND STRESS SITUATIONS IN POLICE WORK

Increasing efforts are being made to develop special stress and conflict management training for police. This results from the fact that police are confronted with stress and conflict situations more than many other vocational groups, and traditionally they have received inadequate education for coping with stress and managing interpersonal conflicts. An analysis of public complaints shows that the legality of police intervention is seldom doubted. However, the verbal and nonverbal behavior of the policeman in conflict situations is a subject of criticism (cf. Trum, 1982). This reflects deficits in the field of conflict management, especially a lack of communicative competency. In addition, several studies indicate that the job of the policeman is characterized more than other jobs by stressful situations. Caplan, Cobb, French, Van Harrison, and Pinneau (1982) emphasized the fact that a key contributory factor to the stress is the high complexity of the policeman's job and the relatively high responsibility attached to it. Similarly, Haritz (1977) has noted the stressful effect of having to take immediate actions which have far-reaching consequences.

Specific stressful aspects of police duties were the subject of a study by the Max-Planck Institute for Psychiatry (Munich) which was carried out in conjunction with the Nordrhein-Westfalen state police (Olszewski, 1984). A total of 893 patrol policemen were asked to name the most stressful aspects of their job. These stress situations were differentiated according to their intensity and frequency. As regards the relationship to superiors, the most frequently mentioned problems were: domineering behaviour, injustice, and poor guidance. In connection with patrol service, the interviewees mentioned severely injured persons in accidents, taking blood tests, confiscation of a driving license, interviewing in family and other disputes, the use of physical restraint, and being a witness in a judicial hearing. As regards the intensity of stress, the following organizational, service, and working aspects were named: the use of physical restraint, shift-work, the necessity of making instant decisions which have far-reaching consequences, interrupted sleep following a night-shift, being overworked, waiting for help in critical situations, finding a murdered child, and living up to the demands of one's own family. These strains frequently cause frustration, lead to negative attitudes toward one's own job and towards other people, and even to psychosomatic disorders (Fullgrabe, 1982). According to Wagner (1979) a relatively frequent reaction to stress in police work is the increased consumption of alcohol which, in turn, becomes a threat to the physical and mental health of police and can result in a pronounced safety risk in everyday work.

SELECTION AND TRAINING OF POLICEMEN IN TERMS OF COMMUNICATION COMPETENCE
AND THE ABILITY TO WITHSTAND STRESS

If stress and conflict situations are typical for police work and if
complaints indicate deficits in managing those situations satisfactorily,
there are consequences for the selection and training of police. In my
view the trainee needs some basic skills, if stress and conflict
management training is to be successful. In other words, not all
deficits in coping with stress and conflict management can be compensated
by training. The candidate for the police officer's job has to fulfill
some special basic requirements. These requirements must include stress
resistance, frustration tolerance, a well developed command of the
language, and social competence such as empathy.

The basic skills need supplementation by psychological instruction in
stress and conflict management. Such training has been offered in the
U.S.A. for more than ten years. Worthy of mention is the police crisis
intervention training described by Mulvey and Reppucci (1981). More than
40 hours of optimal behavior in special conflict situations in everyday
police work is provided in this training. Other programs are concerned
with training in crisis intervention in family disputes (cf. Bard, 1973)
or in general methods to cope with stress (see Sarason, Johnson,
Berberich, & Siegel, 1979; Danish & Brodsky, 1970).

In Europe such training courses are being carried out more and more
frequently, for example a conflict management training course based on
transactional analysis (Berne, 1964) at the Zurich district police in
Switzerland (see chapter by Steiner in this volume) and behavior
modification trainings in West Germany (see Olszewski, 1984). The
following report deals with a stress and conflict management training
course which we operate at the police academy in Rheinland-Pfalz.

ACADEMY STRESS AND CONFLICT MANAGEMENT TRAINING
Goal Definition

The global goal of the training is to improve the ability of police to
respond without an escalation of conflict. To define this global goal,
we have carried out an empirical study, asking 165 men of the municipal
police and detective force for the most stressful and conflict-ridden
situations experienced by young policemen. The results of this study led
to the following specific training goals; they are characterized by
typical situations:

(1) Control of Strong Emotions - Interrogation of violent criminals who
have maltreated or killed a child, or conflict with very aggressive and
hostile citizens.

(2) Police Work Under Group Pressure - Establishment of a disciplinary
offence amongst friends or acquaintances; taking intervention measures
against a group of women; or investigations in the flat of a suspect in
the presence of his relatives.

(3) Neutralize Initial Aggressions - Management of impulsive, hostile
and aggressive verbal behavior in different situations.

(4) Building Up Empathy - Speaking with elderly people, drunken people
and children; giving a person the news of the death of someone with whom
he was closely connected.

(5) Taking Measures Which Are Contrary to One's Own Attitudes - Attitude
conflict at demonstrations; taking measures which are, for the affected
person, of strong social consequence.

(6) Decision Making in Problematical Situations - Decisions whether the
husband should be arrested in the case of family disputes; uncertainty in

decisions concerning consequences of an alcohol test for professional drivers.

Contents and Method of the Training

From the inception of the training we made the assumption that there are two major causes for the police being responsible for the escalation of conflicts whilst carrying out their duty:
(1) There is a lack of skill to cope with the stress which forms a part of all conflict situations;
(2) There is a lack of specific behavior techniques for achieving the above mentioned goals.

On the basis of these deficits the training is divided into two parts:
Part I: General training for overcoming stress
Part II: A situation-specific conflict management training

The theoretical basis of the general training for overcoming stress is the cognitive transactional stress model of Lazarus (1966, 1977). Referring to this model the trainees are instructed about stress phenomena and shown, in particular, the importance of subjective elements in producing stress. In detail the trainees have to work on:
(1) individual stress-situations;
(2) individual short- and long-term reactions concerning the motoric behavior (e.g., muscle tension), the vegetative nervous system (e.g., gastric complaints or faintness), and the cognitive level (e.g., self-related cognitions, self doubts or lapses in concentration).

After the stress diagnosis the participants are trained in stress inoculation techniques relating to the afore-mentioned levels:

Table 1

Level of Reactions	Technique
Motoric behavior	-progressive relaxation (Jacobson, 1938); methods of short term relaxation
Vegetative nervous system	-autogenic training (Schultz, 1970) biofeedback (Schwartz, 1973)
Cognitive level	-self-instructional methods (Meichenbaum, 1977)

The situation-specific conflict-management training concerns specifically the six goals of the training. First, the trainees develop concrete situations experienced in police work related to the mentioned goals. Then they practice behavior techniques to manage these situations adequately. This takes place in four steps:
(1) Without any background information the trainees enact a situation in role-play, which is then recorded on video.
(2) The role-play is analyzed by the group of participants. Behavior techniques which should ensure optimal management of the situation are worked out by group discussion and brain storming.
(3) The psychologist supplies psychological background information to the played situation (e.g., techniques of communication, and characteristics of family disputes). In addition he refers to those methods of the stress-inoculation training which can be applied to the specific situations.

304

(4) Bearing in mind the derived behavior techniques and the relevant methods of stress management the trainees repeat the role-plays according to the method of micro-teaching.

Finally it has to be mentioned that there is no distinct temporal separation of the two training parts. The progressive relaxation, for example, is practiced daily. The whole training lasts one week and one year after the training, a follow-up session, lasting one day, takes place. Here the ex-trainees talk about their experiences and the information is supplemented in the light of experience.

Subjects

Taking into account aspects of economy and the effectiveness of the training, no more than ten trainees should participate at a time. The participants are young policemen who have been active in police patrol not longer than one year. They are trained by one psychologist and one special trained policeman, acting as co-trainer.

Program Evaluation

The implementation of the program is not completely finished yet. Therefore the evaluation has only begun. We are going to carry out an evaluation of process and of outcome (cf. Posavac & Carey, 1980). Concerning the evaluation of outcome, we will make a goal attainment scaling (Kiresuk & Sherman, 1968). This means individual training goals are worked out with the trainees at the beginning of the training. When the training is completed one has to determine whether the predetermined goals have been attained or not. A computed goal attainment score can be used to determine and compare treatment effectiveness. In addition, self and observer ratings of trainees' performance in stressful simulated police activities will be utilized as measures of the effectiveness of the training. Further non- and quasi-experimental approaches to outcome evaluation won't be used. Concerning the process evaluation, we asked the trainees to suggest suitable programme improvements. Nearly every participant expressed the desire to extend the training to two weeks, but organizational conditions made it impossible to lengthen the program. Other proposals were taken into account and involve minor modifications to the program. Finally, I would like to mention that the perceived effectiveness of the training was rated by 4% of the trainees (total n = 32) as being very high, by 68% as being high and 21% rated it as moderately effective.

REFERENCES

Bard, M. (1973). Family crisis intervention. From concept to implementation. Washington, DC: U.S. Department of Justice, U.S. Government Printing Office.

Berne, E. (1964). Games people play. New York: Grove Press, Inc.

Caplan, R.D., Cobb, S., French, J.R.P., Van Harrison, R., & Pinneau, S.R. (1982). Arbeit und Gesundheit. Bern: Huber.

Danish, S.J. & Brodsky, S.H. (1970). Training of policemen in emotional control and awareness. American Psychologist, 25, 268-369.

Fullgrabe, U. (1982). Berufsstreß und Motivation bei Polizeibeamten – Das "Burnout"-Syndrom. Polizei, 73(2), 43-47.

Haritz, J. (1977). Psycholsozialer Stress und Polizeideinst. Polizei, 68(1), 20-22.

Jacobson, E. (1938). Progressive relaxation. Chicago: University of Chicago Press.

Kiresuk, T.J., & Sherman, R.E. (1968). Goal attainment scaling: A general method for evaluating comprehensive community mental health programs. Community Mental Health Journal, 4, 443-453.

Lazarus, R.S. (1966). Psychological stress and the coping process. New York: McGraw Hill.

Lazarus, R.S. (1977). Cognitive and coping processes in emotion. In A. Monat, & R.S. Lazarus (Eds.), Stress and coping. New York: Columbia University Press.

Meichenbaum, D. (1977). Cognitive behavior modification: An integrative approach. New York: Plenum.

Mulvey, E.P., & Reppucci, N.D. (1981). Police crisis intervention training: An empirical investigation. American Journal of Community Psychology, 9(5), 527-546.

Olszewski, H. (1984). Ein Verhaltenstraining für Polizeibeamte Vortrag gehalten an der Polizei-Führungsakademie in Hiltrup.

Posavac, E.J., & Carey, R.G. (1980). Program evaluation methods and case studies. Englewood Cliffs, N.Y.: Prentice-Hall.

Sarason, I.G., Johnson, J.H., Berberich, J.P., & Siegel, J.M. (1979). Helping police officers to cope with stress: A cognitive-behavioral approach. American Journal of Community Psychology, 7(6), 593-603.

Schultz, I.H. (1970). Das autogene training. Stuttgart: Thieme.

Schwartz, G. (1973). Biofeedback as therapy. American Psychologist, 28, 666-673.

Trum, H. (1982). Polizeipsychologie im Rahmen eines institutionalisierten psychologischen Dienstes. In Haase & Molt (Eds.), Handbuch der angewandten psychologie. Band, 3, 101-175.

Wagner, M. (1979). Alcoholism and law enforcement - the provision of counselling-services in the Chicago Police Department. ICAA - Congress, Tours.

INTEGRATING WOMEN INTO LAW ENFORCEMENT

BARBARA TRACY-STRATTON

Although the movement to bring women into the police world has some
unique factors, it can best be understood as part of the overall struggle
for women to gain access to power within a male dominated culture.
Viewing the issue in this perspective eliminates blame and gives a sense
of meaning to the continuing quest for women's equality. By accepting
both the differences and similarities of men and women, understanding
their strengths and weaknesses, society will be able to achieve a new
wholeness based upon dignity and respect for all.

History of Women in the Workplace

Despite the many cultural differences throughout the world, women
universally occupy a lower position than men. Although myths exist
pertaining to Amazons, matriarchies, etc., anthropologists have never
found a culture in which women rule (Kessler, 1976). True, women
sometimes have been elevated to power in the absence of adult male
heirs. In such cases, however, it has been recognized that the aberrant
females were acting out male roles. Queen Hatshepsut of Egypt, for
example, was pictured wearing a beard in order to be seen as occupying a
position normally held by men.

There are three factors used to measure the position of women in
society. They are:
(1) Statements of cultural ideology which explicitly devalue women, their
    products, and their roles.
(2) Symbolic devices such as the concept of defilement associated with
    women.
(3) The exclusion of women from participation in the areas believed to be
    most powerful in the particular society, whether religious or secular
    (Ortner, 1974).
Although some societies practice all three, others may practice only
one or two. Ortner states that "everywhere in every known culture women
are and have been considered, in some degree inferior to men." There is
no question but that women differ from men--physically, emotionally,
psychologically, and in numerous other ways. However, women's
differences traditionally have been regarded as badges of inferiority.

With the development of industry, the exclusion of women from power
began to enter the marketplace. Yet changes in women's status started to
evolve. In the early days of the Industrial Revolution, families
involved in the so-called cottage industries produced many of the
commodities at home. In Java, the Batik industry is still run in this
fashion (Boserup, 1970). This type of economy tended to erode the
division of labor, since all adults and even some children participated.

In England, when cottage labor was replaced by the factory, women and children worked under abominable conditions. During this time there were two distinct statuses for English women: poor or wealthy. The poor, who toiled in factories or did other work in the large cities, had no status and few social agencies, public or private, to look after them; they were driven only by their need to earn money. Women who were born or married into wealth led extremely sheltered lives and were treated with great courtesy; their time was occupied by frivolities, and some became angered by the conditions under which other women worked and lived.

A number of changes took place as machinery became more efficient. Fewer workers were needed. In the United States social legislation was enacted to relieve the conditions of women and children in the workplace. This, however, made women less desirable as workers because they had to be given lighter loads, shorter hours and maternity leaves. Fewer women were employed, competition among men for available jobs increased, and women were virtually eliminated from the job market. As prosperity grew and more men were able to support nuclear families, they began to feel emasculated if their wives also worked.

By the nineteenth century, industry had thus created a rigid class system. Wives of wealthy industrialists were expected to act as displays of their husband's success, consumers par excellence. And, by extension, this was considered the desirable model behavior for women of the middle and lower classes.

Middle-class women whose husbands' jobs were sufficiently lucrative to support the family stayed at home and reared children. There were few "proper" jobs available for women who wanted to work. Marriage was the ideal, and, if some misfortune prevented this, women continued to be dependents of their fathers, or later, their brothers. Women were not encouraged to live alone, and the only jobs they could take were as librarians or elementary school teachers.

Poor women had to work, but even for them jobs were categorized as "proper" or "improper." It was proper to sew, provide domestic services, etc., and improper to sell foods in the market or become actresses. Even among the impoverished the ideal was the "good wife and mother" who stayed home, was adept at household chores, and deferred to her husband. When women did take employment, employers and workers agreed that it was merely temporary, until circumstances improved.

For the most part women served as unpaid, stay-at-home domestic help:
The conversion of women into a cryptoservant class was an economic accomplishment of the first importance. Menially employed servants were available only to a minority of the pre-industrial population: their servant-wife is available democratically, to almost the entire male population (Galbraith, 1973).

In Western industrialized nations, affluence actually depended in part upon the success with which industry persuaded women to stay at home and become conspicuous consumers. Modern industry is based upon the assumption that people constantly wish to acquire objects and will readily replace them if necessary (Kessler, 1976).

Convenient social virtue is accorded women who act as consumer, caretaker or replacer of goods. The idea of women controlling money in our society is fiction. Women don't control money, rather they act as the purchasing agents of men, who hold the power to disperse or withhold resources. Wives of executives are expected to cook, clean, chauffeur, entertain, dress well, and take responsibility for the children's health, education and well-being. In doing so, they dispense money earned by their husbands and acquire prestigious items, thereby fulfilling the purpose of the industrial society.

Galbraith may be accurate in his analysis of the role played by the wife and mother in an industrialized society, but there have been numerous exceptions. There has always been a small proportion of women who rejected the stereotypical model in favor of professional accomplishment. These women were often discouraged by family, friends and male colleagues. Frequently, they were ridiculed and made to feel that they were not considered seriously; yet they persevered and became forerunners for women's equality.

The Beginning of a Fight for Equality

About 1830, corresponding with the abolitionist movement, a women's rights movement had its fledgling origins in the United States. As women began working in earnest for the abolition of slavery, they quickly found that they could not function as political equals with their male counterparts. The brutal and unceasing attacks upon these women reformers convinced them that the issues of freedom for slaves and freedom for women were inextricably linked. However, during the American Civil War, the women's rights advocates were urged to abandon their cause and support the war effort. With the cessation of hostilities, the Radical Republicans of the reconstruction ratified the 13th Amendment to the Constitution and began pressing for passage of a 14th Amendment and the Constitution which would secure all rights, privileges and immunities for male citizens under the law. This was the first introduction of a sexual distinction into the American Constitution, and it provided feminists with a focus for their cause of equal status for women. Due to a generally hostile public attitude, the feminists did not attack the citadels of male strength--the church, family, marriage, etc. Rather, they accepted the male premise of sanctity of the home and fought for equality outside the home.

These early feminists believed that women deserved to vote, not because they were the same as men, but because they were different. "Females were primarily spiritual creates. Hence, their involvement in politics would elevate the moral level of government" (Chafe, 1972). The national was seen as a macrocosm of the home--"politics as enlarged housekeeping." Women could preserve the home and remain good mothers, it was argued, only if they acquired the vote and protected the family through political involvement. Little did these early strategists realize that these self-same arguments of uniqueness and spirituality would later be used to deny women access to certain occupations outside the home.

Women Enter Law Enforcement

Before 1910 United States law enforcement was strictly a man's job based on the military model. State police officers were generally young, unmarried, physically strong, and had military backgrounds. They often lived in barracks, and when they wanted to marry they left law enforcement. Women were relegated to secretarial or clerical roles, or worked as matrons in women's prisons. The New York City Police Department hired its first full-time matron in 1888. Women also were used in social worker roles beginning in the first half of the nineteenth century, when new "social reform" packages were being launched. The Child Saving Movement developed because of a growing concern over the fate of minors who had fallen away from the prevailing social code, and "child-saving" was considered a reputable task for females.

Women, in other words, were able to make these early inroads into policing by serving in custodial, clerical or counseling positions which were consistent with the contemporary perceptions of women's roles. It wasn't until 1910 that Mrs. Alice Stebbin Wells became the first policewoman in the United States, and her duties were limited to enforcing the laws concerning women and juveniles at dance halls, skating rinks, movie theaters and other places of public recreation.

The first women professionals in law enforcement considered themselves unique and different from their male counterparts. People viewed them as social service workers rather than "cops," which brought a philosophy of social reform to law enforcement. Most of the policewomen of this era had at least bachelor's degrees and backgrounds in social work, teaching or nursing. The prevailing male attitude was that, so long as policewomen kept out of the men's way and stayed in the women's bureau under the supervision of a woman, they could be retained as a link between police and the social service agencies. "Real" police work would be done by the male officers.

An important event in the history of the policewomen's movement took place in Baltimore, Maryland, on May 17, 1915, when the International Association of Policewomen was organized. Not surprisingly, Alice Stebbins Wells was one of the initiators of the association, and she became its first president. The association was supported by its older male counterpart, the International Association of Chiefs of Police (IACP). The Policewomen's Association disseminated information about policewomen to police agencies and the general public and promoted the hiring of policewomen to perform preventive and protective work with juveniles and females. Many of the members wanted to be recognized as being separate from male officers, in order to improve their own standards and career mobility and to publicize their existence (Horne, 1980).

At its annual convention in 1922, the IACP, under the innovative and progressive direction of August Vollmer, passed a resolution stating that policewomen were essential members of modern police departments. This helped the policewomen's movement spread into more cities in the 1920s. It was a decade of expansion for women in law enforcement, aided by the success of women officers in training camps during the war, the passage of the 19th Amendment enfranchising women in 1920, and the promotion of policewomen by the International Association of Policewomen.

Entrance into this elite women's corps wasn't easy. Salaries were equal to those of males, and the benefits were generous. However, most departments kept their numbers of women very low. There were separate tests and separate eligibility lists. Qualified male candidates had excellent odds of being accepted because many men were not seriously interested in police work and great numbers ended up being appointed. Women, on the other hand, realizing that competition would be stiff and the numbers appointed would be small, didn't bother to apply unless they were extraordinarily confident and intellectually sharp. This process, consequently, produced a superior cadre of women employees.

Two models of women officers began to develop: the compliant model and the competitive model. The compliant were placed on a pedestal, relegated to specialized tasks or clerical functions. They occupied the youth and detective units, staffed headquarters, and served in policewomen's bureaus.

The competitive model fought for the right to be occupationally fulfilled--to assume as much responsibility, and exercise as much power as their abilities merited. These women were the pioneers of "Women's

Lib" and they forced departments to get a taste of what had to be reckoned with in the future.

The Depression and its wide-ranging economic effects brought the hiring of female officers almost to a standstill. Although Massachusetts became the first state to employ female state police officers in 1930 and Connecticut followed suit in 1942, women were not employed regularly in other state agencies until the late 1960s or '70s. During World War II, women re-entered law enforcement to help supplement the depleted manpower needs of police forces, just as they did in the factories. They usually functioned as women auxilary police, but after the war their use was often terminated.

In the 1950s and '60s police agencies employed greater numbers of women to fill in-house clerical and communications support roles. They were usually civilians, not sworn officers. This was the same status accorded women who were hired to control parking or direct traffic, and the titles ranged from "patrol woman" to "meter maid". Some policewomen were utilized in decoy and undercover assignments. However, there were still few opportunities for policewomen to switch to nontraditional assignments, and promotion opportunities were limited.

In the early 1960s women occupied an extremely marginal place in American policing. Only about 2,400 policewomen were employed nationwide on municipal police departments, mostly on big-city departments. The policewomen's movement was almost totally exhausted. It was not until the late 1960s and early 1970s that the movement revived (Walker, 1977).

By 1971 there were 3,700 women employed full-time in law enforcement. This was approximately 1% of all law enforcement personnel. Characteristically, a significant number of these officers were functioning exclusively in clerical or secretarial capacities. Women were often required to have special education or college degrees and to take different extrance exams because of their "special status." Generally there were quotas on the number of women that departments would hire. Differential treatment began from the moment they applied and continued through training and future assignments. Women received no training in defensive tactics, firearms, sex crimes, and many other areas. Once in the department they were locked into the Women's Bureau, with very little room for advancement (Milton, 1974).

The most significant factors in the growth of feminism in the United States were the 1964 Civil Rights Act and 1972 Title VII of the Civil Rights Act which prohibited discrimination by employers on the basis of race, creed, color, sex and national origin. Under the provisions of the act and the Equal Opportunity Commission guidelines, a police department which did not hire or assign women on the same basis as men was required to prove that sex was a "bona fide occupational qualification" and to demonstrate significant differences between men and women in terms of job performances. Because of these acts, the number of policewomen increased dramatically. In 1971 there were fewer than a dozen policewomen on patrol in the United States and only a few women in police supervisory positions. In 1974 there were close to 1,000 female officers and several hundred women sergeants, lieutenants and captains supervising male and female patrol officers and detectives (Milton, 1974). Women began taking their proportionate place in every aspect of law enforcement. Gail Cobb, in September 1974, was the first United States policewoman to die in the line of duty, providing dramatic evidence of women's involvement in all law enforcement duties.

Along with the changes brought about by the legal system, some people in law enforcement began promoting changes which would create a new police "professionalism." Reformers like Vollmer, Wilson, and Smith pioneered the concept of the professional law enforcement agency which stressed operational efficiency, clean-cut lines of organization, more effective use of police personnel, greater mobility, improved training, increased use of high technology, individual integrity, and higher education for police personnel (Goldstein, 1977).

As a result of these many changes in attitudes, one would expect to find a nearly complete acceptance of women police officers. However, this isn't necessarily the case. Despite the fact that there are increasing numbers of women in the field, there remains a tremendous resistance and direct opposition to their presence. Law enforcement remains a traditional male-dominated profession in which men, because of their physiological characteristics, socialization processes and social acceptance, are at a distinct advantage.

An International Law Enforcement History

The use of women in law enforcement worldwide is as diverse as the various cultures themselves. While some countries have openly encouraged women to join police agencies, many others do not employ women at all and have not considered employing them. In countries where women are employed, there is a great variance in how they are used. These practices range from almost no use of women in such countries as France, Italy and Australia to full utilization in Great Britain, Guyana and Canada (Horne, 1980).

Insistence that women play a more significant role in policing undoubtedly stems from both economic pressures and the feminist movement. With the needs of women to work always increasing, so will their demand for equality in the work world. The role of women in law enforcement generally mirrors the social attitudes and prevailing customs towards women in the society at large. Women will perform highly traditional and typically feminine jobs in those countries where women have never been accorded full social, economic, and political equality. Yet, even in the Middle East, Africa and South America, where there are very rigid beliefs concerning women, there are increasing pressures for admitting them into law enforcement and increasing their opportunities in all levels of society (Horne, 1980).

As various countries employ policewomen and as more empirical evidence is collected, the contributions as well as difficulties of women in law enforcement will become clearer. Even in countries where feminist pressures are minimal, concern with women's rights is increasing.

Women Beginning Law Enforcement Careers

Because of social, economic and legal mandates, the police world is in a state of tremendous change. Departments are being required by law to reflect, ethnically and sexually, the communities they serve. In the United States some cities have been given deadlines for treating women equally and allowing them to do the same jobs as men. These changes are resulting in additional stress for administrators, supervisors, male and female officers and their families.

Women are coming into police work in ever-increasing numbers, perhaps not totally aware of what is expected of them or how they'll be treated once they get there; while, at the same time, males are questioning how women will be able to perform as equals.

The process of selection is where these issues first begin to emerge.

Department interviewers with prejudicial attitudes often put up informal barriers to equality of opportunity. Unofficial quotas, as well as legal quotas, can put women at a disadvantage by restricting the number of those hired. The officer who made the following comment would certainly present a problem to female recruits:

We need people who can show some kind of authority. When you're in a tough situation, how you present yourself physically is what counts. If you appear strong and in control you have a better chance of coming out ahead. Now truthfully, how many women appear strong enough to handle any situation? That's why I believe the force can only handle about 15% or so of them. They're good in certain areas, but basically we need men we can count on.

The question of whether a woman police officer is "economic" becomes a leading concern during the selection process. Talk of wastage rates for women brings special attention to questions about marriage and children, whether they see enforcement as a career, and the projected length of their careers. "We're lucky if we get 10 years out of them with babies, husbands, and then changing their minds about what they want out of life. You can't rely on them because they're too inconsistent," commented one interviewer. Although men may answer these questions similarly to women, prejudicial attitudes may lend a different interpretation to women's answers, putting them at a disadvantage.

If a poor or meaningless selection process exists, then low-caliber officers will be selected, whatever their gender. In fact, the selection standards in many departments are not job-related and therefore not valid. Law enforcement can ill afford to turn away good career candidates—men or women—on the basis of poor standards.

Training is a socialization process molding recruits to the image of the officer-ideal. The image is usually one of a strong male figure which makes women destined to fail in this pursuit. Female images projected by the media continue to be predominately weak, ineffective, manipulative or flirtatious. The model presented and the attitudes displayed aren't conducive to effective policing by women. This is complicated by the fact that few men or women are completely free of deeply ingrained myths about female abilities and roles. Without conscious awareness that these are myths, female recruits under the stresses of training can fall prey to counterproductive influences.

Beyond the difficulties of recruiting qualified women for law enforcement, keeping them is another primary concern, particularly if court mandates are to be satisfied. Too often, women recruits encounter serious difficulties in the academy and end up resigning before they even begin the job.

Academy attrition rates for the Los Angeles Police Department (LAPD) from 1976 through 1980 were 50% for females compared to 17% for males. Other departments throughout the country are experiencing similar results. If the recruitment process has selected qualified women, then questions have to be raised about the philosophy and purpose of training, instructional methods, and their relevance to field work (Saxe & Glaser, 1980). Initially, it was thought that lack of physical ability was the primary reason women quit, but other factors appear to be women's misconceptions about the training academy and police work, outside commitments, and unique and interpersonal problems. Women face the same stresses as men during their academy training, but they also experience these additional problems.

Women recruits must face prejudicial attitudes of many in the training

academy about the appropriateness of females in police work. Many women
begin to question themselves and their motivations and whether they want
to be in an organization where their colleagues and perhaps the
colleagues' families make them feel unwanted. They may have to face
officers who think like this:

What can I say? Women together with men create problems and it's
not our fault. You know how it is--they're there, and you wonder
if it's possible, particularly with the young ones. And you both
get off shift at 1 or 2 am and go have a drink to wind down. And
one thing leads to the next. It's just part of life. And that's
why the wives hate having these women officers around. They see
the divorce rates and they know what's happening.

Some women begin to question if their feminine natures can fit into
their career choices. They may not have fully understood the pressures
of operating in this male world. They may begin to question whether a
female can do a male job rather than understanding that women have
masculine sides of their personalities that can serve them in this
field. During academy training, some women begin to feel the only option
they have is to think, act, and behave like men.

Women who give up their female identities totally during the training
period may end up in confusion and with poor self-esteem. They fail to
see what they have to contribute to the field of law enforcement and try
to fit in in ways that are impossible for them. These women may also
begin to have difficulties with their spouses and other important males
in their lives.

Many women entering the academy have unrealistic expectations about
police work, often romanticizing the job. When they are confronted with
the realities of shift work, community prejudices, difficult physical
training, etc., they may become overwhelmed. If their disillusionment is
not addressed they will become disenchanted, becoming angry rather than
assertive, closed-mouthed rather than communicative, and will not live up
to their potential.

Women may find that upon entering the police world there is a distinct
lack of support from those they respect and love. Even if they entered
the academy with the full support of their families, successful trainees
may find themselves with minimal support as they change. Their
increasing self-confidence, leadership ability, command presence, voice
and demeanor can become threatening to their husbands or boyfriends. Old
expectations are violated. Thus, during the course of training they may
find themselves dealing with failing relationships (Gross, 1984).

Despite the overall commitment of most police agencies to hire women,
police personnel can be less than supportive. They may openly talk about
women not being fit for patrol and may treat women recruits (whom they
believe to be naive) as sex objects or tell degrading jokes in their
presence. These prejudices leave many women feeling like outcasts in a
system where people need to support one another.

During the socialization process in the academy, women are taught to
leave all "lady-like" behavior behind them, since passive and submissive
behavior are anathema to police work. Many women need to work on
becoming assertive, which requires developing authority of voice and
stature. Too often their most important skill--communicating with
people--is replaced by assertive behavior that soon becomes aggressive
behavior. The balance between communication and assertiveness is often
forgotten as the academy staff tries to purge submissive behavior out of
women recruits.

Most women who enter the police academy continue to assume responsibility for housework, meals and caring for their children. Police training is hard work and requires long hours. Recruits must study at home, clean and polish their equipment, and find support to get through the next grueling day. Traditionally, married male recruits have been able to come home to a prepared meal and cared-for children and have private time to study. Female recruits are less likely to have partners who will assume these responsibilities and can become burnt out. One female officer related:

My husband said he thought he could handle being married to a cop, but he couldn't handle my new independence, my friends, or even my hours. I changed and he didn't like it. When times were tough during the academy training instead of coming home to the man who would understand and support me, I came home to another battle. Eventually we split.

Women deal with stress and anxiety differently than men. They may be accustomed to crying, overreacting, or withdrawing in order to cope with an immediate situation, but in the academy they learn that these approaches are unacceptable in the police world. New approaches must be developed or old approaches kept hidden. For example, crying during a child abuse investigation would be inappropriate and ineffective at work. However, they could go home that evening and cry to eliminate some of the pain. This means re-learning methods for dealing with feelings--but NOT denying those feelings, which are essential to their beings. Stress reduction approaches like aerobics, meditation, or proper nutrition could help the women officer. Too often, the training staff doesn't teach these approaches, stressing instead the importance of not expressing feelings.

Law enforcement operates from a mini-max strategy in which maximum force is employed for minimum threat. Officers tend to approach all situations as if their lives are in extreme danger, often resulting in poor interaction with citizens and suspects, and negative attitudes all around.

Approaches that women might take would often include more brain than brawn, more communication than force, and more sensitivity than blunt objectivity. These approaches generally are not taught in the academy. Often the training staff presents situations showing how a wrong decision would result in death. The need to train officers to be cautious is essential. Yet when general patrol is examined, it is not as violent or hazardous as recruits are led to believe. Some instances of violence simply cannot be prevented, and in other situations where the officer can influence the final outcome, strength is not as important as attitude and communication skills.

Another example of prejudice against women is the habit that some men have of drawing a generalization from one negative experience, as in the case of an academy staffer who recalls an instance in which his female partner became afraid and locked herself in the squad car while he was being attacked by a gang. Similar incidents happen to male officers, but they are rarely brought up as examples. Male officers might discuss an incident in which a woman officer was hit in the breast and couldn't support her partner. War stories of all types become exaggerated, and incidents that are relatively rare are presented to recruits as if they happen daily. Statistics aren't emphasized which show that 70% to 90% of police work involves communication skills that can either escalate or defuse a dangerous situation.

Training is the first arena in which men, women and the department begin to confront or ignore the issues of women in the department. Women must find ways to adapt to a male-dominated culture, while at the same time trying to teach that culture the best that femininity has to offer. Becoming part of the culture and working to change it becomes life itself for some women officers.

The impact of group feelings and attitudes is evident in the changes that occur to some women during training. Females enter training fairly self-confident and idealistic about their roles and interactions with male co-workers. However, their feelings about peer relations usually worsen during the initial weeks of training and don't improve significantly after that. The LAPD Academy reports that this happened to 80% of the women it studied. The more traditionally feminine they were, the worse they felt (Saxe & Glaser, 1980).

Unfortunately, as women struggle for acceptance they often perceive a rejection of their female essence. When acceptance is gained it's often at the expense of many of their positive female qualities. One recruit commented, "When I act like one of the boys, I even laugh at officers putting female officers down, and then I feel like a traitor to myself and my sex, but sometimes it's the only way to survive."

Women traditionally have been taught to nurture, to respond to the needs of others, to be caretakers and providers. These qualities are extremely valuable in police work and females should be encouraged to maintain them. During academy training these abilities should be presented as important and beneficial to the total law enforcement effort.

There are issues dealing with physical differences between the sexes that must be confronted honestly and directly if women are to become a valued part of policing. The greatest fear voiced by men is that their female partners won't be strong enough physically to back them up. As one sergeant put it, "They're just not physically capable of doing the same job. I'm not saying they're not smart enough, I'm saying they don't have the strength we have."

This fear is intensified during training because of a strong emphasis on the false belief that most situations are life-and-death. In these situations women are believed to be at a disadvantage, which leads to fears and insecurities for both men and women. Yet, it must be acknowledged, if this issue is to be faced honestly, that women, in fact, aren't as strong, usually, and indeed could be at a disadvantage in those rare situations where muscle counts. Women must also deal with the chemical changes that occur as a result of menstruation. For most women this isn't a particular problem, but for the small percentage who suffer from premenstrual syndrome, the success of their careers can depend, in part, on learning to deal with it. It shouldn't be forgotten that there are also male officers who have to deal with physiological changes that result in mood swings or other psychological symptoms. As one woman officer remarked, "I get tired of hearing about females on the rag. I swear I know plenty of male officers who have the same type of moodiness."

Pregnancy can force women out of the field and into office jobs where they won't be liabilities. Pregnant women may face resentment by male officers for getting such special treatment. Until recently most departments had no pregnancy policy, and women who became pregnant feared being fired.

Special treatment and specialization generally have hindered rather than helped the policewoman. One supervisor who tended to treat women differently made this comment:

Yeah, I know it's true. I just can't do it. If a male officer
screws up, I just let him have it and that's that. But with a
female it's just harder. They might cry and I'd feel bad. I'm
just too soft on the women, but I can't help it.

Male officers will find it easier to accept women if the same rules are
enforced equally, when possible. Perhaps just as women are feeling
overburdened by having to adapt to a male-oriented world, men are feeling
overburdened by having to accept female differences in their world.

Unfortunately, there are some ways women try to enter the culture that
are detrimental to both themselves and the department. Becoming one of
the "boys," drinking heavily at bars, telling war stories, becoming
stiffly unemotional and participating in indiscriminate sexual activity
have all been tried as a means by some women to gain acceptance. Some
women resort to childlike ways, needing too much help and direction from
their male counterparts. This leads male officers to wonder, and with
good reason: "Will they need to be protected in a dangerous situation or
can I count on them?" Or, "I plain don't like it--having a female
partner in a fight situation. Even if she can handle herself, I always
feel like I should protect her." But other women respond like this, "The
best thing a male training officer can do for us is to show us how to
protect ourselves. We want to do our job and don't need protective
fathers as partners."

Men cannot accept a woman who rejects her own feminine nature to become
one of the boys, because they cannot trust her. Yet neither can they
trust a woman who relies too heavily on certain feminine traits. To try
approaches that are generally unhealthy to both male and female officers
in order to be accepted, only loses women credibility. The best approach
for a woman is to respect the masculine nature of the police culture
while also trying to incorporate certain tactics that are part of a
woman's repertoire.

Field Problems for Women Officers

The police are a subculture of males in the prime of life, with a
distinctive locker-room quality about their interactions with each
other. Policemen thrive on their rugged physiques, natty uniforms,
sexually symbolic occupational tools and aura of power, all of which
equal virility. Some react with hostility and despair if they're forced
to even think of having to work with a woman. Although no conclusive
evidence is available on male vs. female performance in law enforcement,
most studies indicate that the biggest obstacle for women's acceptance is
the hostility of policemen (Ainsworth, 1983).

Women entering police service will be scrutinized closely, and poor
performance may be seen as representing all females, confirming men's
negative stereotypes. Policewomen may feel alienated, leading in turn to
underachievement and possible resignation.

Some male officers are threatened if they are forced to work with women
and share their masculine authority. Even the possibility of female
equality in law enforcement can generate anxiety about their own
masculinity in men who foster sexual stereotyping. Generalized
statements like "they just don't fit" or "they're more trouble than
they're worth" are often heard.

Sexist stereotypes influence people's expectations, causing them to see
and remember only behavior that furthers the stereotype. The
expectations of male officers, in other words, can become
self-fulfilling. What's more, sexist assumptions can elicit

stereotypical behavior which confirms the original assumption. The existence of the female stereotype (the weaker sex, overemotional, passive, indecisive) is as fatal to women officers' progress as black stereotypes and myths are to raising of black consciousness and pride.

Male protectiveness is another counter-productive, if well-intentioned, practice of policemen. Stiehm (1985) reports an Air Force general saying that women weren't assigned as squadron officers because, "We can't risk having a woman in that job. We don't know if people will take orders from her." A conclusion of her research was that it's unthinkable to almost every man that a woman could defend him (Stiehm, 1985).

Women have been taught to seek out men for protection, physical safety and security. Yet the need to protect women and the need for women to seek this protection will keep women dependent upon their male partners, rather than encourage them to explore more productive methods to protect their partners and themselves.

Female officers often confront male officers if they feel slighted in the areas of communication, relationships, and social manners. Such issues as swearing, opening doors for women, initiating platonic friendships, deciding who should drive patrol cars, and providing excessive back-up personnel for women are all brought into question and must be addressed or they will magnify.

Woman officers also face problems involving the constant clash between work and personal life. Women have historically been the maintainers of the family unit and intimate relationships, and so a woman officer may find herself drawn in a thousand directions, feeling imperfect as a wife, mother, lover, and then even less perfect in the law enforcement world. She may find herself exhausted, depressed, listless, and without time for spouse and family, and most importantly, herself. She constantly must deal with maintaining the house (studies show that working women still do 80% of the housework), solving children issues (who stays home with a sick child?), and emotionally supporting a husband or boyfriend who may not be happy having "his woman" in law enforcement. For the single woman finding a relationship may be difficult, what with varying shifts, misperceptions of female cops, and their own inabilities to relate to the civilian world.

While male officers may feel reasonably comfortable that their homes are maintained or have less need for emotional support from their loved ones, women officers often don't have this luxury. Generally, they're concerned about their families and have greater needs for outside support. Every woman must be comfortable with the time she commits to her job if both her career and her personal life are to be successful.

Solutions

Integrating women into the work force has created societal turmoil that directly affects individuals, families, corporations, governments and society as a whole. Historically, women have been rejected in the work world except in emergency situations such as World War II--and even then they were expected to return to their rightful place, the home, when the crisis ended. Although the working woman was once viewed as a "Woman's Libber," it is generally accepted today that integrating women into the work world is no longer a "woman's problem."

Daycare centers, flexible work hours, job sharing, and maternity and paternity leaves are new features of the corporate world. Women have helped to revitalize institutions that had neglected the needs of minority groups, individuals and families. They bring feelings and subjectivity to a world that had relied almost exclusively on intellectual solutions.

Integrating women into law enforcement is particularly difficult because of its macho orientation, yet this may be where women are needed most. Their family orientation and their skills in communication and understanding human suffering and pain are sorely needed in a field which can easily become alienated from people and societal needs.

To be sure, there are problems in integrating women into law enforcement, and yet there will be no turning back. Seeking solutions to these problems is the approach that all law enforcement agencies and personnel must take to reach workable understandings for all officers.

The police chief is most responsible for insuring the success of women police officers. The top administrator has the ultimate responsibility for the department and sets the tone. An innovative, imaginative police chief realizes the potential of policewomen and overcomes the obstacles to making effective use of them. He is the role model for his executive staff and the spokesperson to a community that may harbor fears about having policewomen on the streets. The police chief must believe in and be able to explain the benefits that women bring to the department and the community.

After this, the chief must begin a planning process to bring these women into the organization harmoniously. Women must be treated equally in all areas, and a directive from the chief outlining expectations in clear, concise language will get this message across. A chief must try to develop some command-level and middle-management enthusiasm and support for his women officers. The male supervisors who work directly with female officers can make or break a program. One way a chief can help is to bring his team together for periodic seminars which focus on the benefits of having women in the department, allow officers to discuss their fears and feelings about it, and then allow them to develop solutions to the issues that arise.

Because the liabilities that women bring to the department are the focus of many male officers, the direct advantages of women cannot be emphasized enough. Women can reduce the incidence of violence between police officers and citizens. The performance of policewomen in America and abroad, the experiences of women in other hazardous jobs, and social psychological studies all indicate that women tend to defuse volatile situations and provoke less hostility than men (Sherman, 1973). As one well seasoned sergeant said:

I'm one of the holdouts from the old school. I just plain didn't believe that women should be cops. They're too small, too soft, and I didn't want them around. They could never carry their load. They'd be more of a nuisance. Well, over the years I've changed my mind—not totally—you hear, but I'm beginning to see that they have some good points, too. One time I saw my rookie woman partner handle a domestic dispute where she just plain listened and said she understood. We all walked out of there OK. I'm sure I would have blown the dude away if it had been just me. And I've seen them add some humor to a job that can be just damn hard. I still have some doubts about these female cops, but at least now I can see that they might be able to fit in and even add some positive stuff to the department.

The wider use of women—as decoys, detectives and plainclothes patrol officers—can increase a department's crime-fighting capabilities. Patrolwomen can immediately handle and search female suspects at the scene of an arrest, averting the destruction of evidence. Women have been repeatedly praised for their ability to elicit important information from both suspects and victims, especially in sex and juvenile offenses. Because of the rapid increase in the number of female arrests, even more women officers are needed today to perform these most obvious functions. As one female police officer noted:

It's not unusual for an officer to pull me aside, even the most macho ones, and tell me that I did OK or handled a situation really well. I've even had them thank me for helping them when they screwed something up. This happened once after a rape interrogation when he (a male police officer) had the victim totally out of control during the questioning. I stepped in and finished up--and maybe it was because I was a women or whatever--but she was able to answer my questions and stay together. And another time I had to take over after my partner pulled over a car and found a woman naked in the back seat with her partner. He got totally flustered and forgot some procedural regulations. That's just two times that I can remember where I got thanked. Now these guys would never say this in front of their fellow officers, but I think it's a big step where at least individually they said that I'm doing a good job.

Women can improve the image of police through their visible presence, expanded contacts with citizens, and exemplary behavior as public servants who care about people and want to help them. An overall improvement in the quality of patrol service is bound to result. Many men ignore the service concept for "real police work," while many women enjoy the service role and actively seek it.

By hiring personnel who represent the entire population, a department can become more responsive to the needs of all people and more democratic. The majority of citizens served by the police, after all, are women and children, and many of these people prefer to deal with policewomen, particularly in cases involving rape or child molestation. Moreover, most patrol forces are composed of men who have common backgrounds and social attitudes, so introducing women and minorities helps to diversify those attitudes and humanize the policemen themselves (Sherman, 1973).

By introducing women into jobs that have been held exclusively by men, departments are forced to rethink and reevaluate other traditional policies and conventional wisdoms. If a woman needs better physical-defense training, so might a man. If officers of either gender defuse a violent situation without having to make an arrest, shouldn't they be given high ratings for effective performance? Through learning how to assimilate women, departments can move toward improving their selection procedures, relating job standards more closely to training, and developing more accurate measures of performance.

Finally, and most practically, acting in accordance with the United States Constitution avoids discrimination lawsuits. Good-faith experimentation in interchangeably using men and women in order to develop selection, recruitment, and promotional standards demonstrates a department's efforts to follow the law and make it work.

Getting qualified women to apply to the department is extremely important for the success of such a program. In recruitment a realistic picture of what is expected must be presented, and programs can be held with male and female officers who are positive role models. Recruiters must be open, honest and sincere in their answers to applicants' questions.

A top quality training staff--people who are effective communicators, ethnically and sexually diverse, with as few prejudicial attitudes as possible, will exemplify a modern department's high expectations. The trainers must be the best the department has to offer because they will be role models for the recruits.

The curriculum should be representative of what will be required of the recruit to handle the job. Besides physical fitness, firearms training and other traditional academy subjects, more time needs to be spent teaching recruits effective communications techniques. Defusing crisis situations, interacting with ethnic minorities in ways that are respectful, and interviewing victims are all essential skills for effective officers. Women recruits who may feel inadequate in physical altercation exercises often have superior communication abilities, and training officers should promote those skills which come most naturally.

Orientation sessions for new recruits can be used to destroy myths and help the recruits in realistically facing their careers. Family involvement in this process furthers understanding between recruits and spouses, giving the mates an intimate glimpse into the heretofore cloistered police world. Fears that recruits' wives and husbands might have concerning safety or lifestyle changes should be addressed. As one spouse said about his new officer wife:

I may not like all that's going on with her during academy training and probably most of her career, but at least I understand some things better. My greatest fear was not feeling part of her world, and, I guess, losing her to some cop. But after hearing about other law enforcement families who have made it, I think we can, too. Basically, we love each other, and my fears kind of got in the way.

Training sessions for both sexes, in which objections and conflicts are dealt with openly, will allow men and women the opportunity to express their feelings. The different attributes of male and female officers should be emphasized, with special attention paid to the skills women bring to the department. These sessions should recognize and support the philosophy that men and women officers with their combined strengths will make a stronger department.

One of the most important and influential people in any new officer's life is the field training officer. Like the training staff, these officers quickly become role models. Young officers equipped with an idealistic image of police work, and wanting to be accepted, may hurriedly model themselves too closely after their field training officers, and indeed might need to in order to be accepted. For women who have male FTO's, this may be another step in denying their femininity and trying to fit into what they think is expected of them.

Field training officers need to be sensitive to the uniqueness of young officers, aware of their own prejudices, and honest in their evaluations. They need to understand how powerful an influence they are on new officers. Allowing for mistakes, being able to listen, and learning from new recruits is all part of their job.

Because of the newness of having women working alongside men in the police force, special support and assistance throughout their careers could prove helpful. Women are usually denied the strong peer support and cohesiveness that characterize contemporary American law enforcement. Feelings of rejection and inferiority are common. Support groups, either formal or informal, should be encouraged by the department as one of the strongest ways of mitigating the consequences of job-related stress.

The Los Angeles Sheriff's Department has a yearly Ladies' Night Out where women deputies get together to socialize and share feelings and experiences. Women might also appreciate more formal sessions in which selected topics are discussed each week or each month. Linda L., a female officer from a small department, related:

> There were no other women in my department, and I was having a hard time handling my anger, confusion--my career and my social life. I was expected to act like a man in one situation, a woman in the next, and to know exactly when this should be. I began to lose myself. So I called up a girlfriend in another department and she called up a girlfriend of hers, and so on. One Tuesday night six of us got together and just talked. We now meet every other week and have a general topic each session, like "Strategies for Getting Along with a Male Chauvinist," or "How to be a Policewoman and have a Social Life, too." Each week one of us is in charge, and each week we leave feeling better because maybe we learned ways of coping, but mostly we felt understood and supported. It saved me and my career.

Often professional organizations lend the needed support to women officers. Aside from accomplishing specific tasks, women gain much information from the other professionals they meet. They find that other agencies encounter the same situations, and they tend to receive honest assistance from those in other agencies because they're not in competition with them. However women officers choose to get together, encouragement for such activities from the administration is important.

Women Supporting Themselves

While women may expect some type of support from their departments, colleagues and families, they must take primary responsibility for the success of their careers. Awareness that they possess innate and learned traits of behavior that can be counterproductive to success in a male-dominated profession is essential. They need to know when not to exhibit these traits and how to develop new behavioral skills.

Law enforcement officers are both team members and leaders. For most women, being a team member is a more familiar role than being a leader. Thinking like a leader, taking assertive action, being professional in all aspects (behavior, speech, dress, etc.) will assist women in the transition. The desirable image for women officers seems to incorporate both masculine and feminine attributes: a bit of everything and an excess of none.

Today's changing opinion of the woman's role demands that women change their ideas and thoughts about themselves in the world. Because of women who made the sacrifices of being pioneers, career opportunities have steadily increased for women. The first policewomen encountered resistance and humiliation, but today's officers are increasingly earning respect, and it's clear that women will continue to play a greater role in the world of law enforcement as we move toward the twenty-first century.

Summary

The roles women have played throughout history have been explored in order to give a perspective to the difficulties of integrating women into law enforcement. Women initially entered law enforcement in 1888 as matrons in women's prisons and continued to function during the first

half of the twentieth century in very specialized roles. It wasn't until
Title VII of the Civil Rights Act in 1972 that women began to perform on
a more equal basis.

The issues that women bring to the department, with their special
strengths and weaknesses, were discussed. Emphasis has been placed on
solutions to these issues. The chief and his supervisors play a major
role in supporting and planning for the success of women officers.
Selection and training techniques are a major influence on the attitudes
and approaches of all officers. And, women officers themselves must take
responsibility for their success or failure. Women bring with them
skills that are sorely needed in the field of law enforcement, which is
becoming more responsive to society and its needs.

REFERENCES

Ainsworth, P. B. (1983). Sex differences amongst British police
    officers' perceptions of psychology. Paper presented to the British
    Psychological Society London Conference.
Boserup, E. (1970). Woman's role in economic development. London:
    George Allen and Unwin Ltd.
Bouza, A. V. (1975, September). Women in policing. FBI Law
    Enforcement Bulletin.
Chafe, W. H. (1972). The American women. New York: Oxford
    Univerity Press.
DeLucchio, J. L. (1975, April). Female officers on the department.
    Police Chief.
Galbraith, J. K. (1973). Economics and the public purpose.
    Boston: Houghton Mifflin Company.
Goldstein, H. (1977). Policing a free society. Cambridge:
    Ballinger Publishing Co.
Gross, S. (1984, January). Women becoming cops: Developmental
    issues and solutions. The Police Chief.
Harding, M. E. (1970). The way of all women. New York: Harper
    & Row.
Horne, P. (1980). Women in law enforcement. Springfield, IL:
    Charles C. Thomas.
Hurrell, J., & Kroes, W. (1975, May). Stress awareness. Paper
    presented to National Institute of Occupational Health and Safety
    Symposium, Cincinnati.
Janeway, E. (1971). Man's world, women's place. New York:
    William Morrow and Company, Inc.
Jones, S. (1985). Women in policing. England: The Equal
    Opportunities Commission. Unpublished manuscript.
Kessler, E. S. (1976). Women: An anthropological view. New York:
    Holt, Reinhart and Winston.
Lord, L. K. (1981). A discriminative analysis of peace officer
    related stress in female officers. Dissertation.
Milton, C. H. (1974). Women in policing: A manual. Washington,
    DC: Police Foundation.
Ortner, S. (1974). Is female to male as nature is to culture?
    Women, Culture and Society, Sanford, CA: Stanford University Press.
Platt, A. (1969). The child savers. Chicago: University of Chicago
    Press.
Prince, J. J. (1982). A pilot study to select and prepare under-
    privileged minorities and women for employment in law enforcement.
    Journal of Police Science and Administration, 10(3).

324

Ryan, M. P. (1983). _Womanhood in America_. New York: Franklin Watts.

Saxe, S., & Glaser, D. F. (1980). _The psychological training of female police recruits_. Behavioral Science Services, LAPD, unpublished manuscript.

Sherman, L. J. (1973). A psychological view of women in policing. _Journal of Police Science and Administration_, _1_(4).

Stiehm, J. (1985). _Bring me men and women_. California: University of California.

Stratton, J. G. (1984). _Police passages_. Manhattan Beach, CA: Glennon Publishing Company.

Van der Poel, S., & Punch, M. (1981). Everybody's watching: Policewomen in Amsterdam. _Police Review_, _89_(12).

Walker, S. (1977). _A critical history of police reform_. Lexington, MA: Lexington Books.

INTERVIEWING DEVELOPMENT: FACING UP TO REALITY

ERIC SHEPHERD

The Conversational Core

Increasingly police officers, particularly senior police officers, refer, argue, insist that policing is a profession. Clearly to be a police officer implies possession of a body of specialist knowledge, acquired over a period of time, and the delivery of a service to the community—assessing situations, identifying the nature of the 'problem', and bringing to bear a 'solution'. Yet in focussing upon specialist knowledge it is possible to lose sight of the fact that there is another defining property of professions such as policing. Policing, like medicine, nursing, teaching and social work, is a close contact occupation characterized by the necessity to manage discourse, conversational exchanges at the point of contact. This is interviewing: controlling and directing a conversation creatively to achieve a desired purpose whether it be obtaining, passing or clarifying information (Russell, 1972).

If you are a member of a close contact occupation, your interviewing performance is the bottom line. It is the personal reality that you create in your exchanges with members of the public and your colleagues. Indeed, all the specialist knowledge in the world and any amount of prowess with technology, information and otherwise, will not make a close contact professional professional. Unless he or she can manage discourse to alter and to create situations in a manner which builds a psychological bridge with the other(s) involved, then he or she can only ever aspire to efficiency, never effectiveness.

Failure to build a psychological bridge with the interviewee, to manage the discourse towards an effective outcome, not only questions the professionalism of the individual. Cumulatively unprofessional performances serve to erode any claims by a close contact occupation to being a profession. It is because there is what I term a conversational core to being a contact professional. It is where situation defining knowledge, basic conversational skills and investigative interviewing skills interact and emerge as a controlled ex tempore discourse in an encounter—the purpose of which may be defined before or arise from the conversational exchange. This is the reality of interviewing.

Situation Defining Knowledge

Professionals tend to define situations too narrowly. They tend to see a situation in terms of the vocabulary of their specialist knowledge—in the case of a police officer this will be the law, procedures, directives, and the like. Indeed the appraisal systems and forms of many police forces underline this—where the term professional knowledge applies to the breadth of an officer's evidenced ability to assess and act upon his or her typology of incidents and typology of solutions.

Yet there are other knowledges involved in situation defining. Knowledge of people as human beings with respect to the differences in personality, perception, memory, emotion, communication, and the processes of influence. Somewhat more challenging is knowing about being human. This knowledge reflects awareness that personality, memory, and emotion are not only active, they are interactive, with antecedent, concurrent, and prospective perceptions of self, other, and the circumstances bringing these together, accounting for levels of individual pressure, arousal and suggestibility.

Very much more challenging is knowledge of discourse. Essential as it is knowledge of channels of communication and barriers to communication in the sender-message-receiver-noise model is insufficient. A natural language conversation is not a linear 'ping pong' match. It is a stream created by the interaction of the participants emergent, ex tempore, thought into action across an entire encounter. It is a stream where ideational, affective, and dispositional messages are consciously and unconsciously sent, and comprehended, or taken up, as meanings which were intended or unintended by the sender, or the product of pure fantasy by the receiver. Imperative knowledge, therefore, is awareness of the phenomena of natural language in conversational exchanges: expressive and logical imprecision, and the processes of discourse comprehension. A professional must know that even everyday exchanges are characterized by reduced forms, contradiction, vagueness, and ambiguity, and how this far-from-perfect stream is processed sequentially and holistically, and always imaginatively, by the listener/observer to derive a macro-structure of the personal knowledge that the speaker has in his or her mind.

Coming to grips with knowledge of human beings, of being human, and the extent to which oneself creates meanings in discourse are essential steps on the path to self-knowledge. As the philosopher Hora (1959) said: To know another one must know oneself; to know oneself, one must know another. Hence the crucial situation defining knowledge relates to the source of the definition—the one tasked with controlling and directing the interview. An individual who does not reflect, or who has never reflected, upon himself or herself, upon identity, values, origins, aspirations and apprehensions, will be ever blind to the extent to which these affect his or her conversations. He or she will certainly not be motivated to recognize, let alone monitor, his or her own expressive and logical performance whilst seeking to handle the other person involved.

Basic Conversational Skills

Like many professionals police officers tend to see encounters in terms of dominance-submission. They feel they must direct but experience difficulty in handling the interactive nature of encounters. To this end an officer will go to great lengths to reduce conversation to routines which enable sufficient 'facts of the matter' to be derived to fit the circumstances into his or her typologies of 'problems' and 'solutions'. Those other facts of the matter expressed in natural language conversations—the affective and the dispositional—are, however, potential sources of anxiety and aggravation. Problems experienced in coping with these facts lead inexorably to perceptions of winning at all costs, not losing face, and so on.

This creates a paradox. Many close contact professionals acquire rank, seniority and professional experience without ever developing the ability to control a conversation—any conversation—in a socially skilled manner. They experience difficulty combining expressive behaviour which controls the other person's thoughts and deeds, with expressive behaviour which is socially rewarding and therefore relationship building. This other aspect of expressive behaviour, by its person-to-person properties fosters and sustains mutual contact, reinforces conversation—instilling in the other person confidence and commitment.

An individual who focuses upon controlling at the expense of reward, comes across as dominant and excluding, and rapidly alienates the other person in a conversation. In contrast the person who rewards but fails to exert control is forced into a submissive position. Socially skilled performances are characterized by balance, a blend of assertion and listening, the latter rendering the former natural, indeed acceptable. Far too many professionals lack the assertion and listening skills fundamental to conversation and police officers are not alone in essentially conducting conversations which are most frustrating (in all senses of the word) for all involved.

Whilst enactive components such as eye-contact, intonation, gesture, timing and the like are important, the assertion and the listening demand basic social skills in an area poorly recognized by psychologists and practical trainers—observation skills, listening comprehension skills, and auditory and visual memory (Shepherd & Levy-Halford, 1985). Unless one observes and processes changes in a person's expressive behaviour (and the logic, mood and attitudes reflected therein) from initial contact to the close, unless one can triple-component process, unless one can bring to bear visual and auditory memory to identify changes in the other's words and deeds, one cannot hope to comprehend that to which one is "listening", and one certainly runs the risk of asserting oneself inappropriately.

Investigative Interviewing Skills

Any interview implies investigation, finding out, if only finding out the interviewee's reaction to information you have given him or her. Needless to say professionals tend not to be too keen on investigating the effects of their information, or their requests for information!

In certain situations professionals are able to reduce the investigation to a questionnaire-like scenario. Here, say in a traffic violation, it is possible to fit the circumstances into a conversation-reducing, almost conversation-excluding, routine. As I noted earlier the outcome may very well be efficient but it is ineffective. In the case of a police officer, the interviewee is left with little or no respect for the interviewer, and with little desire to co-operate, or even assist, this officer (or any officer) at a future time.

However when circumstances do not fit neatly into a questionnaire-like scenario, professionals experience problems. It demands both discipline and logic to prepare oneself for the investigative task, perhaps with little or no time to prepare. Many individuals embark upon investigative interviews not really knowing what they are looking for, and unable to recognize it when they see or hear it! Because they are unclear of their purpose, their investigative objective, they have the greatest difficulty measuring up to the task of establishing a questioning set—a framework of investigation to enable the attainment of the objective. Framing a clear objective and a questioning set are fundamental investigative skills. Without these the associated skills of structuring the exchange, and exploiting emergent information are rendered problematic.

All too many people believe interviewing is all about questions. Of course it is not. It is all about listening and looking, and exploiting responses from individuals whose personality and present emotional and attitudinal state must be continuously assessed. All too many in the close contact professions, however, tend to exclude issues of personality, arousal and disposition, and emerge as overcontrolling, talk most of the time, fail to look and to listen fully, if at all, to the interviewee's responses and thereby end up with impoverished, distorted or even false impressions, accounts, statements and the like. They fail to understand that in the reply to every question lies the germ of the next. Not for them the interviewing spiral--the systematic opening of topic, the systematic probing of responses, verbal and nonverbal, and the summarizing of comprehension before linking to the next topic. Rather there is the 'camel looking for water' phenomenon moving disjointedly from one topic to another, perhaps even returning to a topic which has been already covered but the responses to which were not attended.

If conversational skills are applied then the psychological bridge is constructed between interviewer and interviewee, the prospect of deriving an account through more flowing conversation is increased. An interviewer who is preoccupied with his or her agenda, or with framing the next question rather than listening to (and looking at) the responses to the present topic, is unlikely to get anything other than a collection of shreds of information. If he or she has not been attending to replies then the prospect of checking for consistency, of identifying logical linkages is not good. In investigations even more so the quantity and the quality of information rest heavily upon basic social skills of attentiveness, observation and memory.

Investigative interviewing, therefore, demands that the interviewer translates into action knowledge of human beings, self-knowledge and personal competence in information processing in the pursuit of information. These are all essential to identify where the interviewee lies along the dimensions of willingness to respond and ability to respond. Without such interviewing skills the unaware interviewer is ever at risk of misinterpreting the situation, unable to distinguish between someone who does not know from someone who is unwilling to say. The interviewer is blind and deaf to the indicators of arousal, insentient to the risks of suggestibility. Hence interviewee responses are interpreted as inadequate, unhelpful, or, obstructive, originating from a "difficult" customer. This often leads to the use of questioning strategies which are believed to break down resistance (Hackett, 1978).

The effectiveness of many of these strategies rests, however, upon the interviewer's awareness of the situation--most particularly the status of the relationship between the interviewer and the interviewee. It is true to say that if the interviewer has not through conversational skills, structuring skills, and attentiveness skills, forged an appropriate relationship with the interviewee then strategies such as frank and friendly, or conspiratorial, or joint problem solving are precarious to say the least, and stress, sweet and sour, and tell and sell strategies are doomed. Furthermore with the advent of interviews being open to public scrutiny (i.e., through tape recording) and time and code of conduct constraints (i.e., under the Police and Criminal Evidence Act, 1984) the most fundamental of interviewing skills--building the psychological bridge--has emerged as the essential component of the conversational core.

Training for the Conversational Core: Traditional Perspectives

Traditionally the police service has an ambivalent view towards training. In simple terms 'experience' is seen as the teacher--and formal training is considered "not real", "a waste of money", and detracts from "learning on the job". Whilst learning on the job--otherwise called 'learning (sitting) by Nellie'--has distinct advantages, it has distinct disadvantages. Perhaps its greatest advantage is that it costs little or nothing. Another advantage is that, in the absence of any system of checking the effectiveness of any given Nellie or the outcome of a period with Nellie, an institution can assume that it is not only cheap it is a wholly effective form of training. Of course a moment's thought (which is never really given) would point to the folly of believing that all Nellies have the skills to be imparted, are motivated to impart these, and have the necessary skills of observation, process identification and analysis, integration of teaching, points and facilitative skills to provide feedback and constructive discussion (Shepherd, 1984).

The police service is what could be accurately described as a working group characterized by unsupervised performances which are not subject to close managerial scrutiny. The prospects of receiving feedback are relatively slight unless things go drastically wrong. In such drastic circumstances this places the officer in the position of either blaming himself or herself or the other person. Not unnaturally it emerges as the other person who was in the wrong, failed to understand the pressures upon the officer, or was being "difficult".

Over a lifetime of being essentially unsupervised, professionals emerge as more and more resistant to feedback. Professionalism is increasingly correlated with situation defining knowledge--most particularly that which characterizes the service to be rendered, in the case of police officers, law and procedure. Whilst training programmes may include material on person knowledge--perception, emotion, memory, communication, influence--this remains at the level it was imparted: cognitive information.

Attempts to bring about behaviour change in basic social skills or interviewing skills are most oddly handled. The material remains very much at the information level, with only an infinitesimal number of officers providing class discussion material by actually enacting in a role play situation and receiving feedback. The truth is that such observation without action destines the lesson to have little or no personal relevance.

There are practical pressures to continue with such an inadequate and inappropriate approach to skills training. The truth is that realistic and relevant skills training implies every trainee enacting the skill and receiving rapid feedback. This translates into unavoidable cost: a low trainee-trainer ratio and time for the trainee to attempt a series of progressive approximations to enable an initial assessment, and subsequent progress to be monitored.

Finally, there is a psychological barrier to the implementation of appropriate training in skills for police officers. It requires the service to acknowledge that many officers across the entire career, rank, experience and seniority spectrum who are assumed to have adequate (if not good) conversational and investigative skills actually may not. The alternative to facing up to this particular reality is to continue in the belief that variability in performance, when blatantly overt or unable to be denied any further, is a personal failing of the officer rather than a failing of the universal system of training by experience.

Facing up to Reality: Interviewing Development

Against the admitted ambivalence which arises from coping with a tradition of opposition to training and the barriers of cost and coming to terms with a process of corporate denial, at this conference you will have learned of the steps which the British police service is nonetheless taking to develop the conversational core. The area of most attention at the moment is basic social skills. The target population is predominantly the recruit and the probationer constable. It has, however, been identified that experienced officers need such skills as well to initiate and guide with confidence an encounter, particularly with those of another race (Police Training Council, 1983). The sheer size of the task is daunting, but given managerial commitment and resource I am convinced it can be achieved.

After nearly two years working upon the development of the present policing skills (human awareness) aspect of the Metropolitan Police Recruit Training syllabus, it became possible to stand back and look at the development of the conversational core across the police career spectrum. I now argue that the professional development of any police officer should follow a course of interviewing development--progressively building upon interviewing skills to fulfill a given operational or administrative role.

The Chief Constable of Merseyside, Mr. Kenneth Oxford, lent his support to this perspective. The result has been the establishment of the Merseyside Interview Development Unit--whose unit badge is the Chinese ideogram for active listening.

This is, we believe, the first police unit in the UK directed at the development of interviewing--through interviewing training and iterative research into all aspects of interviewing.

The Interview Development Unit

This is located at the Force Training Centre in Liverpool. It is staffed by a Detective Inspector and three Detective Sergeants. They constitute a most fortunate convergence of experiences. The Inspector was (and remains) Deputy to the Chief Instructor of the CID Training School located at the Training Centre. One of the sergeants had been materially involved in the tape recording trials and another had attended an Instructors' course in Policing and Community Skills which I conducted at the Training Centre. Three of the four are students on an academic course in psychology.

The officers underwent a course of training in interviewing skills and facilitator training. This enabled them, firstly, to conduct courses using experimental learning, micro-teaching and video-recording techniques and, secondly, to work upon course development and the preparation of training materials.

The Unit accommodation comprises an interviewing suite and dedicated classroom. The suite consists of a 'briefing room' and an interviewing room equipped with video-cameras which are controlled remotely from a four-monitor recording console in the adjacent Control Room. The console is connected to the classroom allowing observation to take place during the conduct of the interview.

The Interview Development Course

It was decided that the priority was a course which was directed at the development of basic interviewing skills. The four officers and I worked as a team for some six months on what is termed the Interview Development Course. It was decided to follow a philosophy which concentrated upon building the psychological bridge because so many of the strategies of questioning directed--with variable efficiency and effectiveness--at influencing the interviewee's decision making are inconsistent with the present Judges' Rules and the new Code of Practice in the Police and Criminal Evidence Act and because they are inherently wasteful given the time constraints of the Act. It was decided to develop approaches to the interviewing process which rely maximally upon an officer's ability to assess personality, to monitor changes in psychological state, to derive an initial account, to detect inconsistency within and between accounts, and to use the quality of the relationship forged with the interviewee to cope with emergent inconsistency and resistance. The whole team worked on the production of video material to inculcate this philosophy.

The course admits eight students, is residential and lasts two weeks. Thirty percent of the course is devoted to theory. This, however, is an unfortunate term since it is directed toward developing self-awareness in parallel to developing awareness of the interactive processes of perception, memory, emotion, influence and conversation. The philosophy of the course is founded upon a mutual contract of complete self-disclosure and frankness of feedback, between students and staff, who are from the outset defined as facilitators not didactic teachers. The philosophy translates into practice as effective communication founded upon openness, empathy, supportiveness, positiveness and equality. Hence every theory session has been designed to be a blend of instruction and experimental exercise. Importantly, students carry out their own personality assessment as an essential step in the process of learning how to assess systematically the personalities of others.

Practical interviewing accounts for sixty percent of the course. The earliest practicals seek to raise the consciousness of the student to a level where personal performance monitoring is accepted as part of the interviewing process. Micro-teaching and micro-counselling are themes of first level practicals. Second level practicals involve realistic length interviews. The exercises for first- and second-level practicals are based on real-life material. Role-players are volunteers drawn from the Force and slotted into character sets which reflect their real-life personalities. The Team put thousands of man-hours into producing the exercises. Speaking from a background of professional investigative interviewing training in the military and internal security settings, I feel obliged to say that these exercises are of the highest calibre I have ever seen.

Review and Prospect

The Interview Development Course represents the essential first step in the IDU role of developing specialist operational and administrative interviewing for the career span. Four validating courses have been conducted and a programme of courses is now underway. The syllabus of the Instructors' course in Policing and Community Skills now incorporates training within the Interview Development Unit. Officers--uniform and CID--are assessed for their potential to become IDU instructors, being finally assessed following an Interview Development Course as an observer and contributing in part to a second. It is acknowledged that non-selection for the role of instructor in the IDU is not a mark of failure. It is a recognition, to use an analogy, that one can be an excellent driver but be unsuited to teaching others to drive.

With regard to research to date students in the unit have contributed to projects examining listening comprehension, and the detection of truth, evasion and deception under conditions of sound only, vision only, and sound and vision, and in the case of vision conditions particular parts of the body. Research projects outside the Unit and which in due course will be examined with students include the links between personality and suggestibility, and the links between personality, physiological arousal and latency in responding to questions.

ACKNOWLEDGEMENTS

I would like to acknowledge that were it not for the Chief Constable of Merseyside, Mr. Kenneth Oxford, his Assistant Chief Constable (Personnel), Miss Alison Halford, and the Team, Detective Inspector George Moffatt and Detective Sergeants Ken Bradley, Frank Kite and Garry Watson, the Merseyside Interview Development Unit would never have emerged to face up to the reality of interviewing development: a unit whose badge summarizes its aims--getting individuals to use eyes, ears, and heart in the process of undivided attention.

REFERENCES
Hackett, P. (1978). Interviewing Skills Training. London: IPM.
Hora, T. (1959, November). Epistemological aspects of existence and psychotherapy. Journal of Individual Psychology, 15, 166-173.
Police Training Council. (1983). Community and race relationship training for the police. Report of the Working Party. London: HMSO.
Russell, L. (1972). The ABC of interviewing. London: Pitman.
Shepherd, W. E. (1984). Values into practice: The implementation and implications of Human Awareness Training. Police Journal, 57, 286-300.
Shepherd, E. W., & Levy-Halford, J. E. (1985). Listening comprehension: The forgotten aspect of interviewing training. (In preparation for submission to the Police Journal)

"SPECIAL CARE QUESTIONING" OF MENTALLY VULNERABLE VICTIMS AND WITNESSES
OF CRIME

BRYAN TULLY

The purpose of this article is to discuss the practical experience of
using 'Special Care Questioning' techniques, developed at the Psychology
Unit of the Royal Hong Kong Police Force. Special Care Questioning
refers to techniques, and the avoidance of identifiable hazards, in
obtaining accurate testimony from mentally vulnerable witnesses. In this
context, 'mentally vulnerable' witnesses may include children, the
mentally impaired, emotionally traumatized victims, and normal adults, in
circumstances where memories of vital information are poor. This latter
group has sometimes been selected to undergo 'forensic hypnosis'
procedures to recover these memories (Ault, 1980). Occasionally, our
category of 'mentally vulnerable' witnesses might include a cooperative
suspect who cannot remember well whether he carried out a certain act in
such a way that it qualifies as a serious crime. If he considers he
might have done, and is questioned in a way to improperly prompt him to
make a false confession to police, he can be considered to be vulnerable
in our sense of the word. This last type of phenomenon has been
identified as a 'memory distrust syndrome' (Gudjonsson & MacKeith,
1982). There have been a number of major unfortunate cases of
miscarriage of justice in the United Kingdom concerning such accused
persons. They are usually of below average intelligence. Our notion of
'mentally vulnerable' witnesses rests on the understanding that such
witnesses hold precariously accessible memories. In such circumstances,
the way the individual is managed, and the manner his or her memory is
examined by questioning, has a significant effect on the hazard of
testimonial error and fabrication.

The Foundations of Special Care Questioning
    The principles of Special Care Questioning can be viewed as a
practical integration of the experimental psychology of human memory, the
developmental psychology of childhood or mental immaturity, and the
social psychology of the interview. By respecting and taking account of
the weakness of human memory and effects thereon of various styles of
questioning, Special Care Questioning constitutes a safeguard against
unnecessarily damaging the veracity of testimony. In this regard Special
Care Questioning has clear advantages over forensic hypnosis. Even the
best planned practice of forensic hypnosis, such as that developed by the
F.B.I. in the United States, has been unable to shake off serious doubts
about its dangers of contributing to the fabrication of testimony through
the creation of an over-imaginative and suggestible 'set' in the
subject. This is acknowledged by an elaborate array of other safeguards
worked out to minimize the potential dangers of the procedure itself. In

the current climate of opinion, it is unlikely that the practice of forensic hypnosis will be accepted beyond the limits it has already reached. However in the effort to accomplish the best standards of forensic hypnosis practice, a number of practitioners have recognized and developed the importance of preparing witnesses appropriately. The emphasis on accomplishing comfort, relaxation, rapport, etc., and setting appropriate attitudes for accuracy and dealing with fears, doubts, and misleading expectations have all been prescribed in detail by the F.B.I. Behavioral Science Unit team (Ault, 1980) and Martin Reiser (1980). In this aspect, Special Care Questioning owes much to these practitioners.

The problem of 'suggestibility', which appeared to render as untrustworthy almost any evidence of witnesses of the kind in whom we are interested, is now much better understood. We can be clear that such generalizations about untrustworthiness are unwarranted. 'Suggestibility' is not a simple one factor 'trait' (Evans, 1967), and under specified circumstances, we now know that children's evidence can be as good as adults, and in some respects better (Dent & Stevenson, 1979; Marin, Holmes, Guth, & Kovack, 1979; Goodman & Michelli, 1981; Sheehy, 1983; Loftus & Davies, 1984). Regardless of the supposed reliability or trustworthiness of child witnesses as such, there now exist very good procedures to assess the veracity structure of statements made in certain kinds of crime, e.g., sex crimes against children (Trankell, 1972; Undeutsch, 1982). A test for "interrogative suggestibility" has been developed recently which assesses adult differences in willingness to change remembered responses under conditions of leading questions and mild pressure to shift recollections. This has permitted the hazard of "interrogative suggestibility" and its relationship with intelligence, initial degree of memory recall, self-esteem, and neuroticism, etc., to be explored (Gudjonsson, 1983, 1984a,b).

There is now a major literature on how eyewitnesses can make errors and how this can be compounded by the content of intervening questioning (Loftus, 1979; Yarmey, 1979; Shepherd, Ellis, & Davies, 1982; Bowers & Bekerian, 1983). This has established how normal adults holding 'precariously accessible memories' may be prone to errors which are easily exacerbated by uncareful questioning. Some researchers have tried to develop memory enhancement techniques that reflect some contemporary memory theory and minimize the vulnerability to errors that the eyewitness memory literature has indicated. One such attempt is the "cognitive interview" developed by Gieselman, Fisher, Firstenberg, Hutton, Sullivan, Avetissian, & Prosk (1984) at the University of California, Los Angeles.

As far as mildly mentally handicapped subjects (i.e., those whose 'handicap' is not necessarily obvious to the police) are concerned, an experimental study carried out by this author (Tully & Cahill, 1984) indicated a whole variety of questioning protocols were capable of eliciting different kinds of error when subjects were questioned about a past incident by police officers. The errors were mostly generated by an interaction of memory weakness and the kinds of questioning protocols employed by some police interviewers. Notwithstanding these findings, good examinable memory was available, and our below average intelligence subjects recalled about three quarters as much as control subjects of average intelligence.

Special Care Questioning owes something to all the above sources. A more detailed discussion of the foundations can be found elsewhere

(Tully, 1985)

Training of Police Investigators
A major part of the dissemination of 'Special Care Questioning' concepts is through teaching sessions provided to the Detective Training School of the Royal Hong Kong Police Force. A summary of this training is provided below. It is expected that detectives will make use of this education in carrying out their duties, and therefore the guidelines have to be usable by police officers. In special cases where assessments and practice requires more advanced application, staff of the Psychology Unit will become involved. The application of Special Care Questioning is broken down into three parts: (1) The assessment and preparation of the witness; (2) The questioning protocols, and their monitoring; and (3) The examination of the statement text after the interview.

The Assessment and Preparation of the Witness
We emphasize that the assessment and preparation of the witness is worth absolutely all the time spent on it. It provides the real guide to the questioning interview and helps avoid doubts and confusions, which can be more difficult to resolve once they have arisen later. Officers are taught to make basic sensible assessments of:
(1) the intellectual competence of the witness
(2) the emotional state and demeanor of the witness
(3) the attitude of the witness.

These involve 'educated judgments', and are not intended to obtain clinically precise measurements. There are sensible ways to evaluate intellectual competence, by paying attention to language content and style, and asking for accounts of witnesses' everyday activities and accomplishments. Similarly, officers are educated to notice signs of nervousness or tendencies to withdraw and give minimal responses. They learn to understand witnesses' unease or guardedness, and attempts to prematurely terminate the interview because of this. Officers are guided also to deal with overly enthusiastic witnesses who elaborate their story ever more wonderfully or tragically as they continue to enjoy being the centre of attention for perhaps one of the few times in their lives.

The attitude of witnesses to their own ability (or inability) to give a clear and helpful account of an incident can affect the degree to which they may employ imaginative guesswork. Police officers are alerted to this, and also to excessive 'social desirability' tendencies, i.e., the inability to admit any faults or failings. This can distort their testimony especially when they are the victims. Shame about a crime of sexual assault or extreme views about the police or criminals may 'colour' the kind of report they give. In addition, other preoccupations and feelings which might conflict with going through with the role of a witness or victim-witness in court need to be elicited by a police investigator if there is a likelihood these will distort what the witness is ready to say.

These assessments then form the foundation for the preparation of the witness. The assessments will have begun the process of relaxation and establishing of rapport. The environmental needs of the witness should have been identified and attended. An appropriate style of language, together with an nonthreatening and nonjudgmental posture should have been worked out. Appropriate expectations (on both sides) may have to be clarified. Management of high levels of anxiety and withdrawal behaviour may not be easy, but the investigator has to learn to be patient, help with relaxation, and patiently further build confidence by easy conversation before embarking on the witness's account. Judgment has to be used as to when to curtail interviews, or when to hold them under other conditions. 'Bluster', excessive self-confidence, and 'showing off' may also have to be managed and talked about in advance so that such a witness is brought down to earth in a tactful way. Some victim-witnesses try to cover up something of their part in the course of events because of their shame of having been deceived, looking foolish, etc. Such attempts may be uncovered in Court, and the rest of their testimony may well be discredited. Police investigators need to reassure such victims that they have simply acted as trusting persons and are not as foolish as they feel. In the face of any strong attitude which creates a likelihood of testimony being distorted, investigators are taught to anchor the importance of veracity of testimony to some compatible value identified in the witness. This may include a "higher" value of truth-telling in spite of legitimate strong feelings which are biasing an account. Alternatively, this may involve the creation of a proper anxiety that a biased account will be exposed in Court, or perhaps a flattering of the witness' intelligence that he can discriminate a particular circumstance from an overall--and perhaps defensible-attitude.

Shame or resentment about being questioned about highly personal or intimate matters calls for much care on behalf of the investigator. He or she must establish as a prerequisite that he or she has genuine sympathy, understanding and respect for how, e.g., a rape victim feels. If the victim needs to share misgivings or fears of disapproval, voyeurism, etc., on the part of the interviewer, then dealing with these is a priority. In this way, better cooperation, both at the investigative stage and at later stages of the criminal justice process, will be forthcoming.

Obtaining Accurate Witness Statements from Mentally Vulnerable Witnesses

Police officers are taught that there is an overwhelming wisdom in collecting an early statement as 'free recall', i.e., entirely in the words of the witness and with absolutely minimal prompting. It is likely to contain the fewest inaccuracies; and in style, content, and extent, it remains an important benchmark measure of memory against which future questionings can be compared.

Such narratives, collected as above, often do lack fullness. However, just how full an account needs to be for its primary purpose is something we counsel investigators to think about. There is a tendency for police officers to try to obtain every scrap of information they possibly can 'in case' some of it may be needed. We have shown in our research that relentless searches for detailed descriptions of everything leads to increasing errors. Officers are taught first to ask open, non-leading and clarifying questions. Investigators are briefed on the variety of hazards to accurate recollection that can occur, and bearing in mind their initial assessments of the witness, they should be able to avoid them. These 'hazards' have been described in detail elsewhere (Tully & Cahill, 1984; Tully, 1985), but they include the following kinds of things. Some witnesses have a tendency to "fill in" a gap in their memory by making inferences based on "common sense" about what must have happened. Some witnesses search for leading 'cues' in questions in order to give a 'right' answer. Where interviewers offer a choice of answers, e.g., was a suspect tall or short, there is a strong tendency for one to be chosen--and then a guesstimate to be made, when in reality that

witness may not have been in a position to judge this. Where
interviewers elicit a string of "don't knows" from some witnesses, there
may be a tendency to offer some kind of gift answer to save
embarrassment. Some fifteen different categories of questioning protocol
have been identified as particularly relevant to witnesses with below
average intelligence levels (Tully & Cahill, 1984).

Investigators are encouraged to record contemporaneously the accounts
they elicit from mentally vulnerable witnesses. If possible, interviews
should be taped.

Examining Statement Texts for Truthfulness in Cases of Alleged Sexual Assaults Against Children and Young Persons

The principles of examining statement texts for truthfulness in cases
of alleged sexual assaults against children is now well established
(e.g., Undeutsch, 1982). We follow these guidelines in looking for
spontaneity in accounts, emotional commentaries and reactions, lack of
competence to invent crime specific details, a plausible context for the
alleged offences, and imperfect memories consistent with the intellectual
status of the person.

A major problem is that in the usual course of events, initial police
statement-takers marshall the accounts they are given into a sanitized,
well ordered and unambiguous format for the benefit and convenience of
their senior investigators and the Courts. Whilst this procedure does
often assist the processing of large volumes of witness materials--for
both investigatory and judicial purposes--in the case of mentally
vulnerable witnesses, it essentially removes most of the idiosyncratic
features necessary for making this kind of textual assessment.
Subsequent interviews may also be affected by the fact that a witness may
have had his or her account collected in such a systematic fashion
several times. One of the last men to be hanged for murder in Great
Britain, and then pardoned posthumously, was Timothy Evans. He was of
below average intelligence and shared a house with John Reginald Christie
who was later convicted of multiple murders. Evans gave several
self-incriminating statements to the British police, and key sections
concerning the actual killing of his wife and child were shown by
linguistic analysis to have a distinct syntactic structure from the rest
of the material. It is very likely that this reflected the influence of
the interviewing police officers. These analyses were not admitted to
Court during his trial, but they were examined by the subsequent
Parliamentary inquiry which finally exonerated Evans. Forensic
linguistics, whilst illuminating in this case, has not become popularized
since then (Svartvik, 1968). However, variants of this methodology have
enabled historians to determine probable authorship of questioned ancient
documents.

Ideally, Special Care Questioning interviews should be carried out as
soon as possible if this textual examination is to be done. In between
the early interview and later Special Care Questioning can occur all
kinds of events and experiences which may distort full veracity. In Hong
Kong some traditional families believe that anything bad or shameful
should be kept quiet and forgotton. If the investigatory process becomes
too intrusive and frequent, a degree of non-cooperation is likely to
emerge. Investigators carrying out follow-up interviews may not realize
that the overriding concern for the family is that ordinary routines,
such as going to school, are not disrupted more than absolutely
necessary, lest some explanation has to be given to others.

The Role of the Psychology Unit of the Royal Hong Kong Police Force in
Supporting the Practice of Special Care Questioning

The Psychology Unit of the Royal Hong Kong Police Force is staffed by
two clinical psychologists. It has also had the benefit of an attachment
of a Chief Inspector of Police who has undergone formal training in
forensic hypnosis at the F.B.I. Behavioral Science Unit. Apart from
teaching, staff from the unit may contribute to the questioning of
vulnerable witnesses on request by criminal investigation units. In one
case a traumatized young nurse was taken back through her recollections
of the murder of her fiancé when they had been out walking together in
the park. There was a strong element of guilt involved as she had spent
some time cradling her dying boyfriend after he was stabbed and had not
noticed that his abdomen was swelling from internal hemorrhaging. Unable
initially to give any description of the attacker, she was eventually
able to reconstruct an identi-kit picture of him. In this case "guided
imagery techniques" were used to enhance recall. There is now
significant evidence of the effectiveness of these techniques if employed
in a context of special care (Malpass & Devine, 1981; Gieselman et al.,
1984). One further interesting and gratifying effect accomplished was
that the young woman witness told us that after this session she felt she
was 'at rest' about this tragic event for the first time.

In another case, a 14-year-old girl was brought to the Psychology
Clinic on the grounds that having been kidnapped for several days and
forcibly sexually assaulted, it was thought she would not be able to
stand up to the stress of a Court appearance and cross examination, etc.
Her mother, who had been present during initial interviews, had declared
that there was no way her daughter could have agreed to get involved with
such terrible acts. What had occurred was the most serious of crimes.
The detectives were, however, not so certain about the girl's story as
she didn't seem distressed enough by what she was telling them. It
turned out that this girl was intimidated by her overstrict mother and
had run away from home and gone voluntarily to stay with some boys she
had met before. She had engaged in sexual relations voluntarily as she
had done on a previous occasion.

In other cases, staff from the psychology unit have interviewed
children who have been sexually assaulted when criminal investigation
teams have raised suspicions as to whether a little girl had been
deliberately unwilling to reveal the name of her attacker out of fear or
shame, or how far a little boy may have suffered emotional damage by a
particularly obscene and prolonged sexual assault. Most recently, we
have been asked to extend our teaching to the teachers and social workers
employed by the Hong Kong Mental Handicap Association. They have
reported cases of their students being sexually molested and the
difficulties which they have had both with the police and the Courts. It
is our hope that 'Special Care Questioning' will provide a bridge between
the vulnerable of society, those who care for them, and the criminal
justice system, which surely should protect them above all.

REFERENCES

Ault, R. (1980, January). Hypnosis, the FBI's team approach. F.B.I. Law
    Enforcement Bulletin, 5-8.
Bowers, J., & Bekerian, D. (1983). When will post-event information
    distort eyewitness testimony? Journal of Applied Psychology.

Dent, H., & Stevenson, G. (1979). An experimental study of the
effectiveness and different techniques of questioning child
witnesses. British Journal of Social and Clinical Psychology, 18,
41-51.

Evans, F. (1967). Suggestibility in the normal waking state.
Psychological Review, 67(2), 114-129.

Gieselman, R., Fisher, R., Firstenberg, I., Hutton, L., Sullivan, S.,
Avetissian, I., & Prosk, A. (1984). Enhancement of eyewitness
memory: An empirical evaluation of the cognitive interview. Journal
of Police Science and Administration, 12, 74-80.

Goodman, G., & Michelli, J. (1981, November). Would you believe a child
witness? Psychology Today, 82-95.

Gudjonsson, G. (1983). Suggestibility, intelligence, memory recall, and
personality: An experimental study. British Journal of Psychiatry,
142, 35-37.

Gudjonsson, G. (1984a). A new scale of interrogative suggestibility.
Personality and Individual Differences, 5, 303-314.

Gudjonsson, G. (1984b). Interrogative suggestibility and its relationship with self-esteem and control. Journal of the Forensic Science
Society, 24, 99-110.

Gudjonsson, G., & MacKeith, J. A. (1982). False confessions.
Psychological effects of interrogation. A discussion paper. In A.
Trankell (Ed.), Reconstructing the past: The role of psychologists in
criminal trials. Stockholm, Sweden: P.A. Norstedt & Söners Forlag.

Loftus, E. (1979). Eyewitness testimony. Cambridge, MA: Harvard
University Press.

Loftus, E., & Davies, G. (1984). Distortions in children's memory.
Unpublished manuscript.

Malpass, R., & Devine, P. (1981). Guided memory in eyewitness
identification. Journal of Applied Psychology, 66, 343-350.

Marin, B., Holmes, D., Guth, M., & Kovack, P. (1979). The potential of
children as eyewitnesses. Law and Human Behavior, 3, 295-305.

Reiser, M. (1980). Handbook of investigative hypnosis. Los Angeles, CA:
LEHI Publishing Co.

Sheehy, N. (1983). The child as witness. Unpublished manuscript,
University of Wales Institute of Science and Technology.

Shepherd, J., Ellis, H., & Davies, G. (1982). Identification evidence.

Svartvik, J. (1968). The Evans statements, a case for forensic
linguistics. Sweden: Gothenberg University Press.

Trankell, A. (1972). Reliability of evidence. Stockholm, Sweden:
Rotobeckman.

Tully, B. (1985). 'Special care questioning'. FBI Law
Enforcement Bulletin.

Tully, B., & Cahill, D. (1984). Police interviewing of the mentally
handicapped: An experimental study. London, UK: The Police
Foundation.

Undeutsch, U. (1982). Statement reality analysis. In A. Trankell,
(Ed.), Reconstructing the past: The role of psychologists in criminal
trials. Stockholm, Sweden: P.A. Norstedt & Söners Forlag.

Yarmey, A. P. (1979). The psychology of eyewitness testimony.
New York: The Free Press.

POLICE AND PUBLIC PERCEPTIONS OF THE POLICE ROLE: MOVING TOWARDS A
REAPPRAISAL OF POLICE PROFESSIONALISM

SANDRA JONES

INTRODUCTION

This outline is arranged in two parts. The first section presents a
brief resume of some relevant findings from a major survey of the police
and the public conducted by the author, which had implications for the
training of British police officers. The second raises for discussion
some of the current work in which I am engaged with my colleagues at the
Centre for the Study of Community and Race Relations at Brunel
University. In particular, it explores the nature of police
professionalism, its appropriateness for policing an increasingly
multi-cultural, complex and ambiguous society, and the mismatch between
present police training and effective professional practice.

POLICE AND PUBLIC PERCEPTIONS: THE HUMAN FACTOR IN POLICING

Following the post-mortem of the 1981 civil disorders in the United
States, one might be excused for believing that dissatisfaction with the
police in Britain is a 'minority' pursuit. Indeed, the numerous surveys
of public opinion over the last two decades would, at face value, provide
support for this comforting assumption. Substantial evidence that this
is a seriously deficient concept of the police-public relationship
problem comes from a survey of the public and the police in two police
force areas (Jones 1983) that appears to represent polar extremes in
policing philosophies. The fact that the general finding about the
quality of relationships apply in both police force areas gives added
significance since it suggests that these relationships are in some
measure independent of the particular policing philosophy or style
adopted by Chief Officers.

Public and Police Evalutions of Police Effectiveness

The research focussed primarily on the relationship between the public
and their local police (though it was concerned also with factors such as
public usage and expectations of service, and public and police
perceptions of crime and policing in general). Within the context of an
attitudinal survey, the approach adopted was to construct an overall
image of the police using three sources of data. The first concerned
public satisfaction with their police and their attitudes towards them,
inferred from an area household sample of 960 people, aged 14 and
upwards. The qualitative reasons given by the public for their expressed
level of satisfaction proved to be of particular interest in this
respect. The second involved an assessment of police estimates of these
public attitudes, inferred from a total sample of 365 police officers,
drawn at random and representative of all ranks up to Superintendent. By
combining these two sources of attitudinal data, it was possible to

highlight the differences between the way the public see their police and how the police believe they are seen. The final dimension of the overall police self-image is derived from a parallel study of police officers' attitudes towards the Police Service as an organization and specifically focuses on their attitudes towards police work as an occupation.

Public explanations for their satisfaction or dissatisfaction with their local police pointed to the importance of the quality of encounters between the public and the police in determining satisfaction since they illustrate that judgments based on these encounters reflect, and are the result of, the image presented by the individual police officer. Regardless of whether the individual's experience of the police had been in connection with service, traffic or crime, it was the interpersonal skills reflected in his/her helpfulness, courtesy, kindness and tolerance which 'personalize' the police image and by which the 'police' are collectively judged. In other words, it is the human quality of police work which has decisive impact on people's personal evaluations.

By way of contrast with these public evaluations, the survey of police officers demonstrated their preoccupation with measures of their professional efficiency. Public satisfaction was attributed to the quick (in terms of response rates) and efficient service that the police provide the public and the fact that the police 'success rate', especially for major crimes, is good. Only a minority of the officers interviewed gave as their principal reason for public satisfaction that it was based on the 'personalized' image of the police. Police officers also substantially and consistently over-estimated the extent of favourable public attitudes toward those aspects of their role which directly reflect the operational dimensions of police work, particularly when these attitudes concerned the police subcultural view of 'real' police work.

The Police Self-Image

Further evidence for this 'technical' self-image comes from the parallel study of police officers' attitudes towards the Police Service as an organization (Jones 1982), including an examination of the way police officers view their occupation. As part of this study, the police officers were asked whether they thought police work was a job, a vocation or a profession, and they were asked to judge the skill level of the work they presently did. A 'professional', managerial viewpoint was prevalent, even amongst the younger, junior ranks. There was an interesting difference between the two police forces in this respect in that although the trend across ranks was the same, more officers of all ranks in the 'traditional', more reactive force viewed police work as a profession than did officers in the force with a community-based style of policing. The technical or 'craft' emphasis of this professional orientation was illustrated by police officers' attitudes towards, for example, the importance of experience and specialization, and their questioning of the relevance of academic achievement to practical policing. Police officers, particularly young junior officers, believe that professional policing skills are best achieved through practical experience, and experience, in this sense includes specialization.

Whilst it is relatively easy to document the salient factors which have contributed to this technically efficient professional self-image*, the

---

* It is important to note that this is not the only model of professionalism which currently exists within the British police service, but it has rapidly become the dominant one, displacing the 'practical' craft professional model which was most prevalent up until the mid-sixties.

importance of these findings lies in their implications for police-community relations. The clear evidence of this survey is that it is the human rather than the efficiency factor which determines whether the police are seen to be effective and by which their success is judged in all their major activities; and this is the case whether relationships are 'good' or 'poor', or whichever policing style is adopted. Of course, it may be that the 'public' takes for granted a high level of technical efficiency which is why they place a premium on presentation.

Implications for Training

It has long been argued (see, for example, Cain, 1973) that the 'new technology of policing' has served to create physical distance between the police and the public. This research suggests, however, that the consequences of this technologically-contrived distance are more far-reaching in that the police already believe that their effectiveness is judged by the public on their technical skills. In other words, there is evidence of psychological distance between the police and the 'majority' of the public which is independent of the style of policing adopted. If this belief is sustained (and reinforced by organizational production pressures such as the need to produce tangible evidence of their efficiency), the result can only be a widening of the gap, both physically and psychologically, between the public and the police. As that gap increases, the logical result is that the police will become even more dependent on organizational, rather than community-based, norms as a frame of reference, thus perpetuating the cycle. There is a real danger, then, that the police will take it for granted that their perception of their role corresponds to that which the public expects them to fulfill. Unless and until the police become more aware that public judgments of their 'collective' role are based on the interpersonal skills of the individual officer, they risk losing 'majority' approval when they encounter the public.

It is self-evident from this research that skill in routine human interactions is a prerequisite for effective policing. Indeed, this is recognized by British recruit training which now incorporates interpersonal skills training as one element of the social skills of policing (SSPO) package. However, whilst this is an important recognition of the value of, and need for, these skills, the question remains about the role of training in developing an 'expert' model of professional policing which stresses the need for technical efficiency in the law-enforcement role often at the expense of the 'publicly' valued 'service' functions of policing. The initial training task must be to convince the police themselves (for the public already are convinced) that these service goals are primary (and, indeed, facilitate their law-enforcement role) and to substitute for their self-image as omnipotent 'expert' professionals, a recognition that their 'professionalism' resides in their ability to maintain public confidence, promote public solidarity (both against crime and for its own sake), to channel information, and, along with other professionals and agencies to respond to public 'wants' rather than to impose a paternalistic concept of public 'needs'. Clearly, this indicates the need for the development, through the training process, of a more flexible and responsive model of professionalism.

COMMUNITY AND RACE RELATIONS TRAINING: EXPLORING PROFESSIONAL PRACTICE

At Brunel we are currently engaged in a collaborative exercise with police managers and trainers to develop Community and Race Relations (C.R.R.) Training following the recommendations of the Police Training Council Working Party Report (Home Office, 1983). Three of the major recommendations were that community and race relations should be an integral part of all training courses (i.e., it should run across the curriculum including law topics rather than be taught as an isolated subject); that it should apply to all ranks and specialists; and importantly, that it should relate to practical policing. Significant criticisms of current training related to the content, context and credibility of C.R.R. training. Apart from stating that what effective police officers need is a full working knowledge of their local community and the right attitude and skills to carry out their duties without giving unnecessary offence, the report says that, in practice, police officers need an "adequate conception of their various, and sometimes conflicting, roles and an appreciation of the part that each can play in cementing relations with the community". Not only is this a recognition of the existence within policing of the tension between the service and law-enforcment roles, it is a clear indication that the professional (and subcultural) ideology of the police should derive from all their various functions rather than just the technical law-enforcement role.

The Mismatch Between Current Training and Effective Professional Practice

The criticisms about the practical applicability of current C.R.R. training suggests that there is a mismatch between the training and effective professional practice. Indeed, much the same criticism can be made of police training generally. It would not be too harsh to suggest that much of current police training not only fails to meet the demands of operational reality but, by the emphasis and value it puts upon the technical and law-based topics, develops and sustains the technically efficient 'expert' model of professionalism which, as research demonstrates, is antithetical to the maintainence of harmonious community relations. In common with other professions which have developed (to varying degrees) an 'expert' model of professional practice, this mismatch leads to a significant credibility gap. That this is a problem shared by other professionals is evidenced by the work of Metcalfe who demonstrates that medical training is designed to produce behaviour which is diametrically opposed to the demands of medical practice and that it produces doctors who are one of two types (Metcalfe, 1979). The first are victims who cannot adjust to the disparity between training and practice and end up by trying to resolve anxiety by maintaining a rigid and authoritarian stance. The second group are those that can maintain flexibility and, thus, capability for growth, in spite of the system.

My colleague, Richard Joss, has adapted this model and applied it to police training. He argues that police trainees carry over the rigidity of thinking referred to by Metcalfe but, in addition, translate this into the operational context by early socialization. The training has the effect of producing convergent thinkers who are subject to a high degree of conformity and who are armed with a high level of informational knowledge of the law rather than effective frameworks for applying this knowledge in interpersonal relationships (Joss, 1985). In policing, this is all the more obvious because of the relative lack of a coherent theory of professional practice or body of 'esoteric' knowledge. It is this credibility gap which leads to the recruit being socialized into the norms and procedures of his working group, and the cynical view of the training school as the 'dream factory'.

It is the analysis of the mismatch between training and practice which provides the starting point for the development of a model of professionalism which is more appropriate to the ever-changing, complex, ambiguous and multi-cultural society within which police and other professionals operate. This would require identifying the characteristics of those professionals who are, in Metcalfe's terms, able to survive and grow. Important characteristics are likely to be the development of independence and divergent thinking, the recognition that encounters are active and interactive, the ability to apply principles (rather than set responses) within situations, an understanding of the processes involved in working situations with clients, the ability to work in high uncertainty areas, the ability to develop effectiveness through personal relationships with clients, the understanding that policing occurs in a public-controlled environment, and, that effective practice requires flexibility and humility.

Training for Effectiveness

It is these characteristics that training for effective professional practice (and not just in policing) should aim to develop. Many of them are implicit in the model of the reflective practitioner developed by Schon (1983) which is being examined in the context of the review of probationer training currently being conducted by MacDonald at the Centre for Applied Research in Education, University of East Anglia. Whilst Schon's model recognizes that there are some practice situations, such as emergencies, etc., where decisive 'expert' action is essential; the self-image is, nevertheless, one in which professionals recognize that their technical expertise is embedded in a context of meanings and that their actions may have different meanings for the client than was intended. It is central to this model that the professional actively seeks to discover, in a collaborative manner with the client, what these meanings are in order to make them accessible to the client. The professional's claim to authority lies in the ability to manifest special knowledge in collaborative interactions with the client. Professional growth and flexibility is achieved through reflection on the thoughts and actions that constitute professional practice. This form of professionalism is based on a reflective contract with the client, and as such, it makes the professional more accountable than the traditional contract. In a reflective contract, the client does not agree to accept the practitioners authority but to suspend disbelief in it. Importantly, the model recognizes the relevance of other people's experience and knowledge in the interactions between clients and professionals. Unlike the practical professional model of policing (which also has an experiential but 'trial and error' craft base), the reflective professional does not seek to take exclusive control of situations; nor does he/she deny the relevance of theoretical principles to professional practice or that these can be learnt other than by long experience of coping with actual situations. And, unlike the 'expert' model in which the professional is presumed to know all the answers, the reflective model also recognizes that uncertainty can be a source of learning.

The training implications of this model derive from the fact that (i) it emphasizes the need for interactive skills, and (ii) responses are situationally dependent. Since reflective practitioners select their responses in the light of their reflection about the situation as it unfolds, there is no single prescribed set of rules for action;

346

guidelines within which discretion operates would be more appropriate. Training should emphasize the principles involved and encourage the use of reflection in order to understand how action is dependent upon and continually modified by context and the meanings ascribed by other participants in the situation. In this way the intuitive processes in which effective professionals engage can be made explicit and built into the training practice. Clearly such a model involves a significant shift away from the mainly information-based training which currently predominates in police training establishments, as well as an examination of the appropriateness of current teaching methods and styles. It involves engaging in what Argyris and Schon (1974) describe as 'double-loop', as contrasted with 'single-loop', learning. It is the appropriateness of this form of professionalism and its implications for training in community and race relations which we are beginning to explore with police training practitioners.

REFERENCES

Argyris, C., & Schon, D. A. (1974). Theory in practice: Increasing professional effectiveness. San Francisco: Jossey-Bass.

Cain, M. E. (1973). Society and the policeman's role. London: Routledge and Kegan Paul.

Jones, S.J. (1983). Police-public relationships: A study of the police and public's perceptions of each other. Unpublished research report by the Department of Social Administration, University College, Cardiff.

Jones, S. J. Police inter-rank attitudes: A survey of police officers' attitudes towards their organization. Unpublished research report prepared by the Department of Social Administration, University College, Cardiff.

Joss, R. A., & Jones, S. J. Toward a mismatch model of police training and operations. In preparation.

Metcalfe, D. (1979, July). The long term view. Paper given at a Symposium on Interprofessional Learning. Nottingham University.

Police Training Council. (1983, February). Working party report on community and race relations training for the police. Home Office.

Schon, D. A. (1983). The reflective practitioner: How professionals think in action. London: Temple Smith.

THE PSYCHOLOGIST AS AN AGENT FOR CHANGE

MARY MANOLIAS

In many Western nations it is scarcely recognized that the psychologist has any role at all with respect to the police organization. In other nations, although the psychologist may occasionally be invited to advise on specific issues, his place remains firmly fixed outside the system. Psychological research into police matters is generally tolerated but it is rarely welcomed. Its findings are more often regarded with suspicion or explained away, rather than noted and acted on. At best the psychologist's services will be viewed as an unnecessary luxury. In the more enlightened environments that exist in places such as Canada and the United States, the psychologist is an accepted part of the police organization, but even there he rarely finds himself in a position to influence the organization. Sometimes he will get quite closely involved in real police activities when his help is required for crime profiling or hostage negotiation, and he may also be able to exert a certain amount of influence through the training medium. However, in the main he is confined to the peripheral roles of gatekeeper and healer with the bulk of his working time devoted to selection and counselling. Clearly, those are both worthy tasks but at the same time an extravagant and inefficient use of valuable psychologial skills.

Clearly, the psychologist has a long way to go, but the psychologist can and should be more closely integrated into the police system. He should be enabled to act as a catalyst to intervene at various levels and nodes within the organization to assist it in functioning more effectively. Target areas for action might range from disagreements between personnel to smoothing the way for the introduction of new technology and to aiding the organization in reacting in a positive way to the ever changing demands of modern society. He does not require any specialist or background in management. His professional understanding of human behaviour and group processes and his training in interpersonal skills put him in an ideal position to act as an organizational catalyst. There is a wide variety of techniques he may choose to employ for his purpose. They include quality circles, simulations and games, workshops and brainstorming methods. In fact, he can make use of any group process which assists the participants in getting a perspective on their problems and formulating a solution.

A small Human Factors group with the United Kingdom Home Office (the equivalent of the Ministry of the Interior or Home Affairs in other countries) has experimented with variations on these techniques over a period of several years. In particular, it has made quite extensive use of the workshop method in the area of Police Research and Development. Most of the applications have been directed toward practical projects such as Control Room Design, training for Command and Control, graded response and status and location encoding.

Workshop groups are usually made up of between twelve and twenty individuals with a common interest in the topic under consideration. Each participant will bring his own unique expertise and experience to the event. They are there to learn together through sharing their knowledge and ideas, and every contribution to that process must be considered to carry the same weight and value. To help put everyone on an equal footing, rank structure and titles are temporarily put aside. Each workshop is a unique event and its actual format depends on the subject chosen and on the requirements of the various parties represented. The participants often become so deeply involved in the discussion topic that the workshop will run itself. Despite the apparent informality, the success of the workshop approach does, in fact, depend on careful preparations beforehand and a well defined underlying structure. Everyone who is expected to attend the workshop is encouraged to direct their attention to the topic well in advance of the actual event. This can be achieved in a variety of ways. For instance, background reading material, a questionnaire, or a series of handouts can be circulated in advance, or delegates can be requested to prepare a short presentation on a selected aspect of the topic.

The basic agenda for each workshop will be determined by the participants at the start of proceedings, but there should always be an experienced co-ordinator present who will have the responsibility for monitoring its progress. The co-ordinator's task is to ensure that each delegate is able to make an effective contribution and that discussion is directed to the stated topic. He also has the authority to extend the time spent on any activity that is going well or to suggest a change of direction or technique if progress becomes difficult. Amongst the techniques that may be employed to promote creative ideas are word charts, round robins and small group projects. These techniques all require that any items discussed are also written down and therefore help to ensure a valid record of the event.

The method has proved extremely popular with police officers. They are not often given the opportunity by police management to express their views, and they appreciate being involved in the decision making process. Instead of having advice dictated to them by outside experts, they are allowed to retain the ownership of both the problem and its solution.

The most ambitious application of the workshop method to date has been in a study of Police Stress carried out on behalf of the Association of Chief Police Officers (ACPO) of England and Wales. This project was initiated in response to the growing concern that had been expressed over several years (from 1975 onwards) by the representative bodies within the Police Service over the whole question of occupational stress and its possible link with the health and effective performance of serving officers. The study was to be a preliminary investigation into the nature and extent of the problem with a view to identifying its causes and effects and, where appropriate, to make recommendations for remedial action. The more usual, traditional research methods with their precise impersonal measurement techniques were rejected as unsuitable for the particular circumstances of the inquiry. Stress was seen to be a problem that concerned every level and every aspect of the police organization and which extended beyond the working environment into the domestic circumstances of individual officers. A rather different approach was required, one which would provide a comprehensive overview of this new (for the UK police) and complex area.

At the same time, it was important that the study should be completed within a reasonably short time span and, if possible, include some suggestions for a start to remedial action. The workshop approach offered a method that could fulfill all these requirements. It also provided an opportunity for actively involving ordinary police officers in the project. Only they had a sufficiently intimate knowledge of the lifestyle and culture to be able to understand the problems associated with police work. An objective viewpoint could be supplied by inviting selected specialist advisers. The workshops would provide an internal setting for interaction and promote the free exchange of ideas and information.

The project was run in three phases. In the first phase a directing workshop produced an overview of the topic. Senior officers (i.e., Chief Superintendent and Superintendents) from five British Police Forces were assisted by a team of specialist advisers. These advisers were drawn from a variety of backgrounds ranging from the psychoanalytic to the experimental with medical and occupational health viewpoints also represented. The workshop process developed a particularly productive relationship between the specialist and the police. Its main value lay in the mutual learning and the joint development of a better understanding of the problem. Together they mapped out the overall workshop and planned a strategy for the enquiry. Several main areas of concern were identified and were assigned to different groups for indepth investigation.

The second phase consisted of five "in force" workshops run in parallel. These were organized by the senior officers who attended the first workshops with backup assistance from the Home Office. The participants were ordinary police officers, mainly constables and sergeants, although other ranks were represented with at least two invited specialists to provide outside "expert" input. It was considered that the contents of the detailed discussions were extremely important and should be recorded and so a team of technical writers was employed to produce a structured and readable report on the proceedings of each workshop.

In phase three of the project, the delegates from the directing workshop reconvened to interpret and organize the data derived from their pooled experiences. The combined findings were distilled into a blueprint for future action on police stress. The conclusions fell into two main categories: those concerned with trauma and those concerned with management.

Exposure to traumatic incidents was identified in this study as a major source of acute stress. Such incidents are by definition unpleasant and disturbing, and challenge the individual's adjustive capacities, posing a significant threat to his or her psychological and physical well-being. Three major types of traumatic incidents were highlighted: criminal violence and abuse, involving both self and others; accident and mutilation, for example, road traffic or suicide casualites; and public order situations, for example, riots.

There were seen to be several points of concern. Firstly, the question of the new recruits' inevitable first encounter with traumatic incidents, their reactions, and the cost of those reactions. Secondly, with repeated encounters officers learned to cope with such incidents and to defend themselves against their impact. Such learning might have a hidden cost (e.g., insensitivity), and the person's coping strategies may not be totally effective.

For some officers and on some occasions, there would be a significant and detectable effect of traumatic incidents. The immediate emotional and behavioural response to the situation might impair the officer's performance and, in conflict situations, aggravate the problem. However, effects on officers might only become obvious later. The duration of these effects could vary considerably from individual to individual, and it was not easy to predict how long they would last.

Several processes appeared to contribute to these problems. First, officers might identify with those involved in the incident, or be directly involved themselves, and thus be threatened. Second, they might become involved with the victims of the trauma, and feel for them, and be frustrated by the constraints on offering help. Third, officers might be totally unable to intervene, for example, they might witness, but be unable to prevent, death; then they feel "helpless", in part, reflecting their unrealistic expectations concerning their powers of intervention. Finally, officers might not be properly prepared for, and supported in, these stressful duties.

Several recommendations were made both for immediate and sustained action. The conclusions reached on management issues came under three main headings: management style, management systems and management support. Management style was defined as the manner in which managers control others and it is influenced by attitudes, behaviour, personality traits and the climate of the organization itself. Poor management styles were identified as producing more widespread and long-term stresses in police officers than did their operational tasks. The pressures of police work together with inadequate training and fear of making mistakes were seen to foster a negative and fault-finding management style. Even the most senior ranks feared criticism and often sought a scapegoat. Excessive attention to minutiae suffocated innovative ability and made people reluctant to exercise discretion in a rapidly changing society.

The aspects of poor management highlighted by the preliminary workshops as specifically affecting the performance and health of all officers were:
- Unjust criticism/scapegoating
- Lack of counselling skills
- Unrealistic expectations
- Attitudes to "PC" rank
- Lack of concern for the individual
- Lack of communication
- Excessive autocracy/lack of consultation

Management systems were described as the framework of processes and procedures which should enable the police force to provide an effective service to the public in a changing society. A good management system would provide both guidance for the efficient management of resources whilst at the same time taking into account the needs of individual officers in the service. It should produce officers who were competent in their role, and provide them with the necessary support to fulfill their functions. It should also enable managers to respond to change. It might do this by stimulating consultation at all levels, providing support and making sure that expectations were at a realistic level in the selection, training and control of the officers in their charge. Many of the pressures in existing systems were perceived to stem from giving officers unrealistic expectations and then perpetrating these expectations via appraisals and boards in a way that lacked openness and an honesty of purpose.

Management support was seen as the support offered to the individual and organization in the areas of health, welfare, education, counselling, role conflicts and service demands on the individual officer and his family. It determines the organizational climate by which the individual police officer can truly feel involved and a committed member of the force. The Force must be seen to be equally committed to the officer's well-being in its policies and by a system of genuine consultation. It should produce the kind of climate which will take into account the operational, personal and professional aspects of the police service. A considerable number of recommendations were made in each of those categories. It is interesting to note that they included suggestions for the wider use of psychologists in selection and counselling, and there was also a demand for the application of the workshop approach in further exploring management methods.

COMMUNITY LIAISON SPECIALISTS - A BRITISH PERSPECTIVE

SUSAN V. PHILLIPS

INTRODUCTION

The study described in this paper was commissioned by the British Home Office during 1980, eventually commenced in 1983 and was completed in 1985. Its initial purpose was to examine the role, function and training of police community liaison officers in England and Wales, with the further aim of making recommendations for the organization of community liaison.

Methodology

The investigation was approached in two stages. The aim of the first stage was to gain a broad overview of the field by seeking information from each of the 43 police forces; some of which were known to have community liaison departments whilst others did not have such departments. A questionnaire was designed to elicit information about the organization of community liaison, the tasks performed by community liaison officers (CLOs), selection and training of CLOs and attitudes towards community liaison.

The second stage of the study aimed to provide the detail and validation inevitably lacking in questionnaire responses. This was achieved through making visits of about 2 weeks duration to a small number of forces. Analysis of the questionnaires returned by 42 of the 43 forces provided the foundation for this second stage.

By the end of 1983, 31 out of the 42 forces (74%) had established community liaison departments and 38 (90%) had appointed community liaison officers. More than half of the departments had been formed since 1981, suggesting that the Scarman Report (1981) following the 1981 disturbances had facilitated development in the community liaison field. Indeed 19 of the 31 forces with community liaison departments recorded organizational changes involving increased initiatives in community liaison work following the Scarman inquiry.

The wide variation in both force and community structure throughout England and Wales meant that it was unrealistic to search for a typical police force for the detailed study. Instead, what was attempted was the selection of a range of forces which would, as far as possible, represent the variety of structures identified in the questionnaire analysis. The factors taken into consideration in the selection of the forces for detailed study were:
- the size of the force
- the policing style adopted (e.g., the force's use of community constables)
- the stability of the community liaison structure
- whether the force area was predominantly urban or rural

- the ethnic and demographic composition of the force area.

The intention was to strike a balance between these factors and the presence or absence of a community liaison department. In addition, training courses identified as being available to officers from more than one force were visited where possible and a few days of the programme sampled.

During the second stage, three research methods were used:
- unstructured open-ended interviews
- participant observation of CLOs pursuing their normal duties or attending courses
- diary analyses completed by the CLOs for 10 working days after the fieldwork visit.

A working definition of community liaison was developed. The practical effect of this definition was to exclude from consideration roles later found placed in some forces within their community liaison departments, e.g., crime prevention, juvenile liaison, press/public relations.

Initially, four forces were to be studied in this kind of detail. In the event six forces were included in order to strike a balance between policing environments--inner city, urban and rural, and organizational approach--that is whether or not a force had a community liaison department or specially designated community liaison officers.

The six forces selected for study were spread across England, no Welsh forces were selected and the Metropolitan force was omitted from consideration because it was felt that a two week visit, which was all that time allowed, would be insufficient to accurately report on the force's approach to community liaison, also much research attention had recently focused on the Metropolitan Police (e.g., the P.S.I. Report of 1983; the Scarman Report on the Brixton riots in 1981). As publicity of this kind tends to get generalized to the police force as a whole, it seemed important to turn attention to the provincial forces. The six forces selected ranged in size from one of the smallest forces with an establishment of 1140 and a population density of 0.70 per acre, to the largest provincial force with an establishment of 6684 and a population density of 12.03 per acre. Three of the forces had long established community liaison departments, i.e., well prior to 1981; one had no department at the time of the study, and two had recently developed departments.

Field work visits in the larger forces were concentrated on two or three divisions which would give a flavour of the force area. These were selected by prior consultation with senior officers and allowed for a pattern of three days on average spent with each CLO out on division and a shorter visit to headquarters.

The level of cooperation experienced was high, with most CLOs relaxing under scrutiny by the end of the first day. Some of the CLOs had little warning of the researcher's visit, others had kept their diaries relatively free of engagements, though none had cancelled commitments. Some officers deliberately made informal visits to their main contacts in the community to enable the researcher to talk with them about police/community liaison. Where meetings were scheduled, the researcher accompanied the CLO and was introduced on arrival. On only one occasion was she asked to leave a meeting. Where the CLO set his own hours, the researcher made the necessary early start or late finish and used the free time to fit in extra interviews. In this way divisional or subdivisional commanders or their deputies, community constables, and shift sergeants were included in the study.

ORGANIZATIONAL STRUCTURE

Typically, community liaison officers are located both at headquarters and on division. Increasingly, the subdivision is becoming a significant organizational unit and some CLO posts are subdivisional. Table 1 summarizes background information and the organizational structure adopted for community liaison in each of the forces studied.

Each force with an existing community liaison department had some structure at headquarters. This varied from what was essentially a 'one man band' to a team embracing a wide range of specialisms.

All the forces agreed that the purpose of a headquarters department was to gain an overall picture of the whole force area. This wide overview is complemented by a coordinating function whereby initiatives originating on divisions can be matched against policy and vice versa. A community liaison presence in headquarters was felt to be important because of the potential for influencing policy decisions. There was a widespread belief that for the community relations ethos to permeate the whole force, there needed to be commitment from officers of high rank. Some divisional community liaison officers were working under commanders who did not see the need for police community relations; in these cases intervention from headquarters was necessary to enable the CLO to function. There was general agreement that headquarters departments performed a 'service' function. The centralizing of facilities, resources, liaison with other centrally organized bodies, offered a back-up service for the divisional CLOs.

Four out of the six forces studied had developed the community liaison function at Divisional level. Force B was, however, moving in the direction of subdivisional posting. There was no debate about the appropriateness of localized posting. As one officer said, 'if ever we're going to be operational, we need to be on division'. Whether the divisional headquarters is the most appropriate place for community liaison officers is, however, open to debate. The divisional headquarters may be seen as a mini-headquarters for overview, policy setting and service vis a vis the subdivisions. However, as one subdivision usually shares premises with the divisional headquarters, there is a danger that the services of the CLO may get monopolized by that subdivision. The potential for conflict exists where the significant managerial unit is subdivision, each subdivisional commander operating autonomously but using a service located on division. In a number of forces there seemed to be a shift in emphasis towards the subdivision as being the significant mangerial unit. There are clear advantages in the localizing of the CLO. On a subdivision, community liaison activities may be more easily geared towards the community as-it-is, rather than the community as-it-is believed-to-be, because the geographical area is smaller, and the smaller organizational unit would facilitate the development of relationships between the subdivisional commander, the CLO and other operational officers. However, the CLO, if not adequately supported, may find himself working in isolation; and because there is little potential for a rank structure among specialists at a local level, his low rank may lead to a sense of powerlessness unless there is a high level of commitment from his superiors.

Rank

There was no consensus between the forces studied on the most appropriate rank for the divisional community liaison specialist. Table 1 records the rank and location of officers. In Force A, most of the

Table 1

Force	Popul-ation	Density of population	Authorized establishment	Pop per officer	CLOs	CL Dept yr.est.	Rank and location of CLOs				
							Chief Supt.	Supt	Chief Insp	Sgt	P.C.
A	2,674,000	12.03	6,684	400	yes	1974	–	HQ	HQ/Div	Div	Div
B	2,065,000	4.1	5,154	401	yes	1974	HQ	HQ	Region	Div (F)	–
C	1,524,000	9.52	4,607	331	yes	1977	HQ	HQ +all sub DN Supts	HQ	–	Sub.div + 'high risk area
D	1,354,000	1.14	3,020	448	yes	1983	–	HQ	HQ	HQ/Div	Div
E	746,000	2.05	1,602	446	developing	1985	–	–	HQ	HQ	Sub.div
F	589,000	0.07	1,140	517	yes	1984	–	–	HQ	Div	–

eleven divisions had community liaison staff of sergeant and constable
rank. In Force B, the 14 divisional officers and two race relations
specialists were Inspectors. Community liaison staff in Force C were
located on subdivision, with the twenty four subdivisional
superintendents as part-time CLOs assisted by full-time PCs known as
ACLOs. In Force D, the eight divisional community liaison inspectors
were located at divisional headquarters. They were assisted by a
sergeant and police constables who had functional responsibilties, e.g.,
full time schools and officers. Both divisions in Force F had a
full-time community liaison inspector.

Two diametrically opposed views on the subject of rank are illustrated
in the following quotes:

"The rank of the ACLO doesn't matter, if you're efficient at your job,
it doesn't matter. It comes down to personalities....I wonder if the
good relationship we have here is there in other forces if they need a
rank structure".

"When dealing with other agencies...there needs to be a matching of
authority, you need someone who can make a response without consulting
upwards".

Officers of lower rank are more dependent for their satisfaction on
intrinsic reward. Autonomy is one such reward. Alongside the rigid
hierarchy which forms the skeleton of the organizational structure of the
police force, there co-exists a high degree of autonomy.

Though examination of policy statements revealed references to the
importance of good relationships between police and community, specific
guidelines were often conspicuously absent. This allowed individual
interpretation to flourish, for where roles are not clearly defined,
individuals resolve ambiguity by developing their roles according to
personal preferences. It may well be that the high level of job
satisfaction encountered among CLOs was related to the amount of freedom
they had to operate, however the cost to the organization is a lack of
continuity with changes in personnel.

Another intrinsic reward is status. It is doubtful that many CLOs
received status reward for their role within the police force. High
status work was related to arrests and successful prosecutions. CLOs
were aware of their low status, and here situations encountered during
the fieldwork supported questionnaire findings. In response to a
question about attitudes towards community liaison within their forces,
26% of respondents had said that attitudes were good or improving whereas
68% felt they were mixed, skeptical or reflected the view that community
liaison was 'soft' policing.

Doubts about whether police forces are responding to the
recommendations of the Scarman Report with more than window-dressing
measures have been expressed. Examination of the level of involvement
and commitment among CLOs suggests that this is not the case, so far as
those particular individuals are concerned. However, an examination of
the response of the organization as a whole often lends weight to this
criticism. There is something of a string and chewing gum approach about
the organizational response, evidenced by a lack of facilitating
structures in terms of managerial directives, provision of means for
integrating community liaison into day-to-day policing, resources and
specific skills training (e.g., all forces were involved to some degree
in schools liaison, but only one supplied training for that function).

ROLE, FUNCTIONS AND OBJECTIVES
Perception of the Community Liaison Officer's Role

Analysis of comments made by senior officers, including those designated as part-time CLOs produced three sets of perceptions, although these are not necessarily mutually exclusive:

(1) Some officers believe that CLOs are necessary only because they have the time to do what every officer should be doing;

(2) Some comments conveyed a view that community liaison is a valid specialty, not simply a compensatory measure;

(3) Other comments describe the community liaison role as an important adjunct to successful management.

There was some agreement in role perceptions between CLOs and senior officers, in particular the view was shared that they were doing what is the job of every police officer.

Among CLOs a commonly held metaphor for their role was a bridge between police and community. 'I am an identifiable bridge that people can get to know, to walk between them and the police service'. Sometimes the bridge seemed to be more firmly anchored in the community than in the force and sometimes there was a feeling that if the bridge was not sufficiently anchored at the force end, the result could be the creation of two police forces, the "goodies" and the "baddies". One officer felt frustrated about the way gypsy raids were handled; he felt that he laboured to build up credit which was then expended unnecessarily on 'mob-handed' behaviour used in raids. A CLO in another force insisted on being involved in both the planning and policing of raids on his multi-racial division. He felt that his presence ensured the proper handling of the raid by the police and was an effective means of countering rumour in the community. Some CLOs perceived their roles as being a compensation for past failures of the police force and society. One CLO, who described himself prior to his appointment as 'the most racially prejudiced, biased, bigoted bastard' in the area, said: "Now that I've gotten to know these people, how they've endured racial prejudice in Britain, I feel that some of the treatment I've meted out in the past, is bad". Contact with members of the ethnic minority communities, supplemented by a Racial Awareness Training Course, had led this officer to perceive his role as a compensatory measure, both personally and on behalf of his force.

The view expressed by senior officers that community liaison was a valid specialty was not necessarily echoed by the CLOs. They tended to express confusion over what they were and why they had been selected for their posts; this was due to inadequate feedback on performance. Not that efforts made on the job were totally unrecognized--they were often recognized as suitable material for publicity. What is being referred to is the direct feedback to the individual, the 'pat on the back' and reassurance when individual efforts were in the right direction, or criticism when they were not. Lack of feedback did not always produce dissatisfaction however, for some officers found the positive response they received from members of the community sufficient comment on their performance.

The Function of the CLO

There was wide variation in function among the CLOs studied, some of which could be attributed to differences in force or local policy, but much of which was an expression of individual differences in background, personality and preference. The questionnaire phase identified 59 different functions sometimes performed by CLOs.

Table 2 records functions which were performed, at least some of the time, by CLOs in over 75% of forces. The fieldwork visits confirmed these functions as being performed by CLOs but also showed that specific functions performed related to the particular structure developed for community liaison within a force. For example, in Force C where the community liaison constables (ACLOs) functioned at subdivisional level, they made contact with local community organizations and individuals but agency contact was made by juvenile liaison constables (JLOs). Their coordinating department at headquarters was entitled Youth and Community Branch and ran separate bimonthly conferences for ACLOs and JLOs. Where CLOs were of Inspector rank, they exercised a supervisory role over officers performing disparate functions, e.g., Crime Prevention and Schools Officers in Force D, or Road Safety and Juvenile Liaison in Force B. The creation of composite departments had meant that community liaison specialists could be given rank, but that did necessitate them covering a wider range of activities, and again led to wide differences between individuals in the way in which they balanced their different duties.

Table 2
Functions Performed by CLOs in over 75% of Forces

Function	Percentage of Forces
Maintaining standards of community liaison work	88
Giving talks on the role of police in society	86
Liaison with statutory agencies to improve relations	86
Involvement in community projects	83
Encouraging operational officers to become more involved with local community organizations and individuals	83
Working with agencies and bodies concerned with community relations and welfare	81
Maintaining contact with local youth	81
Maintaining contact with local uniformed officers for the exchange of information on local community matters	81
Schools liaison at – infant and junior level	81
– middle school level	81
– secondary school level	81
– colleges of higher education	81
Keeping the Chief Constable informed of community trends and tensions	79
Maintaining contact with local community organizations, leaders and individuals	79
Liaison with statutory agencies (juvenile offenders)	79
Preparing visual displays	76
Maintaining contact with local ethnic minority organizations, leaders and individuals	76
Evaluation of community liaison work	76

Objectives for community liaison

Many of the Community Liaison Officers interviewed expressed a lack of clarity about their objectives. The policy statements they received tended to be vague and all embracing, and feedback on their performance was minimal, as a result they were not sure what the organization required of them. The present confusion in the police service about the purpose and practice of community liaison may, in part, be due to the necessary service orientation of this function. Police forces are basically response organizations. The police subculture defines 'real police work' in terms of an aggressive response to calls from the public or other officers, but the preventive side of policing has an uneasy co-existence with this response orientation, which continues to influence the attitudes and expectations of officers, even within the community liaison field. Indeed, it would seem that some of the confusion experienced by CLOs over their role originated in a failure to reconcile what was largely a preventive task with a response orientation. Their maintaining of a reactive style tended to exclude proactive planning or prioritizing of task and this proved inconsistent with the goal of developing relationships with, for example, sections of society believed to have a hostile attitude towards the police.

Objectives are important for two reasons. Firstly, they offer direction; and secondly, they offer a criterion by which success may be evaluated. CLOs were more prone to complain of the lack of feedback than the lack of direction. Possibly, any lack of direction was compensated by their response orientation; and because sections of the community did respond to their initatives, they were kept busy. The point is that without specific guidelines, they were unable to be sure that they were busy with things which best suited the goals of the organization as a whole.

The lack of detailed objectives does not, of course, mean that CLOs had no objectives, though lack of consensus within forces would suggest that CLOs were motivated by a personal interpretation of the purpose of their role.

Discussion and observation led to the identification of four discrete purposes:

(1) Public relations — to create a good impression of the police among members of the public. This did occasionally lead to the identification of 'at risk' groups, but sometimes actually diverted attention from such groups to those who were more amenable to impression management. Failure to adopt a specific policy as to which community groups to aim at led to the situation described by one officer whose department never turned down an invitation to give a talk, and ordered visits on a first-come-first-served basis. As his time was fully occupied by adopting this response mode, planned liaison was effectively excluded.

(2) Explanation of the police role — to explain to members of the public both the extent and the limitations of the police role. This often included defending police action, indeed some CLOs acted as trouble shooters dealing with the first stages in the investigation of a complaint by a member of the public.

(3) Informing about rights — to inform members of the public about the rights and duties of citizens. This was one intention behind a lot of the schools work, but did not occur exclusively in schools. One CLO used his role to inform young people how to stage a demonstration and remain within the law while others, for example, focused on the importance of public cooperation in crime detection and prevention.

(4) <u>Two-way communication</u> - to listen to and understand what members of the different community groups were saying and to produce change within the force where possible as a result of increased understanding. This took place either through on-the-job involvement with other officers or through the training role afforded to many CLOs as part of the force's general community relations training. Typically, this was aimed at probationers during their placement in the Community Liaison Department, or refresher or specialist courses for experienced officers.

While not mutually exclusive logically, many CLOs tended to adopt one or another of these philosophies. In forces where structures were provided to integrate the work of the Community Liaison Department into operational policing, consensus was more likely to exist about the primary purpose of liaison; but where structures were lacking, intra-force differences in approach were extremely diverse and dependent on the personal views of the officers involved.

TRAINING

Questionnaire data had led to the identification of three modes of training used by Community Liaison Officers: attachment to experienced community liaison staff; learning by experience on the job; and training courses. Some courses were run internally, exclusively for the members of a particular force. This tended to occur where there had been a change of policy in the community liaison field, or where new methods or structures were being instigated. Some courses were run by one force but were open to surrounding forces, and four courses were part of a national provision sponsored by the Home Office or the Staff College.

Information about their courses was sought from all forces running the community relations course identified by the questionnaire responses. Four of the more widely available courses were visited and a few days of the programme sampled, as far as possible from the course members' point of view. Courses ranged in length from a few days to four weeks and covered areas such as: public relations, including perhaps a visit to a radio station, or simulation exercises; information about minority groups, all courses included input on some minority ethnic groups; policing issues such as 'policing and racially sensitive division', 'the role of the police community liaison officer'; issues drawn from the social sciences, e.g., 'the Psychology of Prejudice', 'Values and Attitudes in Society;, 'the Role of the Trades Union'; and a variety of specific issues such as Victim Support Schemes, Police Consultative Committees, Solvent Abuse.

Three of the courses visited, and all but one of the courses which supplied detailed information, relied heavily on a didactic teaching style delivered largely by visiting speakers from a wide variety of backgrounds and therefore introducing content requiring considerable conceptual leaps by course members. Tutorial expertise was lacking with tutors acting more as administrators than learning faciltators and, with the exception of one or two exercises, there was little use of a participative teaching style.

The examination of training provision for community liaison officers brought seven problem areas to light:

(1) There is a mismatch between training provision and the rank of CLO. 78% of CLOs are of sergeant and constable rank whereas most nationally available courses are for inspector rank and above.

(2) A crammed programme tends to force out learning, particularly in cases where lecturers seek to introduce concepts foreign to the course

members.

(3) Tutors are ill-equipped to facilitate learning experiences.

(4) Previous experience of police training courses leads course members to expect to be told the right answer and therefore inhibits discussion.

(5) The structure of the course means that course members frequently fail to communicate with speakers and tutors; one effect of this is the underuse of the expertise of visiting speakers.

(6) Attempts to apply course material to practical problems tends to occur in the absence of tutorial guidance.

(7) Courses failed to provide skills training in areas specifically required by the community liaison role. Training provision commensurate with the needs of newly appointed community liaison officers was therefore not available.

Consideration of these points in the light of what is now known about the role of police community liaison officers and the organizational climate in which they work highlights the needs for a thorough evaluation of training programmes. This would be a prerequisite to the development of new training initiatives and could be done under three headings:

- evaluation of the programme as a means of achieving force objectives for community liaison
- evaluation in terms of the personal needs and skills development of community liaison officers
- evaluation of training methods leading to the development of a pedagogy suitable for meeting needs dictated both by force policy and the requirements of individual officers.

CONCLUSIONS

Space does not allow for discussion of the social, psychological and organizatioal issues raised by this study. I will, however, summarize them here:

The Problem of Credibility - The maintenance of both internal and external credibility poses something of a dilemma. Traditional methods of enhancing internal credibility--staff rotation, and the development of posts believed to be springboards for promotion--mitigate against the stability and continuity of relationship required to maintain credibility within the community.

The Problem of Integration - For the CLOs to perform a 'bridge' function, there needs to be the requisite degree of integration into the community balanced by adequate integration into the operational side of policing. This sometimes produces structural and attitudinal requirements not presently available, and means that CLOs tend to identify more closely with the community with the consequence of alienation from the police force.

The Problem of Purpose, Direction and Evaluation - Clarity of purpose was often absent at policy level, leading inevitably to confusion at the level of practical outworkings. Ambiguity is resolved according to the individual preferences of the officers concerned. A lack of objectives at policy level means that effectiveness cannot be evaluated. This is well illustrated in the field of school liaison. Schools liaison activities followed a fairly predictable pattern but generated a diverse rationale with a sometimes tenuous link between activity and purpose.

The Problem of Support - A measure of the value placed on community liaison work by a force is the amount of support made available to CLOs. Support may come in a variety of forms: tangible resources like materials, petrol allowances; skill enhancing resources like training courses; managerial resources creation of suitable structures, giving back-up where needed. Support may be divided into two categories, proactive and reactive. Proactive support means that needs are anticipated and the necessary structures developed in advance of the need but as part and parcel of the decision to create a community liaison department. Examples of proactive support are: provision of a budget with suitable headings; provision of access to existing meetings, e.g., divisional policy conferences; creation of new structures designed to meet the management needs of the department, e.g., forcewide or regional CLO conferences. There was evidence that this kind of support was lacking in all six forces. Reactive support refers to the day-to-day backing required when conflicts arise between the needs and beliefs of one branch of the force, and those of community liaison work. Absence of support of this nature led to a high level of frustration when, having exercised initiative in the direction indicated by general policy statements, officers found they did not receive the backing they needed.

In conclusion, I should like to discuss the definition of community liaison. The definition developed at the outset of the study in order to define the field proved adequate as a working definition but as a statement about the role and function of CLOs in practice, it requires some amendment. Originally community liaison was defined as:

Police initiated liaison efforts which seek to develop and maintain grass roots contact with a wide variety of community organizations and individuals. Its primary purpose is to improve police community relations utilizing a non-crime oriented method. This objective is seen in the context of a long term perspective with implications beyond any specific or immediate operational requirements and is achieved through the development of positive contact with the community in a non-confrontation situation.

Do community liaison officers in these six forces make 'grass roots' contact? It would seem that in most areas they do not, for two reasons. Where CLOs are based on division, they are often not able to contact a wide range of organizations and individuals across the division because of its size, and tend to be either selective about who they relate to, or concentrate on a small geographical area. Secondly, because 'grass roots' local knowledge takes time to gather, and positive relationships take time to establish, the extent of contact is a variable closely related to the length of time a force has had community liaison officers.

Do community liaison officers utilize a 'non-crime oriented method' and develop their contacts in a 'non-confrontational situation'? A number of CLOs took exception to this part of the definition, pointing to occasions when they were involved specifically in confrontations in order to halt or prevent law-breaking, though they agreed that their actions were geared towards 'positive contacts with the community'. There were examples of confrontation-style interventions which served to reduce tension and preclude criminal proceedings. This occurred particularly where CLOs operated as race relations specialists, confrontation being an apt description of some of their negotiations. There were examples of what may be seen as crime oriented confrontational action; one full-time schools officer, for example, detected a two hundred pound burglary and a series of cheque frauds. Senior CLOs at headquarters claimed that they were frequently involved in confrontations where high level negotiations over issues like demonstrations occurred. Though their activities were not crime oriented in the sense that they were aimed at detection, they were certainly concerned with the preventing of criminal action.

A definition which describes what community liaison actually is at present might be:

Police initiated liaison efforts which seek to develop and maintain contact with a selected range of agencies, community organizations and individuals. Its primary purpose is to improve police community relations using specialist skills which may lead to the adoption of both confrontational and non-confrontational methods.

Finally, it may be useful to ask whether the study achieved its objectives. The answer is that it has provided documentation of the role, function and training of police community liaison officers, and a definition of community liaison has been developed as a result of information gained. Recommendations have been made concerning objectives, structure and the integration of this aspect of policing as well as an indication of ways in which officers may be better equipped to perform a community liaison function.

REFERENCES

Brown, C. L., & Cochrane, R. (1984). The role, function and training of police community liaison officers: Interim report. Department of Psychology, University of Birmingham.

Phillips, S. V., & Cochrane, R. (1985). The role, function and training of police community liaison officers: Final report. Department of Psychology, University of Birmingham.

Policy Services Institute Report. Police and people in London, PSI 1983.

Scarman, Lord, The Brixton Disorders, 10-12 April, 1981. London, H.M.S.O., 1.

EVALUATING THE POLICE: ATTITUDES, COMPETENCY AND CREDIBILITY

A. DANIEL YARMEY

Over the last few years this writer has studied various social and professional groups' beliefs and attitudes toward general police capability and, more specifically, beliefs about police capability and credibility as eyewitnesses. A summary of this research program is presented here. Complete descriptions of this research may be found in Yarmey (1984, 1985), Yarmey and Jones (1982) and Yarmey and Rashid (1983).

Police officers often are in unique and contradictory positions when serving and protecting their community, and when testifying in court. The police are a regulatory agency with legitimate authority to control those actions of the public that violate the law. This authority may be a source of conflict between the police and the public when attempts by the police to maintain social order are perceived by citizens as a threat to individual freedom.

Attitudes toward the police are related to the psychological makeup of the individual, social group membership, and the cultural structure of society. Police effectiveness depends upon the quality of the relationship between the police and the public, however, the public tends to hold inconsistent perceptions about the police (White & Menke, 1982). One perception is positive, incorporating respect and support of the police (U.S. President's Commission on Law Enforcement and Administration of Justice, 1967). A second perception is an ambivalent image in which the public is skeptical and distrustful of police power but, at the same time, recognizes their legitimacy and is desirous of police services (Reiss, 1967). Finally, there is a negative image which is most clearly seen in the dissenting attitudes of young, lower-class males belonging to racial minorities (Boggs & Galliher, 1975). Although the public holds many attitudes toward the police, these perceptions are understandable. People are not always rational or logical in their evaluations of others or institutions. Individuals can hold an attitude at a general level, such as a belief in the general honesty of the police, and also hold a related attitude at a more specific level, such as the belief that some police lie and intentionally distort their courtroom testimony.

Witness reports to judges and jurors include the testimony of both citizens and police officers. In contrast to non-police, testimony of police officers typically is perceived with high confidence and trust by jurors and the general public (see State v. Wheeler, 1982). Police may be perceived to be accurate observers of street activities, people, and their actions. It is assumed by some police administrators that common street experiences and instruction transform the police trainee into a veteran officer who is superior in ability to remember, describe, and recognize wanted persons (see Ainsworth, 1981). Some observers also believe that street experiences give police officers a special insight into the critical factors which influence the accuracy and completeness of eyewitness identification (see Brigham & Wolfskeil, 1983).

However, in Anglo-American courts the testimony of police officers is not accepted without question. In some respects, police officers, in addition to defendants, are on trial once they enter the witness stand. Rutledge (1979), a former officer-turned-prosecutor, notes that whenever a police officer testifies in court, his or her credibility, professionalism, policies, and observance of the defendant's rights also are on trial.

Attitudes in the Criminal Justice System

Federal and provincial legislators, appelate courts, and on-line agencies such as the police, prosecutors, defense lawyers, trial court judges, and jurors have their own sphere of influence and autonomy which shape their particular functions within the whole system. Although these relationships are somewhat independent, they also are interactive. However, few systematic analyses of the perceptions of legal subgroups toward each other are available. What, for instance, are the general attitudes of the public (potential jurors) and defence lawyers relative to that of the police toward police officers? An attempt was made to answer this question by surveying samples of defense lawyers, citizens, senior citizens, and the police using the semantic differential technique to test attitudes toward typical police officers, judges, prosecutors, and defense attorneys.

Results showed that police officers are highly valued, but not greatly understood, even by the police themselves. Lawyers rated police officers reliably lower in value than did elderly citizens and police subjects. Lawyers also perceived the police as having little power. As might be expected, the police evaluated police officers most highly relative to the ratings given by the other subject groups. In addition, elderly citizens were found to be highly positive toward police. Elderly citizens appeared to be especially impressed by police activity. Correlational tests revealed that the general public's positive evaluations of police were based on perceived understandability and activity, but not perceived potency. In contrast, police's positive evaluations of police officers were reliably related to their perceived activity but not to potency, or to understandability.

The analysis of police officers' attitudes indicated they considered police officers reliably more valuable, more potent, more active, and more understandable than judges and prosecutors. Police also perceived themselves as reliably more valuable, potent, and understandable than defense lawyers, but indicated that defense lawyers are as active as the police. Judges and prosecutors were equally highly valued by police, and both were reliably more valued than defense attorneys. Judges were perceived by the police as reliably more powerful than defense attorneys, but there were no differences in perceived power between judges and prosecutors, or between prosecutors and defense lawyers. Defense lawyers were seen as reliably more active than judges, but did not differ in perceived activity from prosecutors. Prosecutors were also seen as more active than judges and defense lawyers. The police indicated that they had little understanding of either defense lawyers or judges. However, prosecutors were perceived as more understandable than defense lawyers and judges.

Fallibility of Eyewitness Identification

Although few arrests occur as a result of police actually seeing an offender commit a crime, police officers must be able to evaluate the accuracy and credibility of eyewitness testimony. The likelihood of mistaken identification may be attributed to two major sources. First, human perception and memory are probabilistic and often are unreliable in crime-related situations. Secondly, the police may unintentionally use biased or suggestive procedures in gathering identification evidence (see Clifford & Bull, 1978; Ellison & Buckhout, 1981; Loftus; 1979; Wells & Loftus, 1984; Yarmey, 1979).

How aware are police officers of the influence of such factors as stress, cross-racial differences, subjective certainty, time perception, age, etc., on eyewitness memory? A sample of experienced police officers (N = 26, average length of experience = eight years) was given a questionnaire to test their knowledge or intuitions about several issues related to eyewitness accuracy. Their responses were compared to the responses made by sample of 35 criminal lawyers and eight trial judges, 60 adult citizens, and 16 cognitive psychologists from Canada, the U.K. and the U.S.A., defined as "experts" in the field of eyewitness testimony. Table 1 shows one of the questions used in this survey and the percentage of subjects in each group that responded with a particular answer. Experimental evidence suggests that extreme stress and anxiety will interfere with a person's ability to acquire and process information. Clifford and Scott (1978) found that recall accuracy was superior for details of a nonviolent incident in contrast to a violent one. Although males and females were equally accurate in their recall of details in a non-violent incident, males were superior in recall of a violent event. Results shown in Table 1 indicate that police, as well as lawyers and judges, students, and citizens, are most likely to believe that details of violent crimes rather than details of nonviolent crimes are more easily recalled. In contrast, few "experts" accepted this answer. The correct answer (A) was most frequently selected by the experts, but even experts showed some disagreement in their knowledge or intuitions about this particular eyewitness situation.

In general, the results of this study showed that knowledge about the psychological factors that influence eyewitness identification and testimony does not fall within the province of common knowledge. Police officers, lawyers and trial judges were not superior to ordinary citizens in their accuracy of information related to eyewitness memory.

Perceived Expertness and Credibility of Police Officers

Police officers, lawyers, trial judges and jurors base many of their decisions on the relative likelihood and/or veracity of witness statements. Ordinary citizens most typically are witnesses in court but police officers also may be called to testify as eyewitnesses. For example, police may be asked to describe a suspect they observed committing a crime such as selling drugs, or picking pockets, etc. Recently, this investigator surveyed samples of police officers, lawyers for both the defense and prosecution, ordinary citizens and undergraduate psychology students regarding their beliefs about the perceptual and memory capacities of police. In addition, these five groups were questioned regarding their estimations of the likelihood of police deceitfulness in court when testifying as eyewitnesses.

Table 1
Percentage of Subject Groups that gave each of the Responses to a
Question about Eyewitness Accuracy and a Violent or Nonviolent Crime

"Suppose that a man and a woman both witness two crimes. One crime
involves violence while the other is nonviolent. Which statement do
you believe is true?"

	Experts N=16	Lawyers & Judges N=43	Police N=26	Students N=60	Citizens N=60
*(a) Both the man and the woman will remember the details of the nonviolent crime better than the details of the violent crime	62	37	11	10	7
(b) Both the man and the woman will remember the details of the violent crime better than the details of the noviolent crime	6	42	58	57	60
(c) The man will remember the details of the violent crime better than the details of the nonviolent crime, and the woman will remember the details of the nonviolent crime better than the details of the violent crime	25	9	31	22	22
(d) The woman will remember the details of the violent crime better, and the man will remember the details of the nonviolent crime better	0	9	0	12	12
Invalid	6	2			

*Correct answer

Subjects consisted of 150 individuals, half of them randomly selected from Alberta, Canada, and the remainder from Ontario, Canada. The issues examined in this study were drawn from the psycho-legal research literature on police behavior related to eyewitness testimony and decision-making. A number of scenarios were constructed and each scenario was accompanied by an issue or question and a set of four alternative answers. Subjects' task was to rank order which outcomes were most likely to occur and to state how important they felt that this skill or process would be to police officers relative to citizens. For example, the following scenario was given to subjects:

A police officer is called to the scene of a domestic dispute. One of the people involved is highly intoxicated. Please rank order the following statements from one (least likely to be true) to four (most likely to be true).

_____a) The police officer will be able to accurately predict the person's level of intoxication.

_____b) The police officer will overestimate the person's level of intoxication.

_____c) The police officer will underestimate the person's level of intoxication.

_____d) It would be impossible for the police officer to predict the person's level of intoxication.

The results for this particular question indicated that most subjects know little about judgments of intoxication. The correct answer is (c) (see Pagano & Taylor, 1979). The research literature suggests that police officers are reasonably accurate at predicting low levels of intoxication but cannot discriminate between people who have consumed either high or low alcohol dosage. Furthermore, they strongly underestimate the degree of intoxication of high alcohol dosage [high dosage 1.5 oz. (.0451 l) of 100-proof whiskey per 40 lbs. (18 kg) of body weight; low dosage .75 oz. (.023 l) of 100-proof whiskey per 40 lbs. (18 kg) of body weight]. Langenbucher & Nathan (1983) have confirmed these findings: police officers, with the exception of a special unit of highly experienced, specifically trained, skilled officers, are no better than social drinkers and bartenders in correctly judging level of intoxication.

In our study, answer "a" was most frequently selected, i.e., police officers are accurate in predictions of intoxication. This perception was strongly held by both defense attorneys and crown attorneys. Police officers, in contrast, chose both this answer and the correct answer, i.e., that they would underestimate the level of intoxication, equally often. Citizens and students, on the other hand, chose all four responses equally often. Interestingly, all subject groups felt that it was more important for police than citizens to be able to accurately predict levels of intoxication.

All subject groups believed that police are superior to civilians in short-term retention of information related to criminal cases. That is, police would probably be able to remember 10 chunks of information in contrast to only about 7 chunks for civilians. However, according to Bull and Reid (1975), police best remember about 7 chunks of information in short-term recall which is equal to the basic capacity for recall in most subjects. Also, all subjects thought that it was more important for police than civilians to have better short-term memory for criminal information. Since the question dealt with a police briefing session, the difference in perceived importance seems reasonable.

Regarding the ability of police and civilians to make accurate eyewitness verbal descriptions of a male suspect seen earlier for about 10-15 seconds, all subject groups believed that the police are more accurate than civilians. Defense attorneys, in contrast to police and civilians, felt that 10-15 seconds was too short an observation period for either party to accurately describe a suspect. Of particular interest is the finding that the police, in contrast to all other subject groups, thought that it was important for both citizens and police to be good witnesses. Most subject groups favored police over citizens.

Regarding the ability of police and civilians to make visual identifications of suspects seen earlier in official photographs, all subject groups thought that police are superior to civilians. This belief lacks support in the research literature (see Tickner & Poulton, 1975). In fact, a typical finding is that eyewitnesses are poorer in visual identification for suspects than is generally believed (Loftus, 1979). All subjects thought it was equally important for police and citizens to be able to visually identify a suspect.

Since police officers are trained to be suspicious and to look for details that non-police may ignore, this type of perceptual readiness may lead to an increase in false alarms on the part of the police. We found that defense attorneys, in contrast to prosecutors, believed that police officers are much more likely to perceive crimes when the behavior being observed is not criminal in nature (i.e., police perceived theft in progress when a normal exchange of goods was happening). Police themselves do not believe they overestimate the actual number of thefts when observing everyday activities but, in fact, the research literature suggests they do. Prosecuting attorneys, apparently, have unwarranted confidence in both police and civilians since they believed that neither group misperceives crimes. Interestingly, ordinary citizens believed that police reliably overestimate and misperceive crime.

The last topic I wish to cover is the issue of police credibility. In 1984, the Police Complaints Board of Toronto, Canada, announced their findings and conclusions about the alleged assault of a private citizen by Metropolitan Toronto police officers. Following six days of testimony given by the officers involved, other police witnesses, and the complaintant, the Board stated that they were concerned about the reliability of the evidence of several of the police witnesses. The Board felt that police credibility had been lowered, and they stated that if this practice continued police testimony would have little value.

One specific instance the Board focused upon was the following situation:

All of the officers who testified about the incident were unable to identify any of their colleagues involved in the assault. However, these same police officers were able to identify fellow police officers in cars at a distance. The Board concluded that this testimony indicated deceit on the part of the police in order to protect themselves or their fellow officers.

Other interpretations, of course, based upon the psychology of human perception and memory, rather than deceit, may explain the testimony of the officers. However, for the purpose of our research, if we assume that the Board's interpretation was correct and these officers were deceitful, we wondered how widespread subject groups thought this behavior was among police officers, i.e., what percentage of police officers in their opinion would act deceitfully if they were testifying before a Police Complaints Board in the situation described? Also, what

<u>Figure 1</u>
Estimations of Police Deceitfulness in criminal trials and before police
complaints board hearings.

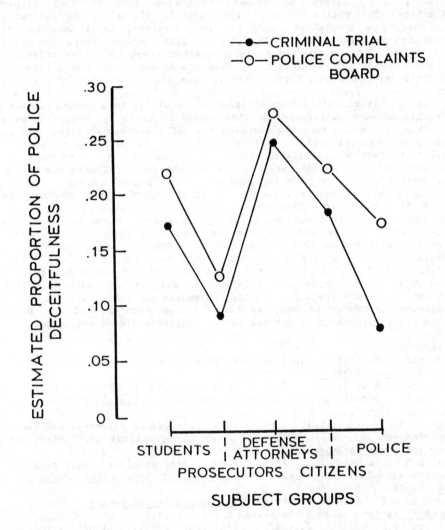

percentage would be deceitful if they were testifying about this matter in a criminal trial. Figure 1 shows the estimated percentages of police deceitfulness as eyewitnesses in the situation described in front of a Police Complaints Board and in a Criminal Trial as a function of the five subject groups. Looking first at the results for testimony given in a criminal trial, police subjects gave the lowest estimations of deceitfulness which differs reliably from the estimations given by students, defense attorneys, and citizens. Defense attorneys and citizens, in contrast to prosecutors, also gave reliably higher estimations for police deceit. The reliable difference in estimated lying before a complaints board and in a criminal trial made by the police group suggests that police differentiate between these two types of inquiry. Prosecutors had reliably greater trust in police officers' testimony before a complaints board than did students, defense attorneys, and citizens. Defense attorneys, as you can see, also differed reliably from police officers.

Focusing only on police deceitfulness as we did in this study, however, is unfair without qualifying our observations. It is my guess that many subject groups would rate the deceitfulness of other professions, such as lawyers and medical doctors, just as highly as the police were rated in similar professionally-related situations. It is also important to emphasize that police officers could have been deceitful when completing this questionnaire by offering the view that police seldom lie in a criminal trial, or before a police complaints board. That they did not do this is a credit to police objectivity.

In conclusion, different social and professional groups have variable beliefs about the memorial capacity and judgmental processes of police officers relative to that of civilians. Some of these beliefs are unrealistic, such as the short-term memory capacity of police. Other beliefs reflect vested interests such as those of defense attorneys, but other perceptions are open to intervention and training such as police judgments of intoxication. Police awareness of the fallibility of eyewitness testimony as well as those system factors that are under police control should be a central part of police training and education.

REFERENCES

Ainsworth, P.B. (1981). Incident perception by British police officers. Law and Human Behavior, 5, 231-236.

Boggs, S.L., & Galliher, J. (1975). Evaluating the police: A comparison of Black Street and household respondents. Social Problems, 22, 393-406.

Brigham, J.C., & Wolfskeil, M.P. (1983). Opinions of attorneys and law enforcement personnel on the accuracy of eyewitness identifications. Law and Human Behavior, 7, 337-349.

Bull, R.H.C., & Reid, R.L. (1975). Recall after briefing: Television versus face-to-face presentation. Journal of Occupational Psychology, 48, 73-78.

Clifford, B.R., & Bull, R. (1978). The psychology of person identification. London: Routledge & Kegan Paul.

Clifford, B.R. & Scott, J. (1978). Individual and situational factors in eyewitness testimony. Journal of Applied Psychology, 63, 352-359.

Ellison, K.W., & Buckhout, R. (1981). Psychology and criminal justice. New York: Harper & Row.

Langenbucher, J.W., & Nathan, P.C. (1983, October). Psychology, public policy and the evidence for alcohol intoxication. American Psychologist, 1070-1077.

Loftus, E.F. (1979). Eyewitness testimony. Cambridge, Mass.: Harvard University Press.

Pagano, M., & Taylor, S. (1979). Police perceptions of alcohol intoxication. Journal of Applied Social Psychology, 10, 166-174.

Reiss, A.J. (1967). Public perceptions and recollections about crime, law enforcement, and criminal justice. In Studies in crime and law enforcement in major metropolitan areas, Vol. 1, Washington, D.C.: U.S. Government Printing Office.

Rutledge, D. (1979). Courtroom survival: The officer's guide to better testimony. Flagstaff, Arizona: Flag Publishing.

State v. Wheeler, 416 So. 2d 78, 79-80 (La. 1982).

Tickner, A.H., & Poulton, E.C. (1975). Watching for people and actions. Ergonomics, 18, 35-53.

U.S. President's Commission on Law Enforcement and Administration of Justice (1967). Task force report: The police. Washington, D.C.: U.S. Government Printing Office.

Wells, G.L., & Loftus, E.F. (1984). Eyewitness testimony: Psychological perspectives. New York: Cambridge University Press.

White, M.F., & Menke, B.A. (1982). On assessing the mood of the public toward the police: Some conceptual issues. Journal of Criminal Justice, 10, 211-230.

Yarmey, A.D. (1979). The psychology of eyewitness testimony. New York: Free Press.

Yarmey, A.D. (1984). Accuracy and credibility of the elderly witness. Canadian Journal on Aging, 3, 79-90.

Yarmey, A.D. (1985, in press). Perceived expertness and credibility of police officers as eyewitnesses. Canadian Police College Journal.

Yarmey, A.D., & Jones, H.T. (1982). Police awareness of the fallibility of eyewitness identification. Canadian Police College Journal, 6, 113 124.

Yarmey, A.D., & Rashid, S. (1983). Perceptions of the public and legal professionals toward police officers. Canadian Police College Journal, 7, 89-95.

INDEX